ADVANCED TEXTS IN ECONOMETRICS

General Editors

C. W. J. GRANGER   G. E. MIZON

LONG-RUN ECONOMIC RELATIONSHIPS

READINGS IN COINTEGRATION

Edited by

R. F. Engle and C. W. J. Granger

OXFORD UNIVERSITY PRESS

1991

Oxford University Press, Walton Street, Oxford OX2 6DP
Oxford New York Toronto
Delhi Bombay Calcutta Madras Karachi
Petaling Jaya Singapore Hong Kong Tokyo
Nairobi Dar es Salaam Cape Town
Melbourne Auckland
and associated companies in
Berlin Ibadan

Oxford is a trade mark of Oxford University Press

Published in the United States
by Oxford University Press, New York

© *R. F. Engle and C. W. J. Granger 1991*

British Library Cataloguing in Publication Data
Data available

Library of Congress Cataloging in Publication Data
Long-run economic relations/edited by R. F. Engle and C. W. J. Granger.
p.   cm.– (Advanced texts in economics)
1. Econometrics.   2. Time-series analysis.   3. Econometric models.
I. Engle, R. F. (Robert F.)   II. Granger, C. W. J. (Clive William
John), 1934–   .   III. Title: Cointegration.   IV. Sereis.
HB139.L66 1991   330'.01'5195–dc20   91-10092
ISBN 0-19-828338-5
ISBN 0-19-828339-3 (Pbk.)

Typeset by Keytec Typesetting Ltd, Bridport, Dorset

Printed in Great Britain by
Bookcraft (Bath) Ltd, Midsomer Norton, Avon

Preface

Cointegration links long-run components of a pair or of a group of series. It can then be used to discuss some types of equilibrium and to introduce those equilibria into time-series models in a fairly controversial way. Since the idea was introduced in the early 1980s, it has generated a lot of interest amongst econometricians and macroeconomists, and the list of papers concerned with the theory and providing applications has expanded rapidly.

For this volume we tried to choose papers that would be of general interest and enable economists with some training in modern econometrics to understand and appreciate recent developments in the field. In general, we have excluded very technical papers and this means that many important workers in the area, such as Peter Philips and Masanao Aoki, are not represented. Due to space limitations, and to keep the price at a reasonable level, we have not been able to include many application papers. We have included an introductory chapter discussing the basic ideas and also some final chapters reviewing recent developments.

We would like to thank all of our friends who agreed to let us use their papers and particularly Sam Yoo and James MacKinnon who have allowed us to use unpublished papers in the volume. We would like to thank Andrew Schuller of Oxford University Press for encouraging us to put this book together. Thanks are also given to Paula Lindsay and Chris Chatfield for typing and editorial help.

ROBERT ENGLE

CLIVE GRANGER

Univ. of California, San Diego

Contents

Contents

1

Introduction

1. Concept and Interpretation of Cointegration

Attractors

To begin, the idea of cointegration will be introduced for a pair of series using just intuitive reasoning rather than precise, mathematically sound arguments.

Let x_t, y_t be a pair of time series, measured at regular time intervals, such as monthly, over a period $t = 1, 2, \ldots, T$. If this sequence of data is plotted as x against y with every time giving a point on the plot, the result is a diagram of the following form:

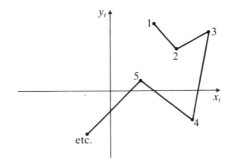

where point 4 is (x_4, y_4), and so forth. There may be some reasons for the economy to prefer these points to lie near some line rather than elsewhere. The reasons may arise from an effective government policy or from the working of some market. An example is a pair of prices of some commodity, say tomatoes, at different parts of a state or country. Let PS_t be the price of tomatoes in Southern California and PN_t the price in Northern California. If these prices are quite different, it would be possible to make a profit by purchasing tomatoes in one region, transporting them to the other region and selling them there. The operation of the markets would tend to increase prices in the region where the extra purchases occur and to lower prices where they are sold. Once the difference between these prices is small enough, further profits cannot be made because of transportation costs, risks, and so forth. Diagrammatically:

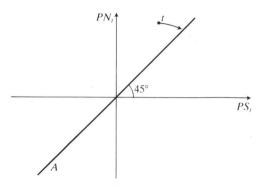

The 45° line, A, acts as an attractor, with some mechanism existing such that if the prices drift away from A, there will be a tendency to get back near to it. Because of uncertainties, sticky prices, contracts, etc., the mechanism may not immediately bring the points exactly to the attractor. At any particular time, shocks to the economy may take it away from the line, but there will be an overall tendency towards it. If the economy lies on A, a shock will take it away. If there is an extended period with no exogenous stocks, the economy will definitely go to the line and remain there. Because of this property, the line A can be thought of as an 'equilibrium', of the centre of gravity type. It is naturally of interest to ask how one can test for the existence of such an attractor and if found how should this existence be acknowledged and included in an econometric model.

   One way to answer these questions is to pretend that there exist just two types of economics series, called long-memory and short-memory. In fact a much richer classification system can be used and this leads to a much more complicated discussion of attractors, but for ease of exposition only the simple classification is considered here. In a short-memory system, an old shock to the series has virtually no effect on the current value of the series, if the shock happened long enough ago. For a long-memory series this is not true, an old shock will still have a noticeable impact on the current value of the series. More formally, suppose that x_t is related to its input innovation series ε_t by

$$x_t = \sum_{j=0}^{\infty} a_j \varepsilon_{t-j} \tag{1.1}$$

then for a short-memory series $a_j \to 0$ as $j \uparrow$ but for a long memory series a_j does not go to 0 as j becomes very large. A simple example is provided by the autoregressive series of order 1, i.e. $x_t \sim AR(1)$, with x_t generated by

$$x_t = ax_{t-1} + \varepsilon_t \qquad (1.2)$$

with a being less than one in modulus, so that $-1 < a < 1$ and ε_t is a white noise series with zero mean, so that $E[\varepsilon_t \varepsilon_{t-k}] = 0$, $k \neq 0$. Solving this equation gives

$$x_t = \sum_{j=0}^{\infty} a^j \varepsilon_{t-j} \qquad (1.3)$$

so that the coefficient on ε_{t-j} declines to zero at an exponential rate, as a is less than one in magnitude. However, if $a = 1$ then x_t is a random walk generated by

$$x_t = x_{t-1} + \varepsilon_t \qquad (1.4)$$

and can be written

$$x_t = \sum_{j=0}^{\infty} \varepsilon_{t-j} \qquad (1.5)$$

so that old shocks have equal weight to new shocks in determining the current value x_t. Thus, a random walk is long-memory. It should be noted that in this case the change in x_t, i.e. $\Delta x_t = x_t - x_{t-1}$, is the white noise ε_t and is consequently short-memory. For ease of exposition it is always assumed in this introduction that the change in a long-memory process is short-memory. Let z_t be a short-memory process; this assumption gives

$$x_t - x_{t-1} = z_t \qquad (1.6)$$

so that

$$x_t = \sum_{j=0}^{\infty} z_{t-j}$$

Thus x_t is the sum of previous z_t's and is called an integrated series. A useful notation is $x_t \sim I(1)$, the one denoting that x_t has to be differenced just once to achieve a short-memory series. A more general case is $x_t \sim I(d)$, meaning that x_t has to be differenced d times to get to a short-memory series. It follows that in this notation a short-memory series is $I(0)$, as it needs differencing zero times. It will be assumed in this introduction that all series are either $I(0)$ or $I(1)$.

These two types of series differ in many ways, other than just having different memory properties. The following three diagrams show three generated series plotted through time. In figure 1.1 x_t is generated by the $AR(1)$ model (1.2) with $a = 0.5$; in figure 1.2, x_t is generated by the random walk (1.4); and in figure 1.3, x_t is generated by 1.6 with z_t being the same $AR(1)$ series shown in figure 1.1.

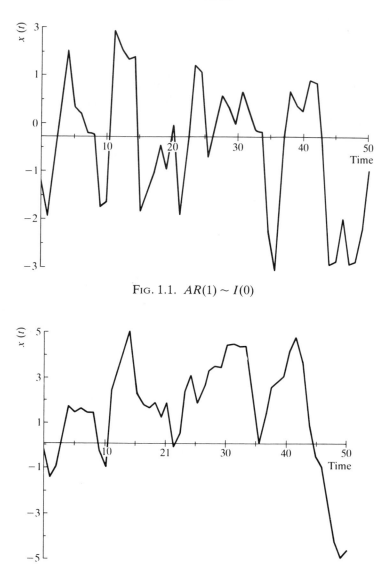

FIG. 1.1. $AR(1) \sim I(0)$

FIG. 1.2. Random Walk $\sim I(0)$

An $I(0)$ will have a mean m and can be considered to have a constant (or bounded) variance. It has a tendency to frequently return to, and cross, the mean value and any value a long way from the mean is inclined to be followed by values nearer to the mean. The value m can thus be thought of as an attractor, although of a rather weak form. For

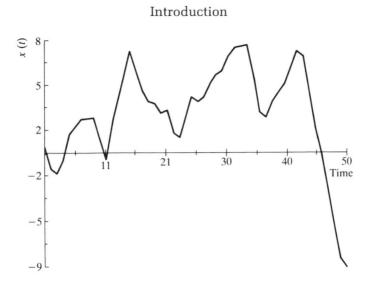

Fig. 1.3. ARIMA $(1, 1, 0) \sim I(1)$

the $AR(1)$ example (1.2), (1.3), the mean is zero and if there are no further shocks after time t, i.e. $\varepsilon_{t+j} = 0$, $j = 1, 2, \ldots$ then x_t will quickly tend to zero, as seen from (1.3) with t replaced by $t + h$, $h = 1, 2, \ldots$

An $I(1)$ series has no attractor. As an example, if x_t is a random walk generated by (1.4) and if the shocks are all zero after time t, then $x_{t+h} = x_t$, $h = 1, 2, \ldots$, so that the series is frozen at its present value and there is no tendency to move in any direction. This is not completely true for the general $I(1)$ process, but the series will tend to some value entirely determined by the value of the series at the time the shocks stop. There is thus no uniform or constant value to which the series is attracted. The example illustrates the differences in appearances of $I(0)$ and $I(1)$ series.

(i) $I(0)$ series are generally less smooth, with more obvious fluctuations than $I(1)$ series;
(ii) an $I(0)$ series will return to the mean value often whereas an $I(1)$ series will rarely return to any particular value, including its starting value.

If an $I(1)$ is believed to start a finite number of time periods ago, and for convenience the series may be thought of as starting at time $t = 0$, then the variance of an $I(1)$ series will be increasing linearly with time. For example, the random walk x_t given by (1.4) has variance $V(x_t) = t\sigma_\varepsilon^2$ whereas if x_t is generated by the $AR(1)$ model (1.2), then $V(x_t) \to \sigma_\varepsilon^2/(1 - a^2)$, which is a constant. Thus, it is seen that $I(0)$ and $I(1)$ processes have several fundamentally different properties.

The categorization of series into these two types has a practical importance in macroeconomics as many macrovariables seem to be long-memory, and can possibly be thought of as $I(1)$, and only a few are $I(0)$.

Cointegration

There are a few simple rules concerning linear combinations of integrated series (where $I(0)$, $I(1)$ are considered as the only alternatives possible):

(a) if $x_t \sim I(0)$ then $a + bx_t$ is $I(0)$
    if $x_t \sim I(1)$ then $a + bx_t$ is $I(1)$
(b) if x_t, y_t are both $I(0)$ then
$$ax_t + by_t \text{ is } I(0)$$
(c) if $x_t \sim I(1)$, $y_t \sim I(0)$ then
$$ax_t + by_t \sim I(1)$$
    This suggests that $I(1)$ is a dominant property.
(d) it is *generally* true that if x_t, y_t are both $I(1)$ then $ax_t + by_t$ is $I(1)$.

However, cases can be found where (d) does not hold and this leads to the following definition

Definition

If x_t, y_t are $I(1)$ but there exists a linear combination

$$z_t = m + ax_t + by_t$$

which is both $I(0)$ and has a zero mean, then x_t, y_t are said to be *cointegrated*.

Cointegration is actually a rather unlikely occurrence and thus when it is observed some interesting special properties may be found. To see how it can occur, consider the following construction

$$\left.\begin{array}{l} x_t = AW_t + \tilde{x}_t \\ y_t = W_t + \tilde{y}_t \end{array}\right\} \tag{1.7}$$

where W_t is $I(1)$, $\tilde{x}_t$, $\tilde{y}_t$ are both $I(0)$ with zero means. It follows from rule (c) that x_t, y_t are both $I(1)$ but

$$z_t = x_t - Ay_t$$
$$= \tilde{x}_t - A\tilde{y}_t$$

is $I(0)$ from rule (b) and has mean zero. Thus, x_t, y_t are cointegrated because their $I(1)$ness arises from the common $I(1)$ factor w_t. In fact it can be shown that this is always true; a pair of $I(1)$ cointegrated series will always have an $I(1)$ common factor representation, such as (1.7). For a pair of actual economic series that are cointegrated it is an interesting question to ask what is the common factor?

Returning to the attractor idea, it follows from the definition that the line $x = Ay$ corresponds to an attractor for the pair of series (x_t, y_t). $z_t = x_t - Ay_t$ is the line indicated in figure 1.4 which takes a positive value when the point is above the line. $\tilde{z}_t = \cos\theta.z_t$ is the orthogonal (signed) distance from the point (x_t, y_t) to the line $x = Ay$. If z_t is $I(0)$ with zero mean as in the definition of cointegration, then so will be $\tilde{z}_t$, from rule (a). If x_t, y_t are individually $I(1)$, then the points (x_t, y_t) will be inclined to move widely around the $x - y$ plane, but as $\tilde{z}_t$ is $I(0)$ with zero mean there will be a tendency for the points to be around the line, and thus for this line to act as an attractor. It is thus seen that cointegration is a sufficient condition for the existence of an attractor, and this attractor can correspond to certain types of equilibrium that arise in macroeconomic theory.

Consideration is next given to a class of models known as *error-correction models*. In the two variables case these are given by

$$\left.\begin{array}{l} \Delta x_t = m_1 + \rho_1 z_{t-1} + lags\ (\Delta x_t, \Delta y_t) + \varepsilon_{x_t} \\ \Delta y_t = m_2 + \rho_2 z_{t-2} + lags\ (\Delta x_t, \Delta y_t) + \varepsilon_{y_t} \end{array}\right\} \quad (1.8)$$

where $(\varepsilon_{x_t}, \varepsilon_{y_t})$ is a bivariate white noise, $z_t = x_t - Ay_t$, and further at least one of ρ_1, ρ_2 is non-zero. If x_t, y_t are cointegrated then each component of each equation is $I(0)$, and so the equations are balanced. Note that if x_t, y_t are $I(1)$ but not cointegrated, then z_t will be $I(1)$ and as $I(1)$ variable (which is long-memory) cannot explain a short-memory, $I(0)$, variable, the equations can only hold if both ρ_1, ρ_2 are zero, which

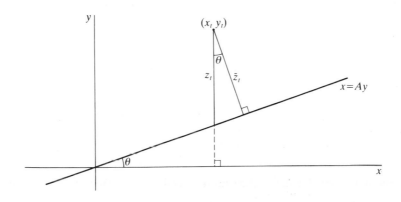

Fig. 1.4.

is excluded by assumption. It is thus seen that cointegration is a necessary condition for the error-correction equation, (1.8) to hold. It can be shown that the reverse also holds, that cointegrated variables can always be thought of as being generated by error-correction equations. In the above interpretation of an attractor as an equilibrium, $\tilde{z}_t$ (and hence z_t) is a measure of the extent to which the system is out of equilibrium, and may be called the 'equilibrium error'. In equation (1.8) the next value of (at least one of) the next change in x_t, y_t will be influenced by the size and sign of the current equilibrium error. This is why the equations are called 'error-correcting'.

It can be noted that if there is a period with no shocks, so that $(\varepsilon_{x_t}, \varepsilon_{y_t})$ is zero, the system will converge so that $\Delta x, \Delta y$ both go to zero, i.e. x_t, y_t will become constants, and z_t will go to zero, so that the points (x_t, y_t) converge so that they lie on the line $x = Ay$. The error-correction equations may be thought of as the disequilibrium mechanism that guides the economy to the equilibrium $x = Ay$.

2. Estimation and Testing

From the preceeding discussion, cointegration seems to be an intuitively plausible characterization of the relation between economic time series. From a theoretical point of view, the power of economic equilibrium as an attractor should force different variables to move together in the long run even if not in the short run and even if they are individually non-stationary. From an empirical view, the observed high correlations among the levels of macroeconomic time series are characteristic of data clustering around a linear attractor and hence cointegrated. The statistical problems of detecting cointegration are complex and non-standard and have been the subject of much research, but fortunately, there are some simple solutions. If cointegration is found between some time series, then new methods for estimating and forecasting can and should be applied.

This introductory chapter will present the simplest solution to these estimation and testing problems. This is the two-step method, introduced by Engle–Granger (1990). As will be seen, it is very easy to carry out and only requires least squares estimation. In the remainder of the book, estimation and testing problems in more complex settings will be addressed. Engle and Yoo (1990a) discuss cointegration tests with more than two variables and Stock and Watson (1990) present tests for multiple cointegrating vectors. Johansen (1990b) unifies these lines of argument by developing a maximum likelihood approach to estimation and testing for multiple cointegrating vectors. Engle, Granger, and Hallman (1990), Hylleberg et al. (1989), and Engle and Yoo (1990b) examine estimation and testing problems with seasonal unit roots and with multiple unit roots.

Engle and Granger (1990) consider estimation and testing for bivariate processes which can therefore have only zero or one cointegrating vector. They ask, for example, whether consumption and income, or wages and prices, or short and long interest rates, or money and nominal GNP, are cointegrated. Campbell and Shiller (1990) examine whether stock prices and dividends and short and long interest rates are cointegrated as would be implied by the simplest present discounted value asset pricing model. Granger and Lee (1990) test for cointegration between production and sales and between inventories and sales. Others have asked whether real exchange rates are cointegrated as a test of purchasing power parity, or whether forward and spot exchange rates are cointegrated.

Estimation of Cointegrated Systems

To begin, consider the problem of fitting a bivariate system of equations when it is known that the variables are cointegrated. In this case the system must have the property that each of the series are integrated of order 1, $I(1)$, while one particular linear combination, the cointegrating relation, is $I(0)$. Even without specifying the dynamic processes of these variables, there is a reasonable approach to estimating the cointegrating relation.

Engle and Granger propose regressing one of the variables on the other using ordinary least squares. This is called the cointegrating regression and is given in (2.1)

$$y_t = \hat{\alpha} x_t + z_t \qquad (2.1)$$

where z_t are the residuals. This algorithm minimizes the residual variance and thus will find a finite variance linear combination if there is one. Since $I(1)$ series will have infinite variance in large samples, and since only one linear combination is stationary and has finite variance, least squares effectively finds a good estimate of the cointegrating coefficient. Least squares is easily shown to be consistent for the true cointegrating coefficient; in fact, Stock (1987) shows even more. The estimate converges to its true value at a rate T^{-1} rather than the usual $T^{-1/2}$ as a consequence of the infinite variance of all other linear combinations. We often call such estimators 'superconsistent'.

The practising econometrician at this moment must be sceptical. It appears that the regression can be run with either variable as the dependent variable, and there is no correction for simultaneous equations bias or serial correlation. The solution to the puzzle is that the R^2

of the regression goes to one asymptotically so that the fit is perfect no matter which way the regression is run and no matter how strong is the simultaneous equations bias. When two series move together and have infinite variance, it is easy for any statistical procedure to find the true relationship. To achieve a consistent estimate it is not necessary to worry about simultaneity or serial correlation.

However, it is important not to use the t-ratios for inference. These do not have limiting normal distributions, and standard attempts to correct for serial correlation will only make the estimator lose its consistency. This ratio has a complicated limiting distribution which Stock suggests tabulating numerically. Fortunately, maximum likelihood estimates of α as proposed by Johansen or as approximated by the Engle–Yoo (1990b) three-step estimator will have t-ratios with normal limits and this is the appropriate way to test hypotheses on the cointegrating coefficient.

The next step in fitting the system of equations is to formulate the dynamics imposing the constraint that they be cointegrated. This is most simply accomplished with the error correction representation. For two variables x_t and y_t which jointly satisfy a $(p+1)^{th}$ order vector autoregression, the equations can be written:

$$\Delta x_t = \gamma_1(y_{t-1} - \alpha x_{t-1}) + \beta_{111}\Delta x_{t-1} + \beta_{112}\Delta y_{t-1} + \cdots$$

$$+ \beta_{1p1}\Delta x_{t-p} + \beta_{1p2}\Delta y_{t-p} + \varepsilon_{xt} \qquad (2.2)$$

$$\Delta y_t = \gamma_2(y_{t-1} - \alpha x_{t-1}) + \beta_{211}\Delta x_{t-1} + \beta_{212}\Delta y_{t-1} + \cdots$$

$$+ \beta_{2p1}\Delta x_{t-p} + \beta_{2p2}\Delta y_{t-p} + \varepsilon_{yt} \qquad (2.3)$$

where ε_{xt} and ε_{yt} may be correlated but are white noise. Notice that these equations have only variables in changes, which are therefore $I(0)$ by assumption, plus the error correction terms $y - \alpha x$. If y and x are cointegrated with parameter α, then this too is $I(0)$ and the equations appropriately are $I(0)$ on both sides. Cointegration implies that the system follows an error correction representation and conversely an error correction system has cointegrated variables. This is proven in Engle and Granger (1990) as the Granger Representation Theorem and again in Engle and Yoo (1990b) using polynomial matrix functions. The exact statement of this result is a little more complicated.

The estimation of equations 2.2 and 2.3 would be simple if α were known since joint estimation of the two equations by seemingly un-related regressions (SUR) is equivalent to ordinary least squares on each because the same variables appear in each. Engle and Granger prove that if a superconsistent estimate of α such as $\hat{\alpha}$ from the cointegrating regression is used, the remaining coefficients (the β's and γ's) will be estimated as efficiently asymptotically as if α were known a priori. The estimate thus proceeds very simply in two steps. First, estimate α from the cointegrating regression, and then take the residuals, z, from this estimate and use these lagged in the vector autoregression of the changes. This is the Engle–Granger two-step estimation method.

Several variations on this procedure should be mentioned as they appear often in applied work. In almost all cases, there should be an intercept in the cointegrating regression. Only strong priors should set it to zero. With seasonal processes which have deterministic seasonals, seasonal dummy variables can be added either in the cointegrating regression or in the error correction form.

Often, it is desirable to introduce the current value of Δx into the first equation making it a 'structural form' equation rather than a 'reduced form' relation. This can always be done but will, of course, change the interpretation of all the coefficients but the cointegrating coefficient. If one were concerned about simultaneity, one could even use instrumental variables to estimate the structural equation. Additional stationary variables can be entered into equations 2.2 and 2.3 and variables which are not significant can be dropped. Of course for full efficiency in this case, SUR estimation would be needed.

Testing for a Unit Root

Turn now to the problem of testing for cointegration between two $I(1)$ variables. For background, tests will first be presented for whether the individual series are $I(1)$. It is important to carry out such tests as otherwise the results of tests of cointegration may be misleading. In the simplest case, the test is computed from a least squares $AR(1)$ model. One runs

$$y_t = \rho y_{t-1} + \varepsilon_t$$

or in other notation:

$$\Delta y_t = (\rho - 1)y_{t-1} + \varepsilon_t \tag{2.4}$$

and tests whether the coefficient of y_{t-1} is zero against the alternative that it is negative. The t-ratio from equation 2.4 is the most familiar version of the Dickey–Fuller test. See Dickey and Fuller (1979) and Fuller (1976). If the null hypothesis that $\rho = 1$ is true, then this regression has an $I(0)$ variable on the left side and an $I(1)$ on the right. For an $I(1)$ random variable, the sums converge in distribution as follows:

$$\sum y_{t-1}^2/T^2 \xrightarrow{D} s_T, \qquad \sum y_{t-1}\varepsilon_t/T \xrightarrow{D} v_T \tag{2.5}$$

where $\sqrt{s_T}$ and v_T are correlated random variables. In fact, under rather general conditions, the limiting distributions in equation 2.5 can be expressed as integrals of Brownian motions as pointed out by Phillips (1987). As a consequence, the t-ratio does not have a limiting normal distribution; it has a distribution now called the 'Dickey–Fuller' distribution. This distribution is skewed to the left and has most of its mass below zero reflecting the fact that values of ρ greater than one could have generated a particular data set only with very low probability.

In practice, one often must include an intercept in equation 2.4 to reflect the possibility that under the alternative of stationarity, the intercept is not zero. This alters the distribution of the test statistic. A further variation introduces a time trend into equation 2.4 to allow the alternative to be trend-stationarity. One can best decide which model is appropriate by thinking of equation 2.4 as the equation under the alternative and the Dickey–Fuller test statistic as being a Wald test. The careful reader may notice that this Wald test is not testing the entire restriction.

A second practical issue is that in most series ε_t is not white noise. There are two popular corrections which might be called a parametric and a non-parametric solution. The parametric solution suggested by Dickey and Fuller (1979) is augmenting the regression (2.4) by adding sufficient terms in Δy_{t-i} to whiten the residuals. Thus the augmented Dickey–Fuller (ADF) test is the t-statistic on y_{t-1} in

$$\Delta y_t = (\rho - 1)y_{t-1} + \sum \theta_i \Delta y_{t-i} + \varepsilon_t. \qquad (2.6)$$

It will have the same asymptotic Dickey–Fuller distribution and will not depend upon θ_i. The investigator, however, is required to pick the order of the autoregression either by a rule, by an automatic data based procedure such as AIC, or by some specification search.

The alternative non-parametric procedure introduced by Phillips (1987) and Phillips and Perron (1988) uses the residuals from the first order model in equation 2.4 to correct the t-statistic. The correction requires estimating only one additional parameter.

$$\sigma_S^2 = E\left[\left(\sum \varepsilon_t\right)^2\right] \qquad (2.7)$$

which can be interpreted as the value of the spectral density of ε at the origin. For finite samples, this can be approximated by various expressions. The most popular is the Newey–West estimator which takes a weighted average of the autocorrelations of ε.

From Monte Carlo evidence Schwert (1989) concludes that the parametric approach gives a more accurate test size even in the case where the true autoregression is infinite. This is not entirely surprising since by specifying and correcting for the autocorrelation, the estimators will be maximum likelihood.

Testing for Non-cointegration

To test whether two series are cointegrated, one must first establish that they are invididually integrated. This is done using the techniques described above. Typically, the test would suppose there to be an intercept. If there is also a trend included then cointegration tests which allow for trends should also be employed as discussed in Engle and Yoo (1990b).

The procedure is simply to test whether there is a unit root in the residual of the cointegrating regression (eqn. 2.1). If the series are not cointegrated then there must be a unit root in these residuals; this is therefore the null of non-cointegration. If the series are cointegrated, then the residuals will be stationary.

The procedure is therefore to run the cointegrating regression, typically with an intercept, and then run an augmented Dickey–Fuller test on the residuals again including an intercept (although this is almost identically zero). The t-ratio from this test, however, no longer has the Dickey–Fuller distribution, since the parameter α has been estimated and therefore makes the residual series appear slightly more stationary than if it were computed at the true α. The distribution of this test was first tabulated by Engle and Granger and has come to be called the Engle–Granger distribution. Tables of critical values are included in Engle and Yoo (1990a,b) and more precise values in MacKinnon (1990). For example, the one tailed critical values for a 5 per cent test of the first order autoregressive coefficient would be -1.64 if it were normal, -2.86 if it were Dickey–Fuller, and -3.34 for the Engle–Granger cointegration test.

If the value of the test statistic is insufficient to. reject the null hypothesis of non-cointegration, then the researcher typically will proceed to estimate a model which imposes non-cointegration by forcing the error correction terms to have zero coefficients in equations 2.2 and 2.3. He simply estimates a model where all the variables are differenced before he begins. If he rejects the null of non-cointegration, it is common to assert that he has found evidence for cointegration, although there could, of course, be other reasons for rejecting the null. Then his model will include both differences and error correction terms.

When the individual series are assumed to be random walks with drift, then it is important to incorporate this information in the testing procedure. In particular, when testing that a series is $I(1)$, it becomes important to include not only an intercept but also a trend and then to use the corresponding Dickey–Fuller tables. This is just equivalent to detrending the series by regressing each on a time trend before computing the Dickey–Fuller test. Similarly, when testing non cointegration of series which have a drift, one can include a time trend in the cointegrating regression which is equivalent to detrending the series first. The critical value is then even higher; the 5 per cent point is now −3.78. Notice, of course, that this is a test that two series are not cointegrated even after extracting a linear time trend.

In practice, it is often desirable to formulate cointegration hypotheses among more than two variables. Under the null hypothesis of non-cointegration, it is possible to follow exactly the same strategy described above. First, estimate the multivariate cointegrating regression and then test for a unit root in the residuals. Now, however, the critical values must again be re-examined. For three variables, the critical value is −3.74 while for five the t-statistic would have to exceed −4.71 to reject non-cointegration. This is a natural consequence of the tendency of least squares to find ever more stationary-looking linear combinations of $I(1)$ variables.

Often researchers would like to include in the cointegrating relationship variables which are not $I(1)$. In principle, inclusion of a stationary variable is prohibited but should not affect the remaining coefficients (assuming it is not the dependent variable). It appears that it also should not affect the asymptotic critical values of the test statistics. More problematical are dummy variables for regime changes or data corrections or seasonality. These cannot be taken as $I(1)$ or $I(0)$ but will be allowable if they do not affect the distribution of the Engle–Granger test. The exact criteria here remain to be developed but presumably depend upon whether the variables have spectral mass at zero frequency.

Several alternative approaches to testing for cointegration have been suggested and are discussed in considerable detail in the remainder of the book. It is worth describing the error in what appears to be a natural alternative approach. Since the hypothesis of cointegration implies the existence of the error correction representation, a natural testing framework is to test for the presence of the error correction terms in equations 2.2 and 2.3. Notice first, that a test in one equation would not enable the investigator to conclude whether or not there was cointegration, since one error correction term is sufficient for cointegration. Only if one assumes that there cannot be such a term in one of the equations, is a test of the other one conclusive. Second, under the null of $\gamma = 0$ which is non-cointegration, the term $y_{t-1} - \alpha x_{t-1}$ will be $I(1)$. Thus the regression will be of an $I(0)$ variable on an $I(1)$ and all the problems of the Dickey–Fuller test statistic remain important. Breaking the error correction terms apart into γy_{t-1} and $\gamma \alpha x_{t-1}$ does not solve this problem. In short, the testing problem is still non-standard; in simulations, Engle and Granger concluded that size corrected tests of this form did not have as good power as the simple Engle–Granger test they recommended.

Conclusions and directions for further research

The theoretical and empirical analysis of cointegrated systems is a rapidly developing and highly exciting field. Many of the techniques which have been developed are already in use and a variety of interesting economic hypotheses have already been phrased and tested in the context of cointegration. Further results can be expected from application to more general systems which had previously been analysed by vector autoregressions or structural econometric models.

This introduction has presented the Engle–Granger two-step approach to estimation and testing in cointegrated systems, but more complex and in some cases more powerful procedures are available and are described in the body of the book. It remains to see how successfully these procedures deal with actual empirical data problems.

References

CAMPBELL, J. Y., and R. J. SHILLER, 'Cointegration and Tests for Present Value Models' reprinted in Chapter 10, this volume.

DICKEY, D., and W. A. FULLER (1979), 'Distribution of the estimators for autoregressive time series with a unit root', *Journal of the American Statistical Association*, **74**, 427–31.

ENGLE, R. F., and C. W. J. GRANGER, 'Cointegration and Error Correction: Representation Estimation and Testing', reprinted in Chapter 5, this volume.

—— —— and J. HALLMAN, 'Merging Short- and Long-run Forecasts', reprinted in Chapter 11, this volume.

—— and B. SAM YOO (1990a), 'Forecasting and Testing in Cointegrated Systems'. (Chapter 6 of this volume.)

—— —— (1990b), 'Cointegrated Economic Time Series: An Overview with New Results'. (Chapter 12 of this volume.)

FULLER, W. A. (1976), *Introduction to Statistical Time Series* (New York, John Wiley).

GRANGER, C. W. J., and T. W. LEE, 'Multicointegration' reprinted in Chapter 9, this volume.

HYLLEBERG, S., R. F. ENGLE, C. W. J. GRANGER, and B. S. YOO (1990), 'Seasonal integration and co-integration', *Journal of Econometrics*.

JOHANSEN, S., 'Statistical Analysis of Cointegration Vectors', reprinted in Chapter 7, this volume.

MacKinnon, James, 'Critical Values for Cointegration Tests', Chapter 13, this volume.

Phillips, P. C. B. (1987), 'Time series regression with a unit root', *Econometrica*, **55**, 277–301.

—— and P. Perron (1988), 'Testing for a unit root in time series regression', *Biometrika*, **75**, 335–46.

Schwert, G. William (1989), 'Test for unit roots: A Monte Carlo investigation', *Journal of Business and Economic Statistics*, **7**, 147–60.

Stock, James (1987), 'Asymptotic properties of least squares estimators of cointegrating vectors', *Econometrica*, **55**, 1035–56.

—— and Mark Watson, 'Testing for Common Trends', reprinted as Chapter 8, this volume.

2

Variable Trends in Economic Time Series

JAMES H. STOCK* and MARK W. WATSON

The two most striking historical features of aggregate output are its sustained long run growth and its recurrent fluctuations around this growth path. Real per capita GNP, consumption and investment in the United States during the postwar era are plotted in Figure 1. Both growth and deviations from the growth trend—often referred to as 'business cycles'—are apparent in each series. Over horizons of a few years, these shorter cyclical swings can be pronounced; for example, the 1953, 1957, and 1974 recessions are evident as substantial temporary declines in aggregate activity. These cyclical fluctuations are, however, dwarfed in magnitude by the secular expansion of output. But just as there are cyclical swings in output, so too are there variations in the growth trend: growth in GNP in the 1960s was much stronger than it was in the 1950s. Thus, changes in long-run patterns of growth are an important feature of postwar aggregate economic activity.

In this article we discuss the implications of changing trends in macroeconomic data from two perspectives. The first perspective is that of a macroeconomist reassessing the conventional dichotomy between growth and stabilization policies. As an empirical matter, does this dichotomy make sense for the postwar United States? What is the relative 'importance' of changes in the trend and cyclical swings in explaining the quarterly movements in economic aggregates? We next adopt the perspective of an econometrician interpreting empirical evidence based on data that contain variable trends. The presence of

* James H. Stock is Assistant Professor of Public Policy, Kennedy School of Government, Harvard University, Cambridge, MA. Mark W. Watson is Associate Professor of Economics, Department of Economics, Northwestern University, Evanston, IL. This article was written while Stock was a National Fellow at the Hoover Institution, Stanford University, Stanford, CA.

Printed with permission of: *Journal of Economic Perspectives*, Volume 2, Number 3, Summer 1988, pp. 147-74.

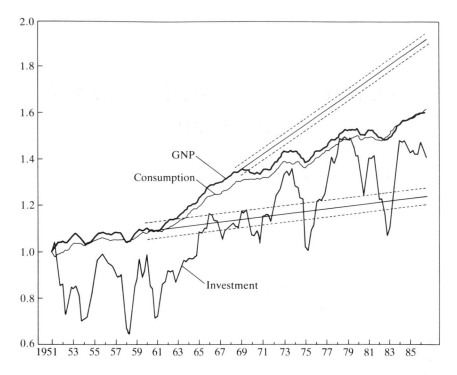

Fig. 1. Postwar real per capita US GNP, total consumption, and gross private investment (in logarithms).

All three series have been arbitrarily set to 1 in 1951:I. The straight solid lines represent two long-run forecasts of GNP, the lower using data from 1951:I–1959:IV and the upper using data from 1960:I–1969:IV. The forecasts were made by extrapolating GNP growth over these periods using a linear deterministic time trend. The dotted lines represent bands of ± two standard deviations of quarterly GNP growth around the long-run forecasts. Were GNP a stationary series about a linear time trend, these bands would provide an approximate long-run 95 per cent confidence interval for the respective GNP forecasts.

variable trends in time series data can lead one to draw mistaken inferences using conventional econometric techniques. How can these techniques—or our interpretation of them—be modified to avoid these mistakes?

The macroeconomist's perspective is adopted in the first major section of the article. Discussions of macroeconomics often treat the concepts of 'trends' and 'cycles' in output separately. On the one hand, theories of growth examine the forces capable of changing long-run trends, while on

the other hand theories of the business cycle attempt to explain shorter
run fluctuations and to determine when macroeconomic policy might
stabilize or exacerbate the swings between expansion and recession. At
one level this dichotomy seems natural, with different theories providing
insights into macroeconomic movements over different horizons. But on
another level this distinction is artificial: theories explaining only growth
or only cycles cannot provide adequate macroeconomic insights if there
are important interactions between the two.

A closer look at Figure 1 suggests that changes in growth trends are
associated with some of the shorter, 'cyclical' swings in the series. For
example, a key turning point between the high-growth 1960s and the
low-growth 1970s and 1980s seems to have been in the early 1970s,
which was also followed by a major recession that saw a particularly
sharp transitory drop in investment. When one formally defines trends
using the 'stochastic trends' concept discussed below, various statistical
measures (introduced in the next section) indicate that a substantial
fraction of the quarterly variation in real GNP is associated with
movements in long run trends rather than being purely transitory
fluctuations. This agrees with the casual inference drawn from Figure 1
that shifts in trends are an important part of changes in GNP.
Moreover, examinations of the co-movements of several macroeconomic
variables indicate that unforecasted shifts in long run economic prospects are associated with short run fluctuations that are similar to
common conceptions of the business cycle. These findings suggest two
conclusions: first, that a key step in understanding the co-movements in
aggregate economic variables is learning about the link between changes
in long run economic trends and cyclical swings; and second, that a
sharp dichotomy between growth and stabilization policies misses an
important connection between the two policy goals.

The econometrician's perspective on variable trends is taken in the
second major section of this article. Variable trends provide numerous
econometric pitfalls and raise difficult methodological issues. Time series
analysts have long recognized that regression analysis can be highly
misleading when applied to series with variable trends. In some cases (as
in Figure 1), the result can be dramatic errors in forecasting. In other
cases, an improper treatment of variable trends can result in false
conclusions about how the economy works. To illustrate this point, we
construct a simple artificial economy and assign two hypothetical inhabitants the task of discovering its true structure. As in many model
economies studied in the modern literature on macroeconomic theory,
these inhabitants happen to be econometricians; but here their training
often fails them simply because they mishandle the variable trends in
their data. Finally, we draw on recent developments in econometric
theory to provide some simple rules-of-thumb that a consumer or

producer of econometric models can use in an attempt to avoid these pitfalls.

What is a 'Variable Trend?'

The basic premise of econometric analysis is that, when viewed together, individual cases and experiences can provide insights into a deeper unifying structure. When analyzing cross sectional data, the individual experiences might be those of different workers or firms; but the only individual experiences we have with the operation of the U.S. economy are historical. For macroeconometric analysis to be of any value, then, it must be that the historical experiences comprising an economic time series are on the one hand sufficiently different from each other that more experiences provide additional information, but on the other hand sufficiently similar that combining individual experiences can elucidate the underlying economic structure. These two require-ments are the essence of the technical assumption that a time series is ergodic and stationary.[1]

The first requirement—that historical experiences be sufficiently un-related—is unlikely to hold for GNP, consumption and investment in Figure 1. The key reason is that the current trend levels of these variables arguably depend on the entire history of these series. For example, were the experiences of the 1950s essentially unrelated to those of the 1980s, except for a perfectly predictable trend, an econo-metric forecaster in 1960 might predict 1987 GNP by extrapolating trend growth during the 1950s out to 1987; an econometrician in 1970 might do the same, only using data from the 1960s. With unchanging trends, these forecasts should be similar, and indeed should be moderately accurate. But, as indicated in Figure 1, these forecasts are close neither to each other nor to the actual value of 1987 GNP. Just as important, the confidence bands around the trend extrapolations in Figure 1—de-signed to capture the uncertainty associated with these forecasts—clearly fail to provide a reliable estimate of the range of future GNP. Thus historical experiences—namely, unforecasted increases in the level of GNP in some past year—appear to have had a dramatic and persistent influence on production today.

On a casual level, the notion that GNP is composed of a variable trend plus some additional cyclical movements seems quite satisfactory.

---

[1] Formally, a time series random variable is said to be stationary if its distribution does not depend on time. As is the convention, we further assume that *stationary* variables have finite variances and autocovariances. See Andrew Harvey (1981, p. 22) or Clive Granger and Paul Newbold (1977, p. 4) for more details.

Time series variables can, without further restrictions, be thought of as composed of a part with a variable trend, plus a part that is not the trend. But a moment's reflection indicates that this decomposition lacks content; without a more precise definition, one economist's 'trend' can be another's 'cycle'. The ambiguity surrounding the definition of a variable trend applies equally to the definition of a 'business cycle'. Indeed, one can imagine extreme views that there is no business cycle, in the sense that all economic fluctuations are merely movements in variable trends—or the reverse view that what appear to be variable macroeconomic trends are but very long cyclical swings. But these extreme views miss valuable notions traditionally associated with the business cycle: that the economy experiences protracted but nonetheless temporary periods of unusually high (or low) output, employment, and inflation across many or all sectors of the economy; that these protracted experiences have important implications for the well-being of people and institutions; and that these changes in well-being often have important political consequences. In referring to business cycles, then, we mean these protracted yet temporary swings in aggregate output.

Then what is a trend? Perhaps the theory of economic growth can provide an operational definition. For example, in a one-sector neoclassical growth model, trends can arise because of technical progress and an increasing labour force and capital stock. If the production technology has constant returns to scale, this suggests that—at least in theory—the trend in output per capita could be represented as a function of the capital-labour ratio, the labour force participation rate, and the stock of 'technology'. Unfortunately, in practice things are not so simple; for example, the capital-labour ratio and the labour force participation rate have cyclical as well as trend components, and the stock of technology cannot be measured directly. Thus, at least at this level of analysis, this approach based on growth theory has little empirical relevance.

It is therefore common to take a different approach to the definition of a variable trend. The specific notion we adopt is a direct extension of a *deterministic linear time trend* (used to compute the forecasts in Figure 1), which increases by some fixed amount (say, 1 per cent) every quarter. In contrast, we model a variable trend as increasing in each quarter by some fixed amount (say, 1 per cent) on average; however, in any given quarter the change in the trend will deviate from its average by some unforecastable random amount. Because it has this unpredictable random component, henceforth we refer to this formulation of a variable trend as a *stochastic trend.* The reader familiar with the random walk theory of stock prices will recognize that this notion of a trend corresponds to a random walk with drift. From a forecasting perspective a key feature of a random walk—in contrast to a stationary time series variable—is that, because of its random growth, forecasts of its level will entail uncertainty that increases as the forecast horizon recedes. With this formulation of a stochastic trend, a (random) change in the trend in one quarter provides a new base from which growth will occur in the next.[2]

While this definition of a stochastic trend might at first seem restrictive, a recent theorem by Stephen Beveridge and Charles Nelson (1981) suggests that it might be broadly applicable to US data. Since George Box and Gwilym Jenkins (1970) proposed their influential autoregressive-integrated-moving average (ARIMA) models for forecasting time series variables, econometricians have generally recognized that many macroeconomic series (when considered one at a time) appear to be *integrated*, that is, their first differences are stationary. ARIMA models are sophisticated yet simple tools for forecasting a single series using only its history. Box and Jenkins referred to integrated variables with autoregressive (AR) or moving average (MA) components as ARIMA($p, 1, q$) processes, where p and q, respectively, denote the orders of the autoregressive and moving average terms and where '1' indicates that the variable is integrated of order one, which means that its first difference (quarterly change) is stationary. ARIMA models are extensions of conventional regression models to time series variables; the AR terms forecast the current variable using p of its lags, and the MA terms forecast using q lags of the error in the process.[3]

[2] A time series variable x_t is a *random walk with drift* if x_t evolves according to

$$x_t = \mu + x_{t-1} + e_t \text{ or } x_t - x_{t-1} = \mu + e_t$$

where e_t has mean zero and variance σ_e^2, and where e_t is serially uncorrelated, i.e. e_t is uncorrelated with e_s for $s \neq t$, so e_t cannot be forecasted using past values of x_t. The 'drift' in the random walk is μ, the average predictable increase in x_t in each period. (For example, from 1951:I to 1986:III, real GNP increased by 3.0 per cent annually; on a per capita basis, the average annual increase was 1.7 per cent). With this definition, a variable y_t that contains a stochastic trend can be written as $y_t = y_t^p + y_t^s$, where y_t^p is a random walk (possibly with drift) and y_t^s is a stationary time series variable; the superscripts 'p' and 's' refer to the 'permanent' (or trend) and 'stationary' (or transitory) components of y_t. A variable that contains a deterministic time trend can be written as $y_t = gt + y_t^s$, where y_t^s is stationary and g is the constant quarterly growth of the deterministic trend.

[3] *Some Useful Definitions*

(i) The variable x_t, is *integrated of order one* (or simply *integrated*) if it is nonstationary and can be written

$$x_t = \mu + x_{t-1} + u_t, \text{ or } x_t - x_{t-1} = \mu + u_t$$

where u_t has mean zero and variance σ_u^2, and where u_t is stationary. It is convenient to let Δx_t, represent $x_t - x_{t-1}$. A variable is said to be *integrated of order d* if it must be differenced d times to be stationary; for example, if Δx_t is not stationary but $\Delta x_t - \Delta x_{t-1}$ is, then x_t is integrated of order 2. The distinction between an integrated process and a random walk is that, if x_t is integrated, u_t is stationary but might be correlated with lagged u_t; if x_t is a random walk, u_t is serially uncorrelated.

(ii) Following Box and Jenkins, an ARIMA($p, 1, q$) model specifies x_t as being integrated of order one and as having a representation of the form,

$$\Delta x_t = c + a_1 \Delta x_{t-1} + \ldots + a_p \Delta x_{t-p} + e_t + b_1 e_{t-1} + \ldots + b_{t-q} e_{t-q}$$

Among time series analysts, a major attraction of ARIMA$(p, 1, q)$ models is their ability to forecast many macroeconomic variables with an accuracy that is impressive among univariate forecasting techniques. Here, however, the importance of ARIMA models is that Beveridge and Nelson prove that every variable having an ARIMA$(p, 1, q)$ representation contains a random walk stochastic trend. Since ARIMA $(p, 1, q)$ models seem to characterize many macroeconomic variables, it follows that the growth in these variables can be described by stochastic trends. Beveridge and Nelson's (1981) trend/cycle decomposition is presented in the Appendix for readers familiar with the mathematical particulars of ARIMA models.

A possible objection to the discussion so far is its emphasis on variables that are integrated of order one, so that the quarterly percentage growth in GNP is modeled as being stationary. Why not treat US data as integrated of order two, so that the second difference of GNP is stationary but the quarterly growth rate itself contains a stochastic trend? Or why not model GNP as stationary but having coefficients that imply almost the same 'stochastic trend' behaviour as an integrated process? Our answer is that the preponderance of evidence currently suggests that the integrated model provides the best approximation of US GNP. This is not to say that US GNP is an integrated process, for this can never be learned with certainty by examining a finite time series; nor is it to say that future research using new techniques or more data could not change this assessment. But, given currently available statistical techniques, modelling GNP as an integrated process seems to provide a good approximation to its long-run properties.[4]

where $a_1, \ldots, a_p$, $b_1, \ldots, b_q$, and c are constant parameters and where e_t is serially uncorrelated.

(iii) A variable that is integrated is said to have a unit root in its autoregressive representation. The term 'unit root' refers to the unit coefficient on x_{t-1} in the formula defining an integrated process. The statements 'x_t has a unit root' an 'x_t is integrated of order one' are equivalent. Box and Jenkins use the term 'nonstationary' to refer to an integrated process. This terminology, while conventional, is unfortunate: while all integrated processes are nonstationary, not all nonstationary processes are integrated.

(iv) An integrated process has a variance that tends to infinity. This is most easily demonstrated for a random walk. Let $x_t = x_{t-1} + e_t$ where e_t is serially uncorrelated and var $(e_t) = \sigma_e^2$, and let $x_0 = 0$. Then $x_t = \sum_{s=1}^{t} e_s$, so that var $(x_t) = t\sigma_e^2$, which tends to infinity with t.

[4] Guy Orcutt (1948) was among the first to suggest that GNP is an integrated process. Using annual US data from 1919 to 1932, he found that many aggregate time series were well described by an ARIMA$(1, 1, 0)$ model with an autoregressive coefficient of 0.3. This argument for the existence of stochastic trends in macroeconomic data is only partly convincing, since Orcutt's and Box and Jenkins's techniques for determining whether the process is integrated require the practitioner to make qualitative judgements. To overcome this drawback, Wayne Fuller (1976) and David Dickey and Fuller (1979) proposed several statistical tests for whether a variable is integrated, against the alternative that it is not (i.e. it is stationary). Nelson and Charles Plosser (1982) provided firm support for what Orcutt

The general success of ARIMA modeling therefore provides a technical motivation for the stochastic trend formulation. But the real motivation is provided by Figure 1, where the long-run forecasts based on a deterministic linear trend are simple, intuitively appealing, and wrong. With a deterministic linear trend, the uncertainty associated with a long-run forecast is limited to the variation in the stationary deviations from that trend. In contrast, with a stochastic trend, the greater the forecasting horizon, the greater is the uncertainty associated with that forecast.

Relations between Trends and Cycles in Macroeconomic Variables

Implicit in many models of the business cycle is the notion that macroeconomic fluctuations are, for the most part, caused by temporary rigidities or misperceptions. These models abstract from economic growth, operating on the implicit assumption that the growth process has little impact on the business cycle. In contrast, an alternative view (exposited clearly by Edward Prescott, 1987) explains economic fluctuations entirely as a reaction to changes in the long-run growth prospects of the economy, with 'business cycles' arising simply as adjustments to new long-run growth paths.

But theoretical debates linking changes in trends to cyclical fluctuations are of little practical interest unless empirical evidence suggests that there is such a link. In this section, we consider two related questions concerning the quantitative importance of changes in long run prospects for short-run economic fluctuations. First, to what extent are quarterly movements in postwar US real per capita GNP associated with variations in its trend? Second, are variations in macroeconomic trends linked to cyclical movements, or are the trend and cyclical variations largely unrelated?

Measuring the Trend in GNP

The first question seems simple enough, especially if we hold ourselves to the 'random walk' concept of stochastic trends. It has, however,

---

and the Box–Jenkins practitioners had suspected: upon applying the formal Dickey–Fuller tests to fourteen annual macroeconomic variables using 60 and 100 years of data, they could not reject the hypothesis that there is a stochastic trend in real and nominal output measures, wages, prices, monetary variables, and asset prices. In their analysis, only the unemployment rate failed to contain a stochastic trend over the twentieth century. Nelson and Plosser also emphasized that the presence of stochastic trends calls into question the validity of the traditional trend/cycle dichotomy used to describe aggregate time series.

generated a heated debate over the importance of the trend component in GNP. Besides being of interest in its own right, this debate highlights central conceptual difficulties that arise in defining trends.

The starting-point for this analysis is to suppose that real GNP consists of two parts: a stochastic trend, plus a part that is transitory, or more precisely, stationary. How important, then, are these two components? Answering this question requires first determining whether the unforecastable changes (technically, the innovations) in the two components are correlated, and second, developing an econometric framework (that is, a model) for interpreting the information contained in historical GNP data.

One would hope that an examination of historical data might shed some light on the correlation between the permanent and stationary innovations. Unfortunately this hope is vain, since this correlation cannot be estimated directly from a single time series; that is, this correlation is not identified in the usual econometric sense. This lack of identification should not be surprising. Broadly speaking, determining the correlation between the trend and stationary innovations in GNP is much like deciding whether the 1975 downturn was a result of a permanent shift in the trend, a transitory fluctuation, or some combination of the two—using only the plot of GNP in Figure 1. Without embarking on a review of the literature, we follow previous authors and consider two extremes: that these innovations are either uncorrelated or perfectly correlated. In the context of the trend-stationary decomposition, assuming the innovations to be uncorrelated implies that the changes in the trend and the transitory fluctuations are unrelated, except of course that they both affect GNP. In contrast, assuming the innovations to be perfectly correlated implies that they arise from the same source.

Although the decision concerning the correlation between the trend and stationary innovations is conceptually distinct from the decision about which model to estimate, in practice the first decision suggests a class of models to choose from. In the introduction, we emphasized that Beveridge and Nelson's theorem shows that all ARIMA(p, 1, q) models imply the presence of a stochastic trend. In fact, their theorem does more than this: it provides an explicit formula for computing a stochastic trend implied by an ARIMA model. An ARIMA model reduces all unforeseen economic events into a single innovation, and the Beveridge–Nelson trend and stationary components are both based on this innovation.

Although they sound complicated, the ARIMA framework and Beveridge–Nelson decomposition are in fact simple. As a concrete example, consider an ARIMA(0, 1, 1) model fit to GNP. Let y_t denote the logarithm of real US GNP, let $\Delta y_t = y_t - y_{t-1}$ denote quarterly real

GNP growth, let e_t denote an unobserved error term, and let SE denote the standard error of the estimate of Δy_t, that is, the standard deviation of the in-sample one-step-ahead forecast error. Because y_t is assumed to be an integrated process, the model is specified using the stationary growth rates, Δy_t. Using data from 1947:II to 1985:IV, we estimated the ARIMA(0, 1, 1) model,[5]

$$\Delta y_t = .008 + e_t + .3e_{t-1}, \; SE = .0106 \qquad (1)$$

In this ARIMA(0, 1, 1) specification, GNP growth is expressed as a weighted moving average of the errors, e_t. According to (1), given e_{t-1} but not e_t, GNP growth would thus be forecasted by $.008 + .3e_{t-1}$. In addition, the Beveridge–Nelson decomposition is particularly easy to apply in this case: using (1) and (A.2) in the Appendix, the permanent, or trend, component in log output (call this y_t^p) is $y_t^p = 1.3\sum_{s=1}^{t}e_s$. The transitory, or stationary, component in log output (call this y_t^s), also given by (1) and (A.2), is $y_t^s = -.3e_t$. Evidently the innovations in the Beveridge–Nelson permanent and stationary components are both e_t, so that the permanent and stationary innovations are perfectly correlated. Although this example is an ARIMA(0, 1, 1) model, their decomposition applies more generally to all ARIMA(p, 1, q) models. In the 'perfect correlation' case then, the choice of model reduces to a choice of p and q.

The choice of a specific model to estimate in the 'zero-correlation' case is conceptually similar. In this class of models, GNP is explicitly represented as the sum of its permanent component, modeled as a random walk with drift, and its transitory component, modeled as a stationary ARMA process (i.e. as an ARIMA(p, 0, q) process). Since neither component is observed directly (only their sum, GNP, is), this model is called an unobserved components ARIMA (UC-ARIMA) model. As a specific example, Watson fit a simple UC-ARIMA model to log real GNP, where the stationary component was assumed to be a second order autoregression (i.e. to be ARMA(2, 0)). Let e_t^s and e_t^p respectively be the innovations in the stationary and permanent components. His model, estimated using data from 1949:I–1984:IV, is:[6]

---

[5] Estimation was performed using the econometrics software package RATS. Let RGNP be the name used for the series, real GNP, in a RATS session. The ARIMA(0, 1, 1) model was estimated using the RATS commands:

set dlrgnp 47:2 85:4 = log(rgnp(t)) − log(rgnp(t − 1))

boxjenk(ar = 0, ma = 1, constant) dlrgnp 47:2 85:4

[6] Estimation of the parameters of UC-ARIMA models is more involved than for ARIMA models. Harvey (1985) provides a complete discussion of specification and estimation of UC-ARIMA models.

$$y_t = y_t^p + y_t^s,$$
$$y_t^p = .008 + y_{t-1}^p + e_t^p, \text{ std. dev. } (e_t^p) = .0057$$
$$y_t^s = 1.5y_{t-1}^s - .6y_{t-2}^s + e_t^s, \text{ std. dev. } (e_t^s) = .0076$$
$$\text{cov}(e_t^s, e_t^p) = 0, \, SE = .0099.$$

(2)

The innovations e_t^s and e_t^p are uncorrelated by assumption. Summarizing, in (2) the permanent component is written as a random walk with a drift of .008, and the stationary term is predicted using two of its lags.

Given a choice of model, the question becomes how to measure the extent to which quarterly movements in GNP are associated with variations in its trend. Since there is no one answer, various measures addressing different aspects of this question are presented in Table 1. The results pertain to different models based on the two assumptions about the correlation between the trend and stationary innovations. The results in the first row are for the ARIMA(0, 1, 1) model reported in (1). The next two results are for other low-order ARIMA models of GNP of the type estimated by John Campbell and Gregory Mankiw (1987a) and Watson (1986), while the following two are for higher order autoregressive models of the type studied by John Cochrane (1986). The final model is a UC-ARIMA model estimated by Peter Clark (1987a) with a stochastic trend plus a stationary AR(2) component, in which the innovations in the trend and stationary components are uncorrelated by assumption.[7]

The first measure of the importance of the trend component in GNP addresses the following question (enunciated most clearly by Campbell and Mankiw, 1987a): supposing that in some quarter GNP were to increase by 1 per cent above its forecasted amount, how would that change one's forecast of the long run level of GNP? If GNP were a stochastic trend with no stationary component, then the answer would be 1 per cent: the best forecast of a random walk arbitrarily far in the future is its current value, and if that value were to change by 1 per cent, so would the long run forecast. In contrast, if GNP were stationary around a purely deterministic time trend, then the answer would be zero per cent: any unpredictable change would have only a transitory effect on forecasts of future GNP.

It turns out that the choice of model by the various researchers makes a big difference in estimating the long-run effect of an innovation in the

---

[7] Model 3 is taken from Campbell and Mankiw (1987a) and Model 6 is taken from Clark (1987a). Cochrane used annual data for his empirical work; the high-order autoregressive models reported here capture his notion of including many lags in an annual specification. Models 1 and 2 were also re-estimated using the full data set. All models produce similar short run forecasts and fit the data well using standard time series diagnostic measures.

trend; the estimates vary by a factor of two. Although this is unsatisfying, it is useful to understand why these estimates vary. Consider first the estimates based on the assumption of a perfect correlation between the trend and stationary innovations. Using the results in the first row of Table 1, suppose that GNP were to grow by an unforecasted 1 per cent in some quarter. This growth will, on average, arise partly from an innovation in the trend and partly from innovations in the stationary component. Since the stationary innovation is perfectly correlated with the trend innovation, the change in the stationary component will either augment or partially offset the permanent innovation, respectively depending on whether the trend innovation induces an increase or a decrease in the stationary component. Using the ARIMA$(0, 1, 1)$ model (1), since $y_t^p = 1.3\sum_{s=1}^{t} e_t$ and $y_t^s = -.3e_t$, an increase in the trend is associated with a decrease in the stationary component using the Beveridge–Nelson decomposition: for a 1.3 per cent increase in the trend, the stationary component would initially drop by 0.3 per cent, leaving a net unforecasted increase in GNP of 1 per cent. Eventually the effect of this innovation on the stationary component will vanish, leaving only the 1.3 per cent permanent increase.

In contrast, when an unforecasted increase in GNP consists of the two uncorrelated innovations, less of an unforecasted quarterly change will be attributed to shifts in the trend. A 1 per cent increase in GNP might

TABLE 1.   Measures of the importance of the trend in real log GNP, estimated using data from 1947:I to 1985:IV

Univariate statistical model	Long-run increase in GNP predicted from a 1% unforeseen increase in GNP in one quarter	Variance ratios	
		$R^2_{corr=1}$	$R^2_{corr=min}$
1. ARIMA$(0, 1, 1)$	1.3	.93	.73
2. ARIMA$(1, 1, 0)$	1.6	.86	.60
3. ARIMA$(2, 1, 2)$	1.5	.80	.70
4. ARIMA$(12, 1, 0)$	1.3	.75	.57
5. ARIMA$(24, 1, 0)$	.9	.79	.64
6. UC-ARIMA	.6	.84	.34

The univariate estimates are based on analysis of GNP. As discussed in the text, the UC-ARIMA model was estimated under the assumption that the trend and stationary innovations are uncorrelated. The R^2 statistics measure the fraction of the variance in the quarterly change in real GNP attributable to changes in its stochastic trend. The minimal correlations used to compute the $R^2_{corr=min}$ statistic for the univariate models are (in order): .85, .9, .95, .9, .8, 0.

Source: authors' calculations, drawing on Campbell and Mankiw (1987a); Clark (1987a); Cochrane; and Gagnon.

have come from a trend or a stationary innovation; since these two innovations on average neither reinforce nor cancel each other, the best guess of either innovation will be less than one. Equivalently, with uncorrelated innovations, the fraction of an unforecasted change that is likely to be permanent will be less than one. Under the uncorrelated assumption, a 1 per cent increase in GNP today will on average therefore lead to a long run increase of less than 1 per cent. In general, then, the initial assumption about this correlation is crucial to ascertaining the relative importance of the two components..

The second pair of measures in Table 1 answers a related question about the relative importance of the trend and stationary components: what fraction of the quarterly variation in GNP is attributable to permanent shifts? Unfortunately, the answer to this is ambiguous, even given an estimated model for GNP, since the fraction of the variance accounted for by the trend depends on the correlation between the trend and stationary innovations. The two measures in the table are 'R-squared' statistics that would arise from regressing the quarterly change in GNP against the change in its true trend which in general is unobserved where the trend is computed under different assumptions about this correlation. The first statistic, $R^2_{\text{corr}=1}$, is from the regression using the trend computed assuming the trend and stationary innovations to be perfectly correlated, so that this trend is computed using Beveridge and Nelson's formula. The second measure is based on the observation that a given ARIMA model cannot be distinguished from (formally, is observationally equivalent to) a UC-ARIMA model with an assumed correlation falling in a certain range, where this range depends on the parameters of the ARIMA model. Accordingly, $R^2_{\text{corr}=\min}$ is computed using the smallest correlation that is capable of generating the estimated ARIMA model from a UC-ARIMA model. Thus these R^2 measures provide a rough range of the fraction of movements in quarterly GNP attributable to shifts in the trend.[8]

---

[8] The observational equivalence of ARIMA and UC-ARIMA models for a range of correlations is not obvious, although as an illustration it is readily derived for the UC-ARIMA model, $y_t = y_t^p + e_t^s$, where $y_t^p = y_{t-1}^p + e_t^p$, $\text{cov}(e_t^s, e_t^p) = 0$, and where e_t^p and e_t^s are serially uncorrelated. This model is observationally equivalent to the ARIMA(0, 1, 1) model: $\Delta y_t = e_t + be_{t-1}$, where $b/(1 + b^2) = -\text{var}(e_t^s)/[\text{var}(e_t^p) + 2\,\text{var}(e_t^s)]$. The observational equivalence follows because both models imply the same autocovariances for Δy_t.

Our variance measures are inspired by Masanao Aoki's (1987) measure of the relative variance of the two components. The correlation for the $R^2_{\text{corr}=\min}$ measure was computed by matching the autocovariances implied by the estimated ARIMA model to those implied by a UC-ARIMA model with various correlations between the two innovations. The R^2 refers to the trend from the UC-ARIMA model with the smallest correlation for which this match was possible, assuming an ARIMA(0, 100) structure for the stationary component in the UC-ARIMA model. The numerical search over trial correlations was carried out using steps of .05. The search was initialized by setting the autocovariances of the stationary process equal to the autocovariances of the innovation in GNP growth.

According to the first, 'perfect correlation' measure, all the univariate models attribute much of the quarterly movements in GNP to shifts in its trend. Indeed, the theoretical maximum of this R^2 is attained in the perfect correlation case. Examining the range of R^2 measures indicates that although the assumed correlation makes a quantitative difference to the estimated fraction of the variance associated with movements in the trend, in all cases it exceeds one-third, and in all but one it exceeds one-half.[9]

Do these calculations resolve the basic question of the extent to which quarterly movements in GNP are associated with variations in its trend? The answer must be both yes and no. Certainly these results provide further substance to the original findings of time series analysts that aggregate economic variables, and in particular GNP, seem to be integrated processes and therefore contain a stochastic trend. Indeed, even the smallest of the R^2 measures (.34) and of the estimates of the change in the long run forecast (.6) are qualitatively quite different from the values of zero that would obtain were the trend in GNP determin-istic rather than stochastic. These statistical measures therefore provide further confirmation of the conclusions drawn from our initial examina-tion of GNP in Figure 1: changes in trends seem to be an important feature of the postwar US experience.

Unfortunately, the ranges of the statistics in Table 1 indicate that the answer must also partially be no. There is nothing intrinsic to this question that rules out the possibility of reaching agreement among the various models. But, at least for the US, the different modeling strategies lead to very different quantitative conclusions.[10]

We have emphasized that a key reason for this ambiguity is the choice of the correlation of the innovations in the permanent and transitory components, likening this to the difficulty of deciding whether the 1975

[9] One approach to resolving the ambiguous results in Table 1 is to develop sensitive statistical measures to assist in choosing one model from another. For example, Cochrane suggested examining the variance of the growth in GNP over several years as a means of estimating the importance of stationary fluctuations in determining the long run behaviour of GNP; Joseph Gagnon (1986) has taken a different statistical approach to the same question. Both provide evidence that the low order ARMA models overstate the importance of the trend component in GNP, essentially for the reasons discussed above. However, Campbell and Mankiw (1987b) provide evidence that variance ratios involving long differences might exhibit substantial small sample bias when based on quarterly data covering 30–40 years.

[10] These different models might yield similar conclusions when applied to data from different countries. In an initial comparison of the stochastic trend behaviour across countries, Clark (1987b) has provided evidence of striking international differences in the relative importance of the trend and stationary components. Indeed, for some countries he suggests that the notion of a stochastic trend as it has been discussed here is inappropriate; following Harvey, he argues for a model in which the trend itself follows a random walk. In this case, GNP would be modeled as being integrated of order two.

downturn was a shift in the permanent or transitory components based solely on visual examination of GNP in Figure 1. Ultimately, however, as economists we should object to having one hand tied behind our back when sorting out trend and stationary movements, in the sense that this analysis focuses solely on the evidence contained in historical GNP. Rather, we might ideally wish to use qualitative evidence about the behaviour of the monetary authorities in response to the quadrupling of oil prices in 1973–4, or about the lasting effect on investment, technology, and human capital of the adjustments made in response to the price hike. Since such information is difficult to use in the context of statistical models, we still might hope to perform a less ambitious analysis using additional aggregate variables such as employment, consumption and investment.

Using Additional Information to Study Macroeconomic Trends

Casual inspection of Figure 1 suggests not only that GNP, consumption and investment appear to contain a stochastic trend, but that they contain a common stochastic trend. Indeed, one indication that the 'trend' in GNP changed betweeen the 1960s and the 1970s is that this shift appears in consumption and investment as well. This suggests that consumption and investment data contain important information about the trend in GNP, so that there is likely to be a statistical payoff to analyzing these series jointly.[11] This section briefly describes some recent work that uses multiple aggregate variables to assess the importance of the trend component in output.

One device used in these multivariate studies to measure the importance of the innovation to the permanent component is the concept of 'variance decompositions', which Christopher Sims (1980a, b) has profitably applied to Vector Autoregressive (VAR) multivariate time series models. When a forecast of GNP (econometric or otherwise) misses its target, and when this forecast error can be traced to a particular factor, it is reasonable to conclude that this factor is important in determining the evolution of GNP—at least within the context of the model that generated the forecast. Forecast error variance decompositions build on this intuition by quantitatively attributing the errors in forecasting the different variables to the various innovations in the system. For example, suppose that, in an empirical multivariate model with permanent and transitory components, forecasts of GNP two years hence are

---

[11] Since government expenditures and net exports are not considered, the national income accounting identity for GNP imposes no restrictions on the number of common trends in GNP, consumption and investment.

typically off by ±1.5 per cent. These forecast errors will, by construction, arise from errors in forecasting the trend, the stationary component, or both. If the errors from forecasting the trend generally
exceed the errors from forecasting the transitory component, then one
might attribute more importance to the permanent than the transitory
component in determining the evolution of GNP two years hence. In
multivariate models with stochastic trends, Sims' forecast error variance
decomposition performs this calculation.

Several recent studies (Oliver Blanchard and Danny Quah, 1987;
Clark, 1987*b*; Campbell and Mankiw, 1987*b*; Andrew Harvey and
Stock, 1987; Matthew Shapiro and Watson, 1988) have used multiple
aggregate variables to shed greater light on the importance of the
permanent component in GNP. Blanchard and Quah (1987) and Robert
King *et al.*, (1987) both use these forecast error variance decompositions
as a guide to assessing the importance of the permanent component.
Blanchard and Quah (1987) identify this component by assuming that it
has no permanent effect on unemployment. In contrast, King *et al.*
identify the permanent component in output by assuming that it is also
the permanent component in consumption and investment. Despite
these and other differences, both papers conclude that between 60 per
cent and 80 per cent of the movements in output at the two- to
four-year horizon are explained by movements in the permanent component. Although this literature is still developing, an emerging conclusion from these multivariate studies is that permanent innovations in
output play an important role in determining the movements of GNP at
horizons typically associated with the business cycle.

Implications

There is a large body of evidence that macroeconomic variables behave
as if they contain stochastic trends. Moreover, the empirical research
outlined here suggests that the innovations in these stochastic trends
play an important role in short-run cyclical movements. Multivariate
empirical analysis suggests that trend variations and business cycle
movements appear to be related. One interpretation of this link is that
business cycle fluctuations might be caused by innovations in growth.
An alternative explanation—equally consistent with the empirical results—
is that cyclical fluctuations cause changes in long run growth. This latter
view is consistent with James Tobin's (1980) argument, 'With respect to
human capital, as well as to physical capital, demand management has
important long run supply-side effects. A decade of slack labour
markets, depriving a generation of young workers of job experience, will
damage the human capital stock far beyond the remedial capacity of
supply-oriented measures.' Given the challenges associated with dif-

ferentiating the trend and cyclical components in the time series models discussed above, however, the logical next step is to bring additional information to bear on distinguishing the complex trend-cycle interactions with which Tobin was concerned.

Interpreting Econometric Evidence when Variables have Stochastic Trends

A Tale of Two Econometricians

Consider the plight of two hypothetical econometricians studying aggregate consumption—but ignorant of the pitfalls that can arise when performing econometric analysis with integrated variables. The econometricians do not, of course, know the true structure of the economy which produced their data; but we do. Specifically, we have constructed for them a simple artificial economy, focusing on aggregate real per capita consumption (C_t), aggregate disposable income (Y_t), and a price index (P_t).

The artificial economy has several key features. First, disposable income consists of two parts: in Milton Friedman's (1957) terminology, permanent and transitory income. The permanent component of disposable income is assumed to follow a random walk, while the transitory component is an independently and identically distributed random variable that is independent of the permanent component. Using the terminology of the previous section, we therefore assume that disposable income has a stochastic trend plus a stationary component, that this stationary component has no serial correlation, and that the correlation between the trend and stationary innovations is zero.

Second, we suppose that consumers know their permanent income and that they behave according to a narrow interpretation of Friedman's permanent income hypothesis, thereby consuming precisely the permanent component of their disposable income (which changes from period to period, since it is a random walk). Finally, price changes—assumed to be random and unforecastable with mean zero—do not confuse these consumers, in the sense that real consumption and disposable income are determined independently of the price level or its changes.

To summarize these assumptions mathematically, let Y_t^p and Y_t^s respectively denote the permanent and stationary (or transitory) components of disposable income (Y_t). The equations describing output, consumption and the price level in this artificial economy are:

$$Y_t = Y_t^p + Y_t^s \tag{3}$$

$$Y_t^p = Y_{t-1}^p + u_t \tag{4}$$

TABLE 2. Regression results using data from the artificial economy (3)–(7)

Typical regression results			Results based on 1000 replications	
Estimated regression equation	R^2	D.W.	Percentage rejections using the usual 10% two-sided t-test	Other statistics
Econometrician no. 1				
1. $C_t = \begin{array}{l} 9.16 \\ (28.7) \end{array} + \begin{array}{l} .40\ P_t \\ (5.12) \end{array}$	.15	.08	Testing $\beta_{P_t} = 0$: 81%	Median R^2 = .15
2. $C_t = \begin{array}{l} 2.48 \\ (6.35) \end{array} + \begin{array}{l} .069\ t \\ (16.9) \end{array}$	.66	.16	Testing $\beta_t = 0$: 91%	Median R^2 = .42
3. $\Delta C_t = \begin{array}{l} .048 \\ (.81) \end{array} + \begin{array}{l} .28\ \Delta Y_t \\ (8.06) \end{array}$	.31	2.27	—	Median $\hat\beta_{\Delta y_t}$ = .33
4. $\Delta Y_t = \begin{array}{l} .41 \\ (2.33) \end{array} - \begin{array}{l} .041\ C_{t-1} \\ (-2.15) \end{array}$	.03	1.98	Testing $\beta_{C_{t-1}} = 0$: 48%	Median $\hat\beta_{C_{t-1}}$ = −.035

TABLE 2. (*Cont.*)

Typical regression results			Results based on 1000 replications	
Estimated regression equation	R^2	D.W.	Percentage rejections using the usual 10% two-sided t-test	Other statistics
Econometrician no. 2				
5. $C_t = .51 + .94 \; Y_t$ $\quad\;\; (2.60) \;\; (-2.74)$	.93	1.88	Testing $\beta_{Y_t} = 1 : 84\%$	Median $\hat\beta_{Y_t} = .94$
6. $C_t = .45 + .97 \; C_{t-1} - .01 \; C_{t-2}$ $\quad\;\; (2.52) \;\; (11.7) \;\;\;\;\;\; (-.13)$	.94	2.01	Testing $\beta_{C_{t-2}} = 0 : 9\%$	Median $\hat\beta_{C_{t-2}} = -.001$
7. $C_t = .41 + 1.03 \; C_{t-1} - .07 \; Y_{t-1}$ $\quad\;\; (2.36) \;\; (14.3) \;\;\;\;\;\; (-.97)$	.94	1.97	Testing $\beta_{Y_{t-1}} = 0 : 10\%$	Median $\hat\beta_{Y_{t-1}} = .005$
8. $C_t = .47 + .95 \; C_{t-1}$ $\quad\;\; (2.21) \;\; (45.0)$ $\quad + .004 \; P_{t-1} + .06 \; \Delta P_{t-1}$ $\quad\;\;\;\; (.17) \;\;\;\;\;\;\; (.87)$	.94	2.00	Testing $\beta_{P_{t-1}} = 0 : 27\%$ Testing $\beta_{\Delta P_{t-1}} = 0 : 9\%$	Median $\hat\beta_{P_{t-1}} = -.003$ Median $\hat\beta_{\Delta P_{t-1}} = -.008$

Notes: The regression results in the left half of the table are based on a typical draw of 150 observations constructed according to (1)–(4) using a random number generator in the statistical package RATS (see footnote 12). R^2 and D.W. respectively denote the regression R-squared and the Durbin–Watson statistic. t-statistics are given in parentheses. The t-statistic on the coefficient in Y_t in regression 5 tests the hypothesis that the coefficient equals one, while all other t-statistics refer to the hypothesis that the coefficient equals zero. The entries in the right half of the table summarize the results of repeating these regressions 1000 times with independently drawn series.

$$C_t = Y_t^p \tag{5}$$

$$P_t = P_{t-1} + v_t. \tag{6}$$

The innovations Y_t^s, u_t, and v_t are assumed to be mutually independent and, for convenience, to be normally distributed with mean zero and unit variance. According to (3), disposable income (Y_t) is the sum of its permanent (Y_t^p) and transitory (Y_t^s) components where, according to (4), the permanent component evolves according to a random walk. The consumption function (5) states that consumers set their consumption (C_t) equal to their permanent income, so that the marginal propensity to consume out of permanent income is one. Finally, (6) states that, like permanent income, the price level (P_t) is a random walk.

We provide our two econometricians with a typical time series comprised of 150 observations (coincidentally, the number of quarters between 1950:I and 1987:II) on the three variables Y_t, C_t and P_t, generated according to (3)–(6) using a pseudo-random number generator on a portable computer.[12] They do not know but seek to uncover the true relations among these variables. What might they learn?

The first econometrician begins by investigating whether consumers change their consumption patterns based on the price level, which he does by regressing C_t against a constant and P_t. Since the t-statistic on P_t (given on the left-hand side of Table 2) of 5.12 far exceeds the conventional 5 per cent two-sided critical value of 1.96, a standard interpretation of his regression is that nominal prices affect consumption. He then checks whether consumption has a linear deterministic time trend by regressing C_t on a constant and time; upon checking the t-statistic, he concludes that it does. However, he recognizes that the low Durbin–Watson statistic from these regressions indicates substantial serial correlation in the residuals (e.g. Robert Pindyck and Daniel Rubinfeld 1981, pp. 158–64). Troubled by these low Durbin–Watson statistics and thinking consumption to have a deterministic time trend,

[12] The following computer program, written for the econometrics package RATS, will produce random time data according to equations (3)–(6):

```
cal 50 1 4
all 0 87:2
dec rect err(150, 3)
matrix err = ran(1.0)
zer yp ; zer ys ; zer p
eval yp(1) = err(1, 1) ; eval ys(1) = err(1, 2) ; eval p(1) = err(1, 3)
do i = (50:2), (87:2)
    eval yp(i) = yp(i − 1) + err(i, 1)
    eval ys(1) = err(i, 2)
    eval p(i) = p(i − 1) + err(i, 3)
end do i
set y / = yp(t) + ys(t); set c/ = yp(t)
diff y / 1 dy; diff c / 1 dc ; diff p / 1 dp
```

he differences the data and attempts to estimate the marginal propensity to consume by regressing the change of consumption on the change of income; he finds that the marginal propensity is small indeed. Finally, he recalls Robert Hall's (1978) famous argument that Friedman's Permanent Income Hypothesis implies that consumption follows a random walk, so that the first difference of consumption should be unpredictable. Accordingly, he checks whether lagged consumption is a useful predictor of future changes in consumption; based on the t-statistic of -2.15, he rejects the random walk hypothesis at the 5 per cent significance level. Summarizing, he concludes that consumers have money illusion, that consumption contains a linear time trend, that the marginal propensity to consume is 0.28, and that past values of consumption are useful in predicting future consumption. That he drew these conclusions is not an artifact of the particular series we gave him to analyse. Repeating this experiment 1000 times using independent draws (the results are summarized on the right-hand side of Table 2) indicates that his findings were typical.

Each of his conclusions is wrong.

The second econometrician estimates different regressions. She estimates the marginal propensity to consume by regressing consumption against income and finds it large, but significantly less than one using the usual 5 per cent critical value for the t-statistic. When she tests the random walk hypothesis by regressing consumption on two of its lags, the second lag has no statistically significant predictive content; the same conclusion obtains if a lag of income is used. Finally, she finds no additional forecasting value of lagged price changes (although, with the benefit of 1,000 replications, we know she would incorrectly reject the hypothesis of no predictive content of the lagged price level 27 per cent of the time using the 10 per cent critical value). She concludes that Hall's interpretation of Friedman's theory is valid and that the marginal propensity to consume is less than one, although this latter finding seems to be more a matter of statistical than economic significance.

Her conclusions, then, are largely right. Participants at a conference at which these two econometricians present their results might find the exchange entertaining. But they might also long for a systematic way to decide which regression results could be trusted and which could not.

Recent Developments in the Theory of Regression with Integrated Variables

It has long been recognized that the usual techniques of regression analysis can result in highly misleading conclusions when the variables contain stochastic trends. In the econometrics literature, since Clive

Granger and Paul Newbold's (1974) influential simulation study, this has been known as the problem of 'spurious regressions'. Largely influenced by the techniques of Box and Jenkins, the accepted 'solution' to the 'problem of nonstationarity' has been to transform the variables so that they appear to be stationary; in practice this typically means using first differences of the series. Unfortunately, by sidestepping the issues raised by stochastic trends, this approach has little to say about the regressions in Table 2. Moreover, simply using first differences of the data in the regressions generally will not suffice to uncover the true relations in the economy, as the first econometrician's regression of changes in consumption on changes in income makes clear.[13]

The past few years have seen important progress associated with the specification and analysis of multivariate models with integrated processes. Much of this stems from Fuller's (1976) and Dickey and Fuller's (1979) development of the first formal tests for the existence of stochastic trends in a single time series, and from three seminal papers by Granger and Andrew Weiss (1982), Granger (1983), and Robert Engle and Granger (1987). These latter papers provide a mathematical framework for analysing variables that contain common stochastic trends. Specifically, they consider the case that two (or more) variables might each contain a stochastic trend, i.e. appear to be integrated: consumption and GNP in Figure 1 are good examples. However, casual inspection suggests that these series contain a common trend—and that, by subtracting out this trend, the difference between the two variables is stationary. Formally, they define two integrated processes to be *cointegrated* if there is some linear combination (that is, weighted average) of them that is stationary. Thus consumption and GNP are arguably individually integrated; indeed, Dickey and Fuller's tests fail to reject this null hypothesis. But, assuming that log consumption less log output is stationary, they are jointly cointegrated; that is, they share a common stochastic trend. These theoretical developments (tests for a series being integrated and the concept of cointegration) spurred an enormous amount of recent research into econometric issues that arise when

---

[13] In a lively discussion of the history of spurious regression, David Hendry (1986) traces the recognition of this problem in the context of integrated processes to G. Yule (1926). In many circumstances, using differences of time series variables has proven very successful. Aside from having the intuitive appeal of modeling the rates of change of variables (when first differences of logarithms of the series are used), modeling differences of variables is arguably well-suited to producing short run forecasts—as dramatized by the early success of Box–Jenkins time series methods when pitted against the large Keynesian econometric models of the 1960s and 1970s. However, restricting econometric attention to differences in series rules out direct examination of the relation among the levels of the series. Even if the objective is to produce short run forecasts, the econometrician might wish to follow Sims (1980a) and use the additional information available in the levels of variables.

cointegrated processes contain unit roots.[14]

To understand the regression results in Table 2, we focus on one of the key lessons of this research: in certain circumstances, even if the right-hand variables (the regressors) are integrated, the usual procedures of OLS analysis can still provide a satisfactory framework for evaluating econometric evidence and for producing forecasts. Furthermore, this research has produced some simple rules-of-thumb that suggest when this is—and is not—likely to be the case.

We first state these rules-of-thumb in a general context, then apply them to the regressions in Table 2.[15] Broadly speaking, the usual assumptions of time series analysis are:

(i) The error term is serially uncorrelated and is uncorrelated with the regressors (i.e. the regressors are either exogenous or predetermined and the error term is i.i.d.).

(ii) All the regressors are either deterministic or stationary random variables.

Under these circumstances, the estimated coefficients will become arbitrarily close to their true values in increasingly large samples (that is, they will be consistent). Furthermore, in large samples the null distribution of regression t- and F-statistics can be approximated by normal and F-distributions, respectively.

When some or all of the regressors are integrated processes, condition (ii) clearly is violated. Perhaps surprisingly, however, in many cases the usual techniques of regression analysis will still apply. Specifically, suppose that one is interested in interpreting a particular coefficient or set of coefficients in the regression equation. Although (ii) does not hold, suppose that (ii') does:

(ii') If there are integrated regressors, either (a) the coefficients of interest are coefficients on mean zero stationary variables; or (b) even if some or all of the coefficients of interest are coefficients on integrated regressors, the regression equation can nevertheless be written in such a way that all the coefficients of interest become coefficients on mean zero stationary variables.

[14] The empirical results of James Davidson *et al.* (1978) provided an important motivation for the development of the theory of cointegration by developing an empirical model of consumption in which consumption and income were implicitly modeled as cointegrated. Granger (1986) and Hendry review recent developments in this area and discuss the link between error-correction models and cointegration.

[15] These rules-of-thumb are drawn from Sims, Stock, and Watson (1986). For expositional simplicity, we assume throughout that all regressions include a constant term for reasons discussed in that paper. All statements assume that the variables are either stationary or integrated of order one, and that the integrated variables have zero drift. The situation with nonzero drift or multiple orders of integration is somewhat more complicated, and the reader is referred to Sims, Stock and Watson or Stock and Kenneth West (1988) for a dicussion of this case.

Even if condition (a) in (ii′) does not hold, condition (b) still might; an example of this is given below. Under (i) and (ii′), the OLS estimator will be consistent. Moreover, the t- and F-statistics for the coefficient(s) of interest have their usual large sample distributions, so (for example) the standard critical values apply.

In some cases it might be impossible to express the coefficient of interest as a coefficient on a mean zero stationary variable, and instead (ii″) might hold:

(ii″) The parameter of interest is a coefficient on an integrated process and cannot be written as a coefficient on a stationary variable.

Under (i) and (ii″), the estimator of the coefficient is consistent, but it does not have the usual normal asymptotic distribution, so the usual critical values do not apply.

When the level of one variable is regressed against the level of another, it might well be the case that the error term is not i.i.d. or independent of the regressors. However, suppose that (i) does not hold, but that (i′) does:

(i′) The integrated dependent variable is cointegrated with at least one of the integrated regressors, so that the error in the regression equation is stationary but not necessarily serially uncorrelated or independent of the regressors.

Under (i′) and (ii″), unless the regressor is strictly exogenous the stationary regressor will typically be correlated with the error term and the parameter estimate will be inconsistent. This is the usual source of 'simultaneous equations bias', 'omitted variables bias', and 'errors-in-variables bias'. However, under (i′) and (ii″), rather remarkably the estimator of the coefficient of interest is consistent, although it does not have an asymptotic normal distribution.

Finally, suppose that the regressor and at least one dependent variable are integrated, but that there is no cointegrating relationship between the dependent variable and the regressors; it follows that the error term in the regression is integrated. In this case the estimated coefficients on regressors satisfying (ii″) will not be consistent; indeed, these coefficients and the R^2 of the regressions converge to random variables. An important example of this case is the regression of one random walk on another independent random walk, which is Granger and Newbold's (1974) spurious regression problem.

While these rules-of-thumb are rather involved, some intuition for why they work can be developed by first considering the familiar case of a single regressor that is stationary and uncorrelated with a serially uncorrelated error term. Under these assumptions, the OLS estimator is consistent because in large samples the average squared residual formed using any trial coefficient is minimized at or near the true coefficient value; for all coefficients except the true one, the average squared residual is larger but finite. In contrast, in time series regression with two cointegrated variables (so that the dependent variable and the regressor are both integrated but the true error term is stationary), because the two series are trending together, the residual constructed using other than the true coefficient will itself be integrated. Since an integrated process has a variance that tends to infinity, the average squared residual formed using a trial coefficient will grow arbitrarily large as the sample size increases, and will remain finite (and therefore be minimized) only for the true parameter value. This suggests that the coefficient on an integrated regressor can be estimated unusually precisely, as long as the error term is stationary. Furthermore, this unusual behaviour of the average squared error suggests that the standard Gaussian asymptotic theory might not apply when there are integrated regressors. In summary, the coefficient in a regression of one integrated variable on another will be consistent if the two variables are co-integrated although, as it turns out, the asymptotic theory is non-standard.[16]

This intuition can be extended to a regression that includes one stationary regressor, one integrated regressor, and a serially uncorrelated error term that is uncorrelated with either regressor. The preceding reasoning suggests that the coefficient on the integrated regressor will be estimated more precisely than usual (and will have a nonstandard asymptotic distribution); indeed, by the logic of cointegrated regressions, this would be so even if the stationary regressor were omitted from the specification. Turning to the coefficient on the stationary regressor, suppose that the stationary and integrated regressors are uncorrelated. Then the usual reasoning for OLS with uncorrelated regressors suggests that this coefficient will have the conventional large-sample properties. While this argument assumed the two regressors to be uncorrelated, this turns out not to be restrictive: it can be shown that, since the stochastic trend dominates the behaviour of an integrated process, the sample correlation between an integrated variable and any mean zero stationary variable tends to zero as the sample

---

[16] This argument applies both when the regressor and the dependent variable are cointegrated and when the regressor is a lagged value of the (integrated) dependent variable. In the latter case, the estimated coefficient will converge to one, even if additional lags in the regression have been omitted, so that the error is stationary but serially correlated. Assuming the process to have no drift, in this case the estimated coefficient will have an asymptotic 'unit root' distribution as discussed by Fuller (1976) and Dickey and Fuller (1979) which differs dramatically from the usual normal distribution, implying substantial bias towards zero in moderate sample sizes. The estimator converges to this distribution at the rate T rather than $T^{1/2}$ as in the case of conventional time series regression. Also see Fuller's discussion of the case that the variable contains a drift.

size increases. Thus the usual tools of time series regression can be used to examine the coefficient on the mean zero stationary regressor even if there are other regressors that are integrated. Finally, this reasoning can be extended to the case that this coefficient can be written as a coefficient on a mean zero stationary regressor by recognizing that the sum of a stationary variable and an integrated variable is itself integrated, so that the previous logic applies directly to the rearranged regression.

We illustrate these general principles by returning to the curious regressions in Table 2.

Understanding the Two Econometricians' Results

These rules-of-thumb provide a simple framework for explaining the results of our two econometricians, especially since we know the true economic structure that generated their data.

By construction, consumption and the price level are integrated processes that do not share a common stochastic trend, so they are not cointegrated. Thus the first regression clearly falls into the category of a spurious regression. As both Granger and Newbold (1974) and Peter Phillips (1986a) have emphasized, an indication of this situation is the extremely low Durbin–Watson statistic—although this statistic does not provide a formal test for a relation between integrated processes.

The second regression also fails to meet any of the criteria for applying the usual asymptotic approximation to the t-statistic, since consumption is not cointegrated with a linear time trend; indeed, from the definition of cointegration, it cannot be, since a linear time trend is not itself an integrated stochastic process. This regression was analyzed theoretically in an influential article by Nelson and Heejoon Kang (1981); in addition to producing a random R^2, with 100–150 quarterly observations the residuals from this regression seem to exhibit cycles with a period similar to one associated with the business cycle. Thus a linearly detrended random walk is likely to exhibit spurious periodicity.

Had our econometrician read Friedman closely, he would have recognized the problem with the third specification: the change in disposable income measures the change in permanent income, but with error, since it includes the change in transitory income as well. Thus the coefficient estimator in the third regression is biased downwards, even in arbitrarily large samples.

His final regression satisfies condition (i) (the true coefficient is zero and the error term is the i.i.d. error in permanent income); however, the regressor C_{t-1} is integrated. Thus the coefficient on C_{t-1} satisfies (ii″). It follows that this coefficient is consistent (indeed, its median estimate is close to its true value of zero), but that it will not have the usual asymptotic distribution. For the hypothetical economy (3)–(6), the t-statistic on C_{t-1} is in fact Dickey and Fuller's proposed test for a unit root in consumption; according to Fuller (1976, Table 8.5.2, p. 373) the correct 10 per cent critical value for a test against the hypothesis that consumption is stationary is -2.57. Had the first econometrician used this critical value, he would have failed to reject the hypothesis that consumption follows a random walk.

Why did the second econometrician fare better? By construction, consumption and income are cointegrated in the artificial economy, so the theoretical rules-of-thumb indicate that her first regression will result in a consistent estimator with a nonstandard distribution. Indeed, the median estimate of the 1000 replications is close to—but less than—one, although the t-statistic clearly has a nonstandard distribution. This is a specific example of Stock's (1987) result about the consistency of OLS estimators of cointegrating vectors, even if the error in the regression equation is serially correlated or not independent of the regressors. Additionally, a moment's reflection will indicate that Trygve Haavelmo's (1943) argument that the OLS estimator of the MPC is consistent because of simultaneous equations bias does not hold when consumption and income are cointegrated; rather, the estimator will be consistent, but will exhibit small sample bias.[17]

Her next test involved a coefficient on an integrated process in a regression equation with an i.i.d. error. However, the coefficient on the second lag of consumption can be rewritten as a coefficient on a stationary variable, so that condition (ii′) applies. To see this, consider that part of the regression involving the lags of consumption, and denote the two coefficients as α and β. Algebraic manipulations show that $\alpha C_{t-1} + \beta C_{t-2} = (\alpha + \beta)C_{t-1} - \beta(C_{t-1} - C_{t-2})$; but $C_{t-1} - C_{t-2}$ is stationary, so β clearly can be written as a coefficient on a stationary variable. Thus the theory predicts that the usual t- and F-distributions will apply, and the simulation results on the right side of Table 2 support this prediction. This argument applies equally to her next regression, except that the stationary combination of regressors is $Y_{t-1} - C_{t-1}$, which is stationary because consumption and income are cointegrated.

Her final regression satisfies (i) and, since ΔP_{t-1} is stationary, its coefficient satisfies (ii′), so that the usual asymptotic theory applies to

---

[17] It is interesting to note that this small sample bias provides an explanation of the difference between estimates of the marginal and average propensities to consume that provided one of the original motivations for Friedman's study of consumption. Specifically, applying nonstandard distribution theory to Friedman's original data, Stock (1986) shows that the marginal propensity to consume has a negative bias of approximately .15; upon adjusting for bias, the marginal and average consumption propensities are both approximately .9.

this coefficient (and indeed appears to work well in moderately sized samples, at least according to these calculations). However, the coefficient on P_{t-1} cannot be written as a coefficient on a mean zero stationary regressor, since there are no other regressors with which P_{t-1} is cointegrated. It follows that this estimator is consistent (converging to zero in this case) but has a nonstandard distribution, so that the usual critical values do not apply.[18]

The rules of thumb thus provide a general framework for evaluating these regression results with integrated variables, assuming the true economic structure to be known.[19]

Evaluating Actual Regression Results

The previous discussion emphasizes the importance of uncovering the stochastic trend properties of actual data to be used in regression analysis. In certain circumstances, economic theory might suggest orders of integration and cointegration among the variables. For example, Campbell (1987) argues that consumption and income being co-integrated is plausible both theoretically and empirically. Often, however, economic theory provides no clear guidance in determining which variables have stochastic trends, which do not, and when the trends are common among those that do.

There are no simple 'recipes' for performing time series analysis with integrated variables. One sensible starting point in analysing time series data in which there might be stochastic trends, however, is to perform a series of initial tests on the data. In particular, Dickey and Fuller's test for a unit root in a single series can provide an important piece of evidence about whether the variable is integrated. Typically an analysis will involve multiple time series, in which case it is important to know their cointegration properties as well. Diagnostic measures for the existence of cointegration have been proposed and analysed by Engle and Granger, Søren Johansen (1987), Phillips and Ouliaris (1987), and Stock and Watson (1986).[20] While these tests certainly are not fool-proof, their judicious application can shed considerable light on the way that stochastic trends enter the time series. This in turn provides a

[18] Interpreting P_t not as the price level but as the Standard and Poor's Stock Price Index, the reader might recognize her final three equations as simplified versions of Hall's tests of the Permanent Income Hypothesis. Stock and West provide further evidence on the finite sample performance of the asymptotic distribution theory that arises in interpreting Hall's regressions.

[19] This discussion has focused on the case of roots exactly equaling one, rather than (say) 0.999 or 1.001. Mathematically, however, similar warnings about the use of usual regression techniques arise for roots close to one; for example, see Cavanagh (1986) or Phillips (1986b). Thus the rules-of-thumb for identifying those coefficients with asymptotic normal distributions can be seen as tools to guard against misleading inferences if one suspects there to be roots close to one.

framework for implementing the rules of thumb described in this section.

Conclusions

Macroeconomic time series appear to contain variable trends. Moreover, modeling these variable trends as random walks with drift seems to provide a good approximation to the long run behaviour of many aggregate economic variables, at least in the US. While this general observation is over thirty years old, the application of recently developed statistical 'magnifying glasses' has led to several important conclusions for developing and testing macroeconomic theories and for formulating macroeconomic policies.

First, variations in growth trends constitute a quantitatively large part of the movements in real per capita GNP in the US. Thus the importance of shifts in long run prospects must be recognized even if one is primarily concerned with a relatively short specific historical episode.

Second, the presence of stochastic trends requires careful thought to avoid important econometric pitfalls. If an econometrician wishes to exploit the additional information contained in levels of variables rather than their differences, it is possible to apply a variety of tests and some simple rules-of-thumb to reduce the possibility of making dramatic errors in inference.

Finally, there is evidence not only that aggregate variables contain a substantial stochastic trend component, but that there is a link between changes in this stochastic trend and business cycle movements. This emphasizes the importance of assessing both the short-run implications of growth policies and the long-run implications of stabilization policies.

The authors thank Francis Bator, Peter Clark, Francis Diebold, Eric Fisher, Joseph Gagnon, Deborah Haas-Wilson, Andrew Harvey, Charles Manski, Danny Quah, Carl Shapiro, Joseph Stiglitz, and Timothy Taylor for helpful comments.

[20] Nelson and Plossser provide a clear discussion of the particulars of applying the Dickey–Fuller test to a single series. One shortcoming of integration or cointegration tests is that, with sample sizes typically encountered in macroeconomic research, they can have a fairly low ability to discriminate between the various hypotheses, particularly with multiple variables. For example, with 150 observations it is difficult to distinguish an integrated process from one that is stationary but highly serially correlated. (One implication of this is that tests based on theoretical cointegrating vectors, if they are known, typically have greater power than tests based on estimated cointegrating vectors.) This is closely related to the statistical difficulties discussed in the previous section with distinguishing stochastic trends from stationary components, since both econometric enterprises involve extracting information about relations among variables over the very long run using only 30 to 40 years of data.

Appendix

Stochastic Trends and Integrated Processes

This appendix presents the mathematical link between ARIMA models and the concept of stochastic trends used in the text.

Beveridge and Nelson show that any ARIMA model can be represented as a stochastic trend plus a stationary component, where a stochastic trend is defined to be a random walk, possibly with drift. This representation is most easily obtained for an ARIMA(0, 1, 1) model. Specifically, suppose that Δy_t (where $\Delta y_t = y_t - y_{t-1}$) is a MA(1) process, so that $\Delta y_t = e_t + be_{t-1}$, where e_t is i.i.d. and b is a constant. Let $y_0 = e_0 = 0$, so that y_t can be written as

$$
\begin{aligned}
y_t &= y_{t-1} + e_t + be_{t-1} \\
&= y_{t-2} + (e_{t-1} + be_{t-2}) + (e_t + be_{t-1}) \\
&= \sum_{r=1}^{t} e_r + b\sum_{r=1}^{t-1} e_r \\
&= (1 + b)\left(\sum_{r=1}^{t} e_r\right) - be_t.
\end{aligned}
\tag{A.1}
$$

Letting $y_t^p = (1 + b)\sum_{r=1}^{t} e_r$ and $y_t^s = -be_t$, one can rewrite the final expression in (A.1) as

$$
y_t = y_t^p + y_t^s, \qquad \text{where } y_t^p = y_{t-1}^p + (1 + b)e_t. \tag{A.2}
$$

Evidently y_t^p is a random walk with no drift and y_t^s is stationary (indeed, here y_t^s is serially uncorrelated). Equation (A.2) gives the Beveridge–Nelson representation of an ARIMA(0, 1, 1) process in terms of a stochastic trend (y_t^p) and a stationary component (y_t^s). Note that the innovations in the two components are both proportional to e_t, i.e. they are perfectly correlated; if $b > 0$, the correlation is -1, whereas if $b < 0$, the correlation is $+1$.

The representation can in fact be obtained for general ARIMA($p, 1, q$) processes. This is most easily shown using lag (or 'backshift') operator notation, where by definition $L^j x_t = x_{t-j}$ and $a(L) = \sum_{j=0}^{p} a_j L^j$. With this notation, an ARIMA($p, 1, q$) model can be written,

$$
a(L)\Delta y_t = f + b(L)e_t \tag{A.3}
$$

where f is a constant and $a(L)$ and $b(L)$ are lag polynomials of order p and q, respectively. Inverting $a(L)$, one can write (A.3) in its infinite moving average form,

$$
\Delta y_t = g + c(L)e_t \tag{A.4}
$$

where $g = f/\sum_{j=0}^{p} a_j$ and $c(L) = b(L)/a(L)$. Next, recursively substitute lagged Δy_t as was done in (A.1) and assume that $y_0 = 0$ and $e_r = 0$ for $r \leq 0$, so that an expression similar to the final one in (A.1) obtains:

$$
y_t = gt + h\sum_{r=1}^{t} e_r + d(L)e_t \tag{A.5}
$$

where $h = \sum_{j=0}^{\infty} c_j$ and $d_i = -\sum_{j=i+1}^{\infty} c_j$. Thus (A.5) can be rewritten as

$$y_t = y_t^p + y_t^s, \text{ where } y_t^p = g + y_{t-1}^p + he_t \text{ and } y_t^s = d(L)e_t \qquad (A.6)$$

which provides the Beveridge-Nelson decomposition for general ARIMA $(p, 1, q)$ processes, where the stochastic trend has drift g. Note that h is easily calculated as $\sum_{j=0}^{q} b_j \sum_{i=0}^{p} a_i$. As in the ARIMA$(0, 1, 1)$ case, the innovations in the trend and the cyclical components are both proportional to e_t, and thus are perfectly correlated.

References

AOKI, MASANAO (1987), 'How to build state space models for nonstationary time series and how to measure random walk components', (University of California–Los Angeles, Department of Economics Working Paper No. 438).

BEVERIDGE, STEPHEN, and CHARLES R. NELSON (1981), 'A new approach to decomposition of economic time series into permanent and transitory components with particular attention to measurement of the "business cycle"', *Journal of Monetary Economics*, 7, 151–74.

BLANCHARD, OLIVIER J., and DANNY QUAH (1987), 'The dynamic effects of aggregate demand and supply disturbances', (manuscript, MIT).

BOX, GEORGE E. P., and GWILYM M. JENKINS (1970), *Time Series Analysis: Forecasting and Control* (San Francisco, Holden-Day).

CAMPBELL, JOHN Y. (1987), 'Does saving anticipate declining labor income? An alternative test of the permanent income hypothesis', *Econometrica*, 55, 1249–74.

—— and N. GREGORY MANKIW (1987a), 'Are output fluctuations transitory', *The Quarterly Journal of Economics*, 102, 857–80.

—— —— (1987b), 'Permanent and transitory components in macroeconomic fluctuations', *The American Economic Review*, 77, 111–17.

CAVANAGH, CHRISTOPHER L. (1986), 'Roots local to unity' (Harvard University Department of Economics Discussion Paper).

CLARK, PETER K. (1987a), 'The cyclical component of U.S. economic activity', *The Quarterly Journal of Economics*, 102, 797–814.

—— (1987b), 'Trend reversion in real output and unemployment' (discussion paper, Graduate School of Business, Stanford University).

COCHRANE, JOHN H. (1988), 'How big is the random walk component in GNP', *Journal of Political Economy*, 96, 893–920.

DAVIDSON, JAMES E. H., DAVID F. HENDRY, FRANK SRBA, and S. YEO (1978), 'Econometric modelling of the aggregate time-series relationship between consumer's expenditure and income in the United Kingdom', *Economic Journal*, 86.

DICKEY, DAVID A. and WAYNE A. FULLER (1979), 'Distribution of the estimators for autoregressive time series with a unit root', *Journal of the American Statistical Association*, 74, 1057–72.

ENGLE, ROBERT F., and CLIVE W. J. GRANGER (1987), 'Co-integration and error correction: Representation, estimation and testing', *Econometrica*, 55, 251–76.

FRIEDMAN, MILTON (1957), *A Theory of the Consumption Function* (Princeton, Princeton University Press).

FULLER, WAYNE A. (1976), *Introduction to Statistical Time Series* (New York, Wiley).

GAGNON, JOSEPH E. (1988), 'Short run models and long run forecasts', *Quarterly Journal of Economics*, (May), **103**.

GRANGER, CLIVE W. J. (1983), 'Co-integrated and error correcting models', (UCSD Discussion Paper no. 83-13a).

—— (1986), 'Developments in the study of cointegrated economic variables', *Oxford Bulletin of Economics and Statistics*, Aug. **48**, no. 3, 213–28.

—— and ANDREW A. WEISS (1982), 'Time series analysis of error-correction models' (UCSD Discussion Paper no. 82-28).

—— and PAUL NEWBOLD (1974), 'Spurious regressions in econometrics', *Journal of Economics*, **2**, 111–20.

—— —— (1977), *Forecasting Economic Time Series* (New York, Academic Press).

HAAVELMO, TRYGVE (1943), 'The statistical implications of a system of simultaneous equations', *Econometrica*, **11**, no. 1, 1–12.

HALL, ROBERT E. (1978), 'Stochastic implications of the life cycle-permanent income hypothesis: Theory and evidence', *Journal of Political Economy*, **86**, no. 6, 971–87.

HARVEY, ANDREW C. (1981), *Time Series Models* (New York, Wiley).

—— (1985), 'Trends and cycles in macroeconomic time series', *Journal of Business and Economic Statistics*, **3**, 216–27.

—— and JAMES H. STOCK (1987), 'Continuous time autoregressive models with common stochastic trends', *Journal of Economic Dynamics and Control*.

HENDRY, DAVID F. (1986), 'Econometric modelling with cointegrated variables: An overview', *Oxford Bulletin of Economics and Statistics* (Aug.), **48**, no. 3, 201–12.

JOHANSEN, SØREN (1987), 'Statistical analysis of cointegrating vectors', *Journal of Economic Dynamics and Control* **12**, 231–54; Chapter 7 this volume.

KING, ROBERT G., CHARLES I. PLOSSER, JAMES H. STOCK, and MARK W. WATSON (1987), 'Stochastic trends and economic fluctuations', (NBER Discussion Paper No. 2229).

NELSON, CHARLES R., and HEEJOON KANG (1981), 'Spurious periodicity in inappropriately detrended time series', *Econometrica*, **49**, 741–51.

—— and CHARLES I. PLOSSER (1982), 'Trends and random walks in macroeconomic time series', *Journal of Monetary Economics*, 129–62.

ORCUTT, GUY H. (1948), 'A study of the autoregressive nature of the time series used for Tindbergen's model of the economic system of the United States, 1919–1932', *Journal of the Royal Statistical Society B*, **10**, no. 1, 1–45.

PHILLIPS, PETER C. B. (1986a), 'Understanding spurious regressions in econometrics', *Journal of Econometrics*, **33**, 311–40.

—— (1986b), 'Towards a unified asymptotic theory of autoregression', (Yale University, Cowles Foundation Discussion Paper no. 782).

—— and S. OULIARIS (1987), 'Asymptotic properties of residual based tests for cointegration', (Yale University, Cowles Foundations Discussion Paper no. 847).

PINDYCK, ROBERT S., and DANIEL L. RUBINFELD (1981), *Econometric Models and Economic Forecasts*, 2nd edn. (New York, McGraw-Hill).

PRESCOTT, EDWARD C. (1987), 'Theory ahead of business cycle measurement' (Carnegie–Rochester Conference on Public Policy).

SHAPIRO, MATTHEW D., and MARK W. WATSON (1988), 'Sources of business cycle fluctuations', *NBER Macroeconomics Annual*.

SIMS, CHRISTOPHER A. (1980a), 'Macroeconomics and reality', *Econometrica* (Jan.) **48**, 1–48.

—— (1980b), 'Comparison of interwar and postwar business cycles: Monetarism reconsidered', *American Economic Review* (May) **70**, 250–7.

—— JAMES H. STOCK, and MARK W. WATSON (1986), 'Inference in linear time series models with some unit roots' (manuscript, Stanford University).

STOCK, JAMES H. (1987), 'Asymptotic properties of least squares estimators of cointegrating vectors', *Econometrica*, **55**, 1035–56.

—— (1988), 'A reexamination of Friedman's consumption puzzle', *Journal of Business and Economic Statistics*, **6**, 401–7.

—— and MARK W. WATSON (*Forthcoming*), 'Testing for common trends', *Journal of the American Statistical Association*, **83**, 1097–1109; Chapter 8 of this book.

—— and KENNETH D. WEST (1988), 'Integrated regressors and tests of the permanent income hypothesis', *Journal of Monetary Economics*, **21**, 85–95.

TOBIN, JAMES (1980), 'Stabilization policy ten years after', *Brookings Papers on Economic Activity*, **1**, 19–90.

WATSON, MARK W. (1986), 'Univariate detrending methods with stochastic trends', *Journal of Monetary Economics*, **18**, 49–75.

YULE, G. U. (1926), 'Why do we sometimes get nonsense-correlations between time-series?', *Journal of the Royal Statistical Society B*, **89**, 1–64.

3

Econometric Modelling with Cointegrated Variables: an Overview

DAVID F. HENDRY

I. Introduction

Until recently, the vast bulk of econometric theory has been based on the assumption that the underlying data processes are stationary and ergodic, despite the manifest non-stationarity of, say, the aggregate time series to which that theory was applied in economics. Over the last century, most economic variables have changed radically in mean and often in variance so that their first two moments are far from constant. The consequences for the statistical properties of estimators and tests are profound as evidenced by the substantial literature on 'spurious regressions' discussed in Section II of this overview.

To overcome such problems, some investigators have suggested differencing the data to remove random walk and trendlike components although others have argued that this loses valuable 'long-run' information in the data. In Section III, the concept of cointegrated series is evaluated as one means of effecting a resolution of such debates.

The last three years have witnessed a veritable explosion of research on cointegration and related topics, most of which had not appeared in print at the time this Special Issue was commissioned. The Editors considered these developments of sufficient practical importance for empirical research to seek an overview with related applications, and this volume is the result. We realise that a large range of problems remains to be resolved and trust that the contributions herein help stimulate a deeper understanding of the empirical analysis of economic time series.

First, however, the basic notion of an integrated series must be clarified.

The simplest example is a random walk:

$$x_t = x_{t-1} + \varepsilon_t \qquad \text{where } \varepsilon_t \sim \text{IN}(0, \sigma^2) \text{ say.} \qquad (1)$$

Printed with permission of: *Oxford Bulletin of Economics and Statistics*, 48, 3, (1986).

Thus:

$$x_t = \sum_{j=0}^{t-1} \varepsilon_{t-j} \qquad\qquad \text{if } x_0 = 0 \qquad\qquad (2)$$

so that x_t is the sum of all the past innovations ε_t, however long ago these occurred. Conversely, $\Delta x_t = \varepsilon_t$ is stationary. If we denote a stationary series as $I(0)$ (integrated of order zero), then another series z_t (say) is $I(k)$ (integrated of order k) if $\Delta^k z_t$ is $I(0)$ (see Granger, 1981). Stationarity is in fact not necessary for $I(0)$ but for this introduction is a convenient simplification. Clearly $I(0) \pm I(1)$ is $I(1)$.

The primary problem which arises from attempting to analyse $z_t \sim I(k)$ if $k > 0$ is that the usual statistical properties of first and second sample moments (e.g. converging to their population counterparts) do *NOT* hold. Thus a different distributional theory is required for non-stationary, non-ergodic processes and a sketch of the issues and developments is provided in Section II. The empirical relevance of $I(1)$ analysis is borne out by Nelson and Plosser (1982).

Next, consider two series x_t and y_t both of which are $I(1)$. It is possible that a linear combination of these: $z_t = \{y_t - \lambda x_t\}$ say, is $I(0)$ in which case y and x are said to be cointegrated (see Granger, 1983). If λ exists, it must be unique since changing it to $(\lambda - \delta)$, say, would drop δx_t which is $I(1)$ and hence z_t must be $I(1)$ also. Otherwise, z_t seems a feasible way to retain 'long-run' information in an $I(0)$ representation compatible with having Δy_t (which is $I(0)$) as the dependent variable.

A number of new problems pertinent to econometric modelling arise from cointegration and some of these are discussed in Section III. For example, the erroneous omission or inclusion of variables could substantially alter the properties of a model in some cases, and have no effect in others; the relative attractiveness of certain other procedures could be radically altered (such as 'autocorrelation corrections'); and the occurrence of both stocks and flows raises 'dimensionality' problems unless they are of the same order of integratedness.

Finally, Section IV provides a brief review of the papers included in this Special Issue. There are contributions by Clive Granger; Stephen Hall; Timothy Jenkinson; Anindya Banerjee, Juan Dolado, David Hendry and Gregor Smith; and César Molinas. Christopher Gilbert provides the Practitioners' Corner paper which exposits closely related methodological issues.

II. Historical Background[1]

The observation that some systematic co-movements of variables may nevertheless be spurious is undoubtedly of ancient origin, even though

---

[1] This section draws heavily on Hendry and Morgan (1986).

formal analyses are relatively recent. In his study of periodic commercial fluctuations, Jevons (1884. p. 3) notes the need 'to avoid any variation due to the time of the year' and also to eliminate 'non-periodic variations'. Hooker (1901) discusses the problems of applying correlation theory 'where the element of time is involved' and argues for analysing 'the deviations from the trend'. His examples show large changes in the values of the correlations depending on whether the original or the 'deviations' series is analysed, specifically focussing on cases where the latter is far *higher* (e.g. due to a negative trend masking a positive relation). Nevertheless, the first formal study is that of Yule (1926) who used both analytical and experimental methods to examine the correlation between two unrelated series such that: (a) the series were white noise $[I(0)]$; (b) their first differences were white noise $[I(1)]$; and (c) their second differences were white noise $[I(2)]$. Correlation theory worked well in case (a), and the correlation distribution was nearly normal, but in case (b) it resembled a semi-ellipse with 'excess frequency' at both ends. In case (c) it was U-shaped so that the most likely correlations for unrelated series were ± 1! This, of course, is what would also occur if the two series were related. Keynes (1939) scathingly referred to this result as 'the mine [Mr Yule] sprang under the contraptions of optimistic statisticians'. Earlier, Working (1934) had lamented that: 'Economic theory has fallen far short of recognising the full implications of the resemblance of many economic time series to random-difference series; and the methods of statistical analysis in general use have given these implications almost no recognition', a worry that was to remain pertinent for most of the next half-century. To improve matters, Working provided a 'standard random difference series'[2] for comparing against the claimed characteristics of economic time series: his artificial data manifested distinct 'trends' and 'cycles', but not a great deal of use has been made of his approach.

No 'solution' to discriminating spurious from 'real' relationships emerged and economists continued to apply standard procedures to economic time series. A shot across the bows of this approach came from Granger and Newbold (1974) based on ideas in Box and Jenkins (1970), concerning differencing data to remove unit roots. Granger and Newbold replicated the gist of Yule's findings but also noted the low values of the Durbin–Watson statistic (see Durbin and Watson 1950, 1971) associated with spurious regressions. They suggested that this seriously biased the conventional tests towards rejecting the null hypothesis of no relation even when it is true. This whole strand was recently subjected to an elegant formal analysis by Phillips (1985b) who developed an asymptotic theory for regressions between general integrated

[2] Now generally referred to as an integrated random process (which is virtually the terminology Working considered and dismissed as ambiguous!) and denoted $I(1)$ above.

random processes. Phillips demonstrated that the distributions of the conventional statistics were not at all like those derived under stationarity. Specifically, the coefficients of the regression do *NOT* converge in probability as the sample size increases: the distribution of the constant diverges and both the regression coefficient and R^2 have non-degenerate distributions. Worse still, the distributions of 't'-tests diverge so that 'there are *no* asymptotically correct critical values for these conventional significance tests' (although an appropriately standardised test can be derived). Finally, the Durbin–Watson test converges on zero (so that the Granger–Newbold findings have a clear theoretical basis), but again a usable distributional result can be derived.

A closely related literature is that concerned with 'time-series versus econometrics' (see e.g. Naylor *et al.* 1972; Cooper 1972; and the discussion in Sims 1977). By analysing *only* the differences of economic time-series, all information about potential (long-run) relationships between the levels of economic variables is lost; this seems a drastic 'solution' to possible spurious regressions. Sargan (1964) had considered a class of models later to be known as error correction mechanisms (ECM–see Davidson *et al.* 1978) which retained levels information in what could have been a non-integrated form. Hendry and Mizon (1978) argued for retaining such variables in econometric models which were sufficiently well specified to have white-noise residuals, and hence avoid the spurious regressions problem. Granger and Weiss (1983) introduced the concept of cointegrated series for variables which are individually $I(1)$ but where some linear combination thereof is $I(0)$. Granger and Engle (1985) proved that cointegrated series have an ECM representation and conversely, that ECM's generate cointegrated series, thus reconciling the two approaches as well as clarifying when levels information could legitimately be retained in econometric equations. Stock (1984) proved that if the variables are cointegrated, then superconsistent (i.e. $O_p(T^{-1})$ rather than $O_p(T^{-1/2})$) estimates results; see Section III below.

The third inter-related literature of considerable relevance is that concerned with the statistical properties of, and tests for, time-series data with unit roots (as $I(1)$ processes must have). The relevant mathematical-statistical literature on serial correlation includes Anderson (1942), Anderson (1948), White (1958), Fuller (1976), Dickey and Fuller (1979), (1981), Hasza and Fuller (1979), Evans and Savin (1981), (1984), Sargan and Bhargava (1983), Bhargava (1983), Phillips (1985a–c, 1986a, b), Phillips and Durlauf (1985) and Durlauf and Phillips (1986). The main practical results are 't'-tests for unit roots in autoregressions based on tabulated critical values (Dickey–Fuller), tests based on the Durbin–Watson statistic (Sargan–Bhargava) and a rapidly increasing body of knowledge of the distributions of estimators and tests when $I(1)$ series are

involved (Phillips). Some of these results are referred to in Section III
below and in other papers in this special issue (see especially the Appendix
in Banerjee *et al.* which applies some of the general distributional results
obtained by Phillips).

III. Econometric Modelling with Cointegrated Variables

(a) *Static Regressions*. Let (y_t, x_t) be two $I(1)$ series such that $\{y_t - \lambda x_t\}$
is $I(0)$. Then the least squares estimator $\hat{\lambda}$ of λ must be normalised by
T to have a non-degenerate distribution: $T(\hat{\lambda} - \lambda) \xrightarrow{\text{D}} D(\mu, \sigma^2)$ where
μ and σ^2 are the mean and variance of this (non-normal) limiting
distribution (see Stock, 1984). Note that $\mu \neq 0$ does not imply that $\hat{\lambda}$ is
inconsistent since the normalisation is T, rather than $\sqrt{T}$. This rapid
convergence is used in Granger and Engle (1985) as the basis of a
two-step procedure for dynamic modelling. Since $\hat{\lambda}$ differs from λ by
terms of $0_p(T^{-1})$, whereas for $I(0)$ variables coefficients vary around
their probability limits by $0_p(T^{-1/2})$, estimating λ and knowing it yields
the same result asymptotically in dynamic models between $I(0)$ variables. Now differencing *must* reduce the order of integration of a
variable by unity, so if Δy_t is related to Δx_t (and perhaps lags of both of
these), then if x and y are cointegrated $(y_{t-1} - \hat{\lambda} x_{t-1})$ is $I(0)$ and can
be included in a model as if $\hat{\lambda}$ were known (i.e. the sampling variance
of $\hat{\lambda}$ can be ignored). Thus the 'spurious regressions problem' is
resurrected in a completely new guise and now to the benefit of
economics! One begins by regressing y_t on x_t to estimate $\hat{\lambda}$; such an
equation will have substantial residual autocorrelation so inference on λ
is invalid, but the ECM can be constructed as $z_t = y_t - \hat{\lambda} x_t$. Now all
variates are $I(0)$ and conventional modelling strategies seem applicable.
   However, there are several steps needing clarification. Firstly, how
can one know that z_t is $I(0)$ or more basically that y_t and x_t are
cointegrated? Certainly, a high R^2 is necessary at the first stage, but by
Yule's findings, not sufficient. Conversely, a low Durbin–Watson (DW)
statistic might be expected as all dynamics are omitted: but it must not
be too low since that is what will occur with $I(1)$ residuals (Phillips
1985*b*). Thus, for example, the results of Sargan and Bhargava (1983)
and Bhargava (1983) can be applied to the use of the DW test against
the null hypothesis of a random walk rather than the null of a white
noise process. Alternatively, any of the tests for a unit root can be
applied to z_t (see e.g. Dickey and Fuller 1979; Granger and Engle 1985,
discuss the various possibilities). Of course, one should first have
checked that y_t and x_t were $I(1)$ and the same tests could be applied in
that case. Applying these tests to the 'rainfall causes inflation' example

in Hendry (1980) confirms its spurious nature (DW is well below the critical value).

A major complication relative to conventional testing theory is that the distribution of the tests tends to be influenced in important ways by unknown features of the data process. For example, if x_t and y_t were $I(0)$, a test on the ECM would use the conventional t-tables; however, if the levels were $I(1)$ with drift, different critical values might be required. Bhargava (1983) stresses the invariance advantages of the Durbin–Watson test relative to the Dickey–Fuller test (where different tables are needed if an intercept is included or not for example), although the distributions of most of the tests have been tabulated only for special cases. Durlauf and Phillips (1986) provide a thorough treatment of the distributions of tests in integrated processes, focussing on discriminating between $I(0)$ and $I(1)$.

Next, $\hat{\lambda}$ is biased for λ, and although that bias is $0(T^{-1})$ it can be substantial. Note that T needs some absolute time units to meaningfully judge μ, since it would be surprising if simple time disaggregation (from years to months, say) helped in the estimation of *long-run* relations. This would suggest that μ was a function of some parameter such as the mean lag of the dynamic adjustment process relating y and x. Banerjee *et al.* show that μ can be extremely large in certain cases and in some simple data processes is a function of the R^2 from the static regression. If R^2 is low, large biases in $\hat{\lambda}$ are likely, cautioning against using the two-step procedure (and indeed being less than fully consistent with the assertion that y_t and x_t are $I(1)$, but cointegrated).

The third problem is that in testing $\{z_t\}$ (or any series) for being $I(1)$ against $I(0)$, one wishes to discriminate between roots on the unit circle and those inside, which may be around 0.95. High power cannot be expected in such situations so that large type II errors are a potential difficulty. Consider the DW test applied to z_t when there are 100 observations: the 5 per cent critical value is around $\frac{1}{4}$ (the 1 per cent around $\frac{1}{3}$), with larger values rejecting the null hypothesis of no-cointegration. But DW $\approx 2(1 - \hat{\rho})$ where $\hat{\rho}$ is the first order serial correlation coefficient, so that $\hat{\rho} < 0.9$ is needed to reject the null at even the 5 per cent level. Conversely, the ECM coefficient (i.e. the coefficient of z_{t-1} in the dynamic model) would have to exceed 0.10 in absolute value, which will generally correspond to a relatively *small* mean lag (unless no Δx coefficients are significant). On the null that z_t is $I(1)$, the usual 't'-test significance levels should not be valid for this ECM coefficient, and some modification based on the Dickey–Fuller tables should be used, usually requiring 't'-values in excess of *three* (but see the simulation results in Banerjee *et al.* 1986). Thus frequent type II mistakes seem likely. Nevertheless, if R^2 is reasonably high (>0.95) and DW is not too low in the static regression, the Granger–Engle 2-step procedure is clearly of interest and is applied below in the papers by Hall and Jenkinson.

The final problem for the static regression is: 'in which direction to regress?' If y and x are cointegrated, then $\{y_t - \lambda x_t\}$ or $\{x_t - 1/\lambda y_t\}$ are equally valid, so that *both* directions are *a priori* valid, and both should yield 'good' estimates of λ. In this bivariate context, the product of the two estimates is R^2, so if that statistic is nearly unity, virtually identical estimates of λ will result: for several aggregate time series, Granger and Engle demonstrate that such a result holds in practice. Moreover, this renormalisation consideration also suggests that the bias in $\hat{\lambda}$ will depend on R^2. Of course, in a multivariate context, the issue is more complex and is discussed by Granger below.

(b) *Autocorrelation Corrections*. Given the intimate connection between cointegrated series and ECM representations, a further insight is provided into the potential difficulties of mechanical 'residual autocorrelation corrections'. Even if z_t is $I(0)$, it will usually be highly autocorrelated: 'mopping up' such autoorrelation by repeated application of (say) Cochran–Orcutt will enforce a mean lag of *zero*, irrespective of the underlying dynamic responses. Worse still, if z_t is $I(1)$ but the autocorrelation correction precludes unit roots, the resulting model will be entirely spurious and very mis-leading inferences can result (see Granger and Newbold 1977; and for a discussion of residual autocorrelation correction see Gilbert below). Again citing Hendry (1980), autocorrelation corrections still left rainfall as a 'significant cause' of inflation (although the common factor test could reject that).

(c) *Multicollinearity*. Similarly, a new gloss is put on the much discussed 'problem' of multicollinearity. If a model involves $I(0)$ and $I(1)$ variables such that the latter are cointegrated, then there will be a 'near singularity' in the second moment matrix (indeed, most $I(1)$ variables will be highly intercorrelated even if they are *not* cointegrated, which is just the spurious regressions problem again.) For example consider:

$$\Delta y_t = \alpha_0 + \alpha_1 \Delta x_t + \alpha_2 y_{t-1} + \alpha_3 x_{t-1} + v_t. \tag{3}$$

In (3), y_{t-1} and x_{t-1} will be 'highly collinear' and neither need have 'significant "t"-values' despite being cointegrated, especially if proper account is taken of their $I(1)$ nature. Dropping either would be a disastrous resolution of this 'problem' since the other *must* now be insignificant if it is $I(1)$, given that the dependent variable is $I(0)$. Being $I(1)$, the second moments of y_{t-1} and x_{t-1} are huge relative to those of the intercept, Δx_t and $z_{t-1} = (y_{t-1} - \lambda x_{t-1})$; thus; when the $(X'X)$ matrix for the regression is inverted, the sub-matrix involving y_{t-1} and

x_{t-1} will indeed have a near-singularity corresponding to the cointegrating vector $(1:-\lambda)$.[3] This is hardly a 'problem'; rather transformation to the appropriate ECM before deleting any levels variables seems essential. Such an analysis strongly supports the static model tests proposed by Granger and Engle.

Conversely, in the static regression, omitting any $I(0)$ variables will be irrelevant to the estimate of λ (as will the presence of $I(0)$ measurement errors, etc.). Further, if z_t is $I(1)$ this could be due to the spurious nature of any linear relationship between y and x; or it may reflect the omission of a further $I(1)$ variable, w_t say, such that $\{y_t - \lambda x_t - \phi w_t\}$ is $I(0)$. Now, omission of a variable is again fatal since no relationship is definable even where an interesting, more general, relation exists. In terms of (3), neither $\hat{\alpha}_2$ nor $\hat{\alpha}_3$ should be significant if w_t is omitted; yet adding this highly collinear variable which induces a near-singularity in $(X'X)$ will (for sufficiently large T) produce a significant ECM coefficient (see Davidson et al. 1978). Thus, considerable care is required when modelling $I(1)$ variables, and to this writer, the moral yet again points towards beginning with relatively general specifications, which are sufficient to ensure $I(0)$ ECM's, despite the potential identification issues discussed by Granger. Equally, it is essential to check that *all* the variables in any static regression are $I(1)$ (and that no subset is cointegrated) if the super-consistency result of Stock (1984) is to apply. Consequently, no 'free lunch' seems in the offing for modellers through the theory of cointegration.

(d) *Stocks and Flows and Functional Form*.[4] By definition, a stock is the integral of some flow, perhaps with a discount factor for depreciation (as with the capital stock). If depreciation is denoted by δ, the stock by S_t and the input by M_t, then:

$$S_t = (1 - \delta)S_{t-1} + M_t \tag{4}$$

Thus, for $\delta > 0$, S_t is of the same order of integration as M_t (e.g. $I(1)$ if M_t is $I(1)$, though potentially more autoregressive; if $\delta = 0$, S_t is $I(1)$ if M_t is $I(0)$. In many cases (inventory accumulation, wealth etc.), M_t is itself the difference between two or more $I(1)$ series; e.g. $M_t = y_t - \lambda x_t$ (as in Savings = Income − Expenditure). If these 'basic' series are cointegrated, M_t is $I(0)$, so for $\delta = 0$, S_t is $I(1)$ and could be cointegrated with x_t or y_t. This is testable as discussed earlier, and hopefully occurs in practice if stock/flow ratios are to be meaningful, let alone constant.

---

[3] This entire analysis can be placed in the context of Frisch's (1934) 'confluence' problem, but with the crucial difference that the variables are $I(1)$, whereas errors are $I(0)$.

[4] This material also draws on Granger (1985).

Finally, the choice of functional form assumes a greater importance than merely convenience as with $I(0)$ processes. As Granger shows below, if x_t and y_t have trends in their means as well as trend-free $I(1)$ components, then they can still be cointegrated if the trends obey the same factor of proportionality as the cointegrating vector of the $I(1)$ components. If the trends are different functions of time, this cannot occur. Thus, if x_t and t_t are of such a form and are cointegrated, then e.g. y_t and $\log x_t$ will generally *not* be cointegrated (even assuming $x_t > 0 \forall_t$).

IV. This Special Issue on Cointegration

The first paper is by Clive Granger and describes a range of recent developments pertinent to the analysis of $I(1)$ variables, some of which have been mentioned above. Following a review of the basic concepts and models, Granger draws six implications of cointegration, which relate that concept to short-term and long-run forecasts, control, Granger-causality and speculative markets. Results are presented for many variables, stock-flow relationships, and non-linear and time-dependent processes.

Next there are two empirical studies by Hall and Jenkinson respectively. The former is a re-analysis of the Sargan (1964) ECM wage equation, extended to incorporate average hours, and productivity. Hall tests and rejects the null of no-cointegration betwen wages, prices, unemployment, hours and productivity. He finds wages and prices are $I(2)$ but cointegrate to real wages being $I(1)$, which in turn cointegrates with the remaining variables to $I(0)$. Hall applies the Granger–Engel 2-stage approach discussed above and develops an interesting dynamic model of wages.

Jenkinson tackles the related topic of labour demand using a similar approach but with less clear-cut results. In testing for cointegration between employment, real product wages, real material costs and the capital stock (all the variables apparently being $I(1)$) the evidence is not sufficient clearly to reject the null of no-cointegration. However, in an ECM representation constructed from the static regression, the error correction coefficient is significant and the dynamic model seems well specified. Nevertheless, Jenkinson concludes that this result arises primarily from the significance of the lagged level of employment (the dependent variable), casting doubt on the original decision that employment was $I(1)$.

The Monte Carlo study by Banerjee, Dolado, Hendry and Smith was undertaken to try and elucidate the actual behaviour of the various cointegration estimators and tests in sample sizes of practical relevance, albeit for rather simple data generation processes. Replicating the process used by Granger and Engle (1985) but for a much wider range of signal/noise ratios, they find that the cointegrating regression estimator can have very large biases and the tests low power to reject non-cointegration. Indeed, the bias in $\hat{\lambda}$ does not appear to decline at the theoretically anticipated rate of T^{-1}, but instead vanishes very slowly. Drawing on the distributional theory in Phillips (1985a, b) and on Nagar (1958) expansions, Banerjee et al. derive approximate analytical expressions for the bias. They find that $(\hat{\lambda} - \lambda)$ depends on $(1 - R^2)$ (which is $0(T^{-1})$) and on a term of $0(T^{-2})$ which is important in accounting for the slow decline in the bias. Similar results obtain for a second data generation process where ECM representations are evaluated and found to exhibit smaller biases (consistent with Stock 1984) and higher test powers. They also consider testing the hypothesis that consumption is a random walk.

As noted above, the appropriate test procedures for integrated series are dependent on unknown characteristics of the underlying data processes even under the null (i.e. the null distributions are functions of nuisance parameters). In the final paper, Molinas considers the behaviour of the various cointegration tests when the process is an integrated moving average rather than a random walk as in (1) above. His Monte Carlo results are dramatically different from those found for random walks and he cautions that cointegration testing is a hazardous procedure.

The basic model Molinas uses takes the following form [IMA(1,1)]:

$$x_t = \alpha + x_{t-1} + \varepsilon_t - \theta\varepsilon_{t-1} \qquad \text{with } \varepsilon_t \sim \text{IN}(0, \sigma^2) \qquad (5)$$

When $\theta = 0$, x_t is a random walk (with drift if $\alpha \neq 0$), whereas if $\theta = 1$, x_t is white noise; thus we can crudely express x_t as $I(1 - \theta)$. Provided $|\theta| < 1$, the mean (if $\alpha \neq 0$) and variance of x_t increase with t, but if $\theta > \frac{1}{2}$, the correlogram of x_t in fact dies out rapidly, unlike the characterisation of an $I(1)$ series offered in, say, Granger's paper. One implication of this is that had the DW statistic been applied to test whether x_t and y_t were themselves $I(1)$, rejection of that hypothesis seems likely, especially for $\theta = 0.9$. Thus, the static regression analysis would not be legitimate since the theory does not apply to $I(0)$ variables; the high rejection rate of the DW test could not be taken to 'prove' that y_t and x_t are really related since all $I(0)$ series are automatically cointegrated. However, if the residuals from the static regression were essentially white-noise, the conventional 't'-test on the regression parameter could be applied (note his finding that the mean DW value converges on 2 as θ tends to unity). It would seem that $I(0)$ and $I(1)$ can be treated as discrete points on a 'continuum' for practical sample sizes, and in Molinas' experiments this 'continuum' seems to be parameterised by $1 - \theta$.

References

ANDERSON, R. L. (1942), 'Distribution of the serial correlation coefficient', *Annals of Mathematical Statistics*, **13**, 1–13.

ANDERSON, T. W. (1948), 'On the theory of testing for serial correlation', *Skandinavisk Aktuarietidskrift*, **31**, 88–116.

BANERJEE, A., J. J. DOLADO, D. F. HENDRY, and G. W. SMITH (1986), 'Exploring equilibrium relationships in econometrics through static models: Some Monte Carlo evidence', *Oxford Bulletin of Economics and Statistics*, **48**, 253–78.

BHARGAVA, A. (1983), 'On the theory of testing for unit roots in observed time series', ICERD Discussion Paper 83/67, London School of Economics.

BOX, G. E P. and G. M. JENKINS (1976), *Time Series Analysis: Forecasting and Control* (San Francisco, Holden-Day).

COOPER, R. L. (1972), 'The predictive performance of quarterly econometric models of the United States', in Hickman, B. (ed.), *Econometric Models of Cyclical Behavior* NBER Studies in Income and Wealth, pp. 36 (Columbia University Press).

DAVIDSON, J., D. F. HENDRY, F. SRBA, and S. YEO (1978), 'Econometric modelling of the aggregate time-series relationship between consumers' expenditure and income in the United Kingdom', *Economic Journal*, **88**, 661–92.

DICKEY, D. A. and W. A. FULLER (1979), 'Distribution of the estimators for auto-regressive time series with a unit root', *Journal of American Statistical Association*, **74**, 427–3.

—— (1981), 'Likelihood ratio statistics for autoregressive time series with a unit root', *Econometrica* **49**, 1057–72.

DURBIN, J., and G. S. WATSON (1950), 'Testing for serial correlation in least squares regression I', *Biometrika*, **37**, 409–28.

—— (1971), 'Testing for serial correlation in least squares regression III', *Biometrika*, **58**, 1–19.

DURLAUF, S. N., and P. C. B. PHILLIPS (1986), 'Trends versus random walks in time series analysis', Cowles Foundation Discussion Paper 788.

EVANS, G. B. A., and SAVIN, N. E. (1981). 'Testing for unit roots: 1', *Econometrica*, **49**, 753–77.

—— (1984), 'Testing for unit roots: 2', *Econometrica*, **52**, 1241–70.

FRISCH, R. (1934), *Statistical Confluence Analysis by Means of Complete Regression Systems*, (University Economics Institute, Oslo).

FULLER, W. A. (1976), *Introduction to Statistical Time Series*, (New York, Wiley).

GRANGER, C. W. J. (1981), 'Some properties of time series data and their use in econometric model specification', *Journal of Econometrics*, **16**, 121–30.

—— (1983), 'Cointegrated variables and error correcting models', UCSD Discussion Paper 83–13a.

—— (1985), 'Multi-cointegrated economic series', manuscript, Nuffield College, Oxford.

—— and P. NEWBOLD (1974), 'Spurious regressions in econometrics', *Journal of Econometrics*, **2**, 111–20.

—— —— (1977), 'The time series approach to econometric model building', in

C. A. Sims (ed), *New Methods in Business Cycle Research,* (Federal Reserve Bank of Minneapolis).

—— and A. A. WEISS (1983), 'Time series analysis of error correction models', in S. Karlin, T. Amemiya, and L. A. Goodman (eds), *Studies in Econometric Time-Series and Multivariate Statistics* (New York, Academic Press, UCSD Discussion Paper 82–28).

—— and R. F. ENGLE (1985), 'Dynamic model specification with equilibrium constraints: Co-integration and error-correction', Mimeo, University of California, San Diego. (Forthcoming, *Econometrica.*); *Chapter 5 of this book.*

HASZA, D. P. and W. A. FULLER (1979), 'Estimation for autoregressive processes with unit roots', *Annals of Statistics,* **7**, 1106–20.

HENDRY, D. F. (1980), 'Econometrics–alchemy or science?', *Economica,* **47**, 387–406.

—— and G. E. MIZON (1978), 'Serial correlation as a convenient simplification, not a nuisance: A comment on a study of the demand for money by the Bank of England', *Economic Journal,* **88**, 549–63.

—— and M. MORGAN (1986), *Classics in The Statistical Foundations of Econometrics,* forthcoming, Cambridge University Press.

HOOKER, R. H. (1901), 'Correlation of the marriage-rate with trade', *Journal of the Royal Statistical Society*, **64,** 485–92.

JEVONS, W. S. (1884), *Investigations in Currency and Finance* (London, Macmillan).

KEYNES, J. M. (1939), 'Professor Tinbergen's method', *Economic Journal*, **49**, 558–68.

NAGAR, A. L. (1959), 'The bias and moment matrix of the general K-class estimators of the parameters in simultaneous systems', *Econometrica,* **27**, 575–95.

NAYLOR, T. H., T. G. SEAKS, and D. W. WICHERN (1972), 'Box–Jenkins methods: An alternative to econometric models', *International Statistics Review*, **40**, 123–37.

NELSON, C. R. and C. PLOSSER (1982), 'Trends and random talk in macroeconomic time series: Some evidence and implications', *Journal of Monetary Economics,* **10**, 139–62.

PHILLIPS, P. C. B. (1985a), 'Time series regression with unit roots', Cowles Foundation Discussion Paper, 740.

—— (1985b). 'Understanding spurious regressions in econometrics', Cowles Foundation Discussion Paper, 757.

—— (1985c), 'Asymptotic expansions in nonstationary vector autoregressions', Cowles Foundation Discussion Paper.

—— (1986a), 'Regression theory for near-integrated time series', Cowles Foundation Discussion Paper, 781.

—— (1986b), 'Towards a unified asymptotic theory for autoregression', Cowles Foundation Discussion Paper, 782.

—— and S. N. DURLAUF (1985), 'Multiple time series regression with integrated processes', Cowles Foundation Discussion Paper, 768.

SARGAN, J. D. (1964), 'Wages and prices in the United Kingdom: A study in econometric methodology', in P. E. Hart, G. Mills, and J. N. Whittaker (eds.), *Econometric Analysis for National Economic Planning*, (London, Butterworths).

—— (1980), 'Some tests of dynamic specification for a single equation', *Econometrica,* **48**, 879–97.

—— and A. BHARGAVA (1983), 'Testing residuals from least squares regression for being generated by the Gaussian random walk', *Econometrica*, **51**, 153–74.

SIMS, C. A. (ed.) (1977), *New Methods in Business Cycle Research* (Federal Reserve Bank of Minneapolis).

STOCK, J. H. (1984), 'Asymptotic properties of a least squares estimator of co-integrating vectors', Harvard University Mimeo.

WHITE, J. S. (1958), 'The limiting distribution of the serial correlation coefficient in the explosive case', *Annals of Mathematical Statistics*, **29**, 1188–97.

WORKING, H. (1934), 'A random difference series for use in the analysis of time series', *Journal of American Statistical Association,* pp. 11–24.

YULE, G. U. (1926), 'Why do we sometimes get nonsense-correlations between time-series? A study in sampling and the nature of time-series', *Journal of the Royal Statistical Society*, **89,** 1–64.

4

Developments in the Study of Cointegrated Economic Variables

C. W. J. GRANGER*

I. Introduction

At the least sophisticated level of economic theory lies the belief that certain pairs of economic variables should not diverge from each other by too great an extent, at least in the long-run. Thus, such variables may drift apart in the short-run or according to seasonal factors, but if they continue to be too far apart in the long-run, then economic forces, such as a market mechanism or government intervention, will begin to bring them together again. Examples of such variables are interest rates on assets of different maturities, prices of a commodity in different parts of the country, income and expenditure by local government and the value of sales and production costs of an industry. Other possible examples would be prices and wages, imports and exports, market prices of substitute commodities, money supply and prices and spot and future prices of a commodity. In some cases an economic theory involving equilibrium concepts might suggest close relations in the long-run, possibly with the addition of yet further variables. However, in each case the correctness of the beliefs about long-term relatedness is an empirical question. The idea underlying cointegration allows specification of models that capture part of such beliefs, at least for a particular type of variable that is frequently found to occur in macroeconomics. Since a concept such as the long-run is a dynamic one, the natural area for these ideas is that of time-series theory and analysis. It is thus necessary to start by introducing some relevant time series models.

Consider a single series x_t, measured at equal intervals of time. Time series theory starts by considering the generating mechanism for the series. This mechanism should be able to generate all of the statistical

* I would like to acknowledge the excellent hospitality that I enjoyed at Nuffield College and the Institute of Economics and Statistics, Oxford whilst this paper was prepared.

properties of the series, or at very least the conditional mean, variance and temporal autocorrelations, that is the 'linear properties' of the series, conditional on past data. Some series appear to be 'stationary', which essentially implies that the linear properties exist and are time-invariant. Here we are concerned with the weaker but more technical requirement that the series has a spectrum which is finite but non-zero at all frequencies. Such a series will be called $I(0)$, denoting 'integrated of order zero'. Some series need to be differenced to achieve these properties and these will be called integrated of order one, denoted $x_t \sim I(1)$. More generally, if a series needs differencing d times to become $I(0)$, it is called integrated of order d, denoted $x_t \sim I(d)$. Let Δ^b denote application of the difference operator b times, if $x_t \sim I(d)$ then the bth difference series $\Delta^b x_t$ is $I(d - b)$. Sometimes a series needs to be integrated (summed) to become $I(0)$, for example the difference of an $I(0)$ series is $I(-1)$ and its integral is again $I(0)$. Most of this paper will concentrate on the practically important cases when $d = 0$ or 1. The simplest example of an $I(0)$ series is a white noise ε_t, so that $\rho_k = \mathrm{corr}(\varepsilon_t, \varepsilon_{t-k}) = 0$ for all $k \neq 0$. Another example is a stationary $AR(1)$ series, x_t generated by

$$x_t = \alpha x_{t-1} + \varepsilon_t \tag{1.1}$$

where $|\alpha| < 1$ and ε_t is white noise with zero mean. The simplest example of an $I(1)$ series is a random walk, where x_t is generated by

$$x_t = x_{t-1} + \varepsilon_t \tag{1.2}$$

as would theoretically occur for a speculative price generated by an informationally efficient market. Here, the first differenced series is white noise. The most general $I(1)$ series replaces ε_t in equation (1.2) by any $I(0)$ series not necessarily having zero mean. Many macro economic series appear to be $I(1)$, as suggested by the 'typical spectral shape' (see Granger 1966), by analysis of Box–Jenkins (1970) modelling techniques or by direct testing, as in Nelson and Plosser (1982). Throughout the paper all error processes, such as those in (1.1), (1.2) are assumed to have finite first and second moments.

There are many substantial differences between $I(0)$ and $I(1)$ series. An $I(0)$ series has a mean and there is a tendency for the series to return to the mean, so that it tends to fluctuate around the mean, crossing that value frequently and with extensive excursions. Auto-correlations decline rapidly as lag increases and the process gives low weights to events in the medium to distant past, and thus effectively has a finite memory. An $I(1)$ process without drift will be relatively smooth, will wander widely and will only rarely return to an earlier value. In fact, for a random walk, for a fixed arbitrary value the expected time until the process again passes through this value is infinite. This does not mean that returns do not occur, but that the distribution of the time to return is very long-tailed. Autocorrelations $\{\rho_k\}$ are all near one in magnitude even for large k; an innovation to the process affects all later values and the process has indefinitely long memory. To see this, note that the pure random walk $I(1)$ solves to give

$$x_t = \varepsilon_t + \varepsilon_{t-1} + \varepsilon_{t-2} + \ldots + \varepsilon_1 \qquad (1.3)$$

assuming the process starts at time $t = 0$, with $x_0 = 0$. Note that the variance of x_t is $t\sigma_\varepsilon^2$ and becomes indefinitely large as t increases and $\rho_k = 1 - |k|/t$.

If x_t is a random walk with 'drift' (1.2) becomes

$$x_t = x_{t-1} + m + \varepsilon_t$$

where ε_t is zero-mean white noise. The solution is now

$$x_t = mt + \sum_{j=0}^{t-1} \varepsilon_{t-j} \qquad (1.4)$$

so that x_t consists of a linear trend plus a drift-free $I(1)$ process (random walk) being the process in (1.3). The only more general univariate process considered in this section is

$$x_t = m(t) + x_t'$$

where x_t' is a drift-free random walk, such as generated by (1.3), and $m(t)$ is some deterministic function of time, being the 'trend in mean' of x_t.

II. Cointegration

Consider initially a pair of series x_t, y_t, each of which is $I(1)$ and having no drift or trend in mean. It is generally true that any linear combination of these series is also $I(1)$. However, if there exists a constant A, such that

$$z_t = x_t - Ay_t \qquad (2.1)$$

is $I(0)$, then x_t, y_t will be said to be cointegrated, with A called the cointegrating parameter. If it exists, A will be unique in the situation now being considered. As z_t has such different temporal properties from those of either of its components it follows that the x_t and y_t must have a very special relationship. Both x_t and y_t have dominating low-frequency or 'long wave' components, and yet z_t does not. Thus, x_t and Ay_t must have low-frequency components which virtually cancel out to produce z_t. A good analogy is two series each of which contain a prominent seasonal component. Generally, any linear combination of these series will also contain a seasonal, but if the seasonals are identical in shape there could exist a linear combination which has no seasonal.

The relationship

$$x_t = Ay_t \tag{2.2}$$

might be considered a long-run or 'equilibrium' relationship, perhaps as suggested by some economic theory, and z_t given by (2.1) thus measures the extent to which the system x_t, y_t is out of equilibrium, and can thus be called the 'equilibrium error'. The term 'equilibrium' is used in many ways by economists. Here the term is not used to imply anything about the behaviour of economic agents but rather describes the tendency of an economic system to move towards a particular region of the possible outcome space. If x_t and y_t are $I(1)$ but 'move together in the long-run', it is necessary that z_t be $I(0)$ as otherwise the two series will drift apart without bound. Thus, for a pair of $I(1)$ series, cointegration is a necessary condition for the ideas discussed in the first section of this paper to hold. In some circumstances, an even stronger condition may be required, such as putting complete bounds on z_t, which will guarantee that it is $I(0)$, but such cases are not considered here.

The extension to series having trends in their means is straightforward. Consider

$$\begin{aligned} x_t &= m_x(t) + x_t' \\ y_t &= m_y(t) + y_t' \end{aligned} \tag{2.3}$$

where x_t', y_t' are both $I(1)$ but without trends in mean, and let

$$\begin{aligned} z_t &= x_t - Ay_t \\ &= m_x(t) - Am_y(t) + x_t' - Ay_t'. \end{aligned}$$

For z_t to be $I(0)$, and x_t, y_t not to drift too far apart, it is necessary both that z_t have no trend in mean, so that

$$m_x(t) = Am_y(t) \tag{2.4}$$

for all t, and that x_t', y_t' be cointegrated with the *same* value of A as the cointegrating parameter. It is seen that if the two trends in mean are different functions of time, such as an exponential and a cubic, then (eqn. 2.4) cannot hold.

One thing that should be noted is that a model of the form

$$x_t = \beta y_t + e_t$$

where x_t is $I(0)$ and y_t is $I(1)$, makes no sense as the independent and dependent variables have such vastly different temporal properties. Theoretically the only plausible value for β in this regression is $\beta = 0$.

If x_t, y_t are both $I(1)$ without trends in mean and are cointegrated it has been proved in Granger (1983) and Granger and Engle (1985) that there always exists a generating mechanism having what is called the 'error-correcting' form:

$$\Delta x_t = -\rho_1 z_{t-1} + \text{lagged } (\Delta x_t, \Delta y_t) + d(B)\varepsilon_{1t}$$
$$\Delta y_t = -\rho_2 z_{t-1} + \text{lagged } (\Delta x_t, \Delta y_t) + d(B)\varepsilon_{2t}$$

(2.5)

where

$$z_t = x_t - Ay_t,$$

$d(B)$ is a finite polynomial in the lag operator B (so that $B^k x_t = x_{t-k}$) and is the same in each equation, and ε_{1t}, ε_{2t} are joint white noise, possibly contemporaneously correlated and with $|\rho_1| + |\rho_2| \neq 0$. Not only must cointegrated variables obey such a model but the reverse is also true; data generated by an error-correction model such as (2.5) must be cointegrated. The reason for this is easily seen, as if x_t, y_t are $I(1)$ their changes will be $I(0)$ and so every term in the equations 2.5 is $I(0)$ provided z_t is also $I(0)$ meaning that x_t, y_t are cointegrated. If z_t is not $I(0)$, i.e. if x_t, y_t are not cointegrated, then the z_t term does not belong in these equations given that the dependent variables are $I(0)$ and hence at least one of ρ_1, ρ_2 does not vanish.

These models were introduced into economics by Sargan (1964) and Phillips (1957) and have generated a lot of interest following the work of Davidson et al. (1978), Hendry and von Ungern Sternberg (1980), Curry (1981), Dawson (1981), and Salmon (1982) amongst others. The models are seen to incorporate equilibrium relationships, perhaps suggested by an economic theory of the long-run, with the type of dynamic model favoured by time-series econometricians. The equilibrium relationships are allowed to enter the model but are not forced to do so. The title 'error-correcting' for equations such as (eqn. 2.5) is a little optimistic. The absolute value of z_t is the distance that the system is away from equilibrium. Equation 2.5 indicates that the amount and direction of change in x_t and y_t take into account the size and sign of the previous equilibrium error z_{t-1}. The series z_t does not, of course, certainly reduce in size from one time period to another but is a stationary series and thus is inclined to move towards its mean. A constant should be included in the equilibrium equation (2.2) and in (2.1) if needed, to make the mean of z_t zero.

There are a number of theoretical implications of cointegratedness that are easily derived from the results so far presented:

(i) If x_t, y_t are cointegrated, so will be x_t and $by_{t-k} + w_t$, for any k where $w_t \sim I(0)$, with a possible change in cointegrating parameter. Formally, if x_t is $I(1)$ then x_t and x_{t-k} will be cointegrated for any k, but this is not an interesting property as it is true for any $I(1)$ process and so does not suggest a special relationship, unlike cointegration of a pair of $I(1)$ series. It follows that if x_t, y_t are cointegrated but are only observed with measurement error, then the two observed series will also be cointegrated if all measurement errors are $I(0)$.

(ii) If x_t is $I(1)$ and $f_{n,h}(J_n)$ is the optimal forecast of x_{n+h}, based on the information set J_n available at time n, then x_{t+h}, $f_{t,h}(J_t)$ are cointegrated if J_n is a proper information set, that is if it includes x_{n-j}, $j \geqslant 0$. If J_n is not a proper information set, x_{t+n} and its optimum forecast are only cointegrated if x_t is cointegrated with variables in J_t.

(iii) If x_{n+h}, y_{n+h} are cointegrated series with parameter A and are optimally forecast using the information set $J_n : x_{n-j}$, y_{n-j}, $j \geqslant 0$, then the h-step forecasts $f_{n,h}^x$, $f_{n,h}^y$ will obey

$$f_{n,h}^x = A f_{n,h}^y$$

as $h \to \infty$ (proved by S. Yoo (1986)). Thus, long-term optimum forecasts of x_t, y_t will be tied-together by the equilibrium relationships. Forecasts formed without cointegration terms such as univariate forecasts will not necessarily have this property.

(iv) If T_t is an $I(1)$ target variable and x_t is an $I(1)$ controllable variable, then T_t, x_t will be cointegrated if optimum control is applied. (See Nickell 1985.)

(v) If x_t, y_t are $I(1)$ and cointegrated, there must be Granger causality in at least one direction, as one variable can help forecast the other. This follows directly from the error-correlation model and the condition that $|\rho_1| + |\rho_2| \neq 0$, as z_{t-1} must occur in at least one equation and thus knowledge of z_t must improve forecastability of at least one of x_t, y_t. Here causality is with respect to the information set J_t defined in (iii).

(vi) If x_t, y_t are a pair of prices from a jointly efficient, speculative market, they cannot be cointegrated. This follows directly from (v) as if the two prices were cointegrated, one can be used to help forecast the other and this would contradict the efficient market assumption. Thus, for example, gold and silver prices, if generated by an efficient market, cannot move closely together in the long-run. Tests of this idea have been conducted by Granger and Escribano (1986).

III. Testing for Cointegration

This topic has been discussed at some length by Granger and Engle (1985) and so only an outline of their conclusions is presented here. It is necessary to start with a test for whether a series x_t is $I(0)$ and a useful test has been provided by Dickey and Fuller (1981). The following regression is formed

$$\Delta x_t = \beta x_{t-1} + \sum_{j=1}^{p} \gamma_j \Delta x_{t-j} + e_t$$

where p is selected to be large enough to ensure that the residual e_t is empirical white noise. The test statistic is the ratio of $\hat{\beta}$ to its calculated standard error obtained from an ordinary least squares (OLS) regression. The null hypothesis is $H_0 : x_t \sim I(1)$. This is rejected if $\hat{\beta}$ is negative and significantly different from zero. However, the test-statistic does *not* have a t-distribution but tables of significance levels have been provided by Dickey and Fuller (1979).

To test for cointegration between a pair of series, that are expected to be $I(1)$, one method is to first form the 'cointegration regression'

$$x_t = c + \alpha y_t + a_t \tag{3.1}$$

and then to test if the residual a_t appears to be $I(0)$ or not. It might be noted that when x_t and y_t are cointegrated, this regression when estimated using, say, OLS should give an excellent estimate of the true cointegrating coefficient A, and large samples. Note that a_t will have a finite (or small) variance only if $\alpha = A$, otherwise a_t will be $I(1)$ and thus have theoretically a very large variance in a large sample. Stock (1984) has shown that when series are cointegrated, OLS estimates of A are highly efficient with variances $0(T^{-2})$ compared to more usual situations where the variances are $0(T^{-1})$, T being the sample size. Stock also shows that the estimates are consistent with an $0(T^{-1})$ bias. However, some recent Monte Carlo simulations by Banerjee *et al.* (1986) suggest that these bias terms can be very substantial in some cases. Two simple tests of the null hypothesis

$$H_0 : x_t, \ y_t \ \text{not cointegrated}$$

are based either on a Durbin–Watson statistic (D/W) for (3.1), but testing if D/W is significantly greater than zero (see Sargan and Bhargara 1983 who provide critical values), or using the previously mentioned Dickey–Fuller test for $\hat{a}_t$. The latter test was found by Granger and Engle (1985) to have more stable critical values from a small simulation study and with $T = 100$ observations approximate significance levels for the pseudo t-statistic testing $\beta = 0$ are, 10 per cent ~ 2.88, 5 per cent ~ 3.17, 1 per cent ~ 3.75. A great deal more experience with these tests, and more extensive simulation studies, are required before confidence in the quality of these, or alternative, testing procedures is assured. Some estimates of power for this test were found to be quite satisfactory for a sample size of 100.

Applying this test, some examples of the outcomes of empirical analysis are (mostly from Granger and Engle 1985)

apparently cointegrated
  US national income and consumption
  US non-durables, production and sales
  US short and long-term interest rates
  UK W, P, H, U, T (Hall—this issue)
  UK Velocity and short-term interest rates (Hendry and Ericsson 1983)
apparently not cointegrated
  US wages and prices
  US durables, production and sales
  US money and prices.

Of course, some of the examples where cointegration was not found strongly suggest that further variables should be included in the investigation, such as the addition of productivity to wages and prices. This extension is considered next.

IV. Generalization: Many Variables and General Cointegration

Let x_t be a vector of N component time series, each without trend in mean and each $I(d)$, $d > 0$. For the moment, it is assumed that the d-differenced vector series is a zero mean, purely non-deterministic stationary process, so that there is a Wold representation

$$(1 - B)^d x_t = C(B)\varepsilon_t \tag{4.1}$$

where this is taken to mean that both sides have the same spectral matrix and ε_t is an $N \times 1$ zero-mean white noise vector with

$$E[\varepsilon_t \varepsilon_s'] = 0 \qquad t \neq s$$

$$= G \qquad t = s$$

so that only contemporaneous correlations can occur. Equation (4.1) is normalized by taking $C(0) = I_N$, the unit matrix.

Then x_t will be said to be cointegrated $CI(d, b)$ if there exists a vector α such that

$$z_t = \alpha' x_t$$

is $I(d - b)$, $b > 0$.

The case considered in earlier sections has $N = 2$, $d = b = 1$. Moving to general values for N, d, b adds a large number of possible interrelationships and models. In particular it is clear that α need no longer be unique, as there can be several 'equilibrium' relationships linking $N > 2$ variables. If there are r vectors α, each of which produces z's integrated of order less than d, then r is called the 'order of cointegration' and it is easily seen that $r \leqslant N - 1$.

For the practically important case $d = b = 1$, it is shown in Granger (1983) and in Granger and Engle (1985) that

(i) $C(1)$ is of rank $N - r$

(ii) there exists a vector autoregressive (VAR) representation

$$A(B)x_t = d(B)\varepsilon_t$$

where $A(1)$ is of rank r with $A(0) = I_N$ and $d(B)$ is a scalar stable lag polynomial. If a finite order VAR model exists, it takes this form but with $d(B) = 1$.

(iii) there exist $N \times r$ matrices α, γ of rank r such that

$$\alpha'C(1) = 0$$

$$C(1)\gamma = 0$$

$$A(1) = \gamma\alpha'$$

(iv) there exists an error-correction representation with

$$z_t = \alpha'x_t$$

and $r \times 1$ stationary vector, of the form

$$A^*(B)(1 - B)x_t = -\gamma z_{t-1} + d(B)\varepsilon_t \qquad (4.2)$$

where $A^*(0) = I_N$, $A^*(1)$ is of full rank and $|A^*(w)| = 0$ has all its roots outside the unit circle. It should be noted that the first term on the right hand side can be written as (given (iii) and (v))

$$\gamma z_{t-1} = A(1)x_{t-1}$$

and so, for all terms in (4.2) to be $I(0)$ it is necessary that $A(1)$ does not have a row consisting of just one non-zero term. A resulting condition on α is mentioned below.

Commenting on these results, (i) concerning the rank of $C(1)$ is a necessary and sufficient condition for cointegration and all other results are derived from it. In (ii) concerning VAR, $A(B)$ is the adjoint matrix of $C(B)$ and $d(B)$ is proportional to the determinant of $C(B)$ after dividing out unit roots. It follows from (ii) that if a VAR model is estimated for cointegrated variables, efficiency will be lost unless $A(1)$ is restricted to being of rank r.

In (iii) it should be noted that the matrices γ, α, are not uniquely defined by the set of equations shown. If θ is an $r \times r$ matrix of full rank, then γ can be replaced by $\gamma\theta$ and α' by $\theta^{-1}\alpha'$ and the equations will still hold. This lack of uniqueness leads to some interpretational problems in the error-correction model (4.2), which are similar to the identification problems of classical simultaneous equations models. To illustrate the problem, suppose that $N = 3$ and $r = 2$ and that α_1, α_2 are a pair of cointegrating vectors, giving

$$z_t(\alpha_1) = \alpha_{11}x_{1t} + \alpha_{12}x_{2t} + \alpha_{13}x_{3t}$$

$$z_t(\alpha_2) = \alpha_{21}x_{1t} + \alpha_{22}x_{2t} + \alpha_{23}x_{3t}$$

as a pair of $I(0)$ variables corresponding to equilibrium relationships $\alpha_1'x_t = 0$, $\alpha_2'x_t = 0$. However, generally any combination of a pair of $I(0)$ variables will also be $I(0)$ and so

$$z_t(\lambda) = (1 - \lambda)z_t(\alpha_1) + \lambda z_t(\alpha_2)$$

will also be $I(0)$ [it is assumed that for no λ will $z_t(\lambda)$ consist of just one component of x_t: this is a constraint on the matrix α preventing $z_t(\lambda) = x_t$, for example, which would make $z_t \sim I(1)$]. Thus, the equilibrium relations are not uniquely identified, and the error-correction models cannot be strictly interpreted as 'correcting' for deviations from a particular pair of equilibrium relationships. The only invariant relationship is the line in the (x_1, x_2, x_3) space defined by

$$z_t(\alpha_1) = 0, z_t(\alpha_2) = 0$$

This same line is given by

$$z_t(\lambda_1) = 0, z_t(\lambda_2) = 0$$

for any $\lambda_1 \neq \lambda_2$ and will be called the 'equilibrium sub-space'. The error-correction model might thus be interpreted as Δx_t being influenced by the distance the system is from the equilibrium sub-space. For general N,r, the equilibrium sub-space will be a hyper-plane of dimension $N - r$.

It is unclear if the identification question can be solved in ways similar to those used with simultaneous equations, that is by adding sufficient zeros to $A(1)$ or by appeals to 'exogeneity'.

For the $N = 3$, $r = 2$ case, λ's can be chosen to give

$$z_t = \alpha_1 x_{1t} + \alpha_2 x_{2t}$$

and

$$z_t = \alpha_3 x_{1t} + \alpha_4 x_{3t}$$

and these seem to provide a natural way for testing for cointegration. For more general N and r, the number of possible combinations becomes extensive and testing will be more difficult, particularly when r is an unknown, as will be usual in practice.

Turning briefly to the most general case, with any N, d, b and r, the error-correction model becomes

$$A^*(B)(1 - B)^d x_t = -\gamma[(1 - (1 - B)^b](1 - B)^{d-b} z_{t-1} + d(B)\varepsilon_t$$

(4.3)

where $d(B)$ is a scalar polynomial in B.

It should be noted that $[1 - (1 - B)^b]$, if expanded in powers of B, has no term in B^0 and so only lagged z_t occur on the right hand side. Again, every term in (4.3) is $I(0)$ when cointegration is present. It is possible to define fractional differencing, as in Granger and Joyeux (1980), and equation (4.3) still holds in this case, although its practical importance has yet to be established.

In the general case (with integer N, b, d, r) Yoo (1986) has considered alternative ways of defining the z_t's possibly using lagged x_t components, for a given $c(B)$ matrix but with some added assumptions about its form. Johanssen (1985) has also found some mathematically exact and attractive results for the general case, which do not rely on the assumption that all components of x_t are integrated of the same order. He points out, for example, that if x_{it} is $I(1)$ and x_{2t} is $I(0)$, then x_{1t} and $\bar{x}_{2t} = \sum_{j=0}^{t} x_{2,t-j}$ could be cointegrated, thus expanding the class of variables that might be tested.

The work of Yoo and Johanssen suggests a more general definition of cointegration. Let $\alpha(B)$ be an $N \times 1$ vector of functions of the lag operator B, such that each component, such as $\alpha_j(B)$ has the property that $\alpha_j(1) \neq 0$. Then if $\mathbf{x}_t$ is a vector of $I(d)$ series such that

$$z_t = \alpha'(B)\mathbf{x}_t$$

is $I(d - b)$, $\mathbf{x}_t$ may be called cointegrated. If a cointegrating vector α occurs, as defined in earlier sections there will be many $\alpha(B)$ that also cointegrate, and so uniqueness is lost but extra flexibility is gained. Consideration of these possibilities does allow for a generalisation that is potentially very important in economics. Suppose that $N = 2$, so that $\mathbf{x}_t$ has just two components, and let α be a cointegrating vector, with $\alpha' = (1, A)$. In this case α will be unique, if it does not depend on B, so that $r = 1$. [Generally, one would expect $r < N$]. However, there may exist another cointegrating vector of quite a different form,

$$\alpha'(B) = \left(1 - \frac{A'}{\Delta}, \frac{AA'}{\Delta}\right)$$

$\alpha' = (1, -A')$ and $\Delta = 1 - B$. An example of this possibility is where $\mathbf{x}_t = (x_t, y_t)$, x_t, y_t are cointegrated with vector α, giving equilibrium error:

$$z_t = x_t - A y_t$$

and x_t, $Sz_t = \sum_{j=0}^{t} z_{t-j}$ are cointegrated, so that $x_t - A'Sz_t$ is $I(0)$. This would correspond to a cointegrating vector of the form

$$\alpha(B) = (1 - SA', \, SAA')$$

where $S = 1/\Delta$ and $\Delta = 1 - B$.

For example, x_t, y_t could be sales and production of some industry, z_t = change in inventory, Sz_t inventory and x_t, y_t could be cointegrated as well as x_t, Sz_t. Another example might be x_t = income, y_t = expenditure, z_t = savings, Sz_t = wealth. Such series might be called 'multi-cointegrated'.

Throughout this section, if the series involved have deterministic trends in mean, these need to be estimated and removed before the concepts discussed can be applied. One method of removing trends of general shape is discussed in Granger (1985).

V. Further Generalizations

The processes considered so far have been linear and with time-invariant parameters. Clearly general models, and possibly more realistic ones, are achieved by removing these restrictions.

As institutions, technology and society changes, so may any equilibrium relationships. In the bivariate case, the cointegrating parameter may be slowly changing with time, for instance. To proceed with analysis of this idea, it is necessary to define time-varying parameter (TVP) $I(0)$ and $I(1)$ processes. Using concepts introduced by Priestley (1981), it is possible to define a time-varying spectrum $f_t(w)$ for a process such as one generated by an ARMA model with TVP. For example, consider

$$x_t = \beta(t)x_{t-1} + \varepsilon_t$$

where $\beta(t)$ is a deterministic function of time, obeying the restriction that $|\beta(t)| < 1$ all t. If $f_t(w)$ is bounded above and also is positive for all t, w, the process may be called TVP $I(0)$. If the change of x_t is TVP $I(0)$, then x_t can be called TVP $I(1)$.

For a vector process x_t that is TVP $I(d)$ and has no deterministic components Cramer (1961) has shown that there exists a generalised Wold representation

$$(1 - B)^d x_t = C_t(B)\varepsilon_t \tag{5.1}$$

where

$$E[\varepsilon_t] = 0$$

$$E[\varepsilon_t \varepsilon_s'] = 0$$

$$E[\varepsilon_t \varepsilon_t'] = \Omega_t$$

$$C_t(0) = I_N$$

and if

$$C_t(B) = \sum C_{jt} B^j$$

it will be assumed that

$$\sum_j C_{jt} \Omega_t C_{jt}' < \infty$$

so that the variance of $(1 - B)^d x_t$ is finite.

Assume now that $C_t(1)$ has rank $N - 1$ for all t, so that the cointegration rank is 1, then there will exist $N \times 1$ vectors $\alpha(t)$, $\gamma(t)$ such that

$$\alpha'(t) C_t(1) = 0$$

$$C_t(1) \gamma(t) = 0.$$

The TVP equilibrium error process will then be

$$z_t = \alpha'(t) x_t. \tag{5.2}$$

The corresponding error-correction models will be as (4.2) but with $A^*(B)$, γ, $d(B)$ all functions of time. A testing procedure would involve estimating the equilibrium regression (5.2) using some TVP techniques, such as a Kalman filter procedure, probably assuming that the components of $\alpha(r)$ are stochastic but slowly changing.

It might be thought that allowing $\alpha(t)$ to change with time can always produce an $I(0) z_t$. For example, suppose that $N = 2$ and consider

$$z_t = x_t - A(t) y_t$$

Taking $A(t) = x_t / y_t$ clearly gives $z_t = 0$, which is an uninteresting $I(0)$ situation. However, it is also clear that taking $\bar{A}(t) = x_t / y_t + \delta$ will produce a z_t that is $I(1)$ in general. Interpretation of any TVP cointegration test will have to consider this possible difficulty.

Turning to the possibility of non-linear cointegration, it might be noted that in the basic error-correlation model (2.5) or (4.2) z_{t-1} terms appear linearly so that changes in dependent variables are related to z_{t-1}, whatever its size. In the actual economy, a more realistic behaviour is to ignore small equilibrium errors but to react substantially to large ones, suggesting a non-linear relationship. An error-correction model that captures this idea is, in the bivariate case,

$$\Delta x_t = f_1(z_{t-1}) + \text{lagged } (\Delta x_t, \Delta y_t) + \varepsilon_{1t}$$

$$\Delta y_t = f_2(z_{t-1}) + \text{lagged } (\Delta x_t, \Delta y_t) + \varepsilon_{2t} \tag{5.3}$$

where

$$z_t = x_t - Ay_t.$$

It is generally true that if z_t is $I(0)$ with constant variance, then $f(z_t)$ will also be $I(0)$. Similarly, if z_t is $I(1)$ then generally $f(z_t)$ is also $I(1)$, provided $f(z)$ has a linear component for large z, i.e. $f/z(z) \rightarrow \sum_{j=0}^{\infty} a_j z^j$ with $a_0 \neq 0$. A rigorous treatment of these results is provided by Escribano (1986). As generally z_t and $f(z_t)$ will be integrated of the same order, if a test suggests that a pair of series are cointegrated, then a non-linear error-correction model of form (5.3) is a possibility. Of course, most of the other results of previous sections do not hold as they are based on the linear Wold representation. Equation (5.3) can be estimated by one of the many currently available non-linear, non-parametric estimation techniques such as that employed in Engle *et al.* (1986).

Error-correction models essentially consider processes whose components drift widely but the joint process has a generalised preference towards a certain part of the process space. In the cases so far considered this preferred sub-space is a hyper-plane but more general preferred sub-spaces could be considered although with considerably increased mathematical difficulty.

VI.   Conclusion

This paper has attempted to expand the discussion about differencing macro-economic series when model building by emphasizing the use of a further factor, the 'equilibrium error', that arises from the concept of cointegration. This factor allows the introduction of the impact of long-run or 'equilibrium' economic theories into the models used by the time-series analysts to explain the short-run dynamics of economic data. The resulting error-correction models should produce better short-run forecasts and will certainly produce long-run forecasts that hold together in economically meaningful ways.

If long-run economic theories are to have useful impact on econometric models they must be helpful in model specification and yet not distract from the short-run aspects of the model. Historically, many econometric models were based on equilibrium relationships suggested by a theory, such as

$$x_t = Ay_t + e_t \qquad (6.1)$$

without any consideration of the levels of integratedness of the observed variables x_t, y_t or of the residual series e_t. If x_t is $I(0)$ but y_t is $I(1)$, for example, the value of A in the resulting regression is forced to be near zero. If e_t is $I(1)$, standard estimation techniques are not appropriate. A test for cointegration can thus be thought of as a pre-test to avoid 'spurious regression' situations. Even if x_t and y_t are cointegrated an equation such as (6.1) can only provide a start for the modelling process, as e_t may be explainable by lagged changes in x_t and y_t, eventually resulting in an error-correction model of the form (2.5). However, there must be two such equations, which again makes the equation (2.5) a natural form. Ignoring the process of properly model-ling the e_t can lead to forecasts from (6.1) that can be beaten by simple time-series models, at least in the short-term.

Whilst the paper has not attempted to link error-correction models with optimizing economic theory, through control variables for example, there is doubtless much useful work to be done in this area.

Testing for cointegration in general situations is still in an early stage of development. Whether or not cointegration occurs is an empirical question but the beliefs of economists do appear to support its existence and the usefulness of the concept appears to be rapidly gaining acceptance.

References

Box, G. E. P., and G. M. Jenkins (1970), *Time Series Analysis Forecasting and Control* (San Francisco, Holden Day).

Cramer, H. (1961), 'On some classes of non-stationary processes', *Proceedings 4th Berkeley Symposium on Math, Stats and Probability,* pp. 157–78 (University of California Press).

Currie, D. (1981), 'Some long-run features of dynamic time-series models', *The Economic Journal*, **363**, 704–15.

Davidson, J. E. H., D. F. Hendry, F. Srba, and S. Yeo (1978), 'Econometric modelling of the aggregate time-series relationship between consumer's expen-diture and income in the United Kingdom', *The Economic Journal*, **88**, 661–92.

Dawson, A. (1981), 'Sargan's wage equation: A theoretical and empirical reconstruction', *Applied Economics,* **13**, 351–63.

Dickey, D. A., and W. A. Fuller (1979), 'Distributions of the estimators for autoregressive time series with a unit root', *Journal of the American Statistical Association*, **74**, 427–31.

—— —— (1981), 'The likelihood ratio statistics for autoregressive time series with a unit root, *Econometrica,* **49**, 1057–72.

Engle, R. F., C. W. J. Granger, J. Rice, and A. Weiss (1986), 'Non-parametric estimation of the relationship between weather and electricity demand', *Journal of the American Statistical Association*, **81**, 310–20.

Escribano, A. (1986), Ph.D. thesis, Economics Department, University of California, San Diego.

GRANGER, C. W. J. (1966), 'The typical spectral shape of an economic variable', *Econometrica*, **34**, 150–61.

—— (1983), 'Co-integrated variables and error-correcting models', UCSD Discussion Paper, pp. 83–13a.

—— and R. F. ENGLE (1985), 'Dynamic specification with equilibrium constraints: cointegration and error-correction' (forthcoming, *Econometrica*). See Chapter 5 of this volume.

—— and A. ESCRIBANO (1986), 'Limitation on the long-run relationship between prices from an efficient market', UCSD Discussion Paper.

—— and R. JOYEUX (1980), 'An introduction to long-memory time series and fractional differencing', *Journal of Time Series Analysis*, **1**, 15–29.

HENDRY, D. F., and N. R. ERICSSON (1983), 'Assertion without empirical basis: An econometric appraisal of "Monetary trends in . . . the United Kingdom" by Milton Friedman and Anna Schwartz', *Bank of England Academic Panel Paper No. 22*.

—— and VON UNGERN-STERNBERG, T. (1981), 'Liquidity and inflation effects on consumer's expenditure', in A. S. Deaton (ed.), *Essays in the Theory and Measurement of Consumer's Behaviour* (Cambridge University Press).

JOHANSSEN, S. (1985), 'The mathematical structure of error-correction models', Discussion Paper, Maths Department, University of Copenhagen.

NELSON, C. R., and C. I. PLOSSER (1982), 'Trends and random walks in macro-economic time series', *Journal of Monetary Economics*, **10**, 139–62.

NICKELL, S. (1985), 'Error-correction, partial adjustment and all that: An expository note', *BULLETIN*, **47**, 119–29.

PHILLIPS, A. W. (1957), 'Stabilization policy and the time forms of lagged responses', *Economic Journal*, **67**, 265–77.

PRIESTLEY, M. B. (1981), *Spectral Analysis of Time Series*, (New York, Academic Press).

SALMON, M. (1982), 'Error correction mechanisms', *The Economic Journal*, **92**, 615–29.

SARGAN, J. D. (1964), 'Wages and prices in the United Kingdom: A study in economic methodology', in P. Hart, G. Mills, and J. N. Whittaker (eds), *Econometric Analysis for National Economic Planning*, (London, Butterworths).

—— and A. BHARGAVA (1983), 'Testing residuals from least squares regression for being generated by the Gaussian random walk', *Econometrica*, **51**, 153–74.

STOCK, J. H. (1984), 'Asymptotic properties of a least squares estimator of co-integrating vectors, manuscript Harvard University.

YOO, S. (1986), Ph.D. thesis, Economics Department, University of California, San Diego.

5

Co-integration and Error Correction: Representation, Estimation, and Testing

ROBERT F. ENGLE and C. W. J. GRANGER[1]

The relationship between co-integration and error correction models, first suggested in Granger (1981), is here extended and used to develop estimation procedures, tests, and empirical examples.

If each element of a vector of time series x_t first achieves stationarity after differencing, but a linear combination $\alpha' x_t$ is already stationary, the time series x_t are said to be co-integrated with co-integrating vector α. There may be several such co-integrating vectors so that α becomes a matrix. Interpreting $\alpha' x_t = 0$ as a long run equilibrium, co-integration implies that deviations from equilibrium are stationary, with finite variance, even though the series themselves are nonstationary and have infinite variance.

The paper presents a representation theorem based on Granger (1983), which connects the moving average, autoregressive, and error correction representations for co-integrated systems. A vector autoregression in differenced variables is incompatible with these representations. Estimation of these models is discussed and a simple but asymptotically efficient two-step estimator is proposed. Testing for co-integration combines the problems of unit root tests and tests with parameters unidentified under the null. Seven statistics are formulated and analyzed. The critical values of these statistics are calculated based on a Monte Carlo simulation. Using these critical values, the power properties of the tests are examined and one test procedure is recommended for application.

In a series of examples it is found that consumption and income are co-integrated, wages and prices are not, short and long interest rates are, and

[1] The authors are indebted to David Hendry and Sam Yoo for many useful conversations and suggestions as well as to Gene Savin, David Dickey, Alok Bhargava, and Marco Lippi. Two referees provided detailed constructive criticism, and thanks go to Yoshi Baba, Sam Yoo, and Alvaro Escribano who creatively carried out the simulations and examples. Financial support was provided by NSF SES–80–08580 and SES–82–08626. A previous version of this paper was entitled 'Dynamic Model Specification with Equilibrium Constraints: Co-integration and Error Correction'.

Printed with permission of: *Econometrica*, Vol. 55, No. 2, March 1987, pp. 251–76.

nominal GNP is co-integrated with M2, but not M1, M3, or aggregate liquid assets.

KEYWORDS: Co-integration, vector autoregression, unit roots, error correction, multi-variate time series, Dickey–Fuller tests.

1.   Introduction

An individual economic variable, viewed as a time series, can wander extensively and yet some pairs of series may be expected to move so that they do not drift too far apart. Typically economic theory will propose forces which tend to keep such series together. Examples might be short and long-term interest rates, capital appropriations and expenditures, household income and expenditures, and prices of the same commodity in different markets or close substitutes in the same market. A similar idea arises from considering equilibrium relationships, where equilibrium is a stationary point characterized by forces which tend to push the economy back toward equilibrium whenever it moves away. If x_t is a vector of economic variables, then they may be said to be in equilibrium when the specific linear constraint

$$\alpha' x_t = 0.$$

occurs. In most time periods, x_t will not be in equilibrium and the univariate quantity

$$z_t = \alpha' x_t$$

may be called the equilibrium error. If the equilibrium concept is to have any relevance for the specification of econometric models, the economy should appear to prefer a small value of z_t rather than a large value.

In this paper, these ideas are put onto a firm basis and it is shown that a class of models, known as error-correcting, allows long-run components of variables to obey equilibrium constraints while short-run components have a flexible dynamic specification. A condition for this to be true, called co-integration, was introduced by Granger (1981) and Granger and Weiss (1983) and is precisely defined in the next section. Section 3 discusses several representations of co-integrated systems, Section 4 develops estimation procedures, and Section 5 develops tests. Several applications are presented in Section 6 and conclusions are offered in Section 7. A particularly simple example of this class of models is shown in Section 4, and it might be useful to examine it for motivating the analysis of such systems.

2. Integration, Co-integration, and Error Correction

It is well known from Wold's theorem that a single stationary time series with no deterministic components has an infinite moving average representation which is generally approximated by a finite autoregressive moving average process. See, for example, Box and Jenkins (1970) or Granger and Newbold (1977). Commonly however, economic series must be differenced before the assumption of stationarity can be presumed to hold. This motivates the following familiar definition of integration:

DEFINITION: A series with no deterministic component which has a stationary, invertible, ARMA representation after differencing d times, is said to be integrated of order d, denoted $x_t \sim I(d)$.

For ease of exposition, only the values $d = 0$ and $d = 1$ will be considered in much of the paper, but many of the results can be generalized to other cases including the fractional model. Thus, for $d = 0$ x_t will be stationary and for $d = 1$ the change is stationary.

There are substantial differences in appearance between a series that is $I(0)$ and another that is $I(1)$. For more discussion see, for example, Feller (1968) or Granger and Newbold (1977).

(a) If $x_t \sim I(0)$ with zero mean then (i) the variance of x_t is finite; (ii) an innovation has only a temporary effect on the value of x_t; (iii) the spectrum of x_t, $f(\omega)$, has the property $0 < f(0) < \infty$; (iv) the expected length of times between crossings of $x = 0$ is finite; (v) the autocorrelations, ρ_k, decrease steadily in magnitude for large enough k, so that their sum is finite.

(b) If $x_t \sim I(1)$ with $x_0 = 0$, then (i) variance x_t goes to infinity as t goes to infinity; (ii) an innovation has a permanent effect on the value of x_t, as x_t is the sum of all previous changes; (iii) the spectrum of x_t has the approximate shape $f(\omega) \sim A\omega^{-2d}$ for small ω so that in particular $f(0) = \infty$; (iv) the expected time between crossings of $x = 0$ is infinite; (v) the theoretical autocorrelations, $\rho_k \to 1$ for all k as $t \to \infty$.

The theoretical infinite variance for an $I(1)$ series comes completely from the contribution of the low frequencies, or long run part of the series. Thus an $I(1)$ series is rather smooth, having dominant long swings, compared to an $I(0)$ series. Because of the relative sizes of the variances, it is always true that the sum of an $I(0)$ and an $I(1)$ will be $I(1)$. Further, if a and b are constants, $b \neq 0$, and if $x_t \sim I(d)$, then $a + bx_t$ is also $I(d)$.

If x_t and y_t are both $I(d)$, then it is generally true that the linear combination

$$z_t = x_t - ay_t$$

will also be $I(d)$. However, it is possible that $z_t \sim I(d - b)$, $b > 0$. When this occurs, a very special constraint operates on the long-run components of the series. Consider the case $d = b = 1$, so that x_t, y_t are both $I(1)$ with dominant long run components, but z_t is $I(0)$ without especially strong low frequencies. The constant a is therefore such that the bulk of the long-run components of x_t and y_t cancel out. For $a = 1$, the vague idea that x_t and y_t cannot drift too far apart has been translated into the more precise statement that 'their difference will be $I(0)$'. The use of the constant a merely suggests that some scaling needs to be used before the $I(0)$ difference can be achieved. It should be noted that it will not generally be true that there is an a which makes $z_t \sim I(0)$.

An analogous case, considering a different important frequency, is when x_t and y_t are a pair of series, each having important seasonal component, yet there is an a so that the derived series z_t has no seasonal. Clearly this could occur, but might be considered to be unlikely.

To formalize these ideas, the following definition adapted from Granger (1981) and Granger and Weiss (1983) is introduced:

DEFINITION: The components of the vector x_t are said to be *co-integrated of order d, b*, denoted $x_t \sim CI(d, b)$, if (i) all components of x_t are $I(d)$; (ii) there exists a vector $\alpha (\neq 0)$ so that $z_t = \alpha' x_t \sim I(d - b)$, $b > 0$. The vector α is called the *co-integrating vector*.

Continuing to concentrate on the $d = 1$, $b = 1$ case, co-integration would mean that if the components of x_t were all $I(1)$, then the equilibrium error would be $I(0)$, and z_t will rarely drift far from zero if it has zero mean and z_t will often cross the zero line. Putting this another way, it means that equilibrium will occasionally occur, at least to a close approximation, whereas if x_t was not co-integrated, then z_t can wander widely and zero-crossings would be very rare, suggesting that in this case the equilibrium concept has no practical implications. The reduction in the order of integration implies a special kind of relationship with interpretable and testable consequences. If however all the elements of x_t are already stationary so that they are $I(0)$, then the equilibrium error z_t has no distinctive property if it is $I(0)$. It could be that $z_t \sim I(-1)$, so that its spectrum is zero at zero frequency, but if any of the variables have measurement error, this property in general cannot be observed and so this case is of little realistic interest. When interpreting the co-integration concept it might be noted that in the $N = 2$, $d = b = 1$ case, Granger and Weiss (1983) show that a necessary and sufficient condition for co-integration is that the coherence between the two series is one at zero frequency.

If x_t has N components, then there may be more than one cointegrating vector α. It is clearly possible for several equilibrium relations to govern the joint behaviour of the variables. In what follows, it will be assumed that there are exactly r linearly independent co-integrating vectors, with $r \leq N - 1$, which are gathered together into the $N \times r$ array α. By construction the rank of α will be r which will be called the 'co-integrating rank' of x_t. *multiple α's*

The close relationship between co-integration and error correcting models will be developed in the balance of the paper. Error correction mechanisms have been used widely in economics. Early versions are Sargan (1964) and Phillips (1957). The idea is simply that a proportion of the disequilibrium from one period is corrected in the next period. For example, the change in price in one period may depend upon the degree of excess demand in the previous period. Such schemes can be derived as optimal behaviour with some types of adjustment costs or incomplete information. Recently, these models have seen great interest following the work of Davidson, Hendry, Srba, and Yeo (1978) (DHSY), Hendry and von Ungern Sternberg (1980), Currie (1981), Dawson (1981), and Salmon (1982) among others.

For a two variable system a typical error correction model would relate the change in one variable to past equilibrium errors, as well as to past changes in both variables. For a multivariate system we can define a general error correction representation in terms of B, the backshift operator, as follows.

DEFINITION: A vector time series x_t has an error correction representation if it can be expressed as:

$$A(B)(1 - B)x_t = - \gamma z_{t-1} + u_t$$

where u_t is a stationary multivariate disturbance, with $A(0) = I$, $A(1)$ has all elements finite, $z_\tau = \alpha' x_\tau$, and $\gamma \neq 0$.

In this representation, only the disequilibrium in the previous period is an explanatory variable. However, by rearranging terms, any set of lags of the z can be written in this form, therefore it permits any type of gradual adjustment toward a new equilibrium. A notable difference between this definition and most of the applications which have occurred is that this is a multivariate definition which does not rest on exogeneity of a subset of the variables. The notion that one variable may be weakly exogenous in the sense of Engle, Hendry, and Richard (1983) may be investigated in such a system as briefly discussed below.

A second notable difference is that α is taken to be an unknown parameter vector rather than a set of constants given by economic theory.

3. Properties of Co-integrated Variables and Their Representations

Suppose that each component of x_t is $I(1)$ so that the change in each component is a zero mean purely nondeterministic stationary stochastic process. Any known deterministic components can be subtracted before the analysis is begun. It follows that there will always exist a multivariate Wold representation:

$$(1 - B)x_t = C(B)\varepsilon t, \qquad (3.1)$$

taken to mean that both sides will have the same special matrix. Further, $C(B)$ will be uniquely defined by the conditions that the function $\det[C(z)]$, $z = e^{i\omega}$, have all zeros on or outside the unit circle, and that $C(0) = I_N$, the $N \times N$ identity matrix (see Hannan, 1970, p. 66). In this representation the ε_t are zero mean white noise vectors with

$$E[\varepsilon_t \varepsilon_s'] = 0, \quad t \neq s,$$

$$= G, \quad t = s,$$

so that only contemporaneous correlations can occur.

The moving average polynomial $C(B)$ can always be expressed as

$$C(B) = C(1) + (1 - B)C^*(B) \qquad (3.2)$$

by simply rearranging the terms. If $C(B)$ is of finite order, then $C^*(B)$ will be of finite order. If $C^*(1)$ is identically zero, then a similar expression involving $(1 - B)^2$ can be defined.

The relationship between error correction models and co-integration was first pointed out in Granger (1981). A theorem showing precisely that co-integrated series can be represented by error correction models was originally stated and proved in Granger (1983). The following version is therefore called the Granger Representation Theorem. Analysis of related but more complex cases is covered by Johansen (1985) and Yoo (1985).

GRANGER REPRESENTATION THEOREM: If the $N \times 1$ vector x_t given in (3.1) is co-integrated with $d = 1$, $b = 1$ and with co-integrating rank r, then:

(1) $C(1)$ is of rank $N - r$.

(2) *There exists a vector ARMA representation*

$$A(B)x_t = d(B)\varepsilon_t \tag{3.3}$$

with the properties that $A(1)$ has rank r and $d(B)$ is a scalar lag polynomial with $d(1)$ finite, and $A(0) = I_N$. When $d(B) = 1$, this is a vector autoregression.

(3) *There exist $N \times r$ matrices, α, γ, of rank r such that*

$$\alpha' C(1) = 0,$$
$$C(1)\gamma = 0$$
$$A(1) = \gamma\alpha'.$$

(4) *There exists an error correction representation with $z_t = \alpha'x_t$, an $r \times 1$ vector of stationary random variables:*

$$A^*(B)(1 - B)x_t = -\gamma z_{t-1} + d(B)\varepsilon_t \tag{3.4}$$

with $A^*(0) = I_N$.

(5) *The vector z_t is given by*

$$z_t = K(B)\varepsilon_t, \tag{3.5}$$
$$(1 - B)z_t = -\alpha'\gamma z_{t-1} + J(B)\varepsilon_t, \tag{3.6}$$

where $K(B)$ is an $r \times N$ matrix of lag polynomials given by $\alpha'C^*(B)$ with all elements of $K(1)$ finite with rank r, and $\det(\alpha'\gamma) > 0$.

(6) *If a finite vector autoregressive representation is possible, it will have the form given by (3.3) and (3.4) above with $d(B) = 1$ and both $A(B)$ and $A^*(B)$ as matrices of finite polynomials.*

In order to prove the Theorem the following lemma on determinants and adjoints of singular matrix polynomials is needed.

LEMMA 1: *If $G(\lambda)$ is a finite valued $N \times N$ matrix polynomial on $\lambda \in [0, 1]$, with rank $G(0) = N - r$ for $0 \leq r \leq N$, and if $G^*(0) \neq 0$ in*

$$G(\lambda) = G(0) + \lambda G^*(\lambda),$$

then

(i) $\det(G(\lambda)) = \lambda^r g(\lambda) I_N$ *with $g(0)$ finite,*
(ii) $Adj(G(\lambda)) = \lambda^{r-1} H(\lambda),$

where I_N is the $N \times N$ identity matrix, $1 \leq \text{rank}(H(0)) \leq r$, and $H(0)$ is finite.

PROOF: The determinant of G can be expressed in a power series in λ as

$$\det(G(\lambda)) = \sum_{i=0}^{\infty} \delta_i \lambda^i.$$

Each δ_i is a sum of a finite number of products of elements of $G(\lambda)$ and therefore is itself finite valued. Each has some terms from $G(0)$ and some from $\lambda G^*(\lambda)$. Any product with more than $N - r$ terms from $G(0)$ will be zero because this will be the determinant of a submatrix of larger order than the rank of $G(0)$. The only possible non-zero terms will have r or more terms from $\lambda G^*(\lambda)$ and therefore will be associated with powers of λ of r or more. The first possible nonzero δ_i is δ_r.

Defining

$$g(\lambda) = \sum_{i=r}^{\infty} \delta_i \lambda^{i-r}$$

establishes the first part of the lemma since δ_r must be finite.

To establish the second statement, express the adjoint matrix of G in a power series in λ:

$$\text{Adj } G(\lambda) = \sum_{i=0}^{\infty} \lambda^i H_i,$$

Since the adjoint is a matrix composed of elements which are determinants of order $N - 1$, the above argument establishes that the first $r - 1$ terms must be identically zero. Thus

$$\text{Adj } G(\lambda) = \lambda^{r-1} \sum_{r-1}^{\infty} \lambda^{i-r+1} H_i$$

$$= \lambda^{r-1} H(\lambda).$$

Because the elements of H_{r-1} are products of finitely many finite numbers, $H(0)$ must be finite.

The product of a matrix and its adjoint will always give the determinant so:

$$\lambda^r g(\lambda) I_N = (G(0) + \lambda G^*(\lambda)) H(\lambda)$$

$$= G(0) H(\lambda) \lambda^{r-1} + h(\lambda) G^*(\lambda) \lambda^r.$$

Equating powers of λ we get

$$G(0) H(0) = 0.$$

Thus the rank of $H(0)$ must be less than or equal to r as it lies entirely in the column null space of the rank $N - r$ matrix $G(0)$. If $r = 1$, the first term in the expression for the adjoint will simply be the adjoint of $G(0)$ which will have rank 1 since $G(0)$ has rank $N - 1$.   Q.E.D.

PROOF OF GRANGER REPRESENTATION THEOREM: The conditions of the Theorem suppose the existence of a Wold representation as in (3.1) for an N vector of random variables x_t which are co-integrated. Suppose the co-integrating vector is α so that

$$z_t = \alpha' x_t$$

is an r-dimensional stationary purely nondeterministic time series with invertible moving average representation. Multiplying α times the moving average representation in (3.1) gives

$$(1 - B)z_t = (\alpha'C(1) + (1 - B)\alpha'C^*(B))\varepsilon_t.$$

For z_t to be $I(0)$, $\alpha'C(1)$ must equal 0. Any vector with this property will be a co-integrating vector; therefore $C(1)$ must have rank $N - r$ with a null space containing all co-integrating vectors. It also follows that $\alpha'C^*(B)$ must be an invertible moving average representation and in particular $\alpha'C^*(1) \neq 0$. Otherwise the co-integration would be with $b = 2$ or higher.

Statement (2) is established using Lemma 1, letting $\lambda = (1 - B)$, $G(\lambda) = C(B)$, $H(\lambda) = A(B)$, and $g(\lambda) = d(B)$. Since $C(B)$ has full rank and equals I_N at $B = 0$, its inverse is $A(0)$ which is also I_N.

Statement (3) follows from recognition that $A(1)$ has rank between 1 and r and lies in the null space of $C(1)$. Since α spans this null space, $A(1)$ can be written as linear combinations of the co-integrating vectors.

$$A(1) = \gamma\alpha'.$$

Statement (4) follows by manipulation of the autoregressive structure. Rearranging terms in (3.3) gives:

$$[\tilde{A}(B) + A(1)](1 - B)x_t = - A(1)x_{t-1} + d(B)\varepsilon_t,$$

$$A^*(B)(1 - B)x_t = - \gamma z_{t-1} + d(B)\varepsilon_t,$$

$A^*(0) = A(0) = I_N$.

The fifth condition follows from direct substitution in the Wold representation. The definition of co-integration implies that this moving average be stationary and invertible. Rewriting the error correction representation with $A^*(B) = I + A^{**}(B)$ where $A^{**}(0) = 0$, and premultiplying by α' gives:

$$(1 - B)z_t = - \alpha'\gamma z_{t-1} + [\alpha'd(B) + \alpha'A^{**}(B)C(B)]\varepsilon_t$$

$$= - \alpha'\gamma z_{t-1} + J(B)\varepsilon_t.$$

For this to be equivalent to the stationary moving average representation the autoregression must be invertible. This requires that $\det(\alpha'\gamma) > 0$. If the determinant were zero then there would be at least one unit root, and if the determinant were negative, then for some value of ω between zero and one,

$$\det (I_r - (I_r - \alpha'\gamma)\omega) = 0,$$

implying a root inside the unit circle.

Condition six follows by repeating the previous steps, setting $d(B) = 1$.   *Q.E.D.*

Stronger results can be obtained by further restrictions on the multiplicity of roots in the moving average representations. For example, Yoo (1985), using Smith Macmillan forms, finds conditions which establish that $d(1) \neq 0$, that $A^*(1)$ is of full rank, and that facilitate the transformation from error correction models to co-integrated models. However, the results given above are sufficient for the estimation and testing problems addressed in this paper.

The autoregressive and error correction representations given by (3.3) and (3.4) are closely related to the vector autoregressive models so commonly used in econometrics, particularly in the case when $d(B)$ can reasonably be taken to be 1. However, each differs in an important fashion from typical VAR applications. In the autoregressive representation

$$A(B)x_t = \varepsilon_t,$$

the co-integration of the variables x_t generates a restriction which makes $A(1)$ singular. For $r = 1$, this matrix will only have rank 1. The analysis of such systems from an innovation accounting point of view is treacherous as some numerical approaches to calculating the moving average representation are highly unstable.

The error correction representation

$$A^*(B)(1 - B)x_t = -\gamma\alpha'x_{t-1} + \varepsilon_t$$

looks more like a standard vector autoregression in the differences of the data. Here the co-integration is implied by the presence of the levels of the variables so a pure VAR in differences will be misspecified if the variables are co-integrated.

Thus vector autoregressions estimated with co-integrated data will be misspecified if the data are differenced, and will have omitted important constraints if the data are used in levels. Of course, these constraints will be satisfied asymptotically but efficiency gains and improved multi-step forecasts may be achieved by imposing them.

As $x_t \sim I(1)$, $z_t \sim I(0)$, it should be noted that all terms in the error correction models are $I(0)$. The converse also holds; if $x_t \sim I(1)$ are generated by an error correction model, then x_t is necessarily co-integrated. It may also be noted that if $x_t \sim I(0)$, the generation process can always be written in the error correction form and so, in this case, the equilibrium concept has no impact.

As mentioned above, typical empirical examples of error correcting behaviour are formulated as the response of one variable, the dependent variable, to shocks of another, the independent variable. In this paper all the variables are treated as jointly endogenous; nevertheless the structure of the model may imply various Granger causal orderings and weak and strong exogeneity conditions as in Engle, Hendry, and Richard (1983). For example, a bivariate co-integrated system must have a causal ordering in at least one direction. Because the z's must include both variables and γ cannot be identically zero, they must enter into one or both of the equations. If the error correction term enters into both equations, neither variable can be weakly exogenous for the parameters of the other equation because of the cross equation restriction.

The notion of co-integration can in principle be extended to series with trends or explosive autoregressive roots. In these cases the co-integrating vector would still be required to reduce the series to stationarity. Hence the trends would have to be proportional and any explosive roots would have to be identical for all the series. We do not consider these cases in this paper and recognize that they may complicate the estimation and testing problems.

4.   Estimating Co-integrated Systems

In defining different forms for co-integrated systems, several estimation procedures have been implicitly discussed. Most convenient is the error correction form (particularly if it can be assumed that there is no moving average term). There remain cross-equation restrictions involving the parameters of the co-integrating vectors; and therefore the maximum likelihood estimator, under Gaussian assumptions, requires an iterative procedure.

In this section, we will propose another estimator which is a two step estimator. In the first step the parameters of the co-integrating vector are estimated and in the second these are used in the error correction form. Both steps require only single equation least squares and it will be shown that the result is consistent for all the parameters. The procedure is far more convenient because the dynamics do not need to be specified until the error correction structure has been estimated. As a byproduct we obtain some test statistics useful for testing for co-integration.

From (3.5) the sample moment matrix of the data can be directly expressed. Let the moment matrix divided by T be denoted by:

$$M_T = 1/T^2 \sum_t x_t x_t'.$$

Recalling that $z_t = \alpha' x_t$, (3.5) implies that

$$\alpha' M_T = \sum_t [K(B)\varepsilon_t] x'_t / T^2.$$

Following the argument of Dickey and Fuller (1979) or Stock (1984), it can be shown that for processes satisfying (3.1),

$$\lim_{T \to \infty} E(M_T) = M \quad \text{a finite nonzero matrix,} \tag{4.1}$$

and

$$\alpha' M = 0, \quad \text{or} \quad (\text{vec } \alpha)'(I \otimes M) = 0. \tag{4.2}$$

Although the moment matrix of data from a co-integrated process will be nonsingular for any sample, in the limit, it will have rank $N - r$. This accords well with the common observation that economic time series data are highly colinear so that moment matrices may be nearly singular even when samples are large. Co-integration appears to be a plausible hypothesis from a data analytic point of view.

Equations (4.2) do not uniquely define the co-integrating vectors unless arbitrary normalizations are imposed. Let q and Q be arrays which incorporate these normalizations by reparametrizing α into θ, a $j \times 1$ matrix of unknown parameters which lie in a compact subset of R^j:

$$\text{vec } \alpha = q + Q\theta \tag{4.3}$$

Typically q and Q will be all zeros and ones, thereby defining one coefficient in each column of α to be unity and defining rotations if $r > 1$. The parameters θ are said to be 'identified' if there is a unique solution to (4.2), (4.3). This solution is given by

$$(I \otimes M)Q\theta = -(I \otimes M)q \tag{4.4}$$

where by the assumption of identification, $(I \otimes M)Q$ has a left inverse even though M does not.

As the moment matrix M_T will have full rank for finite samples, a reasonable approach to estimation is to minimize the sum of squared deviations from equilibrium. In the case of a single co-integrating vector, $\hat{\alpha}$ will minimize $\alpha' M_T \alpha$ subject to any restrictions such as (4.3) and the result will be simply ordinary least squares. For multiple co-integrating vectors, define $\hat{\alpha}$ as the minimizer of the trace $(\alpha' M_T \alpha)$. The estimation problem becomes:

$$\min_{\alpha. s.t. (4.3)} \text{tr } (\alpha' M_T \alpha) = \min_{\alpha. s.t. (4.3)} \text{vec } \alpha'(I \otimes M_T) \text{vec } \alpha$$

$$= \min_{\theta} (q + Q\theta)'(I \otimes M_T)(q + Q\theta),$$

which implies the solution

$$\hat{\theta} = - (Q'(I \otimes M_T)Q)^{-1}(Q'(I \otimes M_T)q), \text{ vec } \hat{\alpha} = q + Q\hat{\theta}. \quad (4.5)$$

This approach to estimation should provide a very good approximation to the true co-integrating vector because it is seeking vectors with minimal residual variance and asymptotically all linear combinations of x will have infinite variance except those which are co-integrating vectors.

When $r = 1$ this estimate is obtained simply by regressing the variable normalized to have a unit coefficient upon the other variables. This regression will be called the 'co-integrating regression' as it attempts to fit the long run or equilibrium relationship without worrying about the dynamics. It will be shown to provide an estimate of the elements of the co-integrating vector. Such a regression has been pejoratively called a 'spurious' regression by Granger and Newbold (1974) primarily because the standard errors are highly misleading. They were particularly concerned about the non-co-integrated case where there was no relationship but the unit root in the error process led to a low Durbin–Watson, a high R^2, and apparently high significance of the coefficients. Here we only seek coefficient estimates to use in the second stage and for tests of the equilibrium relationship. The distribution of the estimated coefficients is investigated in Stock (1984).

When $N = 2$, there are two possible regressions depending on the normalization chosen. The nonuniqueness of the estimate derives from the well known fact that the least squares fit of a reverse regression will not give the reciprocal of the coefficient in the forward regression. In this case, however, the normalization matters very little. As the moment matrix approaches singularity, the R^2 approaches 1 which is the product of the forward and reverse regression coefficients. This would be exactly true if there were only two data points which, of course, defines a singular matrix. For variables which are trending together, the correlation approaches one as each variance approaches infinity. The regression line passes nearly through the extreme points almost as if there were just two observations.

Stock (1984) in Theorem 3 proves the following proposition:

PROPOSITION: *Suppose that x_t satisfies (3.1) with $C^*(B)$ absolutely summable, that the disturbances have finite fourth absolute moments and that x_t is co-integrated* (1, 1) *with r co-integrating vectors satisfying (4.3) which identify θ. Then, defining $\hat{\theta}$ by (4.5),*

$$T^{1-\delta}(\hat{\theta} - \theta) \xrightarrow{P} 0 \quad \text{for} \quad \delta > 0. \quad (4.6)$$

The proposition establishes that the estimated parameters converge very rapidly to their probability limits. It also establishes that the estimates are consistent with a finite sample bias of orders $1/T$. Stock presents some Monte Carlo examples to show that these biases may be important for small samples and gives expressions for calculating the limiting distribution of such estimates.

The two-step estimator proposed for this co-integrated system uses the estimate of α from (4.5) as a known parameter in estimating the error correction form of the system of equations. This substantially simplifies the estimation procedure by imposing the cross-equation restrictions and allows specification of the individual equation dynamic patterns separately. Notice that the dynamics did not have to be specified in order to estimate α. Surprisingly, this two-step estimator has excellent properties; as shown in the Theorem below, it is just as efficient as the maximum likelihood estimator based on the known value of α.

THEOREM 2: *The two-step estimator of a single equation of an error correction system, obtained by taking $\hat{\alpha}$ from (4.5) as the true value, will have the same limiting distribution as the maximum likelihood estimator using the true value of α. Least squares errors will be consistent estimates of the true standard errors.*

PROOF: Rewrite the first equation of the error correction system (3.4) as

$$y_t = \gamma \hat{z}_{t-1} + W_t \beta + \varepsilon_t + \gamma(z_{t-1} - \hat{z}_{t-1}),$$

$$z_t = X_t \alpha,$$

$$\hat{z}_t = X_t \hat{\alpha},$$

where $X_t = x_t'$, W is an array with selected elements of Δx_{t-i} and y is an element of Δx_t so that all regressors are $I(0)$. Then letting the same variables without subscripts denote data arrays,

$$\sqrt{T}\begin{bmatrix} \gamma & -\gamma \\ \beta & -\beta \end{bmatrix} = [(\hat{z}, W)'(\hat{z}, W)/T]^{-1}[(\hat{z}, W)'(\varepsilon + \gamma)(z - \hat{z})]/\sqrt{T}.$$

This expression simplifies because $\hat{z}'(z - \hat{z}) = 0$. From Fuller (1976) or Stock (1984), $X'X/T^2$ and $X'W/T$ are both of order 1. Rewriting,

$$W'(z - \hat{z})/\sqrt{T} = [W'X/T][T(\alpha - \hat{\alpha})][1/\sqrt{T}],$$

and therefore the first and second factors to the right of the equal sign are of order 1 and the third goes to zero so that the entire expression vanishes asymptotically. Because the terms in $(z - \hat{z})/\sqrt{T}$ vanish asymptotically, least squares standard errors will be consistent.

Letting $S = \text{plim} [(\hat{z}, W)'(\hat{z}, W)/T]$,

$$\sqrt{T}\begin{bmatrix} \gamma & -\gamma \\ \beta & -\beta \end{bmatrix} \xrightarrow{A} D(0, \sigma^2 S^{-1})$$

where D represents the limiting distribution. Under additional but standard assumptions, this could be guaranteed to be normal.

To establish that the estimator using the true value of α has the same limiting distribution it is sufficient to show that the probability limit of $[(z, W)'(z, W)/T]$ is also S and that $z'\varepsilon/\sqrt{T}$ has the same limiting distribution as $\hat{z}'\varepsilon/\sqrt{T}$. Examining the off diagonal terms of S first,

$$\hat{z}'W/T - z'W/T = T(\hat{\alpha} - \alpha)'[W'X](1/T).$$

The first and second factors are of order 1 and the third is $1/T$ so the entire expression vanishes asymptotically:

$$(\hat{z} - z)'(\hat{z} - z)/T = z'z/T - \hat{z}'\hat{z}/T$$
$$= T(\hat{\alpha} - \alpha)'[X'X/T^2]T(\hat{\alpha} - \alpha)(1/T).$$

Again, the first three factors are of order 1 and the last is $1/T$ so even though the difference between these covariance matrices is positive definite, it will vanish asymptotically. Finally,

$$(\hat{z} - z)'\varepsilon/\sqrt{T} = T(\hat{\alpha} - \alpha)'[X'\varepsilon/T]1/\sqrt{T},$$

which again vanishes asymptotically.

Under standard conditions the estimator using knowledge of α will be asymptotically normal and therefore the two-step estimator will also be asymptotically normal under these conditions. This completes the proof.

$$Q.E.D.$$

A simple example will illustrate many of these points and motivate the approach to testing described in the next section. Suppose there are two series, x_{1t} and x_{2t}, which are jointly generated as a function of possibly correlated white noise disturbances ε_{1t} and ε_{2t} according to the following model:

$$x_{1t} + \beta x_{2t} = u_{1t}, \quad u_{1t} = u_{1t-1} + \varepsilon_{1t}, \tag{4.7}$$

$$x_{1t} + \alpha x_{2t} = u_{2t}, \quad u_{2t} = \rho u_{2t-1} + \varepsilon_{2t}, \quad |\rho| < 1. \tag{4.8}$$

Clearly the parameters α and β are unidentified in the usual sense as there are no exogenous variables and the errors are contemporaneously correlated. The reduced form for this system will make x_{1t} and x_{2t} linear combinations of u_{1t} and u_{2t} and therefore both will be $I(1)$. The second equation describes a particular linear combination of the random variables which is stationary. Hence x_{1t} and x_{2t} are $CI(1, 1)$ and the question is whether it would be possible to detect this and estimate the parameters from a data set.

Surprisingly, this is easy to do. A linear least squares regression of x_{1t} on x_{2t} produces an excellent estimate of α. This is the 'co-integrating regression'. All linear combinations of x_{1t} and x_{2t} except that defined in equation (4.8) will have infinite variance and, therefore, least squares is easily able to estimate α. The correlation between x_{2t} and u_{2t} which causes the simultaneous equations bias is of a lower order in T than the variance of x_{2t}. In fact the reverse regression of x_{2t} on x_{1t} has exactly the same property and thus gives a consistent estimate of $1/\alpha$. These estimators converge even faster to the true value than standard econometric estimates.

While there are other consistent estimates of α, several apparently obvious choices are not. For example, regression of the first differences of x_1 on the differences of x_2 will not be consistent, and the use of Cochrane Orcutt or other serial correlation correction in the co-integrating regression will produce inconsistent estimates. Once the parameter α has been estimated, the others can be estimated in a variety of ways conditional on the estimate of α.

The model in (4.7) and (4.8) can be expressed in the autoregressive representation (after subtracting the lagged values from both sides and letting $\delta = (1 - \rho)/(\alpha - \beta)$) as:

$$\Delta x_{1t} = \beta\delta x_{1t-1} + \alpha\beta\delta x_{2t-1} + \eta_{1t}, \tag{4.9}$$

$$\Delta x_{2t} = -\delta x_{1t-1} - \alpha\delta x_{2t-1} + \eta_{2t}, \tag{4.10}$$

where the η's are linear combinations of the ε's. The error correction representation becomes:

$$\Delta x_{1t} = \beta\delta z_{t-1} + \eta_{1t}, \tag{4.11}$$

$$\Delta x_{2t} = -\delta z_{t-1} + \eta_{2t}, \tag{4.12}$$

where $z_t = x_{1t} + \alpha x_{2t}$. There are three unknown parameters but the autoregressive form apparently has four unknown coefficients while the error correction form has two. Once α is known there are no longer constraints in the error correction form which motivates the two-step estimator. Notice that if $\rho \to 1$, the series are correlated random walks but are no longer co-integrated.

5. Testing for Co-integration

It is frequently of interest to test whether a set of variables are co-integrated. This may be desired because of the economic implications such as whether some system is in equilibrium in the long run, or it may be sensible to test such hypotheses before estimating a multivariate dynamic model.

Unfortunately the set-up is nonstandard and cannot simply be viewed as an application of Wald, likelihood ratio, or Lagrange multiplier tests. The testing problem is closely related to tests for unit roots in observed series as initially formulated by Fuller (1976) and Dickey and Fuller (1979; 1981) and more recently by Evans and Savin (1981), Sargan and Bhargava (1983), and Bhargava (1984), and applied by Nelson and Plosser (1983). It also is related to the problem of testing when some parameters are unidentified under the null as discussed by Davies (1977) and Watson and Engle (1982).

To illustrate the problems in testing such an hypothesis, consider the simple model in (4.7) and (4.8). The null hypothesis is taken to be no co-integration or $\rho = 1$. If α were known, then a test for the null hypothesis could be constructed along the lines of Dickey and Fuller taking z_t as the series which has a unit root under the null. The distribution in this case is already nonstandard and was computed through a simulation by Dickey (1976). However, when α is not known, it must be estimated from the data. But if the null hypothesis that $\rho = 1$ is true, α is not identified. Thus only if the series are co-integrated can α be simply estimated by the 'co-integrating regression', but a test must be based upon the distribution of a statistic when the null is true. OLS seeks the α which minimizes the residual variance and therefore is most likely to be stationary, so the distribution of the Dickey–Fuller test will reject the null too often if α must be estimated.

In this paper a set of seven statistics is proposed for testing the null of non-co-integration against the alternative of co-integration. It is maintained that the true system is a bivariate linear vector autoregression with Gaussian errors where each of the series is individually $I(1)$. As the null hypothesis is composite, similar tests will be sought so that the probability of rejection will be constant over the parameter set included in the null. See, for example, Cox and Hinkley (1974, pp. 134–6).

Two cases may be distinguished. In the first, the system is known to be of first order and therefore the null is defined by

$$\Delta y_t = \varepsilon_{1t}, \quad \begin{bmatrix} (\varepsilon_{1t}) \\ (\varepsilon_{2t}) \end{bmatrix} \sim N(0, \Omega). \qquad (5.1)$$
$$\Delta x_t = \varepsilon_{2t},$$

This is clearly the model implied by (4.11) and (4.12) when $\rho = 1$ which implies that $\delta = 0$. The composite null thus includes all positive definite covariance matrices Ω. It will be shown below that all the test statistics are similar with respect to the matrix Ω so without loss of generality, we take $\Omega = I$.

In the second case, the system is assumed merely to be a stationary linear system in the changes. Consequently, the null is defined over a full set of stationary autoregressive and moving average coefficients as well as Ω. The 'augmented' tests described below are designed to be asymptotically similar for this case just as established by Dickey and Fuller for their univariate tests.

The seven test statistics proposed are all calculable by least squares. The critical values are estimated for each of these statistics by simulation using 10,000 replications. Using these critical values, the powers of the test statistics are computed by simulations under various alternatives. A brief motivation of each test is useful.

1. CRDW. After running the co-integrating regression, the Durbin Watson statistic is tested to see if the residuals appear stationary. If they are nonstationary, the Durbin Watson will approach zero and thus the test rejects non-co-integration (finds co-integration) if DW is too big. This was proposed recently by Bhargava (1984) for the case where the series is observed and the null and alternative are first order models.

2. DF. This tests the residuals from the co-integrating regression by running an auxiliary regression as described by Dickey and Fuller and outlined in Table 1. It also assumes that the first order model is correct.

3. ADF. The augmented Dickey–Fuller test allows for more dynamics in the DF regression and consequently is over-parametrized in the first order case but correctly specified in the higher order cases.

4. RVAR. The restricted vector autoregression test is similar to the two step estimator. Conditional on the estimate of the co-integrating vector from the co-integrating regression, the error correction representation is estimated. The test is whether the error correction term is significant. This test requires specification of the full system dynamics. In this case a first order system is assumed. By making the system triangular, the disturbances are uncorrelated, and under normality the t statistics are independent. The test is based on the sum of the squared t statistics.

5. ARVAR. The augmented RVAR test is the same as RVAR except that a higher order system is postulated.

6. UVAR. The unrestricted VAR test is based on a vector autoregression in the levels which is not restricted to satisfy the co-integration constraints. Under the null, these are not present anyway so the test is simply whether the levels would appear at all, or whether the model can be adequately expressed entirely in changes. Again by triangularizing the coefficient matrix, the F tests from the two regressions can be made independent and the overall test is the sum of the two F's times their degrees of freedom, 2. This assumes a first order system again.

7. AUVAR. This is an augmented or higher order version of the above test.

To establish the similarity of these tests for the first order case for all positive definite symmetric matrices, Ω, it is sufficient to show that the residuals from the regression of y on x for general Ω will be a scalar multiple of the residuals for $\Omega = I$. To show this, let ε_{1t} and ε_{2t} be drawn as independent standard normals. Then

$$y_t = \sum_{i=1,t} \varepsilon_{1i},$$ (5.2)

$$x_t = \sum_{i=1,t} \varepsilon_{2i},$$

and

$$u_t = y_t - x_t \sum x_t y_t / \sum x_t^2$$ (5.3)

To generate y^* and x^* from Ω, let

$$\varepsilon_2^* t = c\varepsilon_{2t},$$ (5.4)
$$\varepsilon_1^* t = a\varepsilon_{2t} + b\varepsilon_{1t},$$

where

$$c = \sqrt{\omega}_{xx}, \ a = \omega_{yx}/c, \ b^2 = \omega_{yy} - \omega_{yx}^2/\omega_{xx}.$$

Then substituting (5.4) in (5.2)

$$x^* = cx, \ y^* = ay + bx,$$

$$u^* = y^* - x^* \sum y_t^* x_t^* / \sum x_t^{*2}$$

$$= ay + bx - cx \sum (ay_t + bx_t)cx_t / \sum c^2 x_t^2$$

$$= au,$$

thus showing the exact similarity of the tests. If the same random numbers are used, the same test statistics will be obtained regardless of Ω.

In the more complicated but realistic case that the system is of infinite order but can be approximated by a p order autoregression, the statistics will only be asymptotically similar. Although exact similarity is achieved in the Gaussian fixed regressor model, this is not possible in time series models where one cannot condition on the regressors; similarity results are only asymptotic. Tests 5 and 7 are therefore asymptotically similar if the p order model is true but tests 1, 2, 4, and 6 definitely are not even asymptotically similar as these tests omit the lagged regressors. (This is analogous to the biased standard errors resulting from serially correlated errors.) It is on this basis that we prefer not to suggest the latter tests except in the first order case. Test 3 will also be asymptotically similar under the assumption that u, the residual from the co-integration regression, follows a p order process. This result is proven in Dickey and Fuller (1981, pp. 1065–6). While the assumption that the system is p order allows the residuals to be of infinite order, there is presumably a finite autoregressive model, possibly of order less than p, which will be a good approximation. One might therefore suggest some experimentation to find the appropriate value of p in either case. An alternative strategy would be to let p be a slowly increasing nonstochastic function of T, which is closely related to the test proposed by Phillips (1985) and Phillips and Durlauf (1985). Only substantial simulation experimentation will determine whether it is preferable to use a data based selection of p for this testing procedure although the evidence presented below shows that estimation of extraneous parameters will decrease the power of the tests.

In Table 1, the seven test statistics are formally stated. In Table 2, the critical values and powers of the tests are considered when the system is first order. Here the augmented tests would be expected to be less powerful because they estimate parameters which are truly zero under

TABLE 1.   The test statistics: reject for large values

---

1. The Co-integrating Regression Durbin Watson: $y_t = \alpha x_t + c + u_t$

   $\xi_1 = DW$.   The null is $DW = 0$.

2. Dickey–Fuller Regression: $\Delta u_t = -\phi u_{t-1} + \varepsilon_t$.

   $\xi_2 = \tau_\phi$:   the t statistic for ϕ.

3. Augmented DF Regression: $\Delta u_t = -\phi u_{t-1} + b_1 \Delta u_{t-1} + \ldots + b_i \Delta u_t - p + \varepsilon_t$.

   $\xi_3 = \tau_\phi$.

4. Restricted VAR: $\Delta y_t = \beta_1 u_{t-1} + \varepsilon_{1t}, \Delta x_t = \beta_2 u_{t-1} + \gamma \Delta y_t + \varepsilon_{2t}$.

   $\xi_4 = \tau_{\beta1}^2 + \tau_{\beta2}^2$.

5. Augmented Restricted VAR; Same as (4) but with p lags of Δy_t and Δx_t in each equation.

   $\xi_5 = \tau_{\beta1}^2 + \tau_{\beta2}^2$.

6. Unrestricted VAR:
   $\Delta y_t = \beta_1 y_{t-1} + \beta_2 x_{t-1} + c_1 + \varepsilon_{1t}, \Delta x_t = \beta_3 y_{t-1} + \beta_4 x_{t-1} + \gamma \Delta y_t + c_2 + \varepsilon_{2t}$.

   $\xi_6 = 2[F_1 + F_2]$ where F_1 is the F statistic for testing β_1 and β_2 both equal to zero in the first equation, and F_2 is the comparable statistic in the second.

7. Augmented Unrestricted VAR: The same as (6) except for p lags of Δx_t and Δy_t in each equation.

   $\gamma_7 = 2[F_1 + F_2]$.

NOTES: y_t and x_t are the original data sets and u_t are the residuals from the co-integrating regression.

both the null and alternative. The other four tests estimate no extraneous parameters and are correctly specified for this experiment.

From Table 2 one can perform a 5 per cent test of the hypothesis of non-co-integration with the co-integrating regression Durbin–Watson

TABLE 2. Critical values and power

I MODEL: Δy, Δx independent standard normal, 100 observations, 10,000 replications, $p = 4$.

Statistic	Critical values			
	Name	1%	5%	10%
1	CRDW	0.511	0.386	0.322
2	DF	4.07	3.37	3.03
3	ADF	3.77	3.17	2.84
4	RVAR	18.3	13.6	11.0
5	ARVAR	15.8	11.8	9.7
6	UVAR	23.4	18.6	16.0
7	AUVAR	22.6	17.9	15.5

II MODEL: $y_t + 2x_t = u_t$, $\Delta u_t = (\rho - 1)u_{t-1} + \varepsilon_t$, $x_t + y_t = v_t$, $\Delta v_t = \eta_t$; $\rho = .8, .9$, 100 observations, 1,000 replications, $p = 4$.

Statistic	Rejections per 100: $\rho = .9$			
	Name	1%	5%	10%
1	CRDW	4.8	19.9	33.6
2	DF	2.2	15.4	29.0
3	ADF	1.5	11.0	22.7
4	RVAR	2.3	11.4	25.3
5	ARVAR	1.0	9.2	17.9
6	UVAR	4.3	13.3	26.1
7	AUVAR	1.6	8.3	16.3

Statistic	Rejections per 100: $\rho = .8$			
	Name	1%	5%	10%
1	CRDW	34.0	66.4	82.1
2	DF	20.5	59.2	76.1
3	ADF	7.8	30.9	51.6
4	RVAR	15.8	46.2	67.4
5	ARVAR	4.6	22.4	39.0
6	UVAR	19.0	45.9	63.7
7	AUVAR	4.8	18.3	33.4

test, by simply checking DW from this regression and, if it exceeds 0.386, rejecting the null and finding co-integration. If the true model is Model II with $\rho = .9$ rather than 1, this will only be detected 20 per cent of the time; however if the true $\rho = .8$ this rises to 66 per cent. Clearly, test 1 is the best in each of the power calculations and should be preferred for this set-up, while test 2 is second in almost every case. Notice also that the augmented tests have practically the same critical values as the basic tests; however, as expected, they have slightly lower power. Therefore, if it is known that the system is first order, the extra lags should not be introduced. Whether a pre-test of the order would be useful remains to be established.

In Table 3 both the null and alternative hypotheses have fourth order autoregressions. Therefore the basic unaugmented tests now are mis-specified while the augmented ones are correctly specified (although some of the intervening lags could be set to zero if this were known). Notice now the drop in the critical values of tests 1, 4, and 6 caused by their nonsimilarity. Using these new critical values, test 3 is the most powerful for the local alternative while at $\rho = .8$, test 1 is the best closely followed by 2 and 3. The misspecified or unaugmented tests 4 and 6 perform very badly in this situation. Even though they were moderately powerful in Table 2, the performance here dismisses them from consideration.

Although test 1 has the best performance overall, it is not the recommended choice from this experiment because the critical value is so sensitive to the particular parameters within the null. For most types of economic data the differences are not white noise and, therefore, one could not in practice know what critical value to use. Test 3, the augmented Dickey–Fuller test, has essentially the same critical value for both finite sample experiments, has theoretically the same large sample critical value for both cases, and has nearly as good observed power properties in most comparisons, and is therefore the recommended approach.

Because of its simplicity, the CRDW might be used for a quick approximate result. Fortunately, none of the best procedures require the estimation of the full system, merely the co-integrating regression and then perhaps an auxiliary time series regression.

This analysis leaves many questions unanswered. The critical values have only been constructed for one sample size and only for the bivariate case, although recently, Engle and Yoo (1986) have calculated critical values for more variables and sample sizes using the same general approach. There is still no optimality theory for such tests and alternative approaches may prove superior. Research on the limiting distribution theory by Phillips (1985) and Phillips and Durlauf (1985) may lead to improvements in test performance.

TABLE 3. Critical values and power with lags

MODEL I: $\Delta y_t = .8\Delta y_{t-4} + \varepsilon_t, \Delta x_t = .8\Delta x_{t-4} + \eta_t;$ 100 observations, 10,000 replications, $p = 4$, ε_t, η_t, independent standard normal.

Statistic	Critical Values			
	Name	1%	5%	10%
1	CRDW	0.455	0.282	0.209
2	DF	3.90	3.05	2.71
3	ADF	3.73	3.17	2.91
4	RVAR	37.2	22.4	17.2
5	ARVAR	16.2	12.3	10.5
6	UVAR	59.0	40.3	31.3
7	AUVAR	28.0	22.0	19.2

MODEL II: $y_t + 2x_t = u_t$, $\Delta u_t = (\rho - 1)u_{t-1} + .8\Delta u_{t-4} + \varepsilon_t$, $y_t + x_t = v_t$, $\Delta v_t = .8\Delta v_{t-4} + \eta_t$; $\rho = 0.9, 0.8$. 100 observations, 1,000 replications, $p = 4$.

Statistic	Rejections per 100: $\rho = 0.9$			
	Name	1%	5%	10%
1	CRDW	15.6	39.9	65.6
2	DF	9.4	25.5	37.8
3	ADF	36.0	61.2	72.2
4	RVAR	.3	4.4	10.9
5	ARVAR	26.4	48.5	62.8
6	UVAR	.0	.5	3.5
7	AUVAR	9.4	26.8	40.3

Statistic	Rejections per 100: $\rho = 0.8$			
	Name	1%	5%	10%
1	CRDW	77.5	96.4	98.6
2	DF	66.8	89.7	96.0
3	ADF	68.9	90.3	94.4
4	RVAR	7.0	42.4	62.5
5	ARVAR	57.2	80.5	89.3
6	UVAR	2.5	10.8	25.9
7	AUVAR	32.2	53.0	67.7

Nevertheless, it appears that the critical values for ADF given in Table 2 can be used as a rough guide in applied studies at this point. The next section will provide a variety of illustrations.

6.   Examples

Several empirical examples will be presented to show performance of the tests in practice. The relationship between consumption and income will be studied in some detail as it was analysed from an error correction point of view in DHSY and a time series viewpoint in Hall (1978) and others. Briefer analyses of wages and prices, short- and long-term interest rates, and the velocity of money will conclude this section.

DHSY have presented evidence for the error correction model of consumption behaviour from both empirical and theoretical points of view. Consumers make plans which may be frustrated; they adjust next period's plans to recoup a portion of the error between income and consumption. Hall finds that U.S. consumption is a random walk and that past values of income have no explanatory power which implies that income and consumption are not co-integrated, at least if income does not depend on the error correction term. Neither of these studies models income itself and it is taken as exogenous in DHSY.

Using U.S. quarterly real per capita consumption on nondurables and real per capita disposable income from 1947-I to 1981-II, it was first checked that the series were $I(1)$. Regressing the change in consumption on its past level and two past changes gave a t statistic of $+0.77$ which is even the wrong sign for consumption to be stationary in the levels. Running the same model with second differences on lagged first differences and two lags of second differences, the t statistic was -5.36 indicating that the first difference is stationary. For income, four past lags were used and the two t statistics were -0.01 and -6.27 respectively, again establishing that income is $I(1)$.

The co-integrating regressions of consumption (C) on income (Y) and a constant was run. The coefficient of Y was 0.23 (with a t statistic of 123 and an R^2 of 0.99). The DW was however 0.465 indicating that by either table of critical values one rejects the null of 'non-co-integration' or accepts co-integration at least at the 5 per cent level. Regressing the change in the residuals on past levels and four lagged changes, the t statistic on the level is 3.1 which is essentially the critical value for the 5 per cent ADF test. Because the lags are not significant, the DF regression was run giving a test statistic of 4.3 which is significant at the 1 per cent level, illustrating that when it is appropriate, it is a more powerful test. In the reverse regression of Y on C, the coefficient is 4.3 which has reciprocal 0.23, the same as the coefficient in the forward regression. The DW is now 0.463 and the t statistic from the ADF test is 3.2. Again the first order DF appears appropriate and gives a test statistic of 4.4. Whichever way the regression is run, the data rejects the null of non-co-integration at any level above 5 per cent.

To establish that the joint distribution of C and Y is an error correction system, a series of models was estimated. An unrestricted vector autoregression of the change in consumption on four lags of consumption and income changes plus the lagged levels of consumption and income is given next in Table 4. The lagged levels are of the appropriate signs and sizes for an error correction term and are individually significant or nearly so. Of all the lagged changes, only the first lag of income change is significant. Thus the final model has the error correction term estimated from the co-integrating regression and one lagged change in income. The standard error of this model is even lower than the VAR suggesting the efficiency of the parameter restrictions. The final model passes a series of diagnostic tests for serial correlation, lagged dependent variables, non-linearities, ARCH, and omitted variables such as a time trend and other lags.

One might notice that an easy model building strategy in this case would be to estimate the simplest error correction model first and then test for added lags of C and Y, proceeding in a 'simple to general' specification search.

The model-building process for Y produced a similar model. The same unrestricted VAR was estimated and distilled to a simple model with the error correction term, first and fourth lagged changes in C and a fourth lagged change in Y. The error correction is not really significant with a t statistic of -1.1 suggesting that income may indeed be weakly exogenous even though the variables are co-integrated. In this case the standard error of the regression is slightly higher in the restricted model but the difference is not significant. The diagnostic tests are again generally good.

Campbell (1985) uses a similar structure to develop a test of the permanent income hypothesis which incorporates 'saving for a rainy day' behaviour. In this case the error correction term is approximately saving which should be high when income is expected to fall (such as when current income is above permanent income). Using a broader measure of consumption and narrower measure of income he finds the error correction term significant in the income equation.

The second example examines monthly wages and prices in the U.S. The data are logs of the consumer price index and production worker wage in manufacturing over the three decades of the 1950s, 1960s, and 1970s. Again, the test is run both directions to show that there is little difference in the result. For each of the decades there are 120 observations so the critical values as tabulated should be appropriate.

For the full sample period the Durbin Watson from the co-integrating regression in either direction is a notable 0.0054. One suspects that this will be insignificantly different from zero even for samples much larger than this. Looking at the augmented Dickey–Fuller test statistic, for p on w we find -0.6 and for w on p we find $+0.2$. Adding a twelfth lag in the ADF tests improves the fit substantially and raises the test statistics to 0.88 and

TABLE 4. Regressions of consumption and income

Dep. Var.:	C	ΔEC	ΔEC	ΔC	ΔC
Y	.23(123)				
C(−1)				−.19(−2.5)	
Y(−1)				.046(2.5)	
EC(−1)		−.22(−3.1)	−.26(−4.3)		−.14(−2.2)
ΔC(−1)				.092(0.9)	
ΔC(−2)				.017(0.2)	
ΔC(−3)				.16(1.5)	
ΔC(−4)				.009(0.1)	
ΔY(−1)				.059(1.8)	.068(2.5)
ΔY(−2)				−.023(−0.7)	
ΔY(−3)				−.027(−0.8)	
ΔY(−4)				−.020(−0.7)	
ΔEC(−1)		−.13(−1.4)			
ΔEC(−2)		.12(1.4)			
ΔEC(−3)		.03(0.4)			
ΔEC(−4)		−.13(−1.6)			
CONST	.52(85)			.10(2.4)	.003(2.6)
σ	.01628	.00999	.01015	.01094	.01078
DW	.46	2.0	2.2	2.0	1.9

Dep. Var:	Y	ΔEY	ΔEY	ΔY	ΔY
C	4.29(123)				
C(−1)				.15(.67)	
Y(−1)				−.034(.63)	
EY(−1)		−.23(−3.2)	−.26(−4.4)		−.053(−1.1)
ΔC(−1)				.79(2.5)	.66(2.4)
ΔC(−2)				−.48(−1.5)	
ΔC(−3)				.68(2.2)	
ΔC(−4)				.56(1.8)	.60(2.1)
ΔY(−1)				−.027(−.3)	
ΔY(−2)				−.051(−.5)	
ΔY(−3)				.011(.1)	
ΔY(−4)				−.23(−2.5)	−.19(2.1)
ΔEY(−1)		−.13(−1.5)			
ΔEY(−2)		.12(1.4)			
ΔEY(−3)		.03(0.4)			
ΔEY(−4)		−.14(−1.6)			
CONST	2.22(−50)			−.071(−.6)	.016(4.6)
σ	.07012	.04279	.04350	.03255	.03321
DW	.46	2.0	2.2	2.1	2.2

NOTES: Data are from 1947-I to 1981-II. *EC* are the residuals from the first regression and *EY* are the residuals from the sixth regression. *T* ratios are in parentheses.

1.50 respectively. In neither case do these approach the critical values of 3.2. The evidence accepts the null of non-co-integration for wages and prices over the thirty year period.

For individual decades none of the ADF tests are significant at even the 10 per cent level. The largest of these six test statistics is for the 50s regressing p on w which reaches 2.4, which is still below the 10 per cent level of 2.8. Thus we find evidence that wages and prices in the U.S. are not co-integrated. Of course, if a third variable such as productivity were available (and were $I(1)$), the three might be co-integrated.

The next example tests for co-integration between short- and long-term interest rates. Using monthly yields to maturity of 20-year treasury bonds as the long term rate (R_t) and the one month treasury bill rate r_t as the short rate, co-integration was tested with data from February 1952 to December 1982. With the long rate as the dependent variable, the co-integrating regression gave:

$$R_t = 1.93 + .785 \, r_t + ER_t, \quad DW = .126, \quad R^2 = .866,$$

with a t ratio of 46 on the short rate. The DW is not significantly different from zero, at least by Tables 2 and 3; however, the correct critical value depends upon the dynamics of the errors (and of course the sample size is 340—much greater than for the tabulated values). The ADF test with four lags gives:

$$\Delta ER_t = \underset{(-3.27)}{-\ .06} \ ER_{t-1} + \underset{(4.55)}{.25} \ \Delta ER_{t-1} - \underset{(-4.15)}{.24} \ \Delta ER_{t-2}$$
$$+ \underset{(-4.15)}{.24} \ \Delta ER_{t-3} - \underset{(-1.48)}{.09} \ \Delta ER_{t-4}.$$

When the twelfth lag is added instead of the fourth, the test statistic rises to 3.49. Similar results were found with the reverse regression where the statistics were 3.61 and 3.89 respectively. Each of these test statistics exceeds the 5 per cent critical values from Table 3. Thus these interest rates are apparently co-integrated.

This finding is entirely consistent with the efficient market hypothesis. The one-period excess holding yield on long bonds as linearized by Shiller and Campbell (1984) is:

$$EHY = DR_{t-1} - (D-1)R_t - r_t$$

where D is the duration of the bond which is given by

$$D = ((1+c)^i - 1)/(c(1+c)^{i-1}$$

with c as the coupon rate and i the number of periods to maturity. The efficient market hypothesis implies that the expectation of the EHY is a constant representing a risk premium if agents are risk averse. Setting $EHY = k + \varepsilon$ and rearraging terms gives the error correction form:

$$\Delta R_t = (D - 1)^{-1}(R_{t-1} - r_{t-1}) + k' + \varepsilon_t,$$

implying that R and r are co-integrated with a unit coefficient and that for long maturities, the coefficients of the error correction term is c, the coupon rate. If the risk premium is varying over time but is $I(0)$ already, then it need not be included in the test of co-integration.

The final example is based upon the quantity theory equation: $MV = PY$. Empirical implications stem from the assumption that velocity is constant or at least stationary. Under this condition, $\log M$, $\log P$, and $\log Y$ should be co-integrated with known unit parameters. Similarly, nominal money and nominal GNP should be co-integrated. A test of this hypothesis was constructed for four measures of money: $M1$, $M2$, and $M3$, and L, total liquid assets. In each case the sample period was 1959-I to 1981-II, quarterly. The ADF tests statistics were:

$M1$	1.81	1.90
$M2$	3.23	3.13
$M3$	2.65	2.55
L	2.15	2.13

where in the first column the log of the monetary aggregate was the dependent variable while in the second, it was $\log GNP$. For only one of the $M2$ tests is the test statistic significant at the 5 per cent level, and none of the other aggregates are significant even at the 10 per cent level. (In several cases it appears that the DF test could be used and would therefore be more powerful.) Thus the most stable relationship is between $M2$ and nominal GNP but for the other aggregates, we reject co-integration and the stationarity of velocity.

7. Conclusion

If each element of a vector of time series x_t is stationary only after differencing, but a linear combination $\alpha' x_t$ need not be differenced, the time series x_t have been defined to be co-integrated of order $(1, 1)$ with co-integrating vector α. Interpreting $\alpha' x_t = 0$ as a long-run equilibrium, co-integration implies that equilibrium holds except for a stationary, finite variance disturbance even though the series themselves are non-stationary and have infinite variance.

The paper presents several representations for co-integrated systems including an autoregressive representation and an error-correction representation. A vector autoregression in differenced variables is incompatible with these representations because it omits the error correction term. The vector autoregression in the levels of the series ignores cross equation constraints and will give a singular autoregressive operator. Consistent and efficient estimation of error correction models is discussed and a two step estimator proposed. To test for co-integration, seven statistics are formulated which are similar under various maintained hypotheses about the generating model. The critical values of these statistics are calculated based on a Monte Carlo simulation. Using these critical values, the power properties of the tests are examined, and one test procedure is recommended for application.

In a series of examples it is found that consumption and income are co-integrated, wages and prices are not, short and long interest rates are, and nominal *GNP* is not co-integrated with *M*1, *M*3, or total liquid assets, although it is possibly with *M*2.

References

BHARGAVA, ALOK (1984), 'On the theory of testing for unit roots in observed time series', manuscript, ICERD, London School of Economics.

BOX, G. E. P., and G. M. JENKINS (1970), *Time Series Analysis, Forecasting and Control* (San Francisco, Holden Day).

CAMPBELL, JOHN Y. (1985), 'Does saving anticipate declining labor income? An alternative test of the permanent income hypothesis', manuscript, Princetown University.

COX, D. R., AND C. V. HINKLEY (1974), *Theoretical Statistics* (London, Chapman and Hall).

CURRIE, D. (1981), 'Some long-run features of dynamic time-series models', *The Economic Journal*, **91**, 704–15.

DAVIDSON, J. E. H., DAVID F. HENDRY, FRANK SRBA, and STEVEN YEO (1978), 'Econometric modelling of the aggregate time-series relationship between consumer's expenditure and income in the United Kingdom', *Economic Journal*, **88**, 661–92.

DAVIES, R. R. (1977), 'Hypothesis testing when a nuisance parameter is present only under the alternative', *Biometrika*, **64**, 247–54.

DAWSON, A. (1981), 'Sargan's wage equation: A theoretical and empirical reconstruction', *Applied Economics*, **13**, 351–63.

DICKEY, DAVID A. (1976), 'Estimation and hypothesis testing for nonstationary time series', Ph.D. Thesis, Iowa State University, Ames.

—— and WAYNE A. FULLER (1979), 'Distribution of the estimators for autoregressive time series with a unit root', *Journal of the American Statistical Assoc.* **74**, 427–31.

—— (1981), 'The likelihood ratio statistics for autoregressive time series with a unit root', *Econometrica*, **49**, 1057–72.

ENGLE, ROBERT F., DAVID F. HENDRY, and J. F. RICHARD (1983), 'Exogeneity', *Econometrica* **51**, 277–304.

—— and Byung Sam Yoo (1986), 'Forecasting and testing in co-integrated systems', UCSD Discussion Paper.

Evans, G. B. A., and N. E. Savin (1981), 'Testing for unit roots: 1', *Econometrica* **49**, 753–79.

Feller, William (1968), *An Introduction to Probability Theory and Its Applications, Volume I* (New York, John Wiley).

Fuller, Wayne A. (1976), *Introduction to Statistical Time Series* (New York, John Wiley).

Granger, C. W. J. (1981), 'Some properties of time series data and their use in econometric model specification', *Journal of Econometrics*, **16**, 121–30.

—— (1983), 'Co-Integrated variables and error-correcting models', unpublished UCSD Discussion Paper 83–13.

—— and P. Newbold (1974), 'Spurious Regressions in Econometrics', *Journal of Econometrics*, **26**, 1045–66.

—— —— (1977), *Forecasting Economic Time Series* (New York, Academic Press).

—— and A. A. Weiss (1983), 'Time series analysis of error-correcting models', in *Studies in Econometrics, Time Series, and Multivariate Statistics* (New York, Academic Press), 255–78.

Hall, Robert E. (1978), 'A stochastic life cycle model of aggregate consumption', *Journal of Political Economy*, 971–87.

Hannan, E. J. (1970), *Multiple Time Series* (New York, Wiley).

Hendry, David F., and T. von Ungern-Sternberg (1981), 'Liquidity and inflation effects on consumer's expenditure', in *Essays in the Theory and Measurement of Consumer's Behavior*, ed. by A. S. Deaton, (Cambridge, Cambridge University Press).

Johansen, Søren (1985), 'The mathematical structure of error correction models', manuscript, University of Copenhagen.

Nelson, C. R., and Charles Plosser (1982), 'Trends and random walks in macroeconomic time series', *Journal of Monetary Economics*, **10**, 139–62.

Pagan A. R. (1984), 'Econometric issues in the analysis of regressions with generated regressors', *International Economic Review*, **25**, 221–48.

Phillips, A. W. (1957), 'Stabilization policy and the time forms of lagged responses', *Economic Journal* **67**, 265–77.

Phillips, P. C. B. (1985), 'Time series regression with unit roots', Cowles Foundation Discussion Paper No. 740, Yale University.

—— and S. N. Durlauf (1985), 'Multiple time series regression with integrated processes', Cowles Foundation Discussion Paper 768.

Salmon, M. (1982), 'Error correction mechanisms', *The Economic Journal* **92**, 615–29.

Sargan, J. D. (1964), 'Wages and prices in the United Kingdom: A study in econometric methodology', in *Econometric Analysis for National Economic Planning*, ed. by P. E. Hart, G. Mills, and J. N. Whittaker (London, Butterworths).

—— and A. Bhargava (1983), 'Testing residuals from least squares regression for being generated by the Gaussian random walk', *Econometrica*, **51**, 153–74.

Shiller, R. J., and J. Y. Campbell (1984), 'A simple account of the behaviour of long-term interest rates', *American Economic Review*, **74**, 44–8.

STOCK, JAMES H. (1984), 'Asymptotic properties of least squares estimators of co-integrating vectors', manuscript, Harvard University.

WATSON, MARK W., and ROBERT ENGLE (1985), 'A test for regression coefficient stability with a stationary AR(1) alternative', forthcoming in *Review of Economics and Statistics*.

YOO, SAM (1985), 'Multi-co-integrated time series and generalized error correction models', manuscript unpublished, UCSD.

6

Forecasting and Testing in Co-integrated Systems*

ROBERT F. ENGLE and BYUNG SAM YOO

Abstract

This paper examines the behaviour of forecasts made from a co-integrated system as introduced by Granger (1981), Granger and Weiss (1983) and Engle and Granger (1987). It is established that a multi-step forecast will satisfy the co-integrating relation exactly and that this particular linear combination of forecasts will have a finite limiting forecast error variance. A simulation study compares the multi-step forecast accuracy of unrestricted vector autoregression with the two-step estimation of the vector autoregression imposing the co-integration restriction.

To test whether a system exhibits co-integration, the procedures introduced in Engle and Granger (1987) are extended to allow different sample sizes and numbers of variables.

1. Introduction

Vector autoregressions provide a convenient representation for both estimation and forecasting of systems of economic time series. Sims (1980) and Litterman (1986) are two of the influential papers which use VAR's for economic analysis and there are many other examples. The forecasting performance of unrestricted VAR's has not been particularly good and the question of whether to preprocess the data by transformations such as differencing so that the analysis will be conducted on stationary series, has perplexed investigators. In this paper it is proposed that the problems are related and that a useful and simple solution is available.

* This paper was presented in the Lake Arrowhead Econometrics Workshop, February 1986. The authors are indebted to the participants and two referees for helpful comments and especially to Clive Granger who collaborated on the development of many of these ideas. This research was supported by NSF Grant SES-84-20680.
Printed with permission of: *Journal of Econometrics*, 35, (1987), pp. 143–59.

It was first pointed out in Granger, 1981, that a vector of time series, all of which are stationary only after differencing, may have linear combinations which are stationary without differencing. In such a case, those variables are said to be co-integrated (see Granger, 1986 for a survey). For such a system there is obviously a dilemma deciding how much differencing to do as the differencing required depends upon the linear combination under consideration. It is easily shown that if all variables are differenced as would appear appropriate from their uni-variate properties, then the system no longer has a multi-variate linear time series representation with an invertible moving average. Essentially, the system has been over-differenced.

Engle and Granger (1987) establish that a co-integrated system can be represented in an error correction structure which incorporates both changes and levels of variables such that all the elements are stationary. This error correction structure provides the framework for estimation, forecasting and testing of co-integrated systems. They developed a representation theorem which is reproduced in part here, an estimation procedure and testing procedures. This paper will explore the multi-step forecasting behaviour of co-integrated systems and examine the perform-ance of the two-step estimator proposed by Engle and Granger. It will finally extend the tables of test critical values to the multi-variate case for a variety of sample sizes.

2.   Some Properties of Co-integrated Systems

The properties of multi-step forecasts of co-integrated systems differ markedly from either stationary VAR's or VAR's in differences. This section will develop the relationships.

Assumptions
An $N \times 1$ vector process $\{x_t; t = 1,2,3,\ldots\}$ has been generated by

$$(1 - B)x_t = C(B)(\varepsilon_t + m)$$
$$= \mu + C(B)\varepsilon_t, \tag{1}$$

where m is an arbitrary $N \times 1$ vector of constants and $\mu = C(1)m$.

(i) $\varepsilon_j = 0$, $\forall j \leq 0$ and $x_0 = 0$.

(ii) $\{\varepsilon_t\}_1^\infty$ is a vector white noise process with

$$E(\varepsilon_t) = 0, \qquad\qquad \forall t \geq 1,$$
$$E(\varepsilon_j \varepsilon_j') = \Omega \delta(i - j), \qquad \forall i, j \geq 1,$$

where Ω is an $N \times N$ positive definite matrix and δ is the delta function.

(iii) $C(B)$ is an $N \times N$ matrix function in B, the lag operator, given by

$$C(B) = C_0 + C_1 B + C_2 B^2 + \ldots, \text{ such that}$$

(a) no row of $C(1)$ is identically zero,
(b) $C(e^{i\omega})\Omega C'(e^{-i\omega}) < \infty, \qquad \forall \omega \in [0, \pi]$,
(c) $C(0) = I_N$.

(iv) The rank of $C(1) = N - r$.

Assumption (iii) implies that all the elements of x_t need to be differenced once to become individually stationary. Such time series are called integrated of order one and denoted $I(1)$. Assumption (iv) implies that the variables are co-integrated. Any $N \times r$ matrix α which spans the null space of $C(1)$ so that $\alpha' C(1) = 0$, will produce an $r \times 1$ time series $z_t = \alpha' x_t$ which is stationary. To see this, write $C(B) = C(1) + C^*(B)(1 - B)$. Then

$$(1 - B)\alpha' x_t = \alpha' C(1)(\varepsilon_t + m) + (1 - B)\alpha' C^*(B)\varepsilon_t,$$

so that

$$z_t = \alpha' C^*(B)\varepsilon_t \quad \text{with} \quad \alpha' C^*(1) < \infty.$$

In Engle and Granger (1987) it is assumed that all deterministic components are extracted before analysis so that $m = 0$. Here we slightly generalize the notion of co-integration. In particular, even though each element in x_t is $I(1)$ with drift so that it has a deterministic trend and a variance which goes to infinity with t [i.e. $\text{var}(x_t) = O(t)$], the linear combination $\alpha' x_t$ will be stationary. Thus μ must have property that $\alpha' \mu = 0$ so that the same linear combination which eliminates the unit roots will also eliminate the trend.

The time series represented by (1) can be integrated as follows:

$$x_1 = \mu + \varepsilon_1,$$

$$x_2 = 2\mu + \varepsilon_2 + (C_1 + I)\varepsilon_1$$

$$x_3 = 3\mu + \varepsilon_3 + (C_1 + I)\varepsilon_2 + (C_2 + C_1 + I)\varepsilon_1$$

so that

$$x_t = t\mu + \sum_{i=1}^{t} \sum_{j=0}^{t-i} C_j \varepsilon_i, \qquad (2)$$

and finally for $h \geqslant 1$,

$$x_{t+h} = (t + h)\mu + \sum_{i=1}^{t} \sum_{j=0}^{t+h-i} C_j \varepsilon_i + \sum_{i=1}^{h} \sum_{j=0}^{h-i} C_j \varepsilon_{t+i}. \tag{3}$$

This form is the basis for multi-step forecasts.

An alternative and closely related representation is introduced by Stock and Watson (1986) which they call the Common Trends representation. This form is convenient for discussing long-term forecasts. A set of time series can be decomposed into deterministic trends, stochastic trends or unit root processes, and stationary components. To see this, rewrite (2) as

$$x_t = \mu t + (1 + B + B^2 + \ldots + B^{t-1}) C(B) \varepsilon_t.$$

Using $C(B) = C(1) + (1 - B)C^*(B)$ and denoting

$$y_t = \sum_{i=1}^{t} \varepsilon_i, \tag{4}$$

we get

$$x_t = \mu t + C(1) y_t + C^*(B) \varepsilon_t, \tag{5}$$

since $B^t C(B) \varepsilon_t = 0$ by initial conditions.

The deterministic trend is now reflected in μt, while the stochastic trend is given by $C(1) y_t$. The remainder is stationary for large t, if the C_j's are exponentially decaying for large j. This is called a Common Trends representation because the reduced rank of $C(1)$ implies that there are fewer stochastic trends (or unit roots) than variables in the system.

3. Forecasting

Let $\mathcal{F}_t = \sigma(\varepsilon_j; \ j = 1, \ldots, t)$ be the information set generated by the random variables ε_j $(1 \le j \le t)$. We shall consider the orthogonal projection of x_{t+h} on $\mathcal{F}_t$, denoted by $x_{t+h|t}$.

From (3) it follows that

$$x_{t+h|t} = \mu(t + h) + \sum_{i=1}^{t} \sum_{j=0}^{t+h-i} C_j \varepsilon_i. \tag{6}$$

Notice that

$$\lim_{h \to \infty} \sum_{j=0}^{t+h-i} C_j = C(1),$$

so that

$$\lim_{h \to \infty} a' x_{t+h|t} = 0, \tag{7}$$

under the co-integration assumption (iv). Thus the long-run forecasts of co-integrated systems are tied together regardless of the fact that individual forecasts diverge to infinity. The co-integrating relationship will hold exactly in the long-run forecast. This is also implied by the Common Trends representation, where the trends in the individual series are such that the linear combination with weights α has no trend.

Note that $\{C_j; \ j = 0, \ 1, \ \ldots\}$ will typically be an exponentially decaying sequence for large j and therefore the convergence

$$\sum_{j=0}^{t+h-i} C_j \to C(1)$$

will be rather rapid as $h \to \infty$. Hence (7) may be observed in a moderate forecasting horizon. Whenever h is sufficiently large that this limit is satisfied, (6) can be rewritten as

$$x_{t+h|t} = \mu(t + h) + C(1)y_t, \tag{8}$$

using the notation from (4). Thus the trend component at time t can be given by

$$\mu t + C(1)y_t = x_{t+h|t} - \mu h, \quad \text{for } h \text{ sufficiently large.}$$

This is the approach to trend extraction suggested for univariate series by Beveridge and Nelson (1981) and Watson (1986) and extended to the multivariate common trend set-up by Stock and Watson (1986).

We next consider the forecast error variance. Denoting the h-step forecast error by $e_{t+h|t}$, we have

$$e_{t+h|t} \equiv x_{t+h} - x_{t+h|t} = \sum_{i=1}^{h} \sum_{j=0}^{h-i} C_j \varepsilon_{t+i} \tag{9}$$

It follows that

$$\text{var}[e_{t+h|t}] = \sum_{i=1}^{h} \left[\left(\sum_{j=0}^{h-i} C_j \right) \Omega \left(\sum_{j=0}^{h-i} C_j' \right) \right]. \tag{10}$$

From (9), it also follows that

$$e_{t+h|t} - e_{t+h-1|t} = \sum_{i=1}^{h} C_{h-i} \varepsilon_{t+i}.$$

The right-hand-side quantity is $C(B)\varepsilon_{t+h}$ taking $\varepsilon_j = 0$ for all $j \leqslant t$. Therefore the forecast error process has the same stochastic structure as the original process x_t and is co-integrated. Writing the forecast error equation similarly to (5), without the deterministic component, immediately reveals that

$$\text{var}[e_{t+h|t}] = O(h), \tag{11}$$

and

$$\text{var}[\alpha'e_{t+h|t}] = \alpha'K\alpha < \infty, \tag{12}$$

for large h, where the constant matrix K comes from the stationary component of the forecast error.

4. Methods for Forecasting Co-integrated Variables

Multi-step forecasts from co-integrated systems have a property not shared by general integrated systems: linear combinations of forecasts are identically zero for large horizons regardless of the forecast origin, and the forecast error variance for this linear combination remains finite while that for all other linear combinations goes to infinity as the horizon goes to infinity. The practical implications of these observations are best seen when it is assumed that the data follow a finite vector autoregression (VAR). The question of whether the data are co-integrated then becomes a question of how many unit roots are in the population autoregressive polynomial, and the question of whether forecasts from the estimated VAR exhibit the desired properties depends upon the roots of the estimated VAR.

Engle and Granger (1987) present and prove a representation theorem due to Granger (1983) which establishes the connection between the moving average representation in (1) and the VAR when $\mu = 0$. This is briefly presented below.

Granger Representation Theorem

If the $N \times 1$ vector x_t given in (1) satisfies the assumptions (i)–(iv) and is therefore co-integrated with co-integrating rank r, and if this vector can be represented by a finite vector autoregression, then:

(a) $A(1)$ has rank r and $A(0) = I_N$ in

$$A(B)x_t = \varepsilon_t + m. \tag{13}$$

(b) There exist $N \times r$ matrices, α, γ, of rank r such that

$$\alpha'C(1) = 0 \qquad C(1)\gamma = 0, \qquad A(1) = \gamma\alpha'.$$

(c) There exists an error correction representation with $z_t = \alpha'x_t$, an $r \times 1$ vector of stationary random variables:

$$A^*(B)(1 - B)x_t = -\gamma z_{t-1} + \varepsilon_t + m \quad \text{with} \quad A^*(0) = I_N. \tag{14}$$

Eq. (13) describes the unrestricted VAR which can be used to estimate and forecast the vector x_t. This representation, however, has restrictions implied by the $N - r$ unit roots which would not be imposed by such an unrestricted estimation. On the other hand, (14) shows that a VAR in differences is inappropriate as the levels should appear through z. In fact the vector $(1 - B)x_t$ does not have a vector ARMA representation with an invertible moving average. Such a series is 'over-differenced'.

Three alternative approaches to the estimation of this system may be identified:

  (i) Unrestricted estimation of (13) or equivalently of (14) without imposing the restriction that the level variables in z must be the same in each equation. If the lags are the same in each equation this is simply OLS equation by equation. Call this an unrestricted vector autoregression (UVAR).
 (ii) Maximum likelihood of (14) under normality which imposes the cross-equation restrictions and uses SURE estimation.
(iii) Two-step estimation where α is estimated by a static least squares regression called the 'co-integrating regression' and then this value of α is used in estimating (14) thereby imposing the cross-equation constraints. The estimation procedure is again OLS equation by equation including the estimated value of z_{t-1} in each equation. As this was proposed by Engle and Granger we call this the EG 2-step.

It is clear that the second approach is theoretically attractive as it imposes all the restrictions known to be true and estimates the system fully efficiently. The first and third are, however, serious contenders. Engle and Granger introduce the two-step estimator and prove that (in the case $\mu = 0$) it is asymptotically just as efficient an estimate of $A^*(B)$ as the estimator using the true value of α which is of course not a feasible estimator. Phillips and Durlauf (1986) and Said and Dickey (1984) in a more restricted context show that the least squares estimate of (14) without restrictions gives estimates of the parameters of the $A^*(B)$ polynomial which are asymptotically the same as those assuming knowledge of α. Consequently, all three of these estimators have the same limiting distribution for the $A^*(B)$ parameters.

For finite samples however, the three differ in an important fashion. The rank of $A(1)$ will be exactly r for estimates (ii) and (iii), but for (i) it will generally be N except for an event with probability measure zero. In particular, the well-known downward bias of the autoregressive parameter in a univariate model may suggest that $A(B)$ will too often look like it has no unit roots for finite samples.

Differences in the forecasting performance of VAR's of co-integrated systems estimated by (i) and (iii) should therefore show up particularly for small samples and for multi-step forecasts. In the next section a small simulation is carried out to examine this contention.

5. Simulation

To examine the relative forecasting accuracy of models estimated by these methods, a small simulation experiment was designed. Only the least squares methods (i), UVAR, and (iii), EG 2-step, were examined and the problem was set up so that both correctly specified the model. The data generation process is given in three different representations:

Moving Average

$$(1 - B)\begin{pmatrix} x_t \\ y_t \end{pmatrix} = (1 - 0.4B)^{-1}\begin{pmatrix} 1 - 0.8B & 0.8B \\ 0.1B & 1 - 0.6B \end{pmatrix}\varepsilon_t, \quad (15)$$

Autoregressive

$$\begin{pmatrix} 1 - 0.6B & -0.8B \\ -0.1B & 1 - 0.8B \end{pmatrix}\begin{pmatrix} x_t \\ y_t \end{pmatrix} = \varepsilon_t \quad (16)$$

Error Correction

$$(1 - B)\begin{pmatrix} x_t \\ y_t \end{pmatrix} = \begin{pmatrix} -0.4 \\ 0.1 \end{pmatrix}(1 - 2)\begin{pmatrix} x_{t-1} \\ y_{t-1} \end{pmatrix} + \varepsilon_t, \quad (17)$$

where

$$\text{var}(\varepsilon_t) = \begin{pmatrix} 100 & 0 \\ 0 & 100 \end{pmatrix}, \qquad x_0 = y_0 = 0.$$

As can best be seen from the error correction representation in (17), the long-run relation between x and y is $x = 2y$.

One hundred replications of this design were computed in each case, with 100 observations used for fitting the model and 10 observations used for post sample forecasting. The two-step error correction estimation proposed by Engle and Granger (EG) was compared with the unrestricted vector autoregression in terms of mean square error for horizons from 1 to 20 periods. Here the mean square error is the trace of the sample covariance matrix of the forecast errors. The results are presented in table 1.

From these results it is clear that for the shortest-period forecasts there are gains to using the unrestricted vector autoregression. The maximum gain is 16 per cent which occurs at the three-step forecast. Through step 4 there is an apparent advantage to the VAR, however for longer-run forecasts the two-step estimator is more accurate. The increase in forecast accuracy rises to 40 per cent ($1/0.71 = 1.40$) after 20 periods and probably would go to infinity for sufficiently long forecast horizons. The fact that the restricted model performed better than the

TABLE 1. Mean square forecast errors for multi-step forecasts from co-integrated systems.

Horizon	EG 2-step	UVAR	Ratio (%)
1	253	230	110
2	445	392	113
3	608	526	116
4	888	798	111
5	1008	995	101
6	1282	1300	99
7	1350	1445	93
8	1647	1855	89
9	1960	2247	87
10	2164	2574	84
11	2363	2833	83
12	2550	3081	83
13	2712	3371	80
14	3223	4095	79
15	3661	4687	78
16	4022	5158	78
17	4452	5831	76
18	4763	6455	74
19	5012	6870	73
20	4978	7021	71

unrestricted model is expected a priori and hence may not be surprising. However, what is being advocated here is the importance of imposing long-run constraint rather than the restriction per se. One might not expect such a difference in the forecasting performances of two correctly specified models in standard cases. In fact, the two-step procedure does not necessarily lead to better parameter estimates as a whole as revealed in the short-term forecasts. One could imagine that the non-linear least squares estimator which imposes the cross-equation restrictions implicit in the error correction representation would dominate both of these estimators. Much however would depend upon the convergence of this estimator, the starting values chosen and the treatment of forecasts from non-convergent samples.

One could also compare these results with estimates which are obviously misspecified such as least squares on differences or Litterman's (1986) Bayesian Vector Autoregressions which shrinks the parameter vector toward the first difference model which is itself misspecified for this system. The finding that such methods provided inferior forecasts would hardly be surprising.

6. Testing For Co-integration

Engle and Granger (1987) investigated tests for the null hypothesis that a pair of the time series which were each $I(1)$ were 'non-co-integrated' against the alternative that they were co-integrated. That is, the null hypothesis is that the system has two unit roots, while the alternative is one unit root. For a sample size of 100 several test statistics were considered. Monte Carlo methods were used to obtain the finite sample critical values and then to examine the power properties of the tests. In a first-order system, two procedures were found to be the best: a Durbin–Watson (DW) test and a Dickey–Fuller (DF) test. In higher-order systems, it is simple to generalize the Dickey–Fuller test to the Augmented Dickey–Fuller test (ADF) which was the recommendation of Engle and Granger.

The tests are computed by performing two regressions. The first, called the co-integrating regression, fits the static bivariate model

$$y_t = \hat{\varphi} + x_t \hat{\pi} + z_t, \tag{18}$$

where z_t is the residual term which is also interpreted as the co-integrating linear relation. The Durbin–Watson test simply examines the DW of this regression to see if it is significantly greater than zero, which would be its probability limit if z_t contains a unit root as required by the null hypothesis. At the second stage, the DF and ADF tests are obtained respectively as the t-statistics of $\hat{\rho}$ in the following regressions $[\Delta \equiv (1 - B)]$:

$$\Delta \hat{z}_t = \hat{\rho} z_{t-1}, \tag{19}$$

$$\Delta \hat{z}_t = \hat{\rho} z_{t-1} + \sum_{i=1}^{p} \hat{\delta}_i \Delta z_{t-i}. \tag{20}$$

In the next section, similar critical values will be developed for other sample sizes and with more than two variables using a simulation approach. In the remainder of this section we discuss the theoretical results which are available for testing unit roots. If φ and π are known, the problem becomes simply a test for a unit root in a univariate process. The more complex case where φ is unknown has been treated by Dickey and Fuller (1979) and the co-integration problem is therefore seen as a further extension to unknown π.

We assume that (y_t, x_t) is generated by

$$y_t = y_{t-1} + v_t,$$

$$x_t = x_{t-1} + w_t,$$

$$\begin{pmatrix} v_t \\ w_t \end{pmatrix} \sim \text{i.i.d.} \left[0, \begin{pmatrix} \sigma_v^2 & 0 \\ 0 & \sigma_w^2 \end{pmatrix} \right], \qquad y_0 = x_0 = 0.$$

For known φ and π, z_t follows a random walk. In particular, this model implies that z_t is equal to y_t since the true values of φ and π are zero. Note that allowing the initial values of the covariance term to be non-zero results in non-zero values of φ and π. However, provided that the estimators of these parameters are understood to be centered around the true values, relaxing these assumptions will not alter the discussion that follows but will only complicate the notation. Hence we maintain this simple set-up. The weak convergence results for the OLS estimator $\hat{\rho}$ in (19) (White, 1958) and associated t-statistics (Dickey and Fuller, 1979 and Phillips, 1985a) are known to be

$$T\hat{\rho} \xrightarrow{\mathrm{d}} \frac{[V(1)^2 - 1]/2}{\int_0^1 V(t)^2 \mathrm{d}t}, \tag{21}$$

$$t_{\hat{\rho}} \xrightarrow{\mathrm{d}} \frac{[V(1)^2 - 1]/2}{[\int_0^1 V(t)^2 \mathrm{d}t]^{1/2}}, \tag{22}$$

where T is the sample size and $V(t)$ is a standard Brownian motion on the unit interval $[0, 1]$. Therefore, the limiting distribution of $T\hat{\rho}$, for example, is the same as the distribution of the RHS variable in (21). Note that we have a faster convergence rate than the standard rate $\sqrt{T}$. This is because the sample covariance between an $I(1)$ variable and its innovation term is $O_p(1)$, while the sample variance of an $I(1)$ variable is $O_p(T)$. Needless to say, $\hat{\rho}$ is the ratio of these two quantities calculated using the true mean values, zero. Despite the fact that the numerator, which is a simple linear transformation of the χ_1^2 random variable $V^2(1)$, has a distribution which is skewed to the right, the limiting distribution of $T\hat{\rho}$ is highly skewed to the left as shown in Fuller (1976, p. 371). This is also true for the t-statistic in (22), so that the critical values are larger in absolute value than the usual critical values. These critical values are available in Fuller (1976, p. 373) under the name $\hat{\tau}$.

When φ is unknown but π is known to be zero, z_t is equal to the mean-corrected y_t (or equivalently an intercept is allowed in (19)). The sample mean of an $I(1)$ variable is $O_p(T^{1/2})$ so that it diverges as $T \to \infty$. Hence using the sample mean in calculating the variance and the covariance does make a difference in the limiting distributions from the previous case, although the order properties remain the same. Dickey and Fuller (1979) also consider this case and the result in our notation becomes

$$T\hat{\rho} \xrightarrow{\mathrm{d}} \frac{[V(1)^2 - 1]/2 - V(1)\int_0^1 V(t)\,\mathrm{d}t}{\int_0^1 V(t)^2\,\mathrm{d}t - [\int_0^1 V(t)\,\mathrm{d}t]^2}, \tag{23}$$

$$t_{\hat{\rho}} \xrightarrow{\mathrm{d}} \frac{[V(1)^2 - 1]/2 - V(1)\int_0^1 V(t)\,\mathrm{d}t}{\{\int_0^1 V(t)^2\,\mathrm{d}t - [\int_0^1 V(t)\,\mathrm{d}t]^2\}^{1/2}}, \tag{24}$$

$$T^{-1/2}\bar{y} \xrightarrow{\ \mathrm{d}\ } \sigma_v \int_0^1 V(t)\,\mathrm{d}t. \tag{25}$$

The second expressions in the numerators and denominators of (23) and (24) are purely due to the sample mean adjustment in z_t. The empirical distribution of t_ρ of the current case, which is skewed more to the left than the previous one, is also available in Fuller (1976) under the name $\hat{\tau}_\mu$. For comparison, part of the critical values of $\hat{\tau}$ and $\hat{\tau}_\mu$ are reproduced in table 2.

Although our discussion is confined to the case of i.i.d. noise terms, Phillips (1985a) shows that the limiting distributions are also valid for heterogeneous error terms under a mixing condition. However, he shows that, if the noise term is intertemporally dependent, then the limiting distribution depends upon nuisance parameters, namely the variance of v_t and the spectral density of v_t at the zero frequency. When this dependence is autoregressive, Fuller (1976) corrects the problem by including lagged dependent variables in the regression as in (20). See also Said and Dickey 1984 for a more general treatment.

We consider now the case when both φ and π are unknown. The limiting distributions of the OLS estimators of the co-integrating regression (18) has been studied by Stock (1984) and Phillips (1985b):

$$\hat{\pi} \xrightarrow{\ \mathrm{d}\ } \frac{\sigma_v[\int_0^1 V(t)W(t)\,\mathrm{d}t - \int_0^1 V(t)\,\mathrm{d}t \int_0^1 W(t)\,\mathrm{d}t]}{\sigma_w[\int_0^1 W(t)^2\,\mathrm{d}t - (\int_0^1 W(t)\,\mathrm{d}t)^2]} \equiv \frac{\sigma_u}{\sigma_w}\xi, \tag{26}$$

$$T^{-1/2}\hat{\varphi} \xrightarrow{\ \mathrm{d}\ } \sigma_v[\int_0^1 V(t)\,\mathrm{d}t - \xi\int_0^1 W(t)\,\mathrm{d}t] \equiv \sigma_v\eta, \tag{27}$$

where $V(t)$ and $W(t)$ are mutually independent standard Brownian motions on the unit interval $[0, 1]$.

Hence $\hat{\varphi}$ diverges at the same speed as the sample mean $\bar{y}$. On the other hand, $\hat{\pi}$ converges to a random variable. If x_t and y_t were co-integrated, $\hat{\pi}$ would converge to a constant with the convergence rate T which is faster than $T^{1/2}$ of the standard cases (Stock 1984). Following the work of Phillips (1985b) it is a bit tedious but straightforward to show that

$$T\hat{\rho} \xrightarrow{\ \mathrm{d}\ } \theta/\psi, \tag{28}$$

$$t_{\hat{\rho}} \xrightarrow{\ \mathrm{d}\ } \theta/[\psi(1 + \xi^2)]^{1/2}, \tag{29}$$

where

$$\theta = \{[V(1) - \xi W(1)]^2 - 1 - \xi^2\}/2 - \eta[V(1) - \xi W(1)],$$

$$\psi = \int_0^1 V(t)^2\,\mathrm{d}t - \left(\int_0^1 V(t)\,\mathrm{d}t\right)^2$$

$$-\xi\left[\int_0^1 V(t)W(t)\,\mathrm{d}t - \int_0^1 V(t)\,\mathrm{d}t\int_0^1 W(t)\,\mathrm{d}t\right].$$

Had the $\hat{\pi}$ converged to zero (i.e. $\xi = 0$), the limiting behaviour of $\hat{\rho}$ and t_ρ would be the same as those from the mean adjusted Dickey and Fuller regression. In the Dickey–Fuller case, the standard error of the regression converges to a constant almost surely. In the present case, however, this statistic converges to a random variable:

$$s^2 \xrightarrow{\ \mathrm{d}\ } \sigma_v^2(1 + \xi^2), \tag{30}$$

where s is the standard error of the regression, which adds a further complication to the limiting distribution.

The large sample behaviour of the t-statistic, $t\hat{\rho}$, depends on the number of variables in the co-integrating regression. This can be seen from the expressions (26) through (30): the right-hand-side random variables are functions of independent Brownian motions, the number of which is equal to the number of the variables in the co-integrating regression. Intuition also tells us that the critical values will get larger in absolute value because the residual series from the co-integrating regression would look more close to a stationary series as the number of variables increases. In the next section, we examine these critical values.

7. Critical Values for the Co-integration Test

Critical values are first constructed for various values of N, the number of variables, and T, the sample size. We assume that the data are generated by

$$x_t = x_{t-1} + \varepsilon_t, \quad x_0 = 0, \quad x_t' = (x_{1t}, x_{2t}, \ldots, x_{Nt}), \tag{31}$$

with

$$\varepsilon_t \sim \mathrm{IN}(0, I_N),$$

and that the co-integrating regression takes the form

$$x_{1t} = \alpha + \beta_2 x_{2t} + \beta_3 x_{3t} + \ldots + \beta_N x_{Nt} + z_t. \tag{32}$$

It is clear that there is a normalization imposed in the co-integrating regression (32) which would mean that different test statistics could be found from the same data set. Stock and Watson, in testing a related hypothesis on the co-integrating rank r, use principle components estimation rather than OLS. Such a convention eliminates the ambiguity. Because the test statistics have the same distribution for all normalizations and in our experience differ little across such choices, and because it is extremely convenient to use OLS with possibly a natural normalization, we continue in the vein of Engle and Granger to pick a particular normalization for the test. The power property of the test, when $N = 2$, has been examined in their paper.

The covariance matrix of the innovations is taken to be identity without any loss of generality. The test statistics will be the same for any value of the covariance matrix as the tests have the property of 'similarity' as discussed for example by Cox and Hinkley (1974, pp. 134–6).

Table 2 reports the critical values of the t-statistics in the regression (19) omitting minus signs for simplicity. These values as well as those in other tables in this section have been obtained through ten thousand replications. For comparison, we also reproduce the critical values of $\hat{\tau}$ and $\hat{\tau}_\mu$ discussed in the previous section from Fuller 1976, p. 373.

The 95 per cent confidence intervals of these critical values (see Rohatgi, 1984, pp. 496–500) vary little bit. They are mostly less than

TABLE 2.   Critical values for the co-integration test.

Number of var's N	Sample size T	Significance level		
		1%	5%	10%
1[a]	50	2.62	1.95	1.61
	100	2.60	1.95	1.61
	250	2.58	1.95	1.62
	500	2.58	1.95	1.62
	∞	2.58	1.95	1.62
1[b]	50	3.58	2.93	2.60
	100	3.51	2.89	2.58
	250	3.46	2.88	2.57
	500	3.44	2.87	2.57
	∞	3.43	2.86	2.57
2	50	4.32	3.67	3.28
	100	4.07	3.37	3.03
	200	4.00	3.37	3.02
3	50	4.84	4.11	3.73
	100	4.45	3.93	3.59
	200	4.35	3.78	3.47
4	50	4.94	4.35	4.02
.	100	4.75	4.22	3.89
	200	4.70	4.18	3.89
5	50	5.41	4.76	4.42
	100	5.18	4.58	4.26
	200	5.02	4.48	4.18

[a] Critical values of $\hat{\tau}$.
[b] Critical values of $\hat{\tau}_\mu$. Both cited from Fuller 1976, p. 373.

±0.08 about the 1 per cent values, ±0.05 about the 5 per cent values, and ±0.03 about the 10 per cent values.

To examine the movement of critical values in higher-order systems, we have generated data according to the following model in place of (31):

$$x_t = x_{t-1} + U_t,$$

$$u_{it} = 0.8u_{it-4} + \varepsilon_{it}, \qquad i = 1, \ldots, N, \qquad (33)$$

maintaining the assumptions on x_0 and ε_t as before.

The critical values of the t-statistic of the augmented regression (20) with $p = 4$ are reported in table 3. Note that this regression includes more variables (i.e. Δz_{t-i}, $i = 1,2,3$) than necessary. Hence the values are not fully efficient ones but reflect the ignorance about the lag length encountered in practice. Of course, such an inefficiency will disappear in a large sample. In theory, the unknown lag structure in z_t might be handled by allowing p to be a slowly increasing function of the sample size as in Said and Dickey (1984). However, it does not provide practical guidance in the choice of p. A readily available way seems to be to use a standard model selection procedure based upon some information criterion (e.g. AIC).

As expected, these critical values differ from those in table 2 when the sample size is small. It might suggest that the values in table 2 are likely to be conservative in small samples. For a sample of size about two hundred, however, the difference becomes qualitatively negligible

TABLE 3.   Critical values for a higher-order system (33).

Number of var's N	Sample size T	Significance level		
		1%	5%	10%
2	50	4.12	3.29	2.90
	100	3.73	3.17	2.91
	200	3.78	3.25	2.98
3	50	4.45	3.75	3.36
	100	4.22	3.62	3.32
	200	4.34	3.78	3.51
4	50	4.61	3.98	3.67
	100	4.61	4.02	3.71
	200	4.72	4.13	3.83
5	50	4.80	4.15	3.85
	100	4.98	4.36	4.06
	200	4.97	4.43	4.14

so that the values in table 2 seem to be fairly accurate approximations for higher-order systems as well.

We have also examined the behaviour of the Durbin–Watson statistic from the co-integrating regression. Unfortunately, the discrepancy between the critical values for different systems remains significant even for the sample of size two hundred. This is not surprising since the statistic is not asymptotically similar as are the preceding tests. Hence this statistic does not appear to be too useful for testing co-integration. For the sake of illustration, we report in table 4 the critical values obtained from the systems (31) and (33) with $N = 2$.

8. Conclusion

It is commonly believed that many economic time series are tied together even though they are all trending. When a forecasting model is needed for such time series, a vector autoregressive model in differences is inappropriate. This is because, even though the residuals may appear to be white, such a model suffers misspecification and the forecasts will diverge from each other. The VAR formulation (in levels) does not suffer such misspecification. However, conventional estimation techniques appear to underestimate the parameters near the unit circle. Since forecasts are made conditional on estimated parameters, the forecasts from a VAR model are likely to be suboptimal especially in multi-step horizons. Our simulation result in section 5 supports this argument even though more practical experience is needed.

Hence it appears important to build models designed for co-integrated time series. The error correction models provide a simple class. The critical values reported in this paper should be a useful guide to decide when to impose the co-integration constraint. The two-step estimator proposed in Engle and Granger (1987) can then be used to model the error correction structure and achieve the multi-step forecast gains described above.

TABLE 4. Critical values for the Durbin–Watson statistic (number of variables $N = 2$).

Sample size	Canonical system (31)			Higher-order system (33)		
	1%	5%	10%	1%	5%	10%
50	1.00	0.78	0.69	1.49	1.03	0.83
100	0.51	0.39	0.32	0.46	0.28	0.21
200	0.29	0.20	0.16	0.13	0.08	0.06

References

BEVERIDGE, S., and C. R. NELSON (1981), 'A new approach to decomposition of economic time series into permanent and transitory components with particular attention to measurement of the business cycle', *Journal of Monetary Economics*, 7, 151–74.

Cox, D. R., and C. V. HINKLEY (1974), *Theoretical Statistics* (London, Chapman and Hall).

DICKEY, DAVID A. and W. A. FULLER (1979), 'Distribution of estimates for autoregressive time series with unit root', *Journal of the American Statistical Association*, 74, 427–31.

ENGLE, ROBERT F. and C. W. J. GRANGER (1987), 'Cointegration and error correction: Representation, estimation and testing', *Econometrica* 55, 251–76.

FULLER, W. A. (1976), *Introduction to statistical time series* (New York, Wiley).

GRANGER, C. W. J. (1981), 'Some properties of time series data and their use in econometric model specification', *Journal of Econometrics*, 16, 121–30.

—— (1983), 'Cointegrated variables and error-correcting models', discussion paper (University of California, San Diego, CA).

—— (1986), 'Developments in the study of cointegrated economic variables', *Oxford Bulletin of Economics and Statistics*, 48, 213–28.

—— and A. A. WEISS (1983), 'Time series analysis of error-correcting models', in S. Karlin *et al.*, eds., *Studies in Econometrics, Time Series, and Multivariate Analysis* (New York, Academic Press) 255–78.

LITTERMAN, R. B. (1986), 'Forecasting with Bayesian vector autoregressions: Five years of experience', *Journal of Business and Economic Statistics*, 4, 25–38.

PHILLIPS, P. C. B. (1985a), 'Time series regression with unit roots', Cowles Foundation discussion paper no. 740 (Yale University, New Haven, CT).

—— (1985b), 'Understanding spurious regressions in econometrics', Cowles Foundation discussion paper no. 757 (Yale University, New Haven, CT).

—— and S. N. DURLAUF (1986), 'Multiple time series regression with integrated processes', *Review of Economic Studies*, 53, 473–95.

ROHATGI, V. K. (1984), *Statistical Inference* (New York, Wiley).

SAID, S. E., and D. A. DICKEY (1984), 'Testing for unit roots in autoregressive-moving average models of unknown order', *Biometrica*, 71, 599–607.

SIMS, C. A. (1980), 'Macroeconomics and reality', *Econometrica*, 48, 1–48.

STOCK, J. (1984), 'Asymptotic properties of least squares estimators of co-integrating vectors', Mimeo (Harvard University, Cambridge, MA).

—— and M. W. WATSON (1986), 'Testing for common trends', Mimeo (Harvard University, Cambridge, MA).

WATSON, M. W. (1986), 'Univariate detrending methods with stochastic trends', *Journal of Monetary Economics,* 18, 49–75.

WHITE, J. S. (1958), 'The limiting distribution of the serial correlation coefficient in the explosive case', *Annals of Mathematical Statistics*, 29, 1188–97.

7

Statistical Analysis of Cointegration Vectors

SØREN JOHANSEN*

Abstract

We consider a nonstationary vector autoregressive process which is integrated of order 1, and generated by i.i.d. Gaussian errors. We then derive the maximum likelihood estimator of the space of cointegration vectors and the likelihood ratio test of the hypothesis that it has a given number of dimensions. Further we test linear hypotheses about the cointegration vectors.

The asymptotic distribution of these test statistics are found and the first is described by a natural multivariate version of the usual test for unit root in an autoregressive process, and the other is a χ^2 test.

1. Introduction

The idea of using cointegration vectors in the study of nonstationary time series comes from the work of Granger (1981), Granger and Weiss (1983), Granger and Engle (1985), and Engle and Granger (1987). The connection with error correcting models has been investigated by a number of authors; see Davidson (1986), Stock (1987), and Johansen (1988) among others.

Granger and Engle (1987) suggest estimating the cointegration relations using regression, and these estimators have been investigated by Stock (1987), Phillips (1985), Phillips and Durlauf (1986), Phillips and Park (1986a,b, 1987), Phillips and Ouliaris (1986, 1987), Stock and Watson (1987), and Sims, Stock and Watson (1986). The purpose of this paper is to derive maximum likelihood estimators of the cointegration vectors for an autoregressive process with independent Gaussian errors,

* The simulations were carefully performed by Marc Andersen with the support of the Danish Social Science Research Council. The author is very grateful to the referee whose critique of the first version greatly helped improve the presentation.

Printed with permission of: *Journal of Economic Dynamics and Control*, 12, (1988), pp. 231–54.

and to derive a likelihood ratio test for the hypothesis that there is a given number of these. A similar approach has been taken by Ahn and Reinsel (1990).

This programme will not only give good estimates and test statistics in the Gaussian case, but will also yield estimators and tests, the properties of which can be investigated under various other assumptions about the underlying data generating process. The reason for expecting the estimators to behave better than the regression estimates is that they take into account the error structure of the underlying process, which the regression estimates do not.

The processes we shall consider are defined from a sequence $\{\varepsilon_t\}$ of i.i.d. p-dimensional Gaussian random variables with mean zero and variance matrix Λ. We shall define the process X_t by

$$X_t = \Pi_1 X_{t-1} + \ldots + \Pi_k X_{t-k} + \varepsilon_t, \qquad t = 1, 2, \ldots, \qquad (1)$$

for given values of $X_{-k+1}, \ldots, X_0$. We shall work in the conditional distribution given the starting values, since we shall allow the process X_t to be nonstationary. We define the matrix polynomial

$$A(z) = I - \Pi_1 z - \ldots - \Pi_k z^k,$$

and we shall be concerned with the situation where the determinant $|A(z)|$ has roots at $z = 1$. The general structure of such processes and the relation to error correction models was studied in the above references.

We shall in this paper mainly consider a very simple case where X_t is integrated of order 1, such that ΔX_t is stationary, and where the impact matrix

$$A(z)|_{z=1} = \Pi = I - \Pi_1 - \ldots - \Pi_k$$

has rank $r < p$. If we express this as

$$\Pi = \alpha\beta', \qquad (2)$$

for suitable $p \times r$ matrices α and β, then we shall assume that, although ΔX_t is stationary and X_t is nonstationary as a vector process, the linear combinations given by $\beta'X_t$ are stationary. In the terminology of Granger this means that the vector process X_t is cointegrated with cointegration vectors β. The space spanned by β is the space spanned by the rows of the matrix Π, which we shall call the cointegration space.

In this paper we shall derive the likelihood ratio test for the hypothesis given by (2) and derive the maximum likelihood estimator of the cointegration space. Then we shall find the likelihood ratio test of the hypothesis that the cointegration space is restricted to lie in a certain subspace, representing the linear restrictions that one may want to impose on the cointegration vectors.

The results we obtain can briefly be described as follows: the estimation of β is performed by first regressing ΔX_t and X_{t-k} on the lagged differences. From the residuals of these $2p$ regressions we calculate a $2p \times 2p$ matrix of product moments. We can now show that the estimate of β is the empirical canonical variates of X_{t-k} with respect to ΔX_t corrected for the lagged differences.

The likelihood ratio test is now a function of certain eigenvalues of the product moment matrix corresponding to the smallest squared canonical correlations. The test of the linear restrictions involve yet another set of eigenvalues of a reduced product moment matrix. The asymptotic distribution of the first test statistic involves an integral of a multivariate Brownian motion with respect to itself, and turns out to depend on just one parameter, namely the dimension of the process, and can hence be tabulated by simulation or approximated by a χ^2 distribution. The second test statistic is asymptotically distributed as χ^2 with the proper degrees of freedom. It is also shown that the maximum likelihood estimator of β suitably normalised is asymptotically distributed as a mixture of Gaussian variables.

2. Maximum Likelihood Estimation of Cointegration Vectors and Likelihood Ratio Tests of Hypotheses about Cointegration Vectors

We want to estimate the space spanned by β from observations X_t, $t = -k + 1, \ldots, T$. For any $r \leq p$ we formulate the model as the hypothesis

$$H_0: \quad \text{rank}(\Pi) \leq r \quad \text{or} \quad \Pi = \alpha\beta', \tag{3}$$

where α and β are $p \times r$ matrices.

Note that there are no other constraints on $\Pi_1, \ldots, \Pi_k$ than (3). Hence a wide class containing stationary as well as nonstationary processes is considered.

The parameters α and β cannot be estimated since they form an overparametrisation of the model, but one can estimate the space spanned by β.

We can now formulate the main result about the estimation of $\text{sp}(\beta)$ and the test of the hypothesis (3).

THEOREM 1. *The maximum likelihood estimator of the space spanned by β is the space spanned by the r canonical variates corresponding to the r largest squared canonical correlations between the residuals of X_{t-k} and ΔX_t corrected for the effect of the lagged differences of the X process.*

The likelihood ratio test statistic for the hypothesis that there are at most r cointegration vectors is

$$-2\ln(Q) = -T\sum_{i=r+1}^{p}\ln(1 - \hat{\lambda}_i), \qquad (4)$$

where $\hat{\lambda}_{r+1}, \ldots, \hat{\lambda}_p$ are the $p - r$ smallest squared canonical correlations.

PROOF. Before studying the likelihood function it is convenient to reparametrise the model (1) such that the parameter of interest Π enters explicitly. We write

$$\Delta X_t = \Gamma_1\Delta X_{t-1} + \ldots + \Gamma_{k-1}\Delta X_{t-k+1} + \Gamma_k X_{t-k} + \varepsilon_t, \qquad (5)$$

where

$$\Gamma_i = -I + \Pi_1 + \ldots + \Pi_i, \qquad i = 1, \ldots, k.$$

Then $\Pi = -\Gamma_k$, and whereas (3) gives a nonlinear constraint on the coefficients $\Pi_1, \ldots, \Pi_k$, the parameters $(\Gamma_1, \ldots, \Gamma_{k-1}, \alpha, \beta, \Lambda)$ have no constraints imposed. In this way the impact matrix Π is found as the coefficient of the lagged levels in a nonlinear least squares regression of ΔX_t on lagged differences and lagged levels. The maximisation over the parameters $\Gamma_1, \ldots, \Gamma_{k-1}$ is easy since it just leads to an ordinary least squares regression of $\Delta X_t + \alpha\beta'X_{t-k}$ on the lagged differences. Let us do this by first regressing ΔX_t on the lagged differences giving the residuals R_{0t} and then regressing X_{t-k} on the lagged differences giving the residuals R_{kt}. After having performed these regressions the concentrated likelihood function becomes proportional to

$$L(\alpha, \beta, \Lambda) = |\Lambda|^{-T/2}\exp\left\{-\tfrac{1}{2}\sum_{t=1}^{T}(R_{0t} + \alpha\beta'R_{kt})'\Lambda^{-1}(R_{0t} + \alpha\beta'R_{kt})\right\}.$$

For fixed β we can maximise over α and Λ by a usual regression of R_{0t} on $-\beta'R_{kt}$ which gives the well-known result

$$\hat{\alpha}(\beta) = -S_{0k}\beta(\beta'S_{kk}\beta)^{-1}, \qquad (6)$$

and

$$\hat{\Lambda}(\beta) = S_{00} - S_{0k}\beta(\beta'S_{kk}\beta)^{-1}\beta'S_{k0}, \qquad (7)$$

where we have defined product moment matrices of the residuals as

$$S_{ij} = T^{-1}\sum_{t=1}^{T}R_{it}R_{jt}', \qquad i, j = 0, k. \qquad (8)$$

The likelihood profile now becomes proportional to

$$|\hat{\Lambda}(\beta)|^{-T/2},$$

and it remains to solve the minimisation problem

$$\min |S_{00} - S_{0k}\beta(\beta'S_{kk}\beta)^{-1}\beta'S_{k0}|,$$

where the minimisation is over all $p \times r$ matrices β. The well-known matrix relation (see Rao 1973)

$$\begin{vmatrix} S_{00} & S_{0k}\beta \\ \beta'S_{k0} & \beta'S_{kk}\beta \end{vmatrix} = |S_{00}||\beta'S_{kk}\beta - \beta'S_{k0}S_{00}^{-1}S_{0k}\beta|$$

$$= |\beta'S_{kk}\beta||S_{00} - S_{0k}\beta(\beta'S_{kk}\beta)^{-1}\beta'S_{k0}|$$

shows that we shall minimise

$$|\beta'S_{kk}\beta - \beta'S_{k0}S_{00}^{-1}S_{0k}\beta|/|\beta'S_{kk}\beta|$$

with respect to the matrix β.

We now let D denote the diagonal matrix of ordered eigenvalues $\hat{\lambda}_1 > \ldots > \hat{\lambda}_p$ of $S_{k0}S_{00}^{-1}S_{0k}$ with respect to S_{kk}, i.e., the solutions to the equation

$$|\lambda S_{kk} - S_{k0}S_{00}^{-1}S_{0k}| = 0, \tag{9}$$

and E the matrix of the corresponding eigenvectors, then

$$S_{kk}ED = S_{k0}S_{00}^{-1}S_{0k}E,$$

where E is normalised such that

$$E'S_{kk}E = I.$$

Now choose $\beta = E\xi$ where ξ is $p \times r$, then we shall minimise

$$|\xi'\xi - \xi'D\xi|/|\xi'\xi|.$$

This can be accomplished by choosing ξ to be the first r unit vectors or by choosing $\hat{\beta}$ to be the first r eigenvectors of $S_{k0}S_{00}^{-1}S_{0k}$ with respect to S_{kk}, i.e. the first r columns of E. These are called the canonical variates and the eigenvalues are the squared canonical correlations of R_k with respect to R_0. For the details of these calculations the reader is referred to Anderson (1984, ch. 12). This type of analysis is also called reduced rank regression (see Ahn and Reinsel 1987, and Velu, Reinsel and Wichern 1986). Note that all possible choices of the optimal β can be found from $\hat{\beta}$ by $\beta = \hat{\beta}\rho$ for ρ an $r \times r$ matrix of full rank. The eigenvectors are normalised by the condition $\hat{\beta}'S_{kk}\hat{\beta} = I$ such that the estimates of the other parameters are given by

$$\hat{\alpha} = -S_{0k}\hat{\beta}(\hat{\beta}'S_{kk}\hat{\beta})^{-1} = -S_{0k}\hat{\beta}, \tag{10}$$

which clearly depends on the choice of the optimising β, whereas

$$\hat{\Pi} = -S_{0k}\hat{\beta}(\hat{\beta}'S_{kk}\hat{\beta})^{-1}\hat{\beta}' = -S_{0k}\hat{\beta}\hat{\beta}', \tag{11}$$

and

$$\hat{\Lambda} = S_{00} - S_{0k}\hat{\beta}\hat{\beta}'S_{k0} = S_{00} - \hat{\alpha}\hat{\alpha}', \tag{12}$$

and the maximised likelihood as given by

$$L_{max}^{-2/T} = |S_{00}|\prod_{i=1}^{r}(1 - \hat{\lambda}_i),$$ (13)

do not depend on the choice of optimising β.

With these results it is easy to find the estimates of Π and Λ without the constraint (3). These follow from (6) and (7) for $r = p$ and $\beta = I$ and give in particular the maximised likelihood function without the constraint (3):

$$L_{max}^{-2/T} = |S_{00}|\prod_{i=1}^{p}(1 - \hat{\lambda}_i).$$ (14)

If we now want a test that there are at most r cointegrating vectors, then the likelihood ratio test statistic is the ratio of (13) and (14) which can be expressed as (4), where $\hat{\lambda}_{r+1} > \ldots > \hat{\lambda}_p$ are the $p - r$ smallest eigenvalues. This completes the proof of Theorem 1.

Notice how this analysis allows one to calculate all p eigenvalues and eigenvectors at once, and then make inference about the number of important cointegration relations, by testing how many of the λ's are zero.

Next we shall investigate the test of a linear hypothesis about β. In this case we have $r = 1$, i.e. only one cointegration vector, it seems natural to test that certain variables do not enter into the cointegration vector, or that certain linear constraints are satisfied, for instance that the variables X_{1t} and X_{2t} only enter through their difference $X_{1t} - X_{2t}$. If $r \geq 2$, then a hypothesis of interest could be that the variables X_{1t} and X_{2t} enter through their difference only in all the cointegration vectors, since if two different linear combinations would occur then any coefficients to X_{1t} and X_{2t} would be possible. Thus it seems that some natural hypotheses on β can be formulated as

$$H_1: \beta = H\varphi,$$ (15)

where $H(p \times s)$ is a known matrix of full rank s and $\varphi(s \times r)$ is a matrix of unknown parameters. We assume that $r \leq s \leq p$. If $s = p$, then no restrictions are placed upon the choice of cointegration vectors, and if $s = r$, then the cointegration space is fully specified.

THEOREM 2. *The maximum likelihood estimator of the cointegration space, under the assumption that it is restricted to sp(H), is given as the space spanned by the canonical variates corresponding to the r largest squared canonical correlations between the residuals of $H'X_{t-k}$ and ΔX_t corrected for the lagged differences of X_t.*
The likelihood ratio test now becomes

$$-2\ln(Q) = T\sum_{i=1}^{r}\ln\{(1 - \lambda_i^*)/(1 - \hat{\lambda}_i)\}, \tag{16}$$

where $\lambda_1^*, \ldots, \lambda_r^*$ are the r largest squared canonical correlations.

PROOF. It is apparent from the derivation of $\hat{\beta}$ that if $\beta = H\varphi$ is fixed, then regression of R_{0t} on $-\varphi'H'R_{kt}$ is still a simple linear regression and the analysis is as before with R_{kt} replaced by $H'R_{kt}$. Thus the matrix φ can be estimated as the eigenvectors corresponding to the r largest eigenvalues of $H'S_{k0}S_{00}^{-1}S_{0k}H$ with respect to $H'S_{kk}H$, i.e., the solution to

$$|\lambda H'S_{kk}H - H'S_{k0}S_{00}^{-1}S_{0k}H| = 0.$$

Let the s eigenvalues be denoted by λ_i^*, $i = 1, \ldots, s$. Then the likelihood ratio test of H_1 in H_0 can be found from two expressions like (13) and is given by (16), which completes the proof of Theorem 2.

In the next section we shall find the asymptotic distribution of the test statistics (4) and (16) and show that the cointegration space, the impact matrix Π and the variance matrix Λ are estimated consistently.

3. Asymptotic Properties of the Estimators and the Test Statistics

In order to derive properties of the estimators we need to impose more precise conditions on the parameters of the model, such that they correspond to the situation we have in mind, namely of a process that is integrated of order 1, but still has r cointegration vectors β.

First of all we want all roots of $|A(z)| = 0$ to satisfy $|z| > 1$ or possibly $z = 1$. This implies that the nonstationarity of the process can be removed by differencing. Next we shall assume that X_t is integrated of order 1, i.e. that ΔX_t is stationary and that the hypothesis (3) is satisfied by some α and β of full rank r. Correspondingly we can express ΔX_t in terms of the ε's by its moving average representation,

$$\Delta X_t = \sum_{j=0}^{\infty} C_j\varepsilon_{t-j},$$

for some exponentially decreasing coefficients C_j. Under suitable conditions on these coefficients it is known that this equation determines an error correction model of the form (5), where $\Gamma_k X_{t-k} = -\Pi X_{t-k}$ represents the error correction term containing the stationary components of X_{t-k}, i.e. $\beta'X_{t-k}$. Moreover, the null space for $C' = \sum_{j=0}^{\infty}C_j'$ given by $\{\xi|C'\xi = 0\}$ is exactly the range space of Γ_k', i.e., the space spanned by the columns in β and vice versa. We thus have the following representations:

$$\Pi = \alpha\beta' \quad \text{and} \quad C = \gamma\tau\delta', \tag{17}$$

where τ is $(p - r) \times (p - r)$, γ and δ are $p \times (p - r)$, and all three are of full rank, and $\gamma'\beta = \delta'\alpha = 0$. We shall later choose δ in a convenient way (see the references to Granger 1981, Granger and Engle 1985, Engle and Granger 1987, or Johansen 1988 for the details of these results).

We shall now formulate the main results of this section in the form of two theorems which deal with the test statistics derived in the previous section. First we have a result about the test statistic (4) and the estimators derived in (11) and (12).

THEOREM 3. *Under the hypothesis that there are r cointegrating vectors the estimate of the cointegration space as well as Π and Λ are consistent, and the likelihood ratio test statistic of this hypothesis is asymptotically distributed as*

$$\text{tr}\left\{\int_0^1 dBB'\left[\int_0^1 BB'du\right]^{-1}\int_0^1 BdB'\right\}, \tag{18}$$

where B is a $(p - r)$-dimensional Brownian motion with covariance matrix I.

In order to understand the structure of this limit distribution one should notice that if B is a Brownian motion with I as the covariance matrix, then the stochastic integral $\int_0^t BdB'$ is a matrix-valued martingale, with quadratic variation process

$$\int_0^t \text{var}(Bdb') = \int_0^t BB'du \otimes I,$$

where the integral $\int_0^t BB'du$ is an ordinary integral of the continuous matrix-valued process BB'. With this notation the limit distribution in Theorem 3 can be considered a multivariate version of the square of a martingale $\int_0^t BdB'$ divided by its variance process $\int_0^t BB'du$. Notice that for $r = p - 1$, i.e. for testing $p - 1$ cointegration relations one obtains the limit distribution with a one-dimensional Brownian motion, i.e.

$$\left(\int_0^1 BdB\right)^2 \bigg/ \int_0^1 B^2 du = ((B(1)^2 - 1)/2)^2 \bigg/ \int_0^1 B^2 du,$$

which is the square of the usual 'unit root' distribution (see Dickey and Fuller 1979). A similar reduction is found by Phillips and Ouliaris (1987) in their work on tests for cointegration based on residuals. The distribution of the test statistic (18) is found by simulation and given in table 1.

TABLE 1.   The quantiles in the distribution of the test statistic,

$$\text{tr}\left\{\int_0^1 dBB'\left(\int_0^1 B(u)B(u)'\,du\right)^{-1}\int_0^1 B\,dB'\right\},$$

where B is an m-dimensional Brownian motion with covariance matrix I.

m	2.5%	5%	10%	50%	90%	95%	97.5%
1	0.0	0.0	0.0	0.6	2.9	4.2	5.3
2	1.6	1.9	2.5	5.4	10.3	12.0	13.9
3	7.0	7.8	8.8	14.0	21.2	23.8	26.1
4	16.0	17.4	19.2	26.3	35.6	38.6	41.2
5	28.3	30.4	32.8	42.1	53.6	57.2	60.3

A surprisingly accurate description of the results in table 1 is obtained by approximating the distributions by $c\chi^2(f)$ for suitable values of c and f. By equating the mean of the distributions based on 10,000 observations to those of $c\chi^2$ with $f = 2m^2$ degrees of freedom, we obtain values of c, and it turns out that we can use the empirical relation

$$c = 0.85 - 0.58/f.$$

Notice that the hypothesis of r cointegrating relations reduces the number of parameters in the Π matrix from p^2 to $rp + r(p - r)$, thus one could expect $(p - r)^2$ degrees of freedom if the usual asymptotics would hold. In the case of nonstationary processes it is known that this does not hold but a very good approximation is given by the above choice of $2(p - r)^2$ degrees of freedom.

Next we shall consider the test of the restriction (15) where linear constraints are imposed on β.

THEOREM 4.   *The likelihood ratio test of the hypothesis*

$$H_1: \quad \beta = H\varphi$$

of restricting the r-dimensional cointegration space to an s-dimensional subspace of R^p is asymptotically distributed as χ^2 with $r(p - s)$ degrees of freedom.

We shall now give the proof of these theorems, through a series of intermediate results. We shall first give some expressions for variances and their limits, then show how the algorithm for deriving the maximum likelihood estimator can be followed by a probabilistic analysis ending up with the asymptotic properties of the estimator and the test statistics.

We can represent X_t as $X_t = \sum_{j=1}^{t} \Delta X_j$, where X_0 is a constant which we shall take to be zero to simplify the notation. We shall describe the stationary process ΔX_t by its covariance function

$$\psi(i) = \text{var}(\Delta X_t, \Delta X_{t+i}),$$

and we define the matrices

$$\mu_{ij} = \psi(i - j) = E(\Delta X_{t-i} \Delta X'_{t-j}), \quad i, j = 0, \ldots, k - 1,$$

$$\mu_{ki} = \sum_{j=k-i}^{\infty} \psi(j), \quad i = 0, \ldots, k - 1,$$

and

$$\mu_{kk} = - \sum_{j=-\infty}^{\infty} |j| \psi(j).$$

Finally define

$$\psi = \sum_{j=-\infty}^{\infty} \psi(j).$$

Note the following relations:

$$\psi(i) = \sum_{j=0}^{\infty} C_j \Lambda C'_{j+i},$$

$$\psi = \sum_{j=0}^{\infty} C_j \Lambda \sum_{j=0}^{\infty} C'_j = C \Lambda C',$$

$$\text{var}(X_{t-k}) = \sum_{j=-t+k}^{t-k} (t - k - |j|) \psi(j),$$

$$\text{cov}(X_{t-k}, \Delta X_{t-i}) = \sum_{j=k-i}^{t-i} \psi(j),$$

which show that

$$\text{var}(X_T/T^{1/2}) \rightarrow \sum_{i=-\infty}^{\infty} \psi(i) = \psi,$$

and

$$\text{cov}(X_{T-k}, \Delta X_{T-i}) \rightarrow \sum_{j=k-i}^{\infty} \psi(j) = \mu_{ki},$$

whereas the relation

$$\text{var}(\beta' X_{T-k}) = (T - k) \sum_{j=-T+k}^{T-k} \beta' \psi(j) \beta - \sum_{j=-T+k}^{T-k} |j| \beta' \psi(j) \beta$$

shows that

$$\text{var}\,(\beta'X_{T-k}) \to \beta'\mu_{kk}\beta,$$

since $\beta'C = 0$ implies that $\beta'\psi = 0$, such that the first term vanishes in the limit. Note that the nonstationary part of X_t makes the variance matrix tend to infinity, except for the directions given by the vectors in β, since $\beta'X_t$ is stationary.

The calculations involved in the maximum likelihood estimation all centre around the product moment matrices

$$M_{ij} = T^{-1}\sum_{t=1}^{T} \Delta X_{t-i}\Delta X'_{t-j}, \qquad i,j = 0,\ldots, k-1,$$

$$M_{ki} = T^{-1}\sum_{t=1}^{T} X_{t-k}\Delta X'_{t-1}, \qquad i = 0,\ldots, k-1,$$

$$M_{kk} = T^{-1}\sum_{t=1}^{T} X_{t-k}X'_{t-k}.$$

We shall first give the asymptotic behaviour of these matrices, then find the asymptotic properties of S_{ij} and finally apply these results to the estimators and the test statistic. The methods are inspired by Phillips (1985) even though I shall stick to the Gaussian case, which make the arguments somewhat simpler.

The following lemma can be derived by the results in Phillips and Durlauf (1986). We let W be a Brownian motion in p dimensions with covariance matrix Λ.

LEMMA 1.   *As $t \to \infty$, we have*

$$T^{-1/2}X_{[Tt]} \xrightarrow{\ W\ } CW(t), \tag{19}$$

$$M_{ij} \xrightarrow{\text{a.s.}} \mu_{ij}, \quad i,j = 0,\ldots, k-1, \tag{20}$$

$$M_{ki} \xrightarrow{\ W\ } C\int_0^1 W\,dW'C' + \mu_{ki}, \quad i = 0,\ldots, k-1, \tag{21}$$

$$\beta'M_{kk}\beta \xrightarrow{\text{a.s.}} \beta'\mu_{kk}\beta, \tag{22}$$

$$T^{-1}M_{kk} \xrightarrow{\ W\ } C\int_0^1 W(u)W'(u)\,du\,C'. \tag{23}$$

Note that for any $\xi \in R^p$, $\xi'M_{kk}\xi$ is of the order in probability of T unless ξ is in the space spanned by β, in which case it is convergent. Note also that the stochastic integrals enter as limits of the nonstationary part of the process X_t, and that they disappear when multiplied by β since $\beta'C = 0$.

We shall apply the results to find the asymptotic properties of S_{ij}, i, $j = 0$, k, see (8). These can be expressed in terms of the M_{ij}'s as follows:

$$S_{ij} = M_{ij} - M_{i*}M_{**}^{-1}M_{*j}, \qquad i, j = 0, k,$$

where

$$M_* = \{M_{ij}, \ i, j = 1, \ldots, k - 1\},$$
$$M_{k*} = \{M_{ki}, \ i = 1, \ldots, k - 1\},$$
$$M_{0*} = \{M_{0i}, \ i = 1, \ldots, k - 1\}.$$

A similar notation is introduced for the μ_{ij}'s. It is convenient to have the notation

$$\textstyle\sum ij = \mu_{ij} - \mu_{i*}\mu_{**}^{-1}\mu_{*j}, \qquad i, j = 0, k.$$

We now get:

LEMMA 2.   *The following relations hold*

$$\Sigma_{00} = \Gamma_k\Sigma_{k0} + \Lambda, \tag{24}$$

$$\Sigma_{0k}\Gamma'_k = \Gamma_k\Sigma_{kk}\Gamma'_k, \tag{25}$$

and hence, since $\Gamma_k = -\alpha\beta'$.

$$\Sigma_{00} = \alpha(\beta'\Sigma_{kk}\beta)\alpha' + \Lambda \text{ and } \alpha = -\Sigma_{0k}\beta(\beta'\Sigma_{kk}\beta)^{-1}. \tag{26}$$

PROOF   From the defining eq. (5) for the process X_t we find the equations

$$M_{0i} = \Gamma_1 M_{1i} + \ldots + \Gamma_{k-1}M_{k-1,i} + \Gamma_k M_{ki} + T^{-1}\sum_{t=1}^{T} \varepsilon_t\Delta X'_{t-i}, \tag{27}$$

$i = 0, 1, \ldots, k - 1$, and

$$M_{0k} = \Gamma_1 M_{1k} + \ldots + \Gamma_{k-1}M_{k-1,k} + \Gamma_k M_{kk} + T^{-1}\sum_{t=1}^{T} \varepsilon_t X'_{t-k}. \tag{28}$$

Now let $T \to \infty$, then we get the equations

$$\mu_{00} = \Gamma_1\mu_{10} + \ldots + \Gamma_{k-1}\mu_{k-1,0} + \Gamma_k\mu_{k0} + \Lambda, \tag{29}$$

$$\mu_{0i} = \Gamma_1\mu_{1i} + \ldots + \Gamma_{k-1}\mu_{k-1,i} + \Gamma_k\mu_{ki}, \quad i = 1, \ldots, k - 1, \tag{30}$$

$$\mu_{0k}\beta = \Gamma_1\mu_{1k}\beta + \ldots + \Gamma_{k-1}\mu_{k-1,k}\beta + \Gamma_k\mu_{kk}\beta. \tag{31}$$

If we solve the eq. (30) for the matrices Γ_* and insert into (29) and (31), we get (24), (25), and (26).

We shall now find the asymptotic properties of S_{ij}.

LEMMA 3.   *For* $T \to \infty$, *it holds that, if* δ *is chosen such that* $\delta'\alpha = 0$, *then*

$$S_{00} \xrightarrow{\text{a.s.}} \Sigma_{00}, \tag{32}$$

$$\delta' S_{0k} \xrightarrow{\text{w}} \delta' \int_0^1 dW W' C', \tag{33}$$

$$\beta' S_{k0} \xrightarrow{\text{a.s.}} \beta' \Sigma_{k0}, \tag{34}$$

$$T^{-1} S_{kk} \xrightarrow{\text{w}} C \int_0^1 W(u) W'(u) \, du C'. \tag{35}$$

$$\beta' S_{kk} \beta \xrightarrow{\text{a.s.}} \beta' \Sigma_{kk} \beta. \tag{36}$$

PROOF. All relations follow from Lemma 1 except the second. If we solve for Γ_* in the eq. (27), insert the solution into (28), and use the definition of S_{ij} in terms of the M's, then we get

$$S_{0k} = T^{-1} \sum_{t=1}^{T} \varepsilon_t X'_{t-k} + \Gamma_k S_{kk} - \sum_{i=1}^{k-1} \sum_{j=1}^{k-1} T^{-1} \sum_{t=1}^{T} \varepsilon_t \Delta X'_{t-i} M^{ij} M_{jk}. \tag{37}$$

The last term goes a.s. to zero as $T \to \infty$, since ε_t and $\Delta X'_{t-i}$ are stationary and uncorrelated. The second term vanishes when multiplied by δ', since $\delta' \Gamma_k = -\delta' \alpha \beta' = 0$, and the first term converges to the integral as stated.

LEMMA 4. *The ordered eigenvalues of the equation*

$$|\lambda S_{kk} - S_{k0} S_{00}^{-1} S_{0k}| = 0 \tag{38}$$

converge in probability to $(\lambda_1, \ldots, \lambda_r, 0, \ldots, 0)$, *where* $\lambda_1, \ldots, \lambda_r$ *are the ordered eigenvalues of the equation*

$$|\lambda \beta' \Sigma_{kk} \beta - \beta' \Sigma_{k0} \Sigma_{00}^{-1} \Sigma_{0k} \beta| = 0. \tag{39}$$

PROOF. We want to express the problem in the coordinates given by the p vectors in β and γ, where γ is of full rank $p - r$ and $\gamma' \beta = 0$. This can be done by multiplying (9) by $|(\beta, \gamma)'|$ and $|(\beta, \gamma)|$ from the left and right, then the eigenvalues solve the equation

$$\left| \lambda \begin{bmatrix} \beta' S_{kk} \beta & \beta' S_{kk} \gamma \\ \gamma' S_{kk} \beta & \gamma' S_{kk} \gamma \end{bmatrix} - \begin{bmatrix} \beta' S_{k0} S_{00}^{-1} S_{0k} \beta & \beta' S_{k0} S_{00}^{-1} S_{0k} \gamma \\ \gamma' S_{k0} S_{00}^{-1} S_{0k} \beta & \gamma' S_{k0} S_{00}^{-1} S_{0k} \gamma \end{bmatrix} \right| = 0.$$

We define $A_T = (\gamma' S_{kk} \gamma)^{-1/2}$ so that by (35), $A_T \xrightarrow{\text{P}} 0$. Then the eigenvalues have to satisfy the equation

$$\left| \lambda \begin{bmatrix} \beta' S_{kk} \beta & \beta' S_{kk} \gamma A_T \\ A'_T \gamma' S_{kk} \beta & I \end{bmatrix} \right.$$

$$\left. - \begin{bmatrix} \beta' S_{k0} S_{00}^{-1} S_{0k} \beta & \beta' S_{k0} S_{00}^{-1} S_{0k} \gamma A_T \\ A'_T \gamma' S_{k0} S_{00}^{-1} S_{0k} \beta & A'_T \gamma' S_{k0} S_{00}^{-1} S_{0k} \gamma A_T \end{bmatrix} \right| = 0.$$

The coefficient matrices converge in probability by the results in Lemma 3, and the limiting equation is

$$\left| \lambda \begin{bmatrix} \beta'\Sigma_{kk}\beta & 0 \\ 0 & I \end{bmatrix} - \begin{bmatrix} \beta'\Sigma_{k0}\Sigma_{00}^{-1}\Sigma_{0k}\beta & 0 \\ 0 & 0 \end{bmatrix} \right| = 0,$$

or

$$\left| \lambda\beta'\Sigma_{kk}\beta - \beta'\Sigma_{k0}\Sigma_{00}^{-1}\Sigma_{k}\beta \right| |\lambda I| = 0,$$

where I is an identity matrix of dimension $p - r$, which means that the equation has $p - r$ roots at $\lambda = 0$. It is known that the ordered eigenvalues are continuous functions of the coefficient matrices (see Andersson, Brøns and Jensen 1983), and hence the statement of Lemma 4 is proved.

We shall need one more technical lemma before we can prove the more useful results. We decompose the eigenvectors $\hat{\beta}$ as follows: $\hat{\beta}_i = \beta\hat{x}_i + \gamma\hat{y}_i$, where $\hat{x}_i = (\beta'\beta)^{-1}\beta'\hat{\beta}_i$ and $y_i = (\gamma'\gamma)^{-1}\gamma'\hat{\beta}_i$. Let $\hat{x} = (\hat{x}_1, \ldots, \hat{x}_r) = (\beta'\beta)^{-1}\beta'\hat{\beta}$. Note that although we have proved that the eigenvalues λ_i are convergent, the same cannot hold for the eigenvectors $\hat{\beta}_i$ or $\hat{x}_i$, since if the limiting eq. (39) has multiple roots then the eigenvectors are not uniquely defined. This complicates the formulation below somewhat. Let

$$S(\lambda) = \lambda S_{kk} - S_{k0}S_{00}^{-1}S_{0k}.$$

LEMMA 5.   *For* $i = 1, \ldots, r$, *we have*

$$\gamma'S(\hat{\lambda}_i)\gamma/T \xrightarrow{W} \lambda_i\gamma'C\int_0^1 WW'\,duC'\gamma, \tag{40}$$

$$\hat{y}_i \in O_P(T^{-1}), \qquad \hat{x} \in O_P(1), \qquad \hat{x}^{-1} \in O_P(1), \tag{41}$$

$$\beta'S(\hat{\lambda}_i)\beta\hat{x}_i \in O_p(T^{-1}) \tag{42}$$

$$\gamma'S(\hat{\lambda}_i)\beta\hat{x}_i = -\gamma'\left[T^{-1}\sum_{t=1}^{T} X_{t-k}\varepsilon_t' \right]\Sigma_{00}^{-1}\Sigma_{0k}\beta\hat{x}_i + O_p(1). \tag{43}$$

PROOF.   The relation (40) follows directly from (35) in Lemma 3, since by Lemma 4, $\hat{\lambda}_i \xrightarrow{P} \lambda_i > 0$.

The normalisation $\hat{\beta}'S_{kk}\hat{\beta}_i = I$ implies by an argument similar to that of Lemma 4 for the eigenvalues of S_{kk} that $\hat{\beta}$ and hence $\hat{x}_i$ is bounded in probability. The eigenvectors $\hat{\beta}_i$ and eigenvalues $\hat{\lambda}_i$ satisfy

$$\beta'S(\hat{\lambda}_i)\beta\hat{x}_i + \beta'S(\hat{\lambda}_i)\gamma\hat{y}_i = 0, \tag{44}$$

$$\gamma'S(\hat{\lambda}_i)\beta\hat{x}_i + \gamma'S(\hat{\lambda}_i)\gamma\hat{y}_i = 0. \tag{45}$$

Now (40) and (45) imply that $\hat{y}_i \in O_p(T^{-1})$, and hence from (44) we find that $\beta'S(\hat{\lambda}_i)\beta\hat{x}_i \in O_p(T^{-1})$, which shows (42), and also from the normalising condition, that $\hat{x}'\beta'S_{kk}\beta\hat{x} \xrightarrow{P} I$. Hence $|\hat{x}|^2|\beta'S_{kk}\beta| \xrightarrow{P} 1$, which implies that also $\hat{x}^{-1}$ is bounded in probability, which proves (41). From (37) it follows that

$$\gamma'S_{k0} + \gamma'S_{kk}\beta\alpha' = \gamma'T^{-1}\sum_{t=1}^{T} X_{t-k}\varepsilon'_t + r_P(1).$$

Now replace $\alpha = -\Sigma_{0k}\beta(\beta'\Sigma_{kk}\beta)^{-1}$ [see (26)] by the consistent estimate $-S_{0k}\beta(\beta'S_{kk}\beta)^{-1}$, then

$$\gamma'S(\hat{\lambda}_i)\beta\hat{x}_i = \gamma'S_{kk}\beta(\beta'S_{kk}\beta)^{-1}(\hat{\lambda}_i\beta'S_{kk}\beta - \beta'S_{k0}S_{00}^{-1}S_{0k}\beta)\hat{x}_i$$

$$- \gamma'T^{-1}\sum_{t=1}^{T} X_{t-k}\varepsilon'_t\Sigma_{00}^{-1}\Sigma_{0k}\beta\hat{x}_i + O_P(1).$$

The first term contains the factor $\beta'S(\hat{\lambda}_i)\beta\hat{x}_i$ which tends to zero in probability by (42). This completes the proof of Lemma 5.

We shall now choose δ of dimension $p \times (p - r)$ such that $\delta'\alpha = 0$ [see (17)] in the following way. We let $P_\alpha(\Lambda)$ denote the projection of R^p onto the column space spanned by α with respect to the matrix Λ^{-1}, i.e.

$$P_\alpha(\Lambda) = \alpha(\alpha'\Lambda^{-1}\alpha)^{-1}\alpha'\Lambda^{-1}$$

We then choose δ of full rank $p - r$ to satisfy

$$\delta\delta' = \Lambda^{-1}(I - P_\alpha(\Lambda)).$$

Note that $\delta'\alpha = 0$, and that $\delta'\Lambda\delta = I$ of dimension $(p - r) \times (p - r)$. Note also that $P_\alpha(\Lambda) = P_\alpha(\Sigma_{00})$ since Σ_{00} is given by (26). This relation is well known from the theory of random coefficient regression (see Rao 1965 or Johansen 1984).

LEMMA 6. *For $T \to \infty$, we have that $T\hat{\lambda}_{r+1}, \ldots, T\hat{\lambda}_p$ converge in distribution to the ordered eigenvalues of the equation*

$$\left| \lambda\int_0^1 BB'du - \int_0^1 BdB'\int_0^1 dBB' \right| = 0, \tag{46}$$

where B is a Brownian motion in $p - r$ dimensions with covariance matrix I.

PROOF. We shall consider the ordered eigenvalues of the equation

$$\left| \begin{bmatrix} \beta'S_{kk}\beta/T & \beta'S_{kk}\gamma/T \\ \gamma'S_{kk}\beta/T & \gamma'S_{kk}\gamma/T \end{bmatrix} - \mu\begin{bmatrix} \beta'S_{k0}S_{00}^{-1}S_{0k}\beta & \beta'S_{k0}S_{00}^{-1}S_{0k}\gamma \\ \gamma'S_{k0}S_{00}^{-1}S_{0k}\beta & \gamma'S_{k0}S_{00}^{-1}S_{0k}\gamma \end{bmatrix} \right| = 0.$$

For any value of T the ordered eigenvalues are

$$\hat{\mu}_1 = (T\hat{\lambda}_p)^{-1}, \ldots, \hat{\mu}_p = (T\hat{\lambda}_1)^{-1}.$$

Since the ordered eigenvalues are continuous functions of the coefficients, we find from Lemma 3 that $\hat{\mu}_1, \ldots, \hat{\mu}_p$ converge in distribution to the ordered eigenvalues from the equation

$$\left| \begin{bmatrix} 0 & 0 \\ 0 & \gamma' C \int_0^1 WW' \, du C' \gamma \end{bmatrix} - \mu \begin{bmatrix} \beta' \Sigma_{k0} \Sigma_{00}^{-1} \Sigma_{0k} \beta & \beta' \Sigma_{k0} \Sigma_{00}^{-1} F \\ F' \Sigma_{00}^{-1} \Sigma_{0k} \beta & F' \Sigma_{00}^{-1} F \end{bmatrix} \right| = 0$$

where F is the weak limit of $S_{0k} \gamma$.

This determinant can also be written as

$$|\mu \beta' \Sigma_{k0} \Sigma_{00}^{-1} \Sigma_{0k} \beta| \left| \gamma' C \int_0^1 WW' \, du C' \gamma \right.$$
$$\left. - \mu F' [\Sigma_{00}^{-1} - \Sigma_{00}^{-1} \Sigma_{0k} \beta (\beta' \Sigma_{k0} \Sigma_{00}^{-1} \Sigma_{0k} \beta)^{-1} \beta' \Sigma_{k0} \Sigma_{00}^{-1}] F \right|, \qquad (47)$$

which shows that in the limit there are r roots at zero. Now apply (24) and (25) of Lemma 2 and find that

$$\Sigma_{00}^{-1} - \Sigma_{00}^{-1} \Sigma_{0k} \beta (\beta' \Sigma_{k0} \Sigma_{00}^{-1} \Sigma_{0k} \beta)^{-1} \beta' \Sigma_{k0} \Sigma_{00}^{-1}$$

equals

$$\Sigma_{00}^{-1} (I - P_\alpha(\Sigma_{00})) = \Lambda^{-1} (I - P_\alpha(\Lambda)) = \delta \delta',$$

and hence that the second factor of (47) is

$$\left| \gamma' C \int_0^1 WW' \, du C' \gamma - \mu F' \delta \delta' F \right|,$$

which by (33) equals

$$\left| \gamma' C \int_0^1 WW' \, du C' \gamma - \mu \gamma' C \int_0^1 W \, dW' \delta \delta' \int_0^1 dWW' C' \gamma \right|. \qquad (48)$$

Thus the limiting distribution of the $p - r$ largest μ's is given as the distribution of the order eigenvalues of (48).

The representation (17): $C = \gamma \tau \delta'$ for some nonsingular matrix τ now implies, since $|\gamma' \gamma| \neq 0$ and $|\tau| \neq 0$, that

$$\left| \delta' \int_0^1 WW' \, du \delta - \mu \delta' \int_0^1 W \, dW' \delta \delta' \int_0^1 dWW' \delta \right| = 0. \qquad (49)$$

Now $B = \delta' W$ is a Brownian motion with variance $\delta' \Delta \delta = I$, and the result of Lemma 6 is found by noting that the solution of (46) are the reciprocal values of the solutions to the above equation.

COROLLARY. *The test statistic for* $H_0: \Pi = \alpha\beta'$ *given by (4) will converge in distribution to the sum of the eigenvalues given by (46), i.e. the limiting distribution is given by (18):*

$$\mathrm{tr}\left\{\int_0^1 dBB'\left(\int_0^1 BB'du\right)^{-1}\int_0^1 BdB'\right\}.$$

PROOF. We just expand the test statistic (4),

$$-2\ln(Q) = -T\sum_{i=r+1}^p \ln(1-\hat{\lambda}_i) = \sum_{i=r+1}^p T\hat{\lambda}_i + o_P(1),$$

and apply Lemma 6.

We can now complete the proof of Theorem 3.

The asymptotic distribution of the test statistic (4) follows from the above corollary, and the consistency of the cointegration space and the estimators of Π and Λ is proved as follows. We decompose $\hat{\beta} = \beta\hat{x} + \gamma\hat{y}$, and it then follows from (41) that $\hat{\beta}\hat{x}^{-1} - \beta = \gamma\hat{y}\hat{x}^{-1} \in O_P(T^{-1})$. Thus we have seen that the projection of β on to the orthogonal complement of $\mathrm{sp}(\beta)$ tends to zero in probability of the order of T^{-1}. In this sense the cointegration space is consistently estimated. From (11) we find

$$\hat{\Pi} = -S_{0k}\hat{\beta}(\hat{\beta}S_{kk}\hat{\beta})^{-1}\hat{\beta}' = -S_{0k}\hat{\beta}\hat{x}^{-1}\left((\hat{\beta}\hat{x}^{-1})'S_{kk}\hat{\beta}\hat{x}^{-1}\right)^{-1}(\hat{\beta}\hat{x}^{-1})',$$

which converges in probability to

$$-\Sigma_{0k}\beta(\beta'\Sigma_{kk}\beta)^{-1}\beta' = \alpha\beta' = \Pi.$$

From (12) we get by a similar trick that

$$\hat{\Lambda} = S_{00} - S_{0k}\hat{\beta}(\hat{\beta}'S_{kk}\hat{\beta})^{-1}\hat{\beta}'S_{k0}$$

$$\xrightarrow{P} \Sigma_{00} - \Sigma_{0k}\beta(\beta'\Sigma_{kk}\beta)^{-1}\beta'\Sigma_{k0} = \Sigma_{00} - \alpha(\beta'\Sigma_{kk}\beta)\alpha',$$

which by (26) equals Λ. This completes the proof of Theorem 3.

In order to prove the Theorem 4 we shall need an expansion of the likelihood function around a point where the maximum is attained. We formulate this as a lemma:

LEMMA 7. *Let A and B be $p \times p$ symmetric positive definite matrices, and define the function*

$$f(z) = \ln\{|z'Az|/|z'Bz|\},$$

where z is a $p \times r$ matrix. If z is a point where the function attains its maximum or minimum, then for any $p \times r$ matrix h we have

$$f(z+h) = f(z) + \mathrm{tr}\{(z'Az)^{-1}h'Ah - (z'Bz)^{-1}h'Bh\} + O(h^3).$$

PROOF. This is easily seen by expanding the terms in f using that the first derivative vanishes at z.

We shall now give the asymptotic distribution of the maximum likelihood estimator $\hat{\beta}$ suitably normalised. This is not a very useful result in practice, since the normalisation depends on β, but it is convenient for deriving other results of interest.

LEMMA 8. *The maximum likelihood estimate $\hat{\beta}$ has the representation*

$$T[\hat{\beta}(\beta'\hat{\beta})^{-1}\beta'\beta - \beta] =$$

$$= \gamma(\gamma'S_{kk}\gamma/T)^{-1}\gamma'\left[T^{-1}\sum_{t=1}^{T}X_{t-k}\varepsilon_t'\right]\Sigma_{00}^{-1}\Sigma_{0k}\beta(\beta'\Sigma_{k0}\beta)^{-1}$$

$$\times \beta'\Sigma_{kk}\beta + o_P(1), \tag{50}$$

which converges in distribution to

$$\gamma\left(\int_0^1 UU'du\right)^{-1}\int_0^1 U\,dV',$$

where U and V are independent Brownian motions given by

$$U = \gamma'CW \tag{51}$$

$$V = \beta'\Sigma_{kk}\beta(\beta'\Sigma_{k0}\Sigma_{00}^{-1}\Sigma_{0k}\beta)^{-1}\beta'\Sigma_{k0}\Sigma_{00}^{-1}W. \tag{52}$$

The variance of V is given by

$$\mathrm{var}(V) = \beta'\Sigma_{kk}\beta(\beta'\Sigma_{k0}\Sigma_{00}^{-1}\Sigma_{0k}\beta)^{-1}\beta'\Sigma_{kk}\beta - \beta'\Sigma_{kk}\beta. \tag{53}$$

Note that the limiting distribution for fixed U is Gaussian with mean zero and variance

$$\gamma\int_0^1 UU'du\gamma' \otimes \mathrm{var}(V).$$

Thus the limiting distribution is a mixture of Gaussian distributions. This will be used in the derivation of the limiting distributions of the test statistics (see Lemma 9).

PROOF. From the decomposition $\hat{\beta}_i = \beta\hat{x}_i + \gamma\hat{y}_i$ we have from (45)

$$T(\hat{\beta}_i - \beta\hat{x}_i) = T\gamma\hat{y}_i = -T\gamma(\gamma'S(\hat{\lambda}_i)\gamma)^{-1}(\gamma'S(\hat{\lambda}_i)\beta)\hat{x}_i.$$

It follows from (40) and (43) in Lemma 5 that this can be written as

$$\gamma(\gamma'S_{kk}\gamma/T)^{-1}\gamma'\left[T^{-1}\sum_{t=1}^{T}X_{t-k}\varepsilon_t'\right]\Sigma_{00}^{-1}\Sigma_{0k}\beta\hat{x}_i\hat{\lambda}_i^{-1} + o_P(1).$$

Hence for $\hat{x} = (\hat{x}_1, \ldots, \hat{x}_r) = (\beta'\beta)^{-1}\beta'\hat{\beta}$ and $\hat{D}_r = \mathrm{diag}(\hat{\lambda}_1, \ldots, \hat{\lambda}_r)$,

$$T(\hat{\beta} - \beta\hat{x}) =$$

$$\gamma(\gamma'S_{kk}\gamma/T)^{-1}\gamma'\left[T^{-1}\sum_{t=1}^{T} X_{t-k}\varepsilon_t'\right]\Sigma_{00}^{-1}\Sigma_{0k}\beta\hat{x}\hat{D}_r^{-1} + o_P(1). \quad (54)$$

Now multiply by $\hat{x}^{-1}$ from the right and note that it follows from (42) that

$$\beta'S_{kk}\beta\hat{x}\hat{D}_r - \beta'S_{k0}S_{00}^{-1}S_{0k}\beta\hat{x} \in o_P(1),$$

which show that

$$\hat{x}\hat{D}^{-1}\hat{x}^{-1} \xrightarrow{\text{P}} (\beta'\Sigma_{k0}\Sigma_{00}^{-1}\Sigma_{0k}\beta)^{-1}\beta'\Sigma_{kk}\beta.$$

Now insert this into (54) and we obtain the representation (50), which converges as indicated with U and V defined as in (51) and (52). The variance matrix for V is calculated from (52) using the relation (26). Similarly, the independence follows from (26).

LEMMA 9. *The likelihood ratio test of the hypothesis of a completely specified β has an asymptotic representation of the form*

$$-2\ln(Q) = T\,\text{tr}\,\{\text{var}(V)^{-1}(\hat{\beta}(\beta'\hat{\beta})^{-1}\beta'\beta - \beta)'$$
$$\times S_{kk}(\hat{\beta}(\beta'\hat{\beta})^{-1}\beta'\beta - \beta)\} + o_P(1), \quad (55)$$

which converges weakly to

$$\text{tr}\left\{\text{var}(V)^{-1}\int_0^1 dVU'\left(\int_0^1 UU'du\right)^{-1}\int_0^1 UdV'\right\}, \quad (56)$$

where U and V are given by (51) and (52).
The statistic (56) has a χ^2 distribution with $r(p - r)$ degrees of freedom.

PROOF. The likelihood ratio test statistic of a simple hypothesis about β has the form

$$T\{\ln\,[|\beta'(S_{kk} - S_{k0}S_{00}^{-1}S_{0k})\beta|/|\beta'S_{kk}\beta|]$$
$$-\ln\,[|\hat{\beta}'(S_{kk} - S_{k0}S_{00}^{-1}S_{0k})\hat{\beta}|/|\hat{\beta}'S_{kk}\hat{\beta}|]\}.$$

Now replace $\hat{\beta}$ by $\hat{\beta}\hat{x}^{-1} = \tilde{\beta}$, say, which is also a maximum point for the likelihood function. Then the statistic takes the form $T\{f(\beta) - f(\tilde{\beta})\}$ for af02 and $B = S_{kk}$ (see Lemma 7). By the result in Lemma 7 it follows that this can be expressed as

$$T\,\text{tr}\,\{(\tilde{\beta}'A\tilde{\beta})^{-1}(\tilde{\beta} - \beta)'A(\tilde{\beta} - \beta) - (\tilde{\beta}'B\tilde{\beta})^{-1}(\tilde{\beta} - \beta)'B(\tilde{\beta} - \beta)\}$$
$$+ O_P(T(\tilde{\beta} - \beta)^3)$$
$$= T\,\text{tr}\,\{[(\tilde{\beta}'A\tilde{\beta})^{-1} - (\tilde{\beta}'B\tilde{\beta})^{-1}](\tilde{\beta} - \beta)'S_{kk}(\tilde{\beta} - \beta)\}$$
$$- T\,\text{tr}\,\{(\tilde{\beta}'A\tilde{\beta})^{-1}(\tilde{\beta} - \beta)'S_{k0}S_{00}^{-1}S_{0k}(\tilde{\beta} - \beta)\} + O_P(T(\tilde{\beta} - \beta)^3).$$

Now use the result from Lemma 8 that $\tilde{\beta} - \beta \in O_P(T^{-1})$ to see that the last two terms tend to zero in probability. We also get

$$[\tilde{\beta}'(S_{kk} - S_{k0}S_{00}^{-1}S_{0k})\tilde{\beta}]^{-1} - [\tilde{\beta}'S_{kk}\tilde{\beta}]^{-1}$$

$$\xrightarrow{P} [\beta'(\Sigma_{kk} - \Sigma_{k0}\Sigma_{00}^{-1}\Sigma_{0k})\beta]^{-1} - [\beta'\Sigma_{kk}\beta]^{-1} = \mathrm{var}\,(V)^{-1}.$$

Finally, we note that $T(\tilde{\beta} - \beta)'S_{kk}(\tilde{\beta} - \beta)$ converges in distribution to

$$\int_0^1 dV U' \left(\int_0^1 UU' du\right)^{-1} \int_0^1 U dV'.$$

Now use the fact that for given value of U the $(p - r) \times r$ matrix $\int_0^1 U dV'$ is Gaussian with mean zero and variance matrix

$$\int_0^1 UU' du \otimes \mathrm{var}\,(V),$$

hence the distribution of (56) for fixed U is χ^2 with $(p - r)r$ degrees of freedom. Since this result holds independently of the given value of U it also holds marginally. This basic independence and the conditioning argument is also used in the work of Phillips and Park (1986b) in the discussion of the regression estimates for integrated processes.

We can now finally give the proof of Theorem 4.

We want to test the hypothesis H_1: $\beta = H\varphi$.

We now choose $\psi(s \times (s - r))$ to supplement $\varphi(s \times r)$ such that (ψ, φ) $(s \times s)$ has full rank. We can choose ψ such that $H\psi = \gamma\eta$ for some $\eta(p - r) \times (s - r)$.

The test statistic (16) can be expressed as the difference of two test statistics we get by testing a simple hypothesis for β. Thus we can use the representation (55) and (50) for both statistics and we find that it has a weak limit, which can be expressed as

$$-2\ln(Q) \xrightarrow{W} \mathrm{tr}\left\{\mathrm{var}\,(V)^{-1}\int_0^1 dV U'\left(\int_0^1 UU' du\right)^{-1}\int_0^1 U dV'\right.$$

$$\left. - \mathrm{var}\,(V_H)^{-1}\int_0^1 dV_H U_H'\left(\int_0^1 U_H U_H' du\right)^{-1}\int_0^1 U_H dV_H'\right\},$$

where

$$U_H = \psi'H'CW = \eta'\gamma'CW = \eta'U,$$

and

$$V_H = \varphi'H'\Sigma_{kk}H\varphi(\varphi'H'\Sigma_{k0}\Sigma_{00}^{-1}\Sigma_{0k}H\varphi)^{-1}\varphi'H'\Sigma_{k0}\Sigma_{00}^{-1}W = V.$$

Thus

$$-2\ln(Q) \xrightarrow{W} \mathrm{tr}\left\{\left[\int_0^1 dV U'\left(\int_0^1 UU' du\right)^{-1}\int_0^1 U dV'\right.\right.$$

$$- \int_0^1 \mathrm{d}V U' \eta \Big(\eta' \int_0^1 U U' \mathrm{d}u \eta \Big)^{-1} \eta' \int_0^1 U \mathrm{d}V' \Big] \mathrm{var}\,(V)^{-1} \Big\}.$$

For fixed value of U the $(p - r) \times r$ matrix

$$Y = \Big(\int_0^1 U U' \mathrm{d}u \Big)^{-1/2} \int_0^1 U \mathrm{d}V' \, \mathrm{var}\,(V)^{-1/2}$$

is Gaussian with variance matrix $I \otimes I$. Let $\tilde{\eta} = (\int_0^1 U U' \mathrm{d}u)^{-1/2} \eta$, then the decomposition into independent components, given by

$$\mathrm{tr}\,\{Y'Y\} = \mathrm{tr}\,\{Y'(I - \tilde{\eta}(\tilde{\eta}'\tilde{\eta})^{-1}\tilde{\eta}')Y\} + \mathrm{tr}\,\{Y'\tilde{\eta}(\tilde{\eta}'\tilde{\eta})^{-1}\tilde{\eta}'Y\},$$

shows that each term is χ^2 distributed with degrees of freedom $r(p - r)$, $r(p - s)$ and $r(s - r)$, respectively. Thus the limiting distribution of $-2\ln(Q)$ is for fixed U a χ^2 distribution with $(p - s)r$ degrees of freedom. Since this result does not depend on the value of U it holds marginally. Thus the proof of Theorem 4 is completed.

References

AHN, S. K., and G. C. REINSEL (1990), 'Estimation for partially nonstationary multivariate autoregressive model', *J. American Statist. Assoc.* **85**, 815–23.

ANDERSON, T. W. (1984), *An Introduction to Multivariate Statistical Analysis* (New York, Wiley).

ANDERSSON, S. A., H. K. BRØNS, and S. T. JENSEN (1983), 'Distribution of eigenvalues in multivariate statistical analysis', *Annals of Statistics*, **11**, 392–415.

DAVIDSON, J. (1986), 'Cointegration in linear dynamic systems', Mimeo (London School of Economics, London).

DICKEY, D. A., and W. A. FULLER (1979), 'Distribution of the estimators for autoregressive time series with a unit root', *Journal of the American Statistical Association*, **74**, 427–31.

ENGLE, R. F., and C. W. J. GRANGER (1987), 'Cointegration and error correction: Representation, estimation and testing', *Econometrica*, **55**, 251–76.

GRANGER, C. W. J. (1981), 'Some properties of time series data and their use in econometric model specification', *Journal of Econometrics*, **16**, 121–30.

—— and R. F. ENGLE (1985), 'Dynamic model specification with equilibrium constraints', Mimeo (University of California, San Diego, CA).

—— and A. A. WEISS (1983), 'Time series analysis of error correction models', in S. Karlin, T. Amemiya, and L. A. Goodman (eds.), *Studies in Economic Time Series and Multivariate Statistics* (New York, Academic Press).

JOHANSEN, S. (1984), 'Functional relations, random coefficients, and non-linear regression with application to kinetic data', *Lecture Notes in Statistics* (New York, Springer).

—— (1988), 'The mathematical structure of error correction models', *Contemporary Mathematics*, **80**, 359–86.

PHILLIPS, P. C. B. (1985), 'Understanding spurious regression in econometrics', Cowles Foundation discussion paper no. 757.

—— (1987), 'Multiple regression with integrated time series', Cowles Foundation discussion paper no. 852.

—— and S. N. DURLAUF (1986), 'Multiple time series regression with integrated processes', *Review of Economic Studies*, **53**, 473–95.

—— and S. OULIARIS (1986), 'Testing for cointegration', Cowles Foundation discussion paper no. 809.

—— —— (1987), 'Asymptotic properties of residual based tests for cointegration', Cowles Foundation discussion paper no. 847.

—— and J. Y. PARK (1986a), 'Asymptotic equivalence of OLS and GLS in regression with integrated regressors', Cowles Foundation discussion paper no. 802.

—— —— (1986b), 'Statistical inference in regressions with integrated processes: Part 1', Cowles Foundation discussion paper no. 811.

—— —— (1987), 'Statistical inference in regressions with integrated processes: Part 2', Cowles Foundation discussion paper no. 819.

RAO, C. R. (1965), 'The theory of least squares when the parameters are stochastic and its applications to the analysis of growth curves', *Biometrika*, **52**, 447–58.

—— (1973), *Linear Statistical Inference and its Applications*, 2nd edn. (New York, Wiley).

SIMS, A., J. H. STOCK, and M. W. WATSON (1986), 'Inference in linear time series models with some unit roots, Preprint.

STOCK, J. H. (1987), 'Asymptotic properties of least squares estimates of cointegration vectors', *Econometrica*, **55**, 1035–56.

—— and M. W. WATSON (1987), 'Testing for common trends', Working paper in econometrics (Hoover Institution, Stanford, CA).

VELU, R. P., G. C. REINSEL, and D. W. WICHERN (1986), 'Reduced rank models for multiple time series', *Biometrika*, **73**, 105–18.

8

Testing for Common Trends

JAMES H. STOCK and MARK W. WATSON*

Abstract

Cointegrated multiple time series share at least one common trend. Two tests are developed for the number of common stochastic trends (i.e. for the order of cointegration) in a multiple time series with and without drift. Both tests involve the roots of the ordinary least squares coefficient matrix obtained by regressing the series onto its first lag. Critical values for the tests are tabulated, and their power is examined in a Monte Carlo study. Economic time series are often modeled as having a unit root in their autoregressive representation, or (equivalently) as containing a stochastic trend. But both casual observation and economic theory suggest that many series might contain the *same* stochastic trends so that they are cointegrated. If each of n series is integrated of order 1 but can be jointly characterized by $k < n$ stochastic trends, then the vector representation of these series has k unit roots and $n - k$ distinct stationary linear combinations. Our proposed tests can be viewed alternatively as tests of the number of common trends, linearly independent cointegrating vectors, or autoregressive unit roots of the vector process. Both of the proposed tests are asymptotically similar. The first test (q_f) is developed under the assumption that certain components of the process have a finite-order vector autoregressive (VAR) representation, and the nuisance parameters are handled by estimating this VAR. The second test (q_c) entails computing the eigenvalues of a corrected sample first-order autocorrelation matrix, where the correction is essentially a sum of the autocovariance matrices. Previous researchers have found that U.S. postwar interest rates, taken individually, appear to be integrated of order 1. In addition, the theory of the term structure implies that yields on similar assets of different maturities will be cointegrated. Applying these tests to postwar U.S. data on the federal funds rate and the three- and twelve-month treasury bill

* James H. Stock is Assistant Professor of Public Policy, John F. Kennedy School of Government, Harvard University, Cambridge, MA 02138. Mark W. Watson is Associate Professor, Department of Economics, Northwestern University, Evanston, IL 60208. This research was supported in part by National Science Foundation Grants SES-84-08797, SES-85-10289, and SES-86-18984. The authors are grateful to C. Cavanagh, R. F. Engle, J. Huizinga, J. Patel, C. Plosser, P. C. B. Phillips, P. Tsay, the referees, and an associate editor for helpful suggestions.

Printed with permission of: *Journal of the American Statistical Association*, December 1988, Vol. 83, No. 404.

rates provides support for this prediction: The three interest rates appear to be cointegrated.

Keywords: Cointegration; Factor models; Integrated processes; Multiple time series; Unit roots; Yield curve.

1. Introduction

There is considerable empirical evidence that many macroeconomic time series are well described by univariate autoregressive integrated moving average (ARIMA) models, so differencing the data produces a series that appears to be covariance stationary. It has been less clear what transformation should be applied to data used in multivariate models, since (loosely speaking) the number of unit roots in a multiple time series may be less than the sum of the number of unit roots in the constituent univariate series. Equivalently, although each univariate series might contain a stochastic trend, in a vector process these stochastic trends might be common to several of the variables. Empirical evidence concerning the number of these common trends is of interest for several reasons. First, an economic or physical theory might predict that the variables contain common trends, and a test for these common trends would be a test of this implication of the theory. Second, one might wish to impose explicitly the number of common trends when making forecasts. Third, it might be desirable to specify a time series model in which all of the variables are stationary, but in which the data are not 'overdifferenced.' Such overdifferencing would occur were the model specified in terms of the first differences of the variables, because this would ignore the reduced dimensionality of the common trends.

We develop tests of the null hypothesis that an $n \times 1$ time series variable X_t has $k \leq n$ common stochastic trends, against the alternative that it has $m < k$ common trends. It is assumed that each component of X_t is integrated of order 1, but that there are $n - k$ linear combinations of X_t that are integrated of order 0. Engle and Granger (1987) defined such a process to be cointegrated of order (1, 1). If the stationary linear combinations are $\alpha' X_t$, then the columns of α are termed the cointegrating vectors of X_t. Engle and Granger showed that if X_t is cointegrated, then it has a representation in terms of an error-correction model, as developed by Sargan (1964), Davidson, Hendry, Srba, and Yeo (1978), and others.

The concept of cointegration formalizes an older notion that some linear combinations of time series variables appear nonstationary, whereas others appear to be almost white noise. Frisch (1934) referred to those linear combinations of time series data with very small variances as being generated by 'true regressions'; one of his primary concerns was with the 'multiple colinearity' that arose when there was more than one true regression (cointegrating vector) among the vector of variates. Box and Tiao (1977) associated the least predictable linear combinations (i.e. those with the weakest serial dependence) of X_t with 'stable contemporaneous relationships'; they described the most predictable relationships as characterizing dynamic growth common to all of the series.

Cointegrated models can be represented formally in terms of a reduced number of common stochastic trends, plus transitory, or stationary, components. For univariate models, Beveridge and Nelson (1981) showed that any singly integrated ARIMA process has an exactly indentified trend plus transitory representation, in which the trend is a random walk and the transitory component is covariance stationary. Fountis and Dickey (1986) extended this decomposition to vector autoregressive (VAR) models with $k = 1$. In Section 2, we provide a general representation for $k \leq n$. Because of the equivalence between these models, our proposed tests for k versus m common trends can be thought of as tests for the existence of $n - k$ versus $n - m$ linearly independent cointegrating vectors.

Several special cases of this testing problem have been considered elsewhere. The case that has received the most attention has been testing for 1 versus 0 unit roots in a univariate time series (e.g. see Dickey and Fuller 1979; Fuller 1976; Phillips 1987; Solo 1984). In a multivariate setting, a test of $k = 1$ versus $m = 0$ was developed by Fountis and Dickey (1986) for processes with a VAR representation with iid normal errors. Engle and Granger (1987) proposed and compared a variety of tests when $n = k = 2$ and the hypothesis of interest is $k = 2$ versus $m = 1$. Like the other tests in this literature, our test is based on the roots of the estimated autoregressive representation of the time series.

Section 2 presents the cointegrated and common-trends representations of X_t and summarizes our testing strategy. In Sections 3 and 4, two tests of k versus m common stochastic trends are proposed for the special case that $X_0 = 0$ and the process has no drift. These tests are extended in Section 5 to handle an estimated intercept and drift in the relevant regressions. The asymptotic critical values are tabulated in Section 6, and a small Monte Carlo experiment investigating the size and power of these tests is reported in Section 7. The tests are applied to data on postwar U.S. interest rates in Section 8, and our conclusions arc summarized in Section 9.

2.   The Model and Testing Strategy

Let X_t denote an $n \times 1$ time series variable that is cointegrated of order $(1, 1)$. That is, each element of X_t is integrated, but there are r linear combinations of X_t that are stationary. We work with an extension of Engle and Granger's (1987) definition of cointegration that allows for possible drift in X_t. The change in X_t is assumed to have the co-integrated vector moving average representation

$$\Delta X_t = \mu + C(L)\varepsilon_t \qquad \sum_i j|C_j| < \infty, \qquad (2.1)$$

where $C(z) = \sum_{i=0}^{\infty} C_i z^i$ with $C(0) = I_n$ (the $n \times n$ identity matrix), ε_t is iid with mean 0 and covariance matrix G, L is the lag operator, and $\Delta \equiv 1 - L$. $C(1)$ is assumed to have rank $k < n$, so X_t is cointegrated; that is, there is an $n \times r$ matrix α (where $r = n - k$) such that $\alpha'C(1) = 0$ and $\alpha'\mu = 0$. As Engle and Granger pointed out, this implies that the spectral density matrix of ΔX_t at frequency 0, $(2\pi)^{-1} C(1)GC(1)'$, is singular. The columns of α are the cointegrating vectors of X_t.

A representation for the stationary linear combinations $\alpha'X_t$ is readily obtained from (2.1). Let $v_t = G^{-1/2}\varepsilon_t$ and $\xi_t = \sum_{s=1}^{t} v_s$, adopt the conventional assumption (e.g. Dickey and Fuller 1979) that $\varepsilon_s = 0$ ($s \le 0$), and allow X_t to have a nonrandom initial value X_0. Then recursive substitution of (2.1) yields

$$X_t = X_0 + \mu t + C(1)G^{1/2}\xi_t + C^*(L)G^{1/2}v_t, \qquad (2.2)$$

where $C^*(L) = (1 - L)^{-1}(C(L) - C(1))$ so that $C_j^* = -\sum_{i=j+1}^{\infty} C_j$. Because $\alpha'C(1) = 0$ and $\alpha'\mu = 0$, it follows that

$$Z_t \equiv \alpha'X_t = \alpha'X_0 + \alpha'C^*(L)G^{1/2}v_t. \qquad (2.3)$$

With the additional assumption in (2.1) and $C(L)$ is 1-summable (Brillinger 1981), $C^*(L)$ is absolutely summable and Z_t has bounded variance.

The cointegrated process X_t has an alternative representation in terms of a reduced number of common random walks plus a stationary component. This 'common trends' representation is readily derived from (2.2). Because $C(1)$ has rank $k < n$, there is an $n \times r$ matrix H_1 with rank r such that $C(1)H_1 = 0$. Furthermore, if H_2 is an $n \times k$ matrix with rank k and columns orthogonal to the columns of H_1, then $A \equiv C(1)H_2$ has rank k. The $n \times n$ matrix $H = (H_1 H_2)$ is nonsingular and $C(1)H = (0A) = AS_k$, where S_k is the $k \times n$ selection matrix $[0_{k\times(n-k)}I_k]$, where $0_{k\times(n-k)}$ is a $k \times (n - k)$ matrix of zeros. In addition, because $\alpha'C(1) = 0$ and $\alpha'\mu = 0$, μ lies in the column space of $C(1)$ and can be written $\mu = C(1)\tilde{\mu}$, where $\tilde{\mu}$ is an $n \times 1$ vector. Thus (2.2) yields the common-trends representation for X_t:

$$
\begin{aligned}
X_t &= X_0 + C(1)[\tilde{\mu}t + G^{1/2}\xi_t] + C^*(L)G^{1/2}v_t \\
&= X_0 + C(1)H[H^{-1}\tilde{\mu}t + H^{-1}G^{1/2}\xi_t] + a_t \\
&= X_0 + A\tau_t + a_t, \qquad \tau_t = \pi + \tau_{t-1} + v_t, \qquad (2.4)
\end{aligned}
$$

where $a_t = C^*(L)G^{1/2}v_t$, $\tau_t = S_k H^{-1}\tilde{\mu}t + S_k H^{-1}G^{1/2}\xi_t$, $\pi = S_k H^{-1}\tilde{\mu}$, and $v_t = S_k H^{-1}G^{1/2}v_t$. (For different derivation of the common-trends representation (2.4) and further discussion, see King, Plosser, Stock, and Watson (1987).) The common-trends representation expresses X_t as a linear combination of k random walks with drift π, plus some transitory components, a_t, that are integrated of order 0.

The common-trends representation provides a convenient framework in which to motivate our proposed tests. Putting aside for the moment the complications that arise from a nonzero intercept and time trend in (2.2), a natural approach to testing k versus m common stochastic trends would be to examine the first-order serial correlation matrix of X_t. Because X_t is composed of both integrated and nonintegrated components, however, its estimated first-order serial correlation matrix has a nonstandard limiting distribution that generally depends on nuisance parameters in complicated ways. To mitigate this difficulty we examine functions of regression statistics of a linear transformation of X_t, denoted by Y_t, chosen so that under the null hypothesis the first $n - k$ elements of Y_t are not integrated, whereas the final k elements of Y_t can be expressed in terms of the k separate trends. More precisely, let $Y_t = DX_t$, where $D = [\alpha \; \alpha^\dagger]'$, where $\alpha^\dagger$ is an $n \times k$ matrix of constants chosen so that $\alpha^{\dagger\prime}\alpha = 0$ and $\alpha^{\dagger\prime}\alpha^\dagger = I_k$. The first $n - k$ elements of Y_t are Z_t in (2.3). Let W_t denote the final k integrated elements of Y_t. It follows from (2.1) that

$$\Delta W_t = \alpha^{\dagger\prime}\mu + u_t, \tag{2.5}$$

where $u_t = \tilde{C}(L)v_t$, with $\tilde{C}(L) = \alpha^{\dagger\prime}C(L)G^{1/2}$. Combining (2.3) and (2.5),

$$\Delta_k Y_t = \delta + F(L)v_t, \tag{2.6}$$

where

$$\Delta_k = \begin{bmatrix} I_{n-k} & 0 \\ 0 & \Delta I_k \end{bmatrix}, \qquad \delta = \begin{bmatrix} \alpha'X_0 \\ \alpha^{\dagger\prime}\mu \end{bmatrix},$$

$$F(L) = \begin{bmatrix} \alpha'C^*(L)G^{1/2} \\ \tilde{C}(L) \end{bmatrix}.$$

Recursive substitution of (2.6) shows that Y_t can be represented as

$$Y_t = \begin{bmatrix} \alpha'X_0 \\ \alpha^{\dagger\prime}X_0 \end{bmatrix} + \begin{bmatrix} 0_{(n-k)\times1} \\ \alpha^{\dagger\prime}\mu \end{bmatrix}t$$

$$+ \begin{bmatrix} 0_{(n-k)\times n} \\ \tilde{C}(1) \end{bmatrix}\xi_t + \begin{bmatrix} \alpha'C^*(L)G^{1/2} \\ \tilde{C}^*(L) \end{bmatrix}v_t$$

$$= \beta_1 + \beta_2 t + \beta_3\xi_t + \beta_4(L)v_t, \tag{2.7}$$

where $\tilde{C}^*(L) = (1 - L)^{-1}(\tilde{C}(L) - \tilde{C}(1))$.

In terms of W_t, a test of k versus m common trends becomes a test of whether $\tilde{C}(1)$ has rank k against the alternative, that it has rank m. To motivate the proposed tests, suppose that $X_0 = \mu = 0$, and consider the result regressing W_t onto W_{t-1}. Under the null hypothesis, W_t is a linear combination of k integrated processes, so Φ, the probability limit of

$$\tilde{\Phi} = \left[\sum W_t W'_{t-1}\right]\left[\sum W_{t-1} W'_{t-1}\right]^{-1}, \qquad (2.8)$$

has k real unit roots. Under the alternative W_t includes m integrated variables and $k - m$ nonintegrated variables, or equivalently W_t has $k - m$ linearly independent cointegrating vectors. Thus under the alternative Φ has only m unit eigenvalues corresponding to the m integrated variables, and $k - m$ eigenvalues with modulus (and therefore with real parts) less than 1. Letting λ_{m+1} denote the eigenvalue of Φ with the $(m + 1)$th-largest real part, our null and alternative hypotheses are $H_0 : \text{real}(\lambda_{m+1}) = 1$ versus $H_1 : \text{real}(\lambda_{m+1}) < 1$.

Much is known about the properties of $\tilde{\Phi}$ when Φ has some unit roots. When $n = 1$ and u_t is serially uncorrelated, $\tilde{\Phi}$ has the distribution studied by White (1958), Fuller (1976), Dickey and Fuller (1979), and others. Phillips (1987) examined the distribution of $T(\tilde{\Phi} - 1)$ under less restrictive conditions on the errors; this analysis was generalized to the multivariate case by Phillips and Durlauf (1986). Unfortunately, when u_t is serially correlated the distribution of $\tilde{\Phi}$ and its eigenvalues $\tilde{\lambda}$ depends on the autocovariances of u_t. This dependence makes it impossible to tabulate the asymptotic critical values of a statistic based in a practical way. Strategies for circumventing this problem and developing asymptotically similar tests are presented in Sections 3 and 4 for the case ($\beta_1 = 0$, $\beta_2 = 0$) and are extended to the cases ($\beta_1 \neq 0$, $\beta_2 = 0$) and ($\beta_1 \neq 0$, $\beta_2 \neq 0$) in Section 5.

3.   A Test Based on Filtering the Data

This section presents a test statistic in which the nuisance parameters of the process are eliminated by assuming a parametric representation for the process generating W_t. The development of this test parallels Dickey and Fuller's (1979) approach to testing for a unit root in a univariate time series. Specifically, suppose that αW_t has a finite-order VAR representation so that (2.5) can be rewritten as

$$\Pi(L)\Delta W_t = \gamma + \eta_t, \qquad (3.1)$$

where $\Pi(L)$ is a matrix lag polynomial of known order p with all roots outside the unit circle, η_t is iid with mean 0, and $\Pi(0)$ is normalized so that $E\eta_t\eta'_t = I_k$. In this section it is assumed that $W_0 = \gamma = 0$.

First, suppose that D and $\Pi(L)$ are known and let $\zeta = \Pi(L)W_t$. Under (3.1), $\Pi(L)\Delta W_t = \Delta[\Pi(L)W_t] = \eta_t$, so under the null hypothesis the elements of $\Pi(L)W_t$ are random walks. In contrast, under the alternative of $m < k$ common trends, only m components of $\Pi(L)W_t$ are random walks, whereas the remaining elements are integrated of order 0. This suggests testing for k versus m common trends by examining the roots of the first sample auto-correlation matrix formed using ζ_t,

$$\tilde{\Phi}_f = \left[\sum \zeta_t \zeta_{t-1}'\right]\left[\sum \zeta_{t-1}\zeta_{t-1}'\right]^{-1}.$$

Rewriting $\tilde{\Phi}_f$, we have

$$T[\tilde{\Phi}_f - I_f] = \Psi_{kT}'(\Gamma_{kT})^{-1}, \tag{3.2}$$

where $\Psi_{kT} = T^{-1}\sum \zeta_{t-1}\eta_t'$ and $\Gamma_{kT} = T^{-2}\sum \zeta_{t-1}\zeta_{t-1}'$.

The limiting behaviour of Ψ_{kT} and Γ_{kT} has been treated in the univariate case by (for example) White (1958), Solo (1984), and Phillips (1987), and in the multivariate case by Phillips and Durlauf (1986) and Chan and Wei (1988). These random matrices converge weakly to functionals of the k-dimensional Wiener process $B_k(t)$: $\Gamma_{kT} \Rightarrow \Gamma_k = \int_0^1 B_k(t)B_k(t)'dt$ and $\Psi_{kT} \Rightarrow \Psi_k \equiv \int_0^1 B_k(t)dB_k(t)'$, where $\Rightarrow$ denotes weak convergence on the space of continuous functions on $[0, 1]^k$ in the sense of Billingsley (1968). Thus from (3.2), $T[\tilde{\Phi}_f - I_f] \Rightarrow \Psi_k'\Gamma_k^{-1}$; that is, $T[\tilde{\Phi} - I_k]$ converges weakly to a random variable that has the same distribution as $\Psi_k'\Gamma_k^{-1}$. It follows that $T(\tilde{\lambda}_f - 1) \Rightarrow \lambda_*$, where λ_* denotes the vector of ordered eigenvalues of $\Psi_k'\Gamma_k^{-1}$, $\tilde{\lambda}_f$ denotes the vector of ordered eigenvalues of $\tilde{\Phi}_f$, and $\iota = (1\ 1\ \dots\ 1)'$.

If D and $\Pi(L)$ were known a test statistic could be constructed using $\tilde{\lambda}_f$. In applications, however, D and $\Pi(L)$ are typically unknown. This deficiency can be remedied by using estimators $\hat{D}$ and $\hat{\Pi}(L)$ of D and $\Pi(L)$, respectively. For the moment, assume that $\hat{D}$ and $\hat{\Pi}(L)$ exist and that (a) $\hat{D} \xrightarrow{P} RD$ under both H_0 and H_1, where $R = \text{diag}(R_1, R_2)$, where R_1 and R_2 are, respectively, nonsingular $(n-k) \times (n-k)$ and $k \times k$ matrices under the null and $(n-m) \times (n-m)$ and $m \times m$ matrices under the alternative, and (b) $\hat{\Pi}(L) \xrightarrow{P} R_2\Pi(L)R_2^{-1}$ under H_0. Let $\hat{W}_t = S_k\hat{D}X_t$ and $\hat{\zeta}_t = \hat{\Pi}(L)\hat{W}_t$. Then one could consider the ordinary least squares (OLS) estimator

$$\hat{\Phi}_f = \left[\sum \hat{\zeta}_t \hat{\zeta}_{t-1}'\right]\left[\sum \hat{\zeta}_{t-1}\hat{\zeta}_{t-1}'\right]^{-1}.$$

This modified version of $\tilde{\Phi}$, computed using the filtered series $\hat{\zeta}_t$, has a limiting representation in which the nuisance parameters in (3.1) do not appear. Letting $\hat{\lambda}_f$ denote the vector of ordered eigenvalues of $\hat{\Phi}_f$, we have Theorem 3.1.

THEOREM 3.1. Suppose that $\hat{D} \xrightarrow{p} RD$, W_t is generated by (3.1) with $W_0 = \gamma = 0$, $\hat{\Pi}(L) \xrightarrow{p} R_2\Pi(L)R_2^{-1}$, and $\max_t E(\eta_{it}^4 \leq \mu_4 < \infty$. Then, (a) $T(\hat{\Phi}_f - I_k) \Rightarrow R_2\Psi_k'\Gamma_k^{-1}R_2^{-1}$, (b) $T(\hat{\lambda}_f - \iota) \Rightarrow \lambda_*$, and (c) $T(|\hat{\lambda}_f| - \iota) \Rightarrow \text{real}(\lambda_*)$.

PROOF. At the suggestion of the editor the proofs of all lemmas and theorems are omitted but provided in Stock and Watson (1988).

Theorem 3.1 suggests testing for k versus m common trends—or equivalently for k versus m real unit roots in Φ—using the statistic

$$q_f(k, m) = T[\text{real}(\hat{\lambda}_{f,m+1}) - 1],$$

where $\hat{\lambda}_{f,m+1}$ is the $(m + 1)$th element of $\hat{\lambda}_f$. Under the null hypothesis, from Theorem 3.1(b) $q_f(k, m)$ asymptotically has the same distribution as $\text{real}(\lambda_{*m+1})$.

The construction of q_f requires the estimation of RD and the autoregressive matrix polynomial $\Pi(L)$ in (3.1). The $n \times n$ matrix RD can be estimated in a variety of ways. The first $n - k$ rows of D (and thus of RD) are a basis for the space spanned by the cointegrating vectors of X_t under the null. Because the cointegrating vectors form linear combinations of X_t that have bounded variance from the otherwise integrated elements of X_t, they (like the autoregressive coefficient in the univariate unit-root problem or its multivariate analog, discussed in the preceding sections) can be estimated consistently without specifying a particular parametric process for the additional stationary components. As demonstrated in Stock (1987, theorem 2), if X_t has the representation (2.1) with $n - k$ cointegrating vectors and $\max_i E(\varepsilon_{it}^4) \leq \mu_4 < \infty$, then the cointegrating vectors consisting of the columns of α can be estimated by contemporaneous OLS regressions of one element of X_t on the others, after an arbitrary normalization to ensure that the estimates are linearly independent.

We adopt a modification of this approach, in which the cointegrating vectors are constructed to be orthonormal with the first cointegrating vector forming the linear combination of X_t having the smallest variance, the second cointegrating vector having the next smallest variance, and so on. Implementing this procedure simply entails estimating the principal components of X_t; α is estimated by those linear combinations corresponding to the smallest $n - k$ principal components, and $\alpha^\dagger$ is estimated by the linear combinations corresponding to the largest k principal components. Since $\hat{\alpha}$ consistently estimates the cointegrating vectors up to an arbitrary linear transformation, $\hat{D} \xrightarrow{B} RD = [\alpha^\dagger R_1' \alpha^\dagger R_2']'$ for some R_1 and R_2.

Since $\hat{\Phi} \xrightarrow{p} I_k$ under the null [where $\hat{\Phi} = \sum \hat{W}_1\hat{W}_{t-1}' (\sum \hat{W}_{t-1}\hat{W}_{t-1})^{-1}$], the parameters of $R_2\Pi(L)R_2^{-1}$ can be estimated consistently by a VAR(p) regression using either $\Delta \hat{W}_t$ or $\hat{u}_t$, where $\hat{u}_t$ are the residuals from a regression of $\hat{W}_t$ onto $\hat{W}_{t-1}$. In either case, normalizing the VAR coefficient matrices so that the VAR residuals have an identity-contemporaneous covariance matrix ensures that $\hat{\Pi}(L) \xrightarrow{p} R_2 \Pi(L) R_2^{-1}$.

This test is consistent against the alternative that there are m rather than k common trends using either estimator of $\Pi(L)$, even if the process is not autoregressive of order p but satisfies (2.1) with $n - m$ cointegrating vectors. Under the alternative, $\hat{D}$ (constructed using principal components) converges in probability to some matrix D_a, the first $n - m$ rows of which contain the cointegrating vectors of X_t and the final m rows of which are orthogonal to the cointegrating vectors. In addition, under the alternative $\hat{\Pi}(L)$ converges to some (finite-order) matrix lag polynomial $\Pi_a(L)$ even if ΔW_t does not have a VAR(p) representation. From (2.1) and the definition of ζ_t, $\Delta \hat{\zeta}_t = \hat{\Pi}(L) S_k \hat{D} C(L) \varepsilon_t$, where $\hat{\Pi}(L) \xrightarrow{p} \Pi_a(L)$ and $\hat{D} \xrightarrow{p} D_a$. Since $\Pi_a(L)$ has finite order and $C(L)$ is absolutely summable under both the null and the alternative, $\Pi_a(L) S_k D_a C(L)$ is absolutely summable. Furthermore, under the alternative, $\text{rank}(\Pi_a(1) S_k D_a C(1)) \equiv m'$ $\leq \text{rank}(C(1)) = m < k$. Using a construction like (2.6), it can be shown that as the sample size tends to infinity, ζ_t [and, by the convergence of $\hat{\Pi}(L)$ and $\hat{D}$, $\hat{\zeta}_t$] has m' unit roots in its sample first-order autoregressive matrix and $k - m'$ roots less than 1 in modulus and therefore with real parts that are less than 1. In particular, $\text{real}(\hat{\lambda}_{f,m+1}) - 1$ converges in probability to a negative number, so the test is consistent. Note that a consistent test obtains whether the filter is estimated using either $\Delta \hat{W}_t$ or $\hat{u}_t$, assuming that the order of the filter is fixed.

4. A Test Based on Correcting the OLS Autoregressive Matrix

Our second proposed statistic tests for k versus $k - 1$ common trends using a corrected version of $\tilde{\Phi}$, the sample first-order autocorrelation matrix for W_t in (2.8), under the assumption that $\beta_1 = \beta_2 = 0$ in (2.7). In this case, $\tilde{\Phi}$ has the asymptotic representation given in Lemma 4.1.

LEMMA 4.1. If $\max_i E(v_{it}^4) \leq \mu_4 < \infty$ and $\beta_1 = \beta_2 = 0$ in (2.7), then

$$T(\tilde{\Phi} - I_k) - [\tilde{C}(1)\Psi'_{nT}\tilde{C}(1)' + M'][\tilde{C}(1)\Gamma_{nT}\tilde{C}(1)']^{-1} \xrightarrow{p} 0,$$

where $\Psi_{nT} = T^{-1}\sum \xi_{t-1} v'_t$, $\Gamma_{nT} = T^{-2}\sum \xi_t \xi'_t$, and $M = [\sum_{j=0}^{\infty}(\tilde{C}_j^* - \tilde{C}_j) \tilde{C}_j' + \tilde{C}(1)\tilde{C}(1)'] = \sum_{j=1}^{\infty} Eu_{t-j} u'_t$.

This lemma indicates that $T(\tilde{\Phi} - I_k)$ asymptotically consists of two parts. The first, $[\tilde{C}(1)\Psi_{nT}\tilde{C}(1)']'\,[\tilde{C}(1)\Gamma_{nT}\tilde{C}(1)']^{-1}$, is T times the error in the estimate of Φ obtained by regressing the random walk $\tilde{C}(1)\xi_t$ on to its lagged value. The second, $M'[\tilde{C}(1)\Gamma_{nT}\tilde{C}(1)']^{-1}$, is analogous to the $O(T^{-1})$ bias in contemporaneous regressions of cointegrated variables. This bias arises from the correlation between the regressor W_{t-1} and u_t in (2.5). This term is related to the bias in OLS regression estimates when there are stationary lagged dependent variables and serially correlated errors. In the present context, since u_t is not integrated (but is serially correlated) and W_t is integrated, this correlation produces not inconsistency but a component of $\tilde{\Phi}$ that is $O_p(T^{-1})$.

The bias term M is problematic, since its presence means that the distribution of $\tilde{\Phi}$ (and its eigenvalues) depends on M and thus on $\tilde{C}(L)$. Nevertheless, the limiting representation in Lemma 4.1 suggests a solution to this problem: Modify the OLS estimator $\tilde{\Phi}$ using an estimator of M so that the asymptotic distribution of the eigenvalues of the modified OLS estimator depends only on Γ_n and Ψ_n. This approach generalizes to the multivariate-setting Phillips (1987, theorem 5.1) test for a single unit root in a univariate process. Specifically, were W_t observed and M known, a corrected estimator $\tilde{\Phi}_c$ could be computed by subtracting off the troublesome term:

$$\tilde{\Phi}_c = \left[T^{-2}\sum W_t W'_{t-1} - T^{-1}M'\right]\left[T^{-2}\sum W_{t-1}W'_{t-1}\right]^{-1}.$$

Letting $\tilde{\lambda}_c$ denote the vector of the k ordered eigenvalues of $\tilde{\Phi}_c$, we have Lemma 4.2.

LEMMA 4.2. Let Ω by a $k \times k$ matrix such that $\Omega\Omega' = \tilde{C}(1)\tilde{C}(1)'$. Then, under the conditions of Lemma 4.1, (a) $T(\tilde{\Phi}_c - I_k) \Rightarrow \Omega\Psi'_k\Gamma_k^{-1}\Omega^{-1}$ and (b) $T(\tilde{\lambda}_c - \iota) \Rightarrow \lambda_*$.

According to Lemma 4.2, the distribution of the standardized eigenvalues of $\tilde{\Phi}_c$ do not depend on any nuisance parameters and thus can be tabulated. But $\tilde{\Phi}_c$ cannot itself form the basis for a test because it involves W_t, which is not directly observed, and M, which depends on unknown parameters. As we discuss later, however, M can be estimated; suppose that the estimator of M, $\hat{M}$, is such that

$$\hat{M} \xrightarrow{\;p\;} R_2 M R'_2.$$

Let $\hat{Y}_t = \hat{D}X_t$, and use $\hat{W}_t = S_k\hat{Y}_t$ and $\hat{M}$ to form the analog of $\tilde{\Phi}_c$,

$$\hat{\Phi}_c = \left[T^{-2}\sum \hat{W}_t\hat{W}'_{t-1} - T^{-1}\hat{M}'\right]\left[T^{-2}\sum \hat{W}_{t-1}\hat{W}'_{t-1}\right]^{-1}.$$

The consistency of $\hat{D}$ and $\hat{M}$ ensure that the eigenvalues of $\hat{\Phi}_c$, $\hat{\lambda}_c$, are asymptotically equivalent to the eigenvalues of $\tilde{\Phi}_c$.

THEOREM 4.1. Suppose that $\hat{D} \xrightarrow{P} RD$ and $\hat{M} \xrightarrow{P} R_2 M R_2'$. Then, under the assumptions of Lemma 4.1, (a) $T(\hat{\Phi}_c - I_k) \Rightarrow R_2 \Omega \Psi_k' \Gamma_k^{-1} \Omega^{-1} R_2^{-1}$ and (b) $T(\hat{\lambda}_c - \iota) \Rightarrow \lambda_*$.

Part (a) of this theorem presents a limiting representation for the ordered eigenvalues of $\hat{\Phi}_c$. We therefore define the test statistic

$$q_c(k, k - 1) = T[\text{real}(\hat{\lambda}_{c,k}) - 1],$$

where $\hat{\lambda}_{c,k}$ is the kth element of $\hat{\lambda}_c$. Under the null hypothesis, $q_c(k, k - 1)$ converges to the real part of the smallest eigenvalue of the random matrix $\Psi_k' \Gamma_k^{-1}$.

The construction of the q_c statistic requires estimators $\hat{D}$ and $\hat{M}$. Construction of $\hat{D}$ was discussed in Section 3. The second expression for M in Lemma 4.1 suggests an estimator of M based on the sample covariances of the $k > 1$ vector of residuals $\hat{u}_t = \hat{W}_t - \hat{\Phi}\hat{W}_{t-1}$ from the regression of $\hat{W}_t$ onto $\hat{W}_{t-1}$. The estimation of M is clearly related to the problem of estimating the spectral density matrix of u_t at frequency 0, $(2\pi)^{-1}\sum_{j=-\infty}^{\infty} V_j = (2\pi)^{-1}(V_0 + M + M')$ (where $V_j = E u_t u_{t-j}'$), so techniques developed for its estimation can be applied here. Let $\hat{V}_j = T^{-1}\sum_{t=j+1}^{T} \hat{u}_t \hat{u}_{t-j}'$. Then M can be estimated by

$$\hat{M} = \sum_{j=1}^{J} K(j)\hat{V}_j', \tag{4.1}$$

where $K(j)$ is a (time domain) kernel. For a proof of the consistency of $\hat{M}$ in the univariate case for $K(j) = 1$ and $J = o(T^{1/4})$, see Phillips (1987).

The test based on $q_c(k, k - 1)$ is consistent if $\hat{M} \xrightarrow{P} \sum_{j=1}^{\infty} E u_{t-j} u_t'$ under the alternative, where $u_t = W_t - \Phi W_{t-1}$. To demonstrate this consistency, write $\Phi = Q \Lambda Q^{-1}$ under the alternative, where Λ is a diagonal matrix with the roots of Φ on the diagonal so that the first $k - 1$ diagonal elements are 1 and the final element is less than 1 in modulus, and where Q is the $k \times k$ matrix of eigenvectors of Φ. Under the alternative, the last element of the transformed variate QW_t [say $(QW_t)_k$] is a stationary process. Let ρ_j and $f_{(QW_t)k}(\omega)$ denote the jth autocorrelation and the (scalar) spectral density of $(QW_t)_k$, respectively. A calculation using the techniques in Stock and Watson (1988) shows that under the fixed alternative, $\hat{\lambda}_{ck} \xrightarrow{P} 1 - (1 - \rho_1)^2(1 + \sum_1^{\infty} \rho_j) \equiv \lambda_{ck}$. Because $f_{(QW_t)k}(0) = c(1 + 2\sum_1^{\infty} \rho_j) \geq 0$ under the alternative (where c is a positive constant), $\sum_1^{\infty} \rho_j \geq -\frac{1}{2}$, so $\lambda_{ck} \leq 1 - \frac{1}{2}(1 - \rho_1)^2 < 1$ for $|\rho_1| < 1$. Thus $T(\hat{\lambda}_{ck} - 1)$ tends to $-\infty$ under the fixed alternative, demonstrating that the test is consistent.

Not all candidate estimators of the correction term M result in a consistent test. In particular, suppose that $\Delta \hat{W}_t$ rather than $\hat{u}_t$ is used to construct an estimator $\tilde{M}$ so that $\tilde{M} \xrightarrow{P} \sum_{j=1}^{\infty} E[\Delta W_{t-j} \Delta W_t']$ under both the null and the fixed alternative. Under the null, the tests formed using $\tilde{M}$ and $\hat{M}$ are asymptotically equivalent. Under the alternative, however, if corrected using $\tilde{M}$, $\hat{\Phi}_c \xrightarrow{p} I_k$, so in particular real $(\hat{\lambda}_{c,k})$ $\xrightarrow{p} 1$ and a one-sided test based on this root is not consistent.

5.   Modifications for Estimated Intercepts and Drifts

In practice it is desirable to allow for nonzero X_0, and in many applications a more appropriate model might be one in which X_t has a nonzero drift as well as a cointegrated stochastic structure. This section addresses the problem of testing the null hypothesis that the rank of $C(1)$ is k, against the alternative that it is $m < k$ when the intercept and drift may be nonzero. In terms of (2.7), this entails testing that the rank of $\tilde{C}(1)$ is k versus m when either (a) $\beta_2 = 0$ but β_1 might be nonzero (but is nonrandom) or (b) β_1 and β_2 are nonrandom but might both be nonzero. In case (b) under the null X_t has k linear combinations that are random walks with nonzero drifts, whereas under the alternative X_t has m such linear combinations. In a univariate setting macroeconomic data often modeled as stationary in first differences around a constant nonzero mean; as Beveridge and Nelson (1981) showed, this implies that the process can be written as the sum of a random walk with nonzero drift and a mean-0 stationary component. Letting β_1 and β_2 be nonzero both generalizes this univariate specification to the multivariate case and permits testing for common trends against an alternative, in which up to $n - m$ components are stationary around a linear time trend. For a discussion of the macroeconomic implications of stochastic versus deterministic trends in economic time series, see Nelson and Plosser (1982); for an alternative approach in which the drift in the stochastic trend is itself modeled as a random walk (so that the series is stationary only after taking second differences), see Harvey (1985).

We follow Fuller's (1976) and Dickey and Fuller's (1979) univariate treatment of intercepts and time trends and modify the previous test statistics so that an intercept or an intercept and a drift are estimated. Accordingly, let $\hat{Y}_t^\mu = \hat{Y}_t - T^{-1} \sum \hat{Y}_t$, and $\hat{Y}_t^\tau = \hat{Y}_t - \hat{\beta}_1 - \hat{\beta}_2 t$, where $\hat{\beta}_1$ and $\hat{\beta}_2$ are the OLS estimates of β_1 and β_2 obtained by regressing $\hat{Y}_t$ on a constant and t, and let $\hat{W}_t^\mu = S_k \hat{Y}_t^\mu$ and $\hat{W}_t^\tau = S_k \hat{Y}_t^\tau$. The modification to the filtering test entails estimating the autoregressive polynomial $\Pi(L)$ using $\hat{W}_t^\mu$ or $\hat{W}_t^\tau$ rather than $\hat{W}_t$ (as in Sec. 3). Let $\hat{\zeta}_t^\mu = \hat{\Pi}(L)\hat{W}_t^\mu$ and $\hat{\zeta}_t^\tau = \hat{\Pi}(L)\hat{W}_t^\tau$, and define

$$\hat{\Phi}_f^\mu = \left[\sum \hat{\zeta}_t^\mu \hat{\zeta}_{t-1}^{\mu\prime} \right]\left[\sum \hat{\zeta}_{t-1}^\mu \hat{\zeta}_{t-1}^{\mu\prime} \right]^{-1}$$

and

$$\hat{\Phi}^{\tau}_f = \left[\sum \hat{\zeta}^{\tau}_t \hat{\zeta}^{\tau\prime}_{t-1}\right]\left[\sum \hat{\zeta}^{\tau}_{t-1} \hat{\zeta}^{\tau\prime}_{t-1}\right]^{-1}$$

Let $\Psi^{\mu}_k = \int^1_0 B^{\mu}_k(t)\,dB^{\mu}_k(t)'$, $\Gamma^{\mu}_k = \int^1_0 B^{\mu}_k(t)B^{\mu}_k(t)'\,dt$, $\Psi^{\tau}_k = \int^1_0 B^{\tau}_k(t)\,dB^{\tau}_k(t)'$, and $\Gamma^{\tau}_k = \int^1_0 B^{\tau}_k(t)B^{\tau}_k(t)'\,dt$, where $B^{\mu}_k(t) = B_k(t) - \int^1_0 B_k(s)\,ds$ and $B^{\tau}_k(t) = B_k(t) - \int^1_0 a_1(s)B_k(s)\,ds - t\int^1_0 a_2(s)B_k(s)\,ds$, where $a_1(s) = 4 - 6s$ and $a_2(s) = -6 + 12s$. Also, let $\hat{\lambda}^{\mu}_f$, $\hat{\lambda}^{\tau}_f$, λ^{μ}_*, and λ^{τ}_*, respectively, denote the ordered eigenvalues of $\hat{\Phi}^{\mu}_f$, $\hat{\Phi}^{\tau}_f$, $\Psi^{\mu\prime}_k(\Gamma^{\mu}_k)^{-1}$, and $\Psi^{\tau\prime}_k(\Gamma^{\tau}_k)^{-1}$. We now have Theorem 5.1.

THEOREM 5.1. Suppose that $\hat{D} \overset{p}{\longrightarrow} RD$, W_t is generated by (3.1), $\hat{\Pi}(L) \overset{p}{\longrightarrow} R_2\Pi(L)R^{-1}_2$, and $\max_i E(\eta^4_{it}) \leq \mu_4 < \infty$. (a) If $\gamma = 0$ and W_0 is an arbitrary constant, then (i) $T(\hat{\Phi}^{\mu}_f - I_k) \Rightarrow R_2\Psi^{\mu\prime}_k(\Gamma^{\mu}_k)^{-1}R^{-1}_2$, (ii) $T(\hat{\lambda}^{\mu}_f - \iota) \Rightarrow \lambda^{\mu}_*$, and (iii) $T(|\hat{\lambda}^{\mu}_f| - \iota) \Rightarrow \text{real}(\lambda^{\mu}_*)$. (b) If γ and W_0 are arbitrary constants, then (i) $T(\hat{\Phi}^{\tau}_f - I_k) \Rightarrow R_2\Psi^{\tau\prime}_k(\Gamma^{\tau}_k)^{-1}R^{-1}_2$, (ii) $T(\hat{\lambda}^{\tau}_f - \iota) \Rightarrow \lambda^{\tau}_*$, and (iii) $T(|\hat{\lambda}^{\tau}_f| - \iota) \Rightarrow \text{real}(\lambda^{\tau}_*)$.

The counterparts of $q_f(k, m)$ when there might be a nonzero intercept or a nonzero intercept and drift are

$$q^{\mu}_f(k, m) = T[\text{real}(\hat{\lambda}^{\mu}_{f,m+1}) - 1]$$

and

$$q^{\tau}_f(k, m) = T[\text{real}(\hat{\lambda}^{\tau}_{f,m+1}) - 1],$$

which (respectively) have the same limiting distribution under the null as $\text{real}(\lambda^{\mu}_{*,m+1})$ and $\text{real}(\lambda^{\tau}_{*,m+1})$, where $\hat{\lambda}^{\mu}_{f,m+1}$ is the $(m + 1)$th-largest eigenvalue of $\hat{\Phi}^{\mu}_f$, and so on.

The modification to the q_c statistic for a nonzero intercept or drift proceeds similarly. Suppose that D were known, let $Y^{\mu}_t = Y_t - T^{-1}\sum Y_t$ and $Y^{\tau}_t = Y_t - \tilde{\beta}_1 - \tilde{\beta}_2 t$, where $\tilde{\beta}_1$ and $\tilde{\beta}_2$ are the coefficients from regressing Y_t onto $(1, t)$. Let $W^{\mu}_t = S_k Y^{\mu}_t$ and $W^{\tau}_t = S_k Y^{\tau}_t$. By analogy to $\tilde{\Phi}$, define

$$\tilde{\Phi}^{\mu} = \left[T^{-2}\sum W^{\mu}_t W^{\mu\prime}_{t-1}\right]\left[T^{-2}\sum W^{\mu}_{t-1} W^{\mu\prime}_{t-1}\right]^{-1}$$

and

$$\tilde{\Phi}^{\tau} = \left[T^{-2}\sum W^{\tau}_t W^{\tau\prime}_{t-1}\right]\left[T^{-2}\sum W^{\tau}_{t-1} W^{\tau\prime}_{t-1}\right]^{-1}.$$

The treatment of $\tilde{\Phi}^{\mu}$ and $\tilde{\Phi}^{\tau}$ parallels the treatment of $\tilde{\Phi}$ in Section 4. It is first shown that the asymptotic distributions of $\tilde{\Phi}$, $\tilde{\Phi}^{\mu}$, and $\tilde{\Phi}^{\tau}$ depend on the same nuisance parameters, although the random components in the asymptotic representations differ. This makes it possible to construct corrected matrices $\tilde{\Phi}^{\mu}_c$ and $\tilde{\Phi}^{\tau}_c$, the eigenvalues of which have a distribution that is independent of the nuisance parameters.

LEMMA 5.1. Suppose that $\max_i E(v_{it}^4 \leq \mu_4 < \infty$. (a) If $\beta_2 = 0$ in (2.7), and β_1 is an arbitrary constant, then

$$T(\tilde{\Phi}^\mu - I) - [\tilde{C}(1)\Psi_{nT}^{\mu\prime}\tilde{C}(1)' + M'][\tilde{C}(1)\Gamma_{nT}^\mu\tilde{C}(1)']^{-1} \xrightarrow{P} 0.$$

(b) If β_1 and β_2 in (2.7) are arbitrary constants, then

$$T(\tilde{\Phi}^\tau - I) - [\tilde{C}(1)\Psi_{nT}^{\tau\prime}\tilde{C}(1)' + M'][\tilde{C}(1)\Gamma_{nT}^\tau\tilde{C}(1)']^{-1} \xrightarrow{P} 0,$$

where $\Psi_{nT}^\mu = T^{-1}\sum \xi_{t-1}^\mu \Delta\xi_t^{\mu\prime}$, $\Gamma_{nT}^\mu = T^{-2}\sum \xi_t^\mu \xi_t^{\mu\prime}$, $\Psi_{nT}^\tau = T^{-1}\sum \xi_{t-1}^\tau \Delta\xi_t^{\tau\prime}$, and $\Gamma_{nT}^\tau = T^{-2}\sum \xi_t^\tau \xi_t^{\tau\prime}$, where $\xi_t^\mu = \xi_t - T^{1/2}\Theta_{0T}$ and $\xi_t^\tau = \xi_t - T^{1/2}\Theta_{1T} - T^{-1/2}\Theta_{2T}t$, where $\Theta_{iT} = T^{-3/2}\sum_{t=1}^T a_{it}\xi_t$ $(i = 0, 1, 2)$, with $a_{0t} = 1$, $a_{1t} = 4 - 6(t/T)$, and $a_{2t} = -6 + 12(t/T)$.

These limiting representations depend on M, given in Lemma 4.1. This dependence can be eliminated by correcting $\tilde{\Phi}^\mu$ and $\tilde{\Phi}^\tau$ using an estimator of M, $\hat{M}$, as suggested in Section 4. In addition, since D and therefore W_t are unknown, replace W_t with $\hat{W}_t = S_k\hat{D}X_t$. Accordingly, let

$$\hat{\Phi}_c^\mu = \left[T^{-2}\sum \hat{W}_t^\mu \hat{W}_{t-1}^{\mu\prime} - T^{-1}\hat{M}'\right]\left[T^{-2}\sum \hat{W}_{t-1}^\mu \hat{W}_{t-1}^{\mu\prime}\right]^{-1}$$

and

$$\hat{\Phi}_c^\tau = \left[T^{-2}\sum \hat{W}_t^\tau \hat{W}_{t-1}^{\tau\prime} - T^{-1}\hat{M}'\right]\left[T^{-2}\sum \hat{W}_{t-1}^\tau \hat{W}_{t-1}^{\tau\prime}\right]^{-1},$$

and let $\hat{\lambda}_c^\mu$ and $\hat{\lambda}_c^\tau$, respectively, denote the vector of ordered eigenvalues of $\hat{\Phi}_c^\mu$ and $\hat{\Phi}_c^\tau$. We now have Theorem 5.2.

THEOREM 5.2. Suppose that $\hat{D} \xrightarrow{P} RD$, $\hat{M} \xrightarrow{P} R_2MR_2'$, and the assumptions of Lemma 5.1 hold. (a) If $\beta_2 = 0$ in (2.7) and β_1 is an arbitrary constant, then (i) $T(\hat{\Phi}_c^\mu - I) \Rightarrow R_2\Omega\Psi_k^{\mu\prime}(\Gamma_k^\mu)^{-1}\Omega^{-1}R_2^{-1}$, (ii) $T(\hat{\lambda}_c^\mu - \iota) \Rightarrow \lambda_*^\mu$, and (iii) $T(|\hat{\lambda}_c^\mu| - \iota) \Rightarrow \text{real}(\lambda_*^\mu)$. (b) If β_1 and β_2 in (2.7) are arbitrary constants, then (i) $T(\hat{\Phi}_c^\tau - I) \Rightarrow R_2\Omega\Psi_k^{\tau\prime}(\Gamma_k^\tau)^{-1}\Omega^{-1}R_2^{-1}$, (ii) $T(\hat{\lambda}_c^\tau - \iota) \Rightarrow \lambda_*^\tau$, and (iii) $T(|\hat{\lambda}_c^\tau| - \iota) \Rightarrow \text{real}(\lambda_*^\tau)$.

This theorem makes it possible to construct test statistics analogous to $q_c(k, k - 1)$ accounting for either an estimated intercept or an estimated intercept and drift. The only modification is that the tests are, respectively, computed using deviations of $\hat{W}_t$ around its average or the residuals from a regression of $\hat{W}_t$ on to a constant and a linear time trend. Therefore let

$$q_c^\mu(k, k - 1) = T[\text{real}(\hat{\lambda}_{c,k}^\mu) - 1]$$

and

$$q_c^\tau(k, k - 1) = T[\text{real}(\hat{\lambda}_{c,k}^\tau) - 1],$$

where $\hat{\lambda}^{\mu}_{c,k}$ '(or $\hat{\lambda}^{\tau}_{c,k}$) is the kth-largest eigenvalue of $\hat{\Phi}^{\mu}_c$ (or $\hat{\Phi}^{\tau}_c$) Theorems 5.1 and 5.2 imply that under the null hypothesis $q^{\mu}_f(k, m)$ $\Rightarrow \text{real}(\lambda^{\mu}_{*m+1})$, $q^{\tau}_f(K, m) \Rightarrow \text{real}(\lambda^{\tau}_{*m+1})$, $q^{\mu}_c(k, k-1) \Rightarrow \text{real}(\lambda^{\mu}_{*k})$, and $q^{\tau}_c(k, k-1) \Rightarrow \text{real}(\lambda^{\tau}_{*k})$.

6.   Critical Values

Although the preceding asymptotic representations do not provide explicit distributions of the proposed test statistics, they do suggest a simple procedure for computing the asymptotic distributions using Monte Carlo techniques. For example, from Theorem 3.1 (b) and Theorem 4.1 (b), the asymptotic distributions of $q_f(k, k-1)$ and $q_c(k, k-1)$ are the same as the asymptotic distribution of the real part of the smallest root of $\Psi'_{kT}\Gamma^{-1}_{kT}$, which in turn has the same asymptotic distribution as real (λ_{*k}), the real part of the smallest root of $\Psi'_k\Gamma^{-1}_k$. Theorems 5.1 and 5.2 imply that similar remarks apply for the q^{μ}_f, q^{τ}_f, q^{μ}_c, and q^{τ}_c test statistics. Accordingly, the distributions of the real parts of the ordered roots of $\Psi'_{kT}\Gamma^{-1}_{kT}$, $\Psi^{\mu\prime}_{kT}(\Gamma^{\mu}_{kT})^{-1}$, and $\Psi^{\tau\prime}_{kT}(\Gamma^{\tau}_{kT})^{-1}$ were computed using 30,000 Monte Carlo replications with $T = 1,000$. (As a check of whether $T = 1,000$ is sufficiently large, the $k = 3$ entries in the tables were recomputed using 10,000 replications with $T = 2,000$. The discrepancies between the two distributions were negligible.)

Selected quantiles of the distribution of $\text{real}(\lambda_{*j})$ are tabulated in Table 1 for $k = 1, \ldots, 6$ and $j = 1, \ldots, k$; the quantiles for $\text{real}(\lambda^{\mu}_{*j})$ and $\text{real}(\lambda^{\tau}_{*j})$ are given in Tables 2 and 3, respectively. Referring to Table 1, the blocks of rows represent the dimension of λ, or equivalently k, the dimension of W_t used to construct the q_f or q_c tests. The columns of the table denote the jth-largest eigenvalue, corresponding to the eigenvalue on which the test is based when there are $m = j - 1$ unit roots under the alternative. For example, in a test of $k = 4$ versus $m = 3$ unit roots, the $q_f(4, 3)$ or $q_c(4, 3)$ tests would be based on the fourth-largest eigenvalue, so the 5 per cent critical value for the test (taken from Table 1) is -34.4 and the 1 per cent critical value is -43.3. For a test of $k = 4$ versus $m = 1$ unit roots, the $q_f(4, 1)$ test would be based on the second-largest eigenvalue, for which the 5 per cent and 1 per cent critical values are -8.5 and -11.5, respectively. If the q^{μ}_f or q^{μ}_c tests are used, the critical values come from Table 2. If the q^{τ}_f or q^{τ}_c tests are used, the critical values come from Table 3.

The asymptotic null distribution of the $q^{\mu}_f(k, k-1)$ and $q^{\mu}_c(k, k-1)$ statistics [i.e. the distribution of the real part of the smallest eigenvalue of $\Psi^{\mu\prime}_k(\Gamma^{\mu}_k)^{-1}$] is plotted in Figure 1 for $k = 1, \ldots, 6$. The figure emphasizes how severely the cdf's of the smallest eigenvalues are shifted below 0, even when $k = 1$ or 2.

Testing for Common Trends

TABLE 1.   Quantiles of real(λ_*)

Dimension of λ_*	Significance level (%)	Eigenvalue number					
		1	2	3	4	5	6
1	1	−13.8					
	2.5	−10.6					
	5	−8.0					
	10	−5.6					
	15	−4.36					
	50	−.87					
	90	.94					
	95	1.30					
2	1	−6.7	−24.4				
	2.5	−5.1	−20.4				
	5	−3.78	−17.5				
	10	−2.71	−14.3				
	15	−2.10	−12.3				
	50	−.21	−5.8				
	90	1.15	−1.30				
	95	1.50	−.62				
3	1	−4.24	−15.0	−34.6			
	2.5	−3.23	−12.9	−29.7			
	5	−2.53	−11.1	−26.0			
	10	−1.82	−9.2	−22.2			
	15	−1.4	−8.1	−19.9			
	50	.02	−3.97	−11.6			
	90	1.24	−.56	−4.97			
	95	1.58	−.08	−3.83			
4	1	−3.19	−11.5	−22.6	−43.3		
	2.5	−2.5	−9.9	−20.1	−38.3		
	5	−1.95	−8.5	−18.0	−34.4		
	10	−1.4	−7.2	−15.6	−30.0		
	15	−1.07	−6.4	−14.1	−27.2		
	50	.14	−3.13	−8.4	−17.5		
	90	1.29	−.21	−3.57	−9.4		
	95	1.62	.20	−2.74	−7.8		
5	1	−2.67	−9.6	−18.3	−30.1	−51.6	
	2.5	−2.04	−8.3	−16.1	−27.1	−46.2	
	5	−1.64	−7.2	−14.5	−24.7	−41.9	
	10	−1.17	−6.1	−12.6	−22.0	−37.4	
	15	−.88	−5.5	−11.4	−20.2	−34.5	
	50	.22	−2.66	−6.9	−13.4	−23.6	
	90	1.32	−.02	−2.93	−7.3	−14.1	
	95	1.66	.36	−2.25	−6.1	−12.3	

TABLE 1.   (*Cont.*)

Dimension of λ_*	Significance level (%)	Eigenvalue number					
		1	2	3	4	5	6
6	1	−2.25	−8.3	−15.5	−24.5	−38.1	−60.2
	2.5	−1.75	−7.3	−13.8	−22.3	−34.3	−54.6
	5	−1.4	−6.4	−12.4	−20.4	−31.5	−49.8
	10	−1.00	−5.4	−10.9	−18.2	−28.3	−44.8
	15	−.74	−4.84	−9.9	−16.8	−26.3	−41.7
	50	.28	−2.28	−6.0	−11.3	−18.6	−29.7
	90	1.36	.13	−2.5	−6.2	−11.4	−19.1
	95	1.69	.49	−1.89	−5.3	−9.9	−16.8

7.   Size and Power Computations

This section reports the results of a small Monte Carlo experiment that investigates the size and power of the tests in samples of sizes typically encountered in applied work. The $q_f^\mu(2, 1)$ and $q_c^\mu(2, 1)$ tests were studied using two different models for Y_t. In the first, Y_t was generated by the VAR(2)

$$(1 - \phi L)(1 - \Phi L)Y_t = \varepsilon_t, \tag{7.1}$$

and in the second by the mixed-vector (autoregressive moving average) ARMA(1, 1) process

$$(1 - \Phi L)Y_t = (1 + \theta L)\varepsilon_t, \tag{7.2}$$

where in (7.1) and (7.2) $E\varepsilon_t\varepsilon_t' = G$, and where

$$\Phi = \begin{bmatrix} 1 & 0 & 0 \\ 0 & \rho & 0 \\ 0 & 0 & .5 \end{bmatrix}, \qquad G = \begin{bmatrix} 1 & .5 & -.25 \\ .5 & 1 & .5 \\ -.25 & .5 & 1 \end{bmatrix}.$$

Both ϕ and θ are scalars that are less than 1 in absolute value. Under the null hypothesis, $\rho = 1$, so there are two common trends; under the alternative, $|\rho| < 1$, and there is only one common trend. The tests were computed as described in the previous sections, using principal components to construct $\hat{D}$ from the generated Y_t. Although Y_t as generated by (7.1) or (7.2) is not cointegrated (since Y_t is not integrated), because D is computed by principal components numerically equivalent test statistics would be obtained using $X_t = PY_t$, where P is any nonsingular matrix. In particular, P could be chosen so that X_t is cointegrated.

Testing for Common Trends

TABLE 2.   Quantiles of real(λ_*^μ)

Dimension of λ_*^μ	Significance level (%)	Eigenvalue number					
		1	2	3	4	5	6
1	1	−20.6					
	2.5	−16.8					
	5	−14.1					
	10	−11.2					
	15	−9.5					
	50	−4.36					
	90	−.82					
	95	−.11					
2	1	−12.3	−30.9				
	2.5	−10.3	−26.4				
	5	−8.8	−23.0				
	10	−7.2	−19.5				
	15	−6.2	−17.2				
	50	−3.03	−9.7				
	90	−.29	−4.05				
	95	.33	−3.10				
3	1	−9.1	−20.1	−40.2			
	2.5	−7.9	−17.7	−35.4			
	5	−6.8	−15.7	−31.5			
	10	−5.7	−13.5	−27.3			
	15	−4.99	−12.1	−24.8			
	50	−2.53	−7.1	−15.6			
	90	−.07	−2.91	−8.1			
	95	−.53	−2.19	−6.8			
4	1	−7.6	−15.9	−27.7	−49.2		
	2.5	−6.6	−14.1	−24.8	−43.6		
	5	−5.8	−12.6	−22.5	−39.3		
	10	−4.91	−10.9	−19.8	−35.0		
	15	−4.33	−9.9	−18.2	−32.1		
	50	−2.33	−5.8	−11.9	−21.6		
	90	.04	−2.35	−6.3	−12.7		
	95	.64	−1.73	−5.3	−11.0		
5	1	−6.7	−13.5	−22.7	−35.5	−57.1	
	2.5	−5.8	−12.1	−20.3	−32.0	−51.5	
	5	−5.2	−10.8	−18.4	−29.2	−47.0	
	10	−4.45	−9.5	−16.5	−26.4	−42.1	
	15	−3.94	−8.6	−15.2	−24.4	−39.1	
	50	−2.05	−5.1	−10.0	−17.0	−27.8	
	90	.13	−2.02	−5.4	−10.3	−17.6	
	95	.75	−1.43	−4.59	−8.9	−15.5	

TABLE 2.   (*Cont.*)

Dimension of λ_*^μ	Significance level (%)	Eigenvalue number					
		1	2	3	4	5	6
6	1	−6.1	−12.2	−19.7	−29.1	−42.5	−65.5
	2.5	−5.4	−10.9	−17.8	−26.5	−39.1	−59.7
	5	−4.75	−9.7	−16.2	−24.5	−36.1	−54.9
	10	−4.09	−8.6	−14.4	−22.1	−32.8	−49.7
	15	−3.64	−7.8	−13.3	−20.6	−30.7	−46.3
	50	−1.9	−4.62	−8.9	−14.5	−22.3	−34.0
	90	.2	−1.77	−4.83	−8.9	−14.5	−22.8
	95	.79	−1.26	−4.06	−7.8	−12.8	−20.3

The experiments were performed using 2,000 replications with a sample size of $T = 200$. This sample is typical of that found in macroeconomic research; for example, the postwar quarterly National Income and Product Accounts data set from 1947:1 to 1986:4 contains 160 observations, and the monthly financial data set examined in Section 8 has 236 observations. Initial values of $Y_0 = \varepsilon_0 = 0$ were used, and the tests were computed using the generated data $Y_1, \ldots, Y_{200}$. Fewer observations were used to compute the VAR's and convariance matrices entering the correction terms as necessary. The $q_c^\mu(2, 1)$ test statistics were computed using a rectangular window of order J, so $K(j) = 1$ for $|j| \leq J$ and 0 otherwise. When the data were generated by (7.1), the $q_f^\mu(2, 1)$ statistic was computed by filtering the first differences of the integrated (under the null) components using an estimated VAR(1); the correction term M in the $q_c^\mu(2, 1)$ statistic was estimated using a window of order $J = 3$. When the data were generated by (7.2), the $q_f^\mu(2, 1)$ filter was estimated using a VAR(3); the $q_c^\mu(2, 1)$ correction was estimated using $J = 1$. Thus the order of the filter in the $q_f^\mu(2, 1)$ statistic was correct under the null when the data were generated by (7.1), and the order of the window in the $q_c^\mu(2, 1)$ statistic was correct under the null when the data were generated by (7.2). In the other cases, a longer VAR (or additional covariance terms) was incorporated to approximate the covariance structure implied by the vector MA (or AR) in first differences under the null.

Columns A and B of Table 4 contain results for the VAR model (7.1) with $\phi = 4$, and columns C and D contain results for the vector ARMA model (7.2) with $\theta = .4$. The nominal sizes of the q_f^μ test (columns A and C) are somewhat above their actual level, whereas the nominal size of the q_c^μ test is above its level when the data are generated by a VAR

TABLE 3. Quantiles of real(λ_*^τ)

Dimension of λ_*^τ	Significance level (%)	Eigenvalue number					
		1	2	3	4	5	6
1	1	−29.2					
	2.5	−24.8					
	5	−21.7					
	10	−18.2					
	15	−16.1					
	50	−9.0					
	90	−3.8					
	95	−2.7					
2	1	−19.1	−39.2				
	2.5	−16.8	−34.6				
	5	−14.9	−30.8				
	10	−12.9	−26.7				
	15	−11.6	−24.2				
	50	−7.0	−15.1				
	90	−2.94	−7.6				
	95	−1.97	−6.3				
3	1	−15.2	−27.1	−48.7			
	2.5	−13.4	−24.3	−43.5			
	5	−12.1	−22.1	−39.0			
	10	−10.7	−19.5	−34.6			
	15	−9.7	−17.8	−31.8			
	50	−6.2	−11.3	−21.4			
	90	−2.52	−5.9	−12.5			
	95	−1.55	−4.91	−10.7			
4	1	−13.2	−22.0	−35.3	−57.2		
	2.5	−11.8	−19.8	−31.6	−51.7		
	5	−10.7	−18.0	−28.9	−47.0		
	10	−9.5	−16.0	−25.9	−42.0		
	15	−8.7	−14.7	−24.0	−38.9		
	50	−5.7	−9.5	−16.7	−27.6		
	90	−2.23	−5.1	−10.0	−17.4		
	95	−1.32	−4.19	−8.7	−15.3		
5	1	−12.2	−19.0	−28.7	−42.4	−64.6	
	2.5	−10.9	−17.2	−26.3	−38.8	−59.2	
	5	−9.8	−15.7	−24.2	−35.9	−54.5	
	10	−8.7	−14.0	−21.9	−32.6	−49.2	
	15	−8.0	−12.8	−20.4	−30.4	−46.0	
	50	−5.3	−8.4	−14.3	−22.1	−33.7	
	90	−2.12	−4.50	−8.8	−14.2	−22.5	
	95	−1.20	−3.72	−7.7	−12.6	−20.1	

TABLE 3.   (*Cont.*)

Dimension of λ_{*}^{τ}	Significance level (%)	Eigenvalue number					
		1	2	3	4	5	6
6	1	−11.2	−17.0	−25.1	−35.3	−49.7	−73.2
	2.5	−10.1	−15.4	−23.1	−32.7	−45.7	−67.1
	5	−9.1	−14.1	−21.3	−30.2	−42.5	−62.4
	10	−8.1	−12.6	−19.3	−27.7	−38.9	−56.8
	15	−7.5	−11.6	−18.0	−26.0	−36.7	−53.2
	50	−4.99	−7.5	−12.9	−19.1	−27.6	−39.9
	90	−2.00	−4.05	−8.0	−12.5	−18.8	−27.8
	95	−1.06	−3.36	−7.0	−11.0	−16.9	−25.2

(column B) and somewhat below its level when the data are generated by a vector MA (column D). In addition, the $q_f^\mu(2, 1)$ test exhibits greater nominal power than the approximate $q_c^\mu(2, 1)$ test with the VAR data-generation process, whereas the reverse is true when the data are generated by the vector ARMA process.

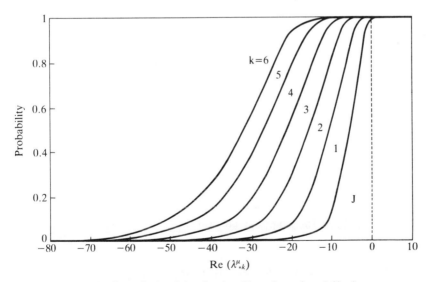

FIG. 1. Cumulative Distribution Function of real (λ_{*k}^{μ}).

TABLE 4. Monte Carlo Experiment Results: Rejection Probabilities

ρ	Level (%)	Data-generating process			
		(7.1), with $\phi = .4$		(7.2), with $\theta = .4$	
		A, $q_f^\mu(2, 1)$	B, $q_c^\mu(2, 1)$	C, $q_f^\mu(2, 1)$	D, $q_c^\mu(2, 1)$
1.00	5	.03	.03	.03	.07
	10	.07	.06	.06	.13
.95	5	.11	.10	.08	.22
	10	.21	.18	.19	.35
.90	5	.40	.34	.30	.60
	10	.59	.50	.51	.74
.80	5	.92	.82	.86	.99
	10	.97	.90	.95	.99

Note: The results were computed using 2,000 Monte Carlo draws with a sample size of $T = 200$.

8.   Common Trends in Postwar U.S. Interest Rates

In this section we test for the number of common trends among three U.S. interest rates with different maturities. The data are 236 monthly observations from January 1960 to August 1979 on the federal funds rate (FF) (an overnight interbank loan rate), the 90-day treasury bill rate (TB3), and the one-year treasury bill rate (TB12). The treasury bill rates are secondary market rates, and all rates are on an annualized basis. All three rates were obtained from the Citibase financial data base.

The theory of the term structure of interest rates suggests that there is at most one common stochastic trend underlying these rates: Because the expected return on a multiperiod instrument in theory equals the expected return obtained from rolling over a sequence of one-period instruments, a stochastic trend in the short-term rate is inherited by the longer-term rate.

Table 5 presents various tests for unit roots in these interest rates. Although all three rates appear to contain a unit root, the differences among them (the spreads) seem to be stationary. [Application of the Dickey–Fuller $\hat{\tau}\mu(4)$ test to the first difference of each interest rate rejects the null of a second unit root at the 1 per cent level.] This suggests that there is a single common trend. The multivariate results

TABLE 5   Integration and Cointegration Tests on Three Monthly Interest Rates, 1960:1–1979:8

| Series | Univariate results | | | |
| | Sample autocorrelations | | | |
	Lag 1	Lag 2	Lag 3	$\hat{\tau}_\mu(4)$
FF	.975	.941	.899	−1.79
TB3	.971	.936	.899	−1.44
TB12	.972	.935	.898	−1.34
FF–TB3	.902	.825	.741	−3.17[b]
FF–TB12	.932	.863	.801	−2.82[c]
TB3–TB12	.851	.727	.614	−4.09[a]

Common trend tests
$q_f^\mu(3, 1)$; $p = 2$, $−22.6^a$; $p = 4$, $−21.6^a$
$q_f^\mu(2, 1)$; $p = 2$, $−23.2^b$; $p = 4$, $−23.5^b$
$q_c^\mu(2, 1)$; $J = 2$, $−24.7^b$; $J = 4$, $−29.6^b$

Note: $\hat{\tau}_\mu(4)$ denotes the Dickey–Fuller (1979) t test for a unit root in a univariate series including an estimated constant with an AR(4) correction. The q_c^μ statistics were computed using a flat kernel for $K(j)$ in (4.1) to weight the J estimated autocovariances. FF denotes the federal funds rate, TB3 denotes the 90-day treasury bill rate, and TB12 denotes the one-year treasury bill rate.

  [a] Significant at the 1 per cent level.
  [b] Significant at the 5 per cent level.
  [c] Significant at the 10 per cent level.

confirm this suspicion. Testing for 3 versus 1 common trend using the $q_f^\mu(3, 1)$ statistic, from Table 2 the 5 per cent critical value is $−15.7$ and the 1 per cent critical value is $−20.1$. The report test statistics are more negative than both of these critical values, indicating rejection at the 1 per cent level. Tests of the more refined hypothesis of 2 versus 1 also reject the null in favour of a model in which these three rates contain a single common trend.

9. Conclusions

The procedures proposed in this article provide a way to test for a reduced number of common trends in a multivariate time series model. Although the tests developed apply to real unit roots, they can be applied to certain cointegrated seasonal models. In particular, suppose that $(1 − L)$ in (2.1) is replaced by a seasonal difference $(1 − L^d)$, where d is some integer. Since $(1 - L^d) = (1 - L)(1 + L + \ldots + L^{d-1})$, the tests and asymptotic theory apply directly to the transformed series $(1 + L + \ldots + L^{d-1})X_t$. This approach only tests for cointegration at frequency 0; however, it is possible that alternative tests could be developed for cointegration at seasonal frequencies.

The derivation of the tests and the Monte Carlo results suggest that the q_f test might perform better than the q_c test if under the null the data are generated by a VAR, whereas the reverse is true if the data are generated by a vector moving average process. Further simulation studies are needed to characterize more fully the circumstances in which the tests are likely to perform well.

References

BEVERIDGE, S., and C. R. NELSON (1981), 'A new approach to decomposition of economic time series into permanent and transitory components with particular attention to measurement of the business cycle', *Journal of Monetary Economics*, **7**, 151–74.

BILLINGSLEY, P. (1968), *Convergence of Probability Measures* (New York, John Wiley).

BOX, G. E. P., and G. C. TIAO (1977), 'A canonical analysis of multiple time series', *Biometrika*, **64**, 355–65.

BRILLINGER, D. P. (1981), *Time Series Analysis and Theory* (San Francisco, Holden-Day).

CHAN, N. H., and C. Z. WEI (1988), 'Limiting distributions of least squares estimates of unstable autoregressive processes', *The Annals of Statistics*, **16**, 367.

DAVIDSON, J. E. H., D. F. HENDRY, F. SRBA, and S. YEO (1978), 'Econometric modelling of the aggregate time-series relationship between consumer's expenditure and income in the United Kingdom', *Economic Journal*, **88**, 661–92.

DICKEY, D. A., and W. A. FULLER (1979), 'Distribution of the estimators for autoregressive time series with a unit root', *Journal of the American Statistical Association*, **74**, 427–31.

ENGLE, R. F., and C. W. J. GRANGER (1987), 'Cointegration and error correction: representation, estimation, and testing', *Econometrica*, **55**, 251–76.

FOUNTIS, N. G., and D. A. DICKEY (1986), 'Testing for a unit root nonstationarity in multivariate autoregressive time series', mimeo, North Carolina State University, Dept. of Statistics.

FRISCH, R. (1934), *Statistical Confluence Analysis by Means of Complete Regression Systems* (Oslo, Universitets Økonomiske Institutt).

FULLER, W. A. (1976), *Introduction to Statistical Time Series*, (New York, John Wiley).

HARVEY, A. C. (1985), 'Trends and cycles in macroeconomic time series', *Journal of Business & Economic Statistics*, **3**, 216–27.

KING, R., C. I. PLOSSER, J. H., STOCK and M. W. WATSON (1987), 'Stochastic trends and economic fluctuations', Working Paper 2229, National Bureau of Economic Research, Cambridge, MA.

NELSON, C. R., and C. I. PLOSSER (1982), 'Trends and random walks in macroeconomic time series', *Journal of Monetary Economics,* **10**, 139–62.

PHILLIPS, P. C. B. (1987), 'Time series regression with unit roots', *Econometrica,* **55**, 277–302.

—— and S. N. DURLAUF (1986), 'Multiple time series regression with integrated processes', *Review of Economic Studies,* **53**, 473–96.

SARGAN, J. D. (1964), 'Wages and prices in the United Kingdom: a study in econometric methodology', in *Econometric Analysis for National Economic Planning,* eds. P. E. Hart, G. Mills, and J. N. Whittaker (London, Butterworth), pp. 25–63.

SOLO, V. (1984), 'The order of differencing in ARIMA models', *Journal of the American Statistical Association,* **79**, 916–21.

STOCK, J. H. (1987), 'Asymptotic properties of least squares estimators of cointegrating vectors', *Econometrica,* **55**, 1035–56.

—— and M. W. WATSON (1988), 'Testing for common trends: technical appendix', Discussion Paper 167D, Harvard University, Kennedy School of Government.

WHITE, J. S. (1958), 'The limiting distribution of the serial correlation coefficient in the explosive case', *Annals of Mathematical Statistics,* **29**, 1188–97.

9

Multicointegration

C. W. J. GRANGER and TAE-HWY LEE

Abstract

This paper introduces a deeper level of cointegration, which might be expected to occur in economics. It can arise from special optimal control situations and can improve short- and long-run forecasts. It seems to be particularly appropriate for considerations of inventory.

1. Introduction

If Q_t is a stationary series with finite variance, then its accumulated sum

$$y_t = \sum_{j=0}^{t} Q_{t-j}$$

is called integrated of order one, denoted $y_t \sim I(1)$. It is assumed that Q_t has a spectrum $f(\omega)$ with the property that $0 < f(\omega) < \infty$, and Q_t is called integrated of order zero, denoted $Q_t \sim I(0)$. The change of an $I(0)$ series will be denoted $I(-1)$, so that if $Q_t \sim I(0)$, then $\Delta Q_t \sim I(-1)$. An $I(-1)$ series will have spectrum having a zero at zero frequency and, of course, its accumulation will be $I(0)$. A series may be nonstationary and still be $I(0)$, but discussion of such possibilities is not necessary in this paper. A stationary series will have no trend, will frequently cross its mean value, will have short memory, and will be relatively unsmooth. An $I(1)$ series will (generally) have an increasing variance, will contain dominant long-swing components (from its infinite spectrum at zero frequencies) and so be smooth, will have long memory (the optimum forecast of y_{n+h} will involve y_n nontrivially for all h), and will not regularly cross any particular level. Thus $I(0)$ and $I(1)$ series have quite different appearances and, generally, the regression of one on the other will result in an (asymptotically) zero regression coefficient. It is an interesting empirical fact that many macroeconomic series appear to be $I(1)$, although possibly with a trend.

Printed with permission of: *Advances in Econometrics*, Vol. 8, (1989) pp. 71–84

If x_t, y_t are both $I(1)$ then it is typically true that any linear combination $x_t + by_t$ will also be $I(1)$. However, for some pairs of $I(1)$ series there does exist a linear combination

$$z_t = x_t - Ay_t \tag{1.1}$$

that is $I(0)$. When this occurs, x_t, y_t are said to be cointegrated. This will only occur when the two series have a decomposition of the form

$$x_t = AW_t + x_{1t},$$

$$y_t = W_t + y_{1t},$$

where x_{1t}, y_{1t} are both $I(0)$ and W_t is $I(1)$. Thus the $I(1)$ property of x_t, y_t comes from the single $I(1)$ common factor W_t. Further, if x_t, y_t are cointegrated they may be considered to be generated by an error-correcting model of the form

$$\Delta x_t = \rho_1 z_{t-1} + \text{lagged}(\Delta x_t, \Delta y_t) + \varepsilon_{xt},$$

$$\Delta y_t = \rho_2 z_{t-1} + \text{lagged}(\Delta x_t, \Delta y_t) + \varepsilon_{yt},$$

where at least one of ρ_1, ρ_2 nonzero, z_t is from (1.1), and $\varepsilon_{xt}, \varepsilon_{yt}$ are jointly white noise.

These properties of cointegrated series, their generalizations to $I(d)$ processes, and testing questions are discussed in Granger 1983, 1986 and Engle and Granger 1987.

It is generally true that for any vector X_t of $NI(1)$ series, there will be at most r vectors α such that $\alpha'X_t$ is $I(0)$, with $r \leq N - 1$. However, it is also true that any pair of $I(1)$ series may be cointegrated, and this does allow the possibility of a deeper form of cointegration occurring, which can be illustrated in the following bivariate case. Suppose that x_t, y_t are both $I(1)$, have no trend, and are cointegrated, so that $z_t = x_t - Ay_t$ is $I(0)$. It follows that

$$S_t = \sum_{j=0}^{t} z_{t-j}$$

will be $I(1)$ and x_t, y_t will be said to be *multicointegrated* if S_t and x_t are also cointegrated. It follows that S_t and y_t will also be cointegrated. As S_t is a function of x_t, y_t and their lags, multicointegration allows two cointegrations at different levels, between just two series. A possible example might be $x_t =$ income, $y_t =$ total consumption, $z_t = x_t - y_t$ being savings, S_t being wealth, and wealth and consumption being cointegrated. The example investigated in this paper has $x_t =$ sales, $y_t =$ production, for some industry, $z_t = y_t - x_t =$ change in inventory (apart from a constant, being the initial inventory), and inventory and production being cointegrated.

Section II discusses some properties of multicointegrated processes,

Section III relates them to some optimization and control situations; Section IV discusses an empirical example, and finally Section V is a conclusion. Only the bivariate case is considered; the extension to higher-order vectors is straightforward. The models considered here are special cases of the general dynamic cointegration process considered by Yoo (1987) and by Johansen (1988). In this paper a simple case that is most likely to be of relevance in economics is considered in some detail.

2.   Properties of Multicointegrated Process

Suppose that x_t, y_t are $I(1)$ and cointegrated, with

$$z_t = x_t - Ay_t \sim I(0).$$

The standard common factor representation is

$$x_t = AW_t + x_{1t}, \qquad y_t = W_t + y_{1t},$$

where W_t is $I(1)$ and x_{1t}, y_{1t} are both $I(0)$. It follows that

$$S_t = \sum_{j=0}^{t} z_{t-j} = \sum_{j=0}^{t} (x_{1,t-j} - Ay_{1,t-j}),$$

and to be cointegrated with x_t it is necessary that this variable has ΔW_t as a component. This will occur if the full decompositions are

$$x_t = AW_t + \alpha_1 \Delta W_t + x_{2t}, \quad y_t = W_t + \alpha_2 \Delta W_t + y_{2t},$$

where x_{2t}, y_{2t} are both $I(-1)$, giving

$$S_t = CW_t + \delta x_{2t} - A\delta y_{2t},$$

where $C = \alpha_1 - A\alpha_2 \neq 0$, $\delta = \Delta^{-1}$, and $\delta x_{2t} - A\delta y_{2t}$ is $I(0)$, being the accumulation of $I(-1)$ variables. It follows that

$$p_t = x_t - DS_t \sim I(0),$$

where $D = A/C$. It should be noted that, using $\delta = \Delta^{-1}$,

$$p_t = x_t - D\delta z_t = (1 - D\delta \quad AD\delta)X_t,$$

where $X_t = (x_t \quad y_t)'$.

The Cramer representation of the vector $I(0)$ series is

$$\Delta X_t - C(B)\varepsilon_t. \tag{2.1}$$

It was shown in Granger (1983) and Engle and Granger (1988) that for the components of X_t to be cointegrated it is necessary and sufficient that the determinant of $C(B)$ has a root $(1 - B)$. It is shown in Appendix A that the requirement for X_t to be multicointegrated is that the determinant of $C(B)$ has a root $(1 - B)^2$. If

$$\det C(B) = (1 - B)^2 d(B),$$

and if $A(B)$ is the adjunct matrix of $C(B)$, then (2.1) may then be written

$$A(B)\Delta X_t = (1 - B)^2 d(B)\varepsilon_t. \tag{2.2}$$

Using the notation

$$A(B) = A(1) + \Delta A^*(B), \qquad A^*(B) = A^*(1) + \Delta A^{**}(B),$$

then after some algebra outlined in Appendix B, (2.2) can be written

$$\bar{A}(B)\Delta X_t = -\gamma_1 p_{t-1} - \gamma_2 z_{t-1} + d(B)\varepsilon_t, \tag{2.3}$$

where

$$p_t = (1 - D\delta \quad AD\delta)X_t, \qquad \delta = \Delta^{-1},$$

$$z_t = \alpha' X_t, \quad \alpha' = (1 \quad -A),$$

$$\gamma\alpha' = A(1), \quad \gamma = \begin{pmatrix} A_{11}(1) \\ A_{21}(1) \end{pmatrix}$$

$$\gamma_1 = -D^{-1}\gamma, \quad \gamma_2 = \gamma - A^{-1}\begin{pmatrix} A_{12}^*(1) \\ A_{22}^*(1) \end{pmatrix}$$

$$\bar{A}(B) = A(1) + A^*(1) + A^{**}(B).$$

Equation (2.3) is the error correction model for a pair of multicointegrated series, in which changes of X_t are related to the pair of lagged cointegration errors $z_t = x_t - A y_t$ and $p_t = x_t - DS_t$. For multicointegrator, ΔX_t is generated by (2.3), with the necessary condition that at least one component of each of γ_1 and γ_2 is nonzero. Equation (2.3) is the generalized error correction model for multicointegrated series. It should be noted that the extra term in the error correction representation does lead to potentially improved forecasts of component of ΔX_t.

An example of a generating process that produces a pair of multicointegrated series is

$$\Delta X_t = \begin{bmatrix} A + \Delta(1 - A) & -A^2(1 - \Delta) \\ 1 - \Delta & -A + \Delta(1 + A) \end{bmatrix} \varepsilon_t.$$

In this case $\alpha' = (1 - A)$, $D = A$, and the error correction models are

$$\Delta x_t = -p_{t-1} + \varepsilon_{1t}, \qquad \Delta y_t = -\lambda p_{t-1} + \lambda z_{t-1} + \varepsilon_{2t},$$

where $\lambda = A^{-1}$.

So far, the series have been assumed to be without trends in mean. To generalize this case, the common factor W_t can be assumed to be the sum of a trend $m(t)$, plus an $I(1)$ component without drift. Thus, multicointegration does allow trends, but of a very limited form.

3.   Generation from Optimum Control

As an example of how multicointegration can arise from an optimum control situation, involving both proportional and integral control, consider the following situation: y_t is a series that one is attempting to control (e.g. inflation); y^*_{t-1} is the target series for y_t, determined at time $t-1$ by the controller; $e_t = y_t - y^*_{t-1}$ is the control error, being the extent to which the target is missed, perhaps due to imperfect control; c_t is the control series, whose value is set at time t by the controller.

Assume that y_t and c_t are related by the 'plant equation'

$$y_t = c_{t-1} + x_{t-1} + \varepsilon_t, \tag{3.1}$$

where x_t is some unspecified set of predetermined variables (possibly including expectations made at time $t-1$ of some contemporaneous variables).

The accumulated control error is

$$S_t = \sum_{j=0}^{t} e_{t-j},$$

and it is assumed this series also has a target series S^*_{t-1}. Costs to the controller will arise from three sources: the size of e_t (i.e. $y_t - y^*_{t-1}$), the size of the control error for S_t (i.e. $S_t - S^*_{t-1}$), and the amount of change in c_t, the cost of changing the control series. Assuming quadratic costs, the quantity to be minimized is thus

$$J = E[(y_{t+1} - y^*_t)^2 + \lambda_1(S_{t+1} - S^*_t)^2 + \lambda_2(c_t - c_{t-1})^2], \tag{3.2}$$

the expectation being made at time t conditional on quantities known at time t. It is naturally assumed that both λ_1, λ_2 are $\geqslant 0$.

Using $S_{t+1} = y_{t+1} - y^*_t + S_t$ and substituting from (3.1) with t replaced by $t+1$ gives

$$J = (1 + \lambda_1)\sigma^2_\varepsilon + (c_t + x_t - y^*_t)^2 + \lambda_1(c_t + x_t - y^*_t + S_t - S^*_t)^2$$
$$+ \lambda_2(c_t - c_{t-1})^2.$$

Differentiating with respect to c_t and equating to zero gives

$$c_t = \theta[(1 + \lambda_1)y^*_t - (1 + \lambda_1)x_t - \lambda_1 S_t + \lambda_2 c_{t-1} + \lambda_1 S^*_t],$$

where $\theta = (1 + \lambda_1 + \lambda_2)^{-1}$, substituting for c_{t-1} from (3.1) gives

$$c_t = \theta[(1 + \lambda_1)y^*_t - (1 + \lambda_1)x_t - \lambda_1(S_t - S^*_t) + \lambda_2 y_t - \lambda_2 x_{t-1} - \lambda_2 \varepsilon_t].$$

Finally, replacing t by $t-1$ substituting into the plant equation (3.1) gives

$$\Delta y_t = -\theta(1 + \lambda_1)(y_{t-1} - y^*_{t-1}) - \theta\lambda_1(S_{t-1} - S^*_{t-1})$$
$$+ \theta\lambda_2\Delta x_{t-1} + d(B)\varepsilon_t, \tag{3.3}$$

where $d(B) = 1 - \theta\lambda_2 B$, and it should be noted that $0 \leqslant \theta\lambda_2 < 1$.

If it is assumed that the two target series y_t^* and S_t^* are both $I(1)$, (3.3) is consistent with y_t, S_t being cointegrated with y_t^*, S_t^*, respectively. For (3.3) to be consistent with multicointegration one has to add the condition that y_t^* and S_t^* are cointegrated. It is thus seen that multicointegration can arise from a special control situation. See also Granger, 1988.

For the inventory example, y_t^* would be expected sales, y_t actual production, c_t planned production, $x_t = 0$, e_t change in inventory, S_t level of inventory, S_t^* planned level to inventory, which is linearly related to planned production or expected sales.

4. Empirical Example: Inventories

The question considered in this section is the form of the relationships between sales, production, and inventory. For a company there is an obvious identity

$$\text{production} - \text{sales} = \text{change in inventory}, \tag{4.1}$$

and if sales is $I(1)$ and the change in inventory is $I(0)$ then production and sales will be cointegrated with a known cointegrating vector $(1 - 1)$. For multicointegration, inventory and sales (and hence production) will also need to be cointegrated. For this particular situation, standard tests for cointegration can be used between inventories and sales as the cointegrating vector at the first level is known. If, using the notation of Section II, both A and D are estimated, new test critical levels for D, the second level, may need to be found. Fortunately, this question can be left for later study. A further advantage of this example is that the first level of cointegration, identity (4.1), will aggregate perfectly from an individual company to an industry and to gross macro variables. The second level of cointegration will not necessarily aggregate unless the D values are (virtually) identical across companies. Aggregation questions are considered by Gonzalo (1989).

The general process of testing for multicointegration and its modeling is based on the methods discussed in Engle and Granger 1987. For a pair of series x_t, y_t the steps are

1. test that both x_t, y_t are $I(1)$,
2. run a least-squares regression

$$x_t = a + b y_t + \text{residual } (z_{1t})$$

to estimate a, b,
3. test that the residual (z_{1t}) is $I(0)$,
4. run the OLS regression

$$x_t = c + dS_{1t} + \text{residual } (w_{1t}),$$

where $S_{1t} = \sum_{j=0}^{t} z_{1,t-1}$, and
5. test if that residual (w_{1t}) is $I(0)$.

The test used in (1) is the augmented Dickey–Fuller (ADF) test in which an OLS regression

$$\Delta x_t = \beta x_{t-1} + \text{lags of } \Delta x_t \qquad (4.2)$$

is run and the t-statistic of β used as the test statistic. The null is $\beta = 0$, which corresponds to $x_t \sim I(1)$. The t-statistic does not have the t-distribution, so that critical values provided by Dickey and Fuller (1979) have to be used. In step (3) the same test statistic is used with x_t in (4.2) replaced by z_t, but as b is estimated somewhat different critical values have to be used, as provided by Engle and Granger (1987). Presumably as b and d are both estimated, the critical values of the ADF test will require further modification. However, for our empirical example, step (2) is unnecessary, and thus regular ADF test can be used in steps (1) and (3) and the Engle–Granger modified test used in step (5). It may be noted that b and d are estimated with extra efficiency, as proved by Stock (1987), when the series involved are cointegrated. The error correction model takes the form

$$\Delta x_t = \rho_1 z_{1,t-1} + \rho_2 w_{1,t-1} + \text{lagged}(\Delta x_t, \Delta y_t) + \text{white noise residual},$$

which is estimated by OLS and the significance of ρ_1, ρ_2 can be tested using standard t-tests. It has become standard practice to repeat all the steps, reversing x_t, y_t in (2), to give z_{2t} for use in (3) and similarly in steps (4) and (5), giving as new residual w_{1t}. The error correction model for Δy_t, then uses z_{2t}, w_{2t} in its construction.

To produce an example, series are taken from the U.S. Department of Commerce, Bureau of Economic Analysis, as available on the Citibank data tape. Monthly figures for the period 1967:1 to 1987:4 for final sales in manufacturing and trade in constant (1982) dollars provide the sales figures. The same tables provide figures for inventories in constant dollars and the 'production' series is then generated by the identity (4.1). The sample size is 244 observations.

The notation used in p_t is production, s_t sales, z_t change in inventory and I_t inventory $= \sum_{j=0}^{t} z_{t-j}$. Note that I_t is the inventory level apart from the initial level I_0, which appears as a constant throughout the sample period.

Using the manufacturing and trade data described above, the ADF test for p_t, s_t both indicated that they are $I(1)$, with test statistics having values -0.55 and -0.41, respectively. Twelve lags were used in the test, and the 95 per cent critical value is approximately 2.88. For z_t, the change in inventory, the ADF test statistic takes the value -4.28, which

allows rejection of the null of $I(1)$ at least at a 99 per cent level. These
initial tests thus indicate that sales and production are cointegrated, z_t is
$I(0)$, and I_t will be $I(1)$. To back up the ADF test, it might be noted
that the first six autocorrelations of the z_t series are 0.432, 0.317, 0.452,
0.304, 0.230, and 0.232.

The regression relating production and the level of inventory gave

$$p_t = 13.77 + 0.62 I_t + w_{1t}, \qquad \bar{R}^2 = 0.93, \qquad DW = 0.10$$

w_{1t} has an ADF test statistic of -3.44, suggesting that the null
hypothesis that w_{1t} is $I(1)$ can be rejected at the 5 per cent level. The
first six autocorrelations of w_{1t} are 0.943, 0.894, 0.841, 0.776, 0.712, and
0.646. The corresponding error correction model is

$$\Delta p_t = \quad 1.90 \quad - \quad 0.81\, z_{t-1} + \quad 0.08 w_{1t-1} + \quad 0.18 \Delta p_{t-1}$$
$$\qquad (5.07) \quad (3.96) \qquad (3.00) \qquad (1.15)$$

$$\qquad - 0.36 \Delta s_{t-1} + \text{residual}, \qquad \bar{R}^2 = 0.06, \qquad DW = 1.97$$
$$\qquad (2.09)$$

(moduli of t-values are shown below).

Reversing p_t, s_t in this sequence gives a residual to step (4) w_{1t} that is
also $I(0)$ at the 5 per cent level, with an ADF statistic of -3.32 and
giving an error correction model

$$\Delta s_t = \quad 0.99 \quad - \quad 0.03 z_{t-1} + \quad 0.02 w_{1,t-1} - \quad 0.42 \Delta s_{t-1}$$
$$\qquad (2.79) \quad (0.16) \qquad (0.63) \qquad (2.47)$$

$$\qquad + \; 0.24 \Delta p_{t-1} + \text{residual}, \qquad \bar{R}^2 = 0.03, \qquad DW = 2.01.$$
$$\qquad (1.51)$$

It is seen that the error correction models indicate that the corrections
occur and are significant only in the production equation.

The results are generally supportive of multicointegration being present between gross production and sales.

The same analysis has been conducted for production and sales of
each of 27 U.S. industries plus industrial groupings with generally
similar conclusions. These results will be presented elsewhere (Ganger
and Lee 1989).

5. Conclusion

This paper has introduced a deeper level of cointegration, which might
be expected to occur in economics, at least in theory. It can arise from

special optimal control situations and, if present, can further improve short- and long-run forecasts. It does seem to be particularly appropriate for considerations of inventory, as illustrated by the empirical example. The extent to which it is found in other economic series can only be established by further empirical work.

Appendix A. Proof of $(1 - B)^2$ root in det $C(B)$

The Cramer representation has

$$\Delta X_t = C(B)\varepsilon_t, \tag{A.1}$$

and using the notation

$$C(B) = C(1) + \Delta C^*(B), \qquad C^*(B) = C^*(1) + \Delta C^{**}(B), \tag{A.2}$$

and

$$C(B) = \begin{bmatrix} C_{11}(B) & C_{12}(B) \\ C_{21}(B) & C_{22}(B) \end{bmatrix}, \tag{A.3}$$

it is found that

$$\det C(B) = E_0 + E_1\Delta + O(\Delta^2),$$

where

$$E_0 = C_{11}(1)C_{22}(1) - C_{12}(1)C_{21}(1)$$
$$E_1 = [C_{11}(1)C_{22}^*(1) + C_{22}C_{11}^*(1) - C_{21}(1)C_{12}^*(1) - C_{12}(1)C_{21}^*(1)].$$

It should be noted that

$$p_t = x_t - DS_t = (1 - D\Delta^{-1})x_t + D\Delta\Delta^{-1}y_t.$$

Substitution from (A.2) and (A.3) gives

$$p_t = \{-D\Delta^{-1}[C_{11}(1) - AC_{21}(1)] - [C_{11}(1) - DC_{11}^*(1) + ADC_{21}^*(1)]$$
$$+ O(\Delta)\}\Delta^{-1}\varepsilon_{1t}$$
$$+\{-D\Delta^{-1}[C_{21}(1) - AC_{22}(1)] + [C_{12}(1) - DC_{12}^*(1) + ADC_{22}^*(1)]$$
$$+ O(\Delta)\}\Delta^{-1}\varepsilon_{2t}.$$

For p_t to be $I(0)$, terms in Δ^{-1} and Δ^{-2} must be zero, giving the conditions

$$C_{11}(1) = AC_{21}(1), \qquad C_{12}(1) = AC_{22}(1), \tag{A.4}$$

which ensure that $E_0 = 0$, and

$$C_{11}(1) = D[C_{11}^*(1) - AC_{21}^*(1)], \qquad C_{12}(1) - D[C_{12}^*(1) - AC_{22}^*(1)], \tag{A.5}$$

which ensure that $E_0 = 0$, hence giving the result that $\det C(B) = O(\Delta)^2$ as required. Conditions (A.4) are sufficient to ensure that $z_t \sim I(0)$ and conditions (A.4) and (A.5) together are those required on $C(B)$ to guarantee multicointegration.

Appendix B. The error correction model

If x_t, y_t are multicointegrated, denoting $X_t = (x_t \quad y_t)'$ as a 2×1 vector the Cramer representation is

$$\Delta X_t = C(B)\varepsilon_t.$$

If $A(B)$ is the adjunct matrix of $C(B)$ this may then be written using the result of Appendix A as

$$A(B)\Delta X_t = d(B)\Delta^2 \varepsilon_t,$$

i.e.

$$A(B)X_t = d(B)\Delta\varepsilon_t. \tag{B.1}$$

Using the expansions

$$A(B) = A(1) + \Delta A^*(B), \qquad A^*(B) = A^*(1) + \Delta A^{**}(B),$$

we have

$$A(B) = A(1)B + \Delta\tilde{A}(B), \tag{B.2}$$

$$\tilde{A}(B) = \tilde{A}(1)B + \Delta\bar{A}(B), \tag{B.3}$$

where

$$\tilde{A}(B) = A(1) + A^*(B), \qquad \bar{A}(B) = A(1) + A^*(1) + A^{**}(B).$$

Let

$$z_t = x_t - Ay_t = (1 \quad -A)X_t, \qquad p_t = x_t - D\delta z_t = (1 - D\delta \quad AD\delta)X_t,$$

where $\delta = \Delta^{-1}$.

Using (B.2), (B.1) can be written

$$\tilde{A}(B)\Delta X_t = -\gamma z_{t-1} + d(B)\Delta\varepsilon_t, \tag{B.4}$$

since $A(1) = \gamma\alpha'$ (see Engle and Granger, 1987). If $\alpha' = (1 - A)$ and

$$A(1) = \begin{bmatrix} A_{11}(1) & A_{12}(1) \\ A_{21}(1) & A_{22}(1) \end{bmatrix},$$

then

$$\gamma = \begin{pmatrix} A_{11}(1) \\ A_{21}(1) \end{pmatrix}.$$

Dividing (B.4) by Δ gives

$$\tilde{A}(B)X_t = -\gamma\delta z_{t-1} + d(B)\varepsilon_t.$$

Substitution from (B.3) by Δ gives

$$\bar{A}(B)\Delta X_t = -\tilde{A}(1)X_{t-1} - \gamma\delta z_{t-1} + d(B)\varepsilon_t$$

$$= -\tilde{A}(1)X_{t-1} - \gamma D^{-1}(x_{t-1} - p_{t-1}) + d(B)\varepsilon_t$$

$$= -[\tilde{A}(1) + D^{-1}\gamma i']X_{t-1} + D^{-1}\gamma p_{t-1} + d(B)\varepsilon_t,$$

where $i' = (1 \quad 0)$. Let

$$\tilde{A}(1) + D^{-1}\gamma i' = \gamma_2\alpha', \qquad D^{-1}\gamma = -\gamma_1,$$

so that

$$\bar{A}(B)\Delta X_t = -\gamma_1 p_{t-1} - \gamma_2 z_{t-1} + d(B)\varepsilon_t.$$

Since

$$\tilde{A}(1) + D^{-1}\gamma i' = \begin{bmatrix} (1 + D^{-1})A_{11}(1) + A_{11}^*(1) & -AA_{11}(1) + A_{12}^*(1) \\ (1 + D^{-1})A_{21}(1) + A_{21}^*(1) & -AA_{21}(1) + A_{22}^*(1) \end{bmatrix},$$

then

$$\gamma_2 = (1 + D^{-1})\gamma + \begin{pmatrix} A_{11}^*(1) \\ A_{21}^*(1) \end{pmatrix} \tag{B.5}$$

or

$$\gamma_2 = \gamma - A^{-1}\begin{pmatrix} A_{12}^*(1) \\ A_{22}^*(1) \end{pmatrix}. \tag{B.6}$$

Finally, it suffices to show that the columns of $A^*(1)$ satisfy that (B.5) = (B.6). Noting that $A(B)$ is the adjunct matrix of $C(B)$, i.e.

$$A(B) = \begin{bmatrix} C_{22}(B) & -C_{12}(B) \\ -C_{21}(B) & C_{11}(B) \end{bmatrix},$$

the relation (B.5) = (B.6) can be written

$$(1 + D^{-1})C_{22}(1) + C_{22}^*(1) = C_{22}(1) = A^{-1}C_{12}^*(1),$$
$$(1 + D^{-1})C_{21}(1) + C_{21}^*(1) = C_{21}(1) + A^{-1}C_{11}^*(1),$$

i.e.

$$C_{22}(1) = DA^{-1}[C_{12}^*(1) - AC_{22}^*(1)],$$
$$C_{21}(1) = DA^{-1}[C_{11}^*(1) - AC_{21}^*(1)],$$

which hold if x_t and y_t are multicointegrated, since then (A.4) and (A.5) hold.

Acknowledgements

Support was provided for this work on NSF Grant SES-87-04669. We would like to thank David Hendry for helpful remarks about Section 3.

References

DICKEY, D. A. and W. A. FULLER (1979), 'Distribution of estimates for autoregressive time series with unit root', *Journal of American Statistical Association*, 427–31.
ENGLE, R. F. and C. W. J. GRANGER (1987), 'Cointegration and error correction: representation, estimation and testing', *Econometrica*, **55**, 251–71.
—— and B.-S. YOO (1987), 'Forecasting and testing in cointegrated systems', *Journal of Econometrics*, **35**, 143–59.

GONZALO, J. (1988), 'Cointegration and aggregation', unpublished Working Paper, University of California, San Diego.

GRANGER, C. W. J. (1983), 'Cointegrated variables and error correcting models', University of California, San Diego.

—— (1986), 'Developments in the study of cointegrated economic Variables', *Oxford Bulletin of Economics and Statistics*, **48**, 213–28.

—— (1988), 'Causality, cointegration and control', *Journal of Economic Dynamics and Control*, **12**, 551–9.

——and T.-H. LEE (1988), 'Investigation of production, sales and inventory relationships using multicointegration and nonsymmetric error correction models', *Journal of Applied Econometrics*, **4**, 5145–59.

JOHANSEN, S. (1988), 'The mathematical structure of the error correction models', *Contemporary Mathematics*, American Math. Assoc.

STOCK, J. (1987), 'Asymptotic properties of least squares estimators of cointegrating Vectors', *Econometrica*, **55**, 1035–56.

YOO, B.-S. (1987), 'Cointegrated time series structure, forecasting and testing', Ph.D. dissertation, University of California, San Diego.

10

Cointegration and Tests of Present Value Models

JOHN Y. CAMPBELL and ROBERT J. SHILLER*

Abstract

Application of some advances in econometrics (in the theory of cointegrated vector autoregressive models) enables us to deal effectively with two problems in rational expectations present value models: nonstationarity of time series and incomplete data on information of market participants. With U.S. data, we find some relatively encouraging new results for the rational expectations theory of the term structure and some puzzling results for the present value model of stock prices.

Present value models are among the simplest dynamic stochastic models of economics. A present value model for two variables, y_t and Y_t, states that Y_t is a linear function of the present discounted value of expected future y_t:

$$Y_t = \theta(1 - \delta)\sum_{i=0}^{\alpha} \delta^i E_t y_{t+i} + c, \qquad (1)$$

where c, the constant, θ, the coefficient of proportionality, and δ, the discount factor, are parameters that may be known a priori or may need to be estimated. Here and in what follows, E_t denotes mathematical expectation, conditional on the full public information set $\mathbf{I}_t$, which includes y_t and Y_t themselves and in general exceeds the information set $\mathbf{H}_t$ available to the econometrician. Models of this form include the expectations theory for interest rates (Y_t is the long-term yield and y_t the one-period rate), the present value model of stock prices (Y_t is the

* We are grateful to Don Andrews, Gregory Chow, Rob Engle, Dick Meese, Peter Phillips, Ken West, and an anonymous referee and to participants in seminars at the University of California, Berkeley, Columbia University, the Federal Reserve Bank of Philadelphia, the National Bureau of Economic Research, Princeton University, Rice University, and the University of Virginia for helpful comments on an earlier version of this paper. We are responsible for any remaining errors. We acknowledge support from the National Science Foundation.

Printed with permission of: *Journal of Political Economy*, Vol. 95, No. 5, (1987).

stock price and y_t the dividend), and, with some modification, the permanent income theory of consumption.[1]

Despite the simplicity of their structure, there is a surprising degree of controversy about the validity of present value models for bonds, stocks, and other economic variables.[2] The controversy seems to be stimulated by three problems that arise in testing equation (1). First, there are several test procedures in the literature: these include single-equation regression tests, tests of cross-equation restrictions on a vector autoregression (VAR), and variance bounds tests. It is not clear how these alternative approaches are related to one another.

Second, a statistical rejection of the model (1) may not have much economic significance. It is entirely possible that the model explains most of the variation in Y_t even if it is rejected at the 5 per cent level. Most work on present value models concentrates on statistical testing rather than informal evaluation of the 'fit' of the models.

Finally, the variables y_t and Y_t usually require some transformation before the theory of stationary stochastic processes can be applied. One approach is to remove a deterministic linear trend, but this can bias test procedures against the model (1) if in fact y_t and Y_t are nonstationary in levels.[3]

In this paper we develop a test of the present value relation that is valid when the variables are stationary in first differences.[4] Hansen and Sargent (1981a), Mankiw et al. (1985), and West (1986, 1987) have also studied this case. We follow Hansen and Sargent and differ from Mankiw et al. and West by using a relatively large information set $\mathbf{H}_t$. We include in $\mathbf{H}_t$ current and lagged values not just of y_t but also of Y_t.

Our choice of information set has several advantages. By including Y_t in the vector stochastic process for analysis, we in effect include *all* relevant information of market participants, even if we econometricians do not observe all their information variables. We can test *all* the implications of the model for the bivariate (y_t, Y_t) process, giving a

---

[1] The discounted sum in eq. (1) extends to an infinite horizon. Most of the methods in this paper can be applied to the finite horizon case, at the cost of some additional complexity. Throughout this paper we will treat conditional expectations as equivalent to linear projections on information.

[2] For bonds, see Sargent (1979), Shiller (1979, 1981a, 1987), Hansen and Sargent (1981a), Shiller, Campbell, and Schoenholtz (1983), and Campbell and Shiller (1984). For stocks, see LeRoy and Porter (1981), Shiller (1981b, 1984), Mankiw, Romer, and Shapiro (1985), Scott (1985), Marsh and Merton (1986), and West (1987, 1988).

[3] This point is made for stocks by Kleidon (1986) and Marsh and Merton (1986). Mankiw and Shapiro (1985) present a similar argument for the permanent income theory of consumption.

[4] It might be attractive to model the variables y and Y as stationary in log first differences. However, since the model (1) is linear in levels, a log specification is intractable unless one is willing to focus on a special case (Kleidon 1986) or to approximate the model (Campbell and Shiller 1986).

natural extension of Fama's (1970) notion of a 'weak-form' test. We can exploit the recently developed theory of cointegrated processes (Phillips and Durlauf 1986; Phillips and Ouliaris 1986; Engle and Granger 1987; Stock 1987). Our test procedure can be interpreted as a single-equation regression or as a test of restrictions on a VAR. We propose a way to assess the economic significance of deviations from (1), comparing the forecast of the present value of future y_t embodied in Y_t with an unrestricted VAR forecast. Because the information set $\mathbf{H}_t$ includes Y_t the two forecasts should be equal if the model is true.

We examine the present value models for bonds and stocks, while a companion piece by one of us (Campbell 1987) studies the permanent income theory of consumption. The paper is organized as follows. Section 1 discusses alternative tests of the present value relation when y_t and Y_t are stationary in first differences rather than levels. Section 2 is an introduction to the literature on cointegration, summarizing the results we use in testing the present value model. Section 3 applies the method to data on bonds and stocks. Section 4 presents conclusions.

1. Alternative Tests of the Present Value Relation

One straightforward way to test the model (1) is to use it to restrict the behaviour of the variable $\xi_t \equiv Y_t - (1/\delta)[Y_{t-1} - \theta(1 - \delta)y_{t-1}]$. Substituting from (1) shows that

$$\xi_t = Y_t - E_{t-1}Y_t + c\left(1 - \frac{1}{\delta}\right). \tag{2}$$

Apart from a constant, ξ_t is the true innovation at time t in Y_t (i.e. the innovation with respect to the full market information set $\mathbf{I}_t$). The model has the striking implication that this innovation is observable when only Y_t, Y_{t-1}, y_{t-1}, and the parameters c, θ, and δ are known.[5] In the applications of this paper, ξ_t has the economic interpretation of an asset return. In the term structure it is the excess return on long bonds over short bills, while in the stock market it is the excess return on stocks over a constant mean, multiplied by the stock price.

Since the right-hand side of (2), adjusted for a constant, is orthogonal to all elements of the information set $\mathbf{I}_{t-1}$, one can test the present value relation by regressing ξ_t on variables in this set and testing that the coefficients are jointly zero. This approach is standard in the literature and seems attractively simple. However, there are some econometric pitfalls and issues of interpretation that need careful handling.

---

[5] The variable ξ_t can also be written as a constant plus the true innovation in the expected present value of all future y_t. We note, however, that in general the model does *not* identify the true innovation in y_t itself.

First, the regressors used to predict ξ_t must be stationary if conventional asymptotic distribution theory is to apply. Of course, there are many stationary elements of $\mathbf{I}_{t-1}$, but one may want to choose variables that summarize the joint history of y_t and Y_t. It is not clear how the stationarity requirement can be reconciled with this objective if y_t and Y_t are themselves nonstationary.

Second, while (1) implies (2), the reverse is not true. Equation (2) is consistent with a more general form of (1) that includes a 'rational bubble', a random variable b satisfying $b_t = \delta E_t b_{t+1}$. Recently there has been considerable interest in testing (1) against the alternative that Y_t is influenced by a rational bubble (Blanchard and Watson 1982; Hamilton and Whiteman 1985; Quah 1986; West 1988).

Third, it is not clear what are the implications for Y_t of nonzero coefficients in a regression of ξ_t on information. Predictability of returns has consequences for asset price behaviour, and one may want to calculate these explicitly.

Further insight into these issues can be gained by defining a new variable $S_t \equiv Y_t - \theta y_t$. We will refer to S_t as the 'spread'. In the case of the term structure, it is just the spread between long- and short-term interest rates; for stocks, it is the difference between the stock price and a multiple of dividends. The spread can also be written as a linear combination of the variables ΔY_t, Δy_t, and ξ_t:$S_t = [1/(1 - \delta)]\Delta Y_t - \theta \Delta y_t - [\delta/(1 - \delta)]\xi_t$.

The present value model (1) implies two alternative interpretations of the spread. Subtracting θy_t from both sides of equation (1) and rearranging, one obtains

$$S_t = E_t S_t^* + c, \qquad (3)$$

where

$$S_t^* = \theta \sum_{i=1}^{\infty} \delta^i \Delta y_t + i,$$

and

$$S_t = \left(\frac{\delta}{1 - \delta}\right) E_t \Delta Y_{t+1} + c. \qquad (4)$$

Equation (3) says that the spread is a constant plus the optimal forecast of S_t^*, a weighted average of future changes in y; equation (4) says that the spread is linear in the optimal forecast of the change in Y.

Equation (4) can be used in an alternative test of the present value model, in which one regresses ΔY_t on a constant, S_{t-1}, and other variables. The coefficient on S_{t-1} should be $(1 - \delta)/\delta$, and the coefficients on the other variables should be zero. This regression is just a linear transformation of the regression that has ξ_t as the dependent variable, and it yields the same test statistic.

Equations (3) and (4) help to resolve the issues raised above. If Δy_t is stationary, it follows from (3) that S_t is stationary; (4) then implies that ΔY_t is stationary. Thus one can use S_t and Δy_t, or S_t and ΔY_t, as stationary variables that summarize the bivariate history of y_t and Y_t in a regression test of the model. (The pair Δy_t and ΔY_t is also stationary, but by using these one would lose information on the relative levels of y_t and Y_t.) Our strategy is to work with S_t and Δy_t.

The effect of a 'rational bubble' alternative is easily seen using (3) and (4). If a term b_t is added to the right-hand side of equation (1), satisfying $b_t = \delta E_t b_{t+1}$, it appears on the right-hand side of (3) but does not affect equations (2) and (4). The term b_t is explosive by construction, so it causes explosive behaviour of S_t by (3), and this is passed through to ΔY_t by (4).[6]

One way to test for the importance of rational bubbles is therefore to test the stationarity of S_t and ΔY_t. This approach has been proposed by Diba and Grossman (1984), among others. As we noted above, S_t can be written as a linear combination of ΔY_t, Δy_t, and ξ_t. Therefore, independent of any model, if three of the variables S_t, ΔY_t, Δy_t, and ξ_t are stationary, the fourth must be also. This linear dependence needs to be taken into account in testing for stationarity.

Finally, (3) and (4) suggest a way to compute the implications for Y_t of predictable ξ_t. Consider estimating a VAR representation for Δy_t and S_t (with their means removed):

$$\begin{bmatrix} \Delta y_t \\ S_t \end{bmatrix} = \begin{bmatrix} a(L) & b(L) \\ c(L) & d(L) \end{bmatrix} \begin{bmatrix} \Delta y_{t-1} \\ S_{t-1} \end{bmatrix} + \begin{bmatrix} u_{1t} \\ u_{2t} \end{bmatrix}, \tag{5}$$

where the polynomials in the lag operator $a(L)$, $b(L)$, $c(L)$, and $d(L)$ are all of order p. This VAR can be used for multiperiod forecasting of Δy_t, and it includes the variable S_t, which, according to (3), is the optimal forecast of the present value of future Δy_t.

To simplify notation, (5) can be stacked into a first-order system

$$\begin{bmatrix} \Delta y_t \\ \cdot \\ \Delta y_{t-p+1} \\ S_t \\ \cdot \\ S_{t-p+1} \end{bmatrix} = \begin{bmatrix} a_1 & \cdots & a_p & b_1 & \cdots & b_p \\ 1 & & & & & \\ & \ddots & & & & \\ & & 1 & & & \\ c_1 & \cdots & c_p & d_1 & \cdots & d_p \\ & & & 1 & & \\ & & & & \ddots & \\ & & & & & 1 \end{bmatrix} \begin{bmatrix} \Delta y_{t-1} \\ \cdot \\ \Delta y_{t-p} \\ S_{t-1} \\ \cdot \\ S_{t-p} \end{bmatrix} + \begin{bmatrix} u_{1t} \\ 0 \\ \cdot \\ 0 \\ u_{2t} \\ 0 \\ \cdot \\ 0 \end{bmatrix},$$

$$\tag{6}$$

[6] Quah (1986) gives an example in which b_t satisfies $b_t = \delta E_t b_{t+1}$ but is stationary. However, this example violates the equivalence of conditional expectations and linear projections, which we assume here.

where blank elements are zero. This can be written more succinctly as $\mathbf{z}_t = \mathbf{A}\mathbf{z}_{t-1} + \mathbf{v}_t$. The matrix $\mathbf{A}$ is called the companion matrix of the VAR. For all i, $E(\mathbf{z}_{t+i}|\mathbf{H}_t) = \mathbf{A}^i\mathbf{z}_t$, where $\mathbf{H}_t$ is the limited information set containing current and lagged values of y_t and Y_t or, equivalently, of $\mathbf{z}_t$. As elsewhere in the paper, we are taking conditional expectations to be linear projections on information.

We can now discuss the implications of the present value relation for the VAR system. A rather weak implication is that S_t must linearly Granger-cause Δy_t unless S_t is itself an exact linear function of current and lagged Δy_t (which is a stochastic singularity we do not observe in the data; it would require, e.g., that the variance-covariance matrix of u_{1t} and u_{2t}, $\mathbf{\Omega}$, be singular).

The intuitive explanation for this result is that S_t is an optimal forecast of a weighted sum of future values of Δy_t, conditional on agents' full information set. Therefore, S_t will have incremental explanatory power for future Δy_t if agents have information useful for forecasting Δy_t beyond the history of that variable. If agents do not have such information, they form S_t as an exact linear function of current and lagged Δy_t.[7]

The full set of restrictions of the present value model is more demanding. We obtain these restrictions by projecting equation (3) on to the information set $\mathbf{H}_t$, noting that the left-hand side is unchanged because S_t is in $\mathbf{H}_t$ and rewriting as

$$\mathbf{g}'\mathbf{z}_t = \theta\sum_{i=1}^{\infty} \delta^i\mathbf{h}'\mathbf{A}^i\mathbf{z}_t,$$

where $\mathbf{g}'$ and $\mathbf{h}'$ are row vectors with $2p$ elements, all of which are zero except for the $p + 1$st element of $\mathbf{g}'$ and the first element of $\mathbf{h}'$, which are unity. If this expression is to hold for general $\mathbf{z}_t$ (i.e. for nonsingular $\mathbf{\Omega}$), it must be the case that

$$\mathbf{g}' = \theta\sum_{i=1}^{\infty} \delta^i\mathbf{h}'\mathbf{A}^i = \theta\mathbf{h}'\delta\mathbf{A}(\mathbf{I} - \delta\mathbf{A})^{-1}. \tag{7}$$

Here the second equality follows by evaluating the infinite sum, noting that it must converge because the variables Δy_t and S_t are stationary under the null.[8]

The restrictions of equation (7) appear to be highly nonlinear cross-equation restrictions of the type described by Hansen and Sargent (1981b) as the 'hallmark' of rational expectations models. However, it

---

[7] A formal proof is as follows. Suppose that S_t does not Granger-cause Δy_t. Then $E(\Delta y_{t+i}|\mathbf{H}_t = E(\Delta y_{t+i}|\Delta y_t, \Delta y_{t-1}, \ldots)$ for all i, and from (3), $E(S_t|\mathbf{H}_t) = E(S_t|\Delta y_t, \Delta y_{t-1}, \ldots)$, an exact linear function of current and lagged Δy_t. But because S_t is itself in the information set $\mathbf{H}_t$, $S_t = E(S_t|\mathbf{H}_t)$.

[8] Under an explosive bubble alternative this infinite sum will not converge, and the matrix $(\mathbf{I} - \delta\mathbf{A})$ will be singular.

turns out that (7) can be simplified so that (taking θ and δ as given) its restrictions are linear and easily interpreted. Postmultiplying both sides of (7) by $(\mathbf{I} - \delta\mathbf{A})$, one obtains

$$\mathbf{g}'(\mathbf{I} - \delta\mathbf{A}) = \theta\mathbf{h}'\delta\mathbf{A}. \tag{8}$$

From the structure of the matrix $\mathbf{A}$, the constraints imposed by (8) on individual coefficients are $c_i = -\theta a_i$, $i = 1, \ldots, p$; $d_1 = (1/\delta) - \theta b_1$; and $d_i = -\theta b_i$, $i = 2, \ldots, p$. By adding $\theta\Delta y_t$ to S_t, one can interpret these restrictions. They state that $\xi_t = S_t - (1/\delta)S_{t-1} + \theta\Delta y_t$ is unpredictable given lagged Δy_t and S_t, which is what equation (2) implies for the information set $\mathbf{H}_t$. In our empirical application, we obtain a Wald test statistic for equation (8) that is numerically identical to the Wald test statistic for a regression of ξ_t on lagged Δy_t and S_t.[9]

The major advantage of the VAR framework is that it can be used to generate alternative measures of the economic importance, not merely the statistical significance, of deviations from the present value relation. To see this more clearly, suppose that the present value model is false so that $E_t\xi_{t+i} \neq 0$ for $i \geq 1$. Then equations (3) and (4) no longer hold. We define the 'theoretical spread', S_t', as the optimal forecast, given the information set $\mathbf{H}_t$, of the present value of all future changes in y:

$$S_t' \equiv E(S_t^*|\mathbf{H}_t) = \theta\mathbf{h}'\delta\mathbf{A}(\mathbf{I} - \delta\mathbf{A})^{-1}\mathbf{z}_t. \tag{9}$$

We then have, ignoring constant terms,

$$S_t - S_t' = \sum_{i=1}^{\infty} \delta^i E(\xi_{t+i}|\mathbf{H}_t) \tag{10}$$

and

$$S_t - \left(\frac{\delta}{1-\delta}\right)E(\Delta Y_{t+1}|\mathbf{H}_t = \left(\frac{1}{1-\delta}\right)E(\xi_{t+1}|\mathbf{H}_t). \tag{11}$$

Equations (10) and (11) measure deviations from the model in two different ways. The metric of equation (11) is the difference between S_t and the optimal forecast, given the information set $\mathbf{H}_t$, of the one-period change in Y. Equation (11) shows that this difference is large if excess returns are predictable one period in advance.

The metric of equation (10) is the difference between S_t and the theoretical spread, which is large if the present value of all future excess returns is predictable. By this measure, a large deviation from the model requires not only that movements in ξ be predictable one period in

---

[9] However, this statistic is not numerically identical to the Wald statistic for a test of eq. (7), even though (7) and (8) are algebraically equivalent restrictions. Nonlinear transformations of restrictions can change the numerical values of Wald statistics and, as Gregory and Veall (1985) point out, can dramatically alter their power. We report Wald statistics for (8) in the tables that summarize our empirical results and Wald statistics for (7) in notes.

advance but that they be predictable many periods in advance. Loosely speaking, predictable excess returns must be persistent as well as variable.[10]

We use the VAR framework not only to conduct statistical tests of the present value relation but also to evaluate its failures using the metric of equation (10). We display time-series plots of the spread S_t and the theoretical spread S_t', the unrestricted VAR forecast of the present value of future changes in y. If the present value model is true, these variables should differ only because of sampling error. Large observed differences in the time-series movements of the two variables imply (subject to sampling error) economically important deviations from the model.

The VAR framework can also be used to test the present value model against more specific alternatives. Volatility tests, for example, are designed to test against the alternative that Y_t or some transformation of it 'moves too much'.

We present two different volatility tests. The first is just a test that the ratio $\mathrm{var}(S_t)/\mathrm{var}(S_t')$ is unity. This ratio, together with its standard error, can be computed from the VAR system. Under the present value model, the ratio should be one but would be larger than one if the spread is too volatile relative to information about future y. A statistic that complements this is the correlation between S_t and S_t' since if the variance ratio and correlation both equal one, then S_t must equal S_t' and the model is satisfied.[11]

We obtain a second volatility test, following West (1987), as follows. Let us define ξ_t' as θ times the innovation from $t-1$ to t in the expected present value of Δy, conditional on the VAR information set:

$$\xi_t' \equiv \theta \sum_{i=0}^{\infty} \delta^i [E(\Delta y_{t+i}|\mathbf{H}_t) - E(\Delta y_{t+i}|\mathbf{H}_{t-1})] \tag{12}$$

$$= S_t' - \left(\frac{1}{\delta}\right) S_{t-1}' + \theta \Delta y_t.$$

Under the present value model, $\xi_t' = \xi_t$ since $S_t' = S_t$. We construct the ratio $\mathrm{var}(\xi_t)/\mathrm{var}(\xi_t')$, again with standard error.[12] The model implies that this ratio should be one, while the notion that stock prices are too

---

[10] The terminology of our earlier paper (Campbell and Shiller 1984) may be helpful in understanding (10) and (11). The right-hand side of (11) is proportional to what we called the one-period 'holding premium', and the right-hand side of (10) is what we called the 'rolling premium'.

[11] We compute the levels variance ratio and correlation from the sample moments of S_t and S_t'. We report numerical standard errors that are conditional on the sample moments of $\mathbf{z}_t$ and take account of sampling error only in the coefficients of the estimated VAR.

[12] We use the estimated variance-covariance matrix of the VAR to compute the innovations variance ratio. The standard error takes account of sampling error in this matrix as well as in the VAR coefficients.

volatile suggests that it will be greater than one. We call the first of our variance ratios the 'levels variance ratio' and the second the 'innovations variance ratio'.

The fact that a linear combination S_t of y_t and Y_t is stationary in its level, even though y_t and Y_t are individually stationary only in first differences, turns out to be important for understanding present value models. In the language of time-series analysis, the vector $\mathbf{x}_t = (y_t \ Y_t)'$ is cointegrated. Cointegrated vectors have a number of important properties, which we now discuss.

2. Properties of Cointegrated Vectors

In this section we summarize the theory of cointegrated processes and show how it applies to present value models.

DEFINITION (Engle and Granger 1987). A vector $\mathbf{x}_t$ is said to be cointegrated of order (d, b), denoted $\mathbf{x}_t \text{CI}(d, b)$, if (i) all components of $\mathbf{x}_t$ are integrated of order d (stationary in dth differences) and (ii) there exists at least one vector $\boldsymbol{\alpha}$ ($\neq 0$) such that $\boldsymbol{\alpha}' \mathbf{x}_t$ is integrated of order $d - b$, $b > 0$.

When y_t is stationary in first differences, the vector $\mathbf{x}_t = (y_t \ Y_t)'$ is $\text{CI}(1, 1)$ if the present value model holds. The $\text{CI}(1, 1)$ case is the one that has been studied almost exclusively in the theoretical literature, and the results that follow apply to it.

Cointegrated systems of order $(1, 1)$ have two unusual properties. These concern the existence of well-behaved vector time-series representations for the cointegrated variables and the estimation of unknown elements of the vector $\boldsymbol{\alpha}$. Both properties turn out to be relevant for testing present value models.

The first important property of a cointegrated vector is that the vector moving average (VMA) representation of the first difference $\Delta \mathbf{x}_t$ is noninvertible. Equivalently, the spectral density matrix of $\Delta \mathbf{x}_t$ is singular at zero frequency. This singularity is what 'holds together' the elements of $\mathbf{x}_t$ so that a linear combination is stationary.

More formally, write $\Delta \mathbf{x}_t = \mathbf{K}(L)\boldsymbol{\varepsilon}_t = \mathbf{I}\boldsymbol{\varepsilon}_t + \mathbf{K}_1 \boldsymbol{\varepsilon}_{t-1} + \ldots$. The matrix $\mathbf{M} = \mathbf{K}(1)\mathbf{K}(1)'$, where $\mathbf{K}(1) = \mathbf{I} + \mathbf{K}_1 + \mathbf{K}_2 + \ldots$, is the spectral density matrix of $\Delta \mathbf{x}_t$ at zero frequency. Now if the variance of $\boldsymbol{\alpha}' \mathbf{x}_t$ exists, it will be given by

$$\text{var}(\boldsymbol{\alpha}' \mathbf{x}_t) = \sum_{i=0}^{x} \boldsymbol{\alpha}' \mathbf{C}_i \mathbf{V} \mathbf{C}_i' \boldsymbol{\alpha},$$

where $\mathbf{V}$ is the variance-covariance matrix of $\boldsymbol{\varepsilon}_t$ and $\mathbf{C}_i =$

$\mathbf{I} + \mathbf{K}_1 + \ldots + \mathbf{K}_i$. Ignoring the degenerate case in which $\mathbf{V}$ is singular, the summation above converges only if $\boldsymbol{\alpha}'\mathbf{C}_i$ converges to zero. But the limit of $\mathbf{C}_i$ as $i \rightarrow \infty$ is $\mathbf{K}(1)$, so for convergence we must have $\boldsymbol{\alpha}'\mathbf{K}(1) = 0$, which requires $\mathbf{K}(1)$, and hence $\mathbf{M}$, to be singular.

It follows from this that if an economic theory imposes cointegration on a set of nonstationary variables, simple first differencing of all the variables can lead to econometric problems. Noninvertibility of the VMA destroys the usual argument for using a finite VAR representation, that a finite VAR can approximate the true VMA arbitrarily well. Intuitively, the problem arises because a cointegrated system has fewer unit roots than variables, so first differencing all the variables amounts to overdifferencing the system. [13]

Fortunately, there is a simple solution to the difficulty, which is to include $\boldsymbol{\alpha}'\mathbf{x}_t$ in a VAR along with a subset of the elements of $\Delta\mathbf{x}_t$. An equation that relates the change in an element of $\mathbf{x}_t$ to its own lags and lags of $\boldsymbol{\alpha}'\mathbf{x}_t$ is called an error-correction model for that element of $\mathbf{x}_t$. The VAR proposed in the previous section to test present value models is an error-correction model for y_t, along with an equation describing the evolution of $\boldsymbol{\alpha}'\mathbf{x}_t$.

The second major result from the theory of cointegration concerns the 'cointegrating vector' $\boldsymbol{\alpha}$. In a present value model, $\boldsymbol{\alpha}$ is unique up to a scalar normalization and is proportional to $(-\theta\ 1)'$. Stock (1987) and Phillips and Ouliaris (1986) prove that a variety of methods provide estimates that converge to the true parameter at a rate proportional to the sample size T (rather than $\sqrt{T}$ as in ordinary cases). The reason for this is that, asymptotically, all linear combinations of the elements of $\mathbf{x}_t$ other than $\boldsymbol{\alpha}'\mathbf{x}_t$ have infinite variance.

The practical implication is that an unknown element of $\boldsymbol{\alpha}$ may be estimated in a first-stage regression and then treated as known in second-stage procedures, whose asymptotic standard errors will still be correct. This is extremely useful in carrying out the VAR tests of the previous section. In the case of stock prices, for example, the present value model constrains $\theta = \delta/(1 - \delta)$, so one can estimate the discount factor from a preliminary regression and then treat it as known in testing the model.

Two types of preliminary regression have been proposed for estimating the unknown parameter θ. The first, called the cointegrating regression by Engle and Granger (1987), is just a regression of Y_t on y_t. The second is an 'error-correction' regression of Δy_t or ΔY_t on lagged changes in and levels of y_t and Y_t. In the first case, one estimates θ as

---

[13] Shiller (1981*b*) and Melino (1983) criticized Sargent (1979) on this ground (and on the ground that he failed to test the implications of the model for the relative levels of y_t and Y_t). Baillie, Lippens, and McMahon (1983) also overdifferenced their system. Hansen and Sargent (1981*a*) corrected the problems with Sargent's procedure.

the coefficient on y_t, while in the second case one takes the ratio of the coefficient on lagged y_t to that on lagged Y_t.

One might argue that use of the error-correction regression is preferable because it accounts more fully for the short-run dynamics of Y_t and y_t. However, it has an important disadvantage. For any cointegrated vector with two elements, there are two possible error-correction regressions, one for Δy_t and one for ΔY_t. Cointegration alone does not rule out that, in one of these regressions, lagged Y_t and y_t have zero coefficients in the population, so that the coefficient ratio fails to identify the desired parameter.[14] Of course, under the present value model the error-correction equation for Δy_t has nonzero coefficients (because $\alpha' x_t$ Granger-causes Δy_t), but this is not implied by all plausible alternatives. Accordingly, we rely primarily on the cointegrating regression to identify θ.

One may want to conduct a formal statistical test of the null hypothesis that x_t is not cointegrated. This turns out to pose some difficult statistical problems. If a candidate for the cointegrating vector α is available, the null hypothesis is that $\alpha' x_t$ is nonstationary, and one can use a modified Dickey–Fuller (1981) test, regressing the change in $\alpha' x_t$ on a constant and a single lagged level. The t-statistics and F-statistic are corrected for serial correlation in the equation residual as proposed by Phillips and Perron (1986) and Phillips (1987) and then compared with significance levels computed numerically by Dickey and Fuller. If the statistics are sufficiently high, the null hypothesis is rejected.

If the cointegrating vector is not known but must be estimated from a cointegrating regression, the Dickey–Fuller significance levels are no longer appropriate. Engle and Granger (1987) analyse a variety of tests that use the residual from the cointegrating regression, an estimate of $\alpha' x_t$. We report two of their test statistics, one based on the Dickey–Fuller regression and one that augments that regression with four lagged dependent variables. Engle and Granger provide significance levels for these tests, based on a Monte Carlo study.[15]

Phillips and Ouliaris (1986) propose an alternative test procedure for the null hypothesis of no cointegration. Their method involves computing the matrix $\mathbf{M}$, the spectral density matrix at zero frequency, nonparametrically. As discussed above, this matrix will be nonsingular under the null and singular under the alternative of cointegration. Unlike the Engle–Granger procedures, their test statistics have a

---

[14] Cointegration does rule out that the coefficients are zero in both error-correction regressions.

[15] The Monte Carlo results are based on 10,000 replications of 100 observations of independent random walks, with four lagged residual changes included in the test.

distribution that is asymptotically free of nuisance parameters. They applied their methods to our data, and we note their results below.

3. Testing the Model in Bond and Stock Markets

In this section we apply the methods developed above to test present value models for bonds and stocks. The model for bonds, usually referred to as the 'expectations theory of the term structure', is a special case of equation (1) in which the parameters θ and δ are known a priori (θ equals one, and δ is a parameter of linearization), while the constant c is a liquidity premium unrestricted by the model.[16]

We test the present value model for bonds on a monthly U.S. Treasury 20-year yield series, available from 1959 to 1983 from Salomon Brothers' *Analytical Record of Yields and Yield Spreads*. The short rate used is a one-month Treasury bill rate, obtained from the *Treasury Bulletin* for dates prior to 1982 and from the *Wall Street Journal* thereafter.[17] These data were previously studied in Campbell and Shiller (1984); Shiller *et al.* (1983) worked with very similar data. We present empirical results both for the full sample 1959:1–1983:10 and for a short sample ending in 1978:8, which is more likely to correspond to a single interest rate regime.[18]

The present value model for stocks is a special case of equation (1) in which θ is known to equal $\delta/(1 - \delta)$. The model restricts the constant c to be zero. The discount factor δ is not known a priori but can be inferred by estimating the cointegrating vector for stock prices and dividends; a consistent estimate is also provided by the sample mean return on stocks.[19]

One difficulty with this formulation for stocks is that Y_t and y_t are not measured contemporaneously. The term Y_t is a beginning-of-period stock price, and y_t is paid sometime within period t. Literal application of the methods outlined in Section I would require us to assume that y_t is known to the market at the start of period t; but, as pointed out by West (1987) and others, this might lead us to a spurious rejection of the model if in fact y_t is known only at the start of period $t + 1$. Intuitively,

---

[16] The linearization required to write the expectations theory in this form is explained in Shiller (1979) and Shiller *et al.* (1983).

[17] The *Treasury Bulletin* and *Wall Street Journal* data are consistent with one another at dates when they are both available.

[18] For both samples, the parameter of linearization δ is set equal to $1/(1 + R)$, with R at $0.0587/12$ (the mean 20-year bond rate in the short sample, expressed at a monthly rate). Our subsequent empirical results are conditional on a fixed value of δ.

[19] The sample mean return converges to the population mean only at rate $\sqrt{T}$ and therefore should not strictly be taken as known in second-stage procedures. However, we ignore this problem in our empirical work.

it is not hard to 'predict' excess returns using ex post information. In order to avoid this problem, we modify the procedures of Section 1 by constructing a variable $SL_t \equiv = Y_t - \theta y_{t-1}$. We use this variable in our tests and alter the cross-equation restrictions appropriately. The dependent variables in the VAR are now SL_t and Δy_{t-1}, both of which are in the information set at the start of time t but not at the start of time $t - 1$ under our conservative assumption about the market's information.[20] Since $SL_t = S_t + \theta \Delta y_t$, it is of course stationary if S_t and Δy_t are.

We tested the model for stocks using time-series data for real annual prices and dividends on a broad stock index from 1871 to 1986. The term Y_t is the Standard and Poor's composite stock price index for January, divided by the January producer price index scaled so that the 1967 producer price index equals 100. (Before 1900 an annual average producer price index was used.) The nominal dividend series is, starting in 1926, dividends per share adjusted to index, fourquarter total, for the Standard and Poor's composite index. The nominal dividend before 1926 was taken from Cowles (1939), who extended the Standard and Poor's series back in time.[21] Finally, y_t is the nominal dividend series, divided by the annual average producer price index scaled so that the 1967 producer price index equals 100.

As shown in table 1, parts A and B, we ran unit root tests on our raw data and the various linear combinations discussed in Section 1. This is an important preliminary because our approach is appropriate only if y_t is integrated of order one. We present test statistics that are based on the t-statistic on the lagged level in a Dickey–Fuller regression, corrected for fourth-order serial correlation as proposed by Phillips and Perron (1986) and Phillips (1987).[22] We ran the Dickey–Fuller regression with and without a time trend; the former is appropriate when the alternative hypothesis is that the series is stationary around a trend, the latter when the alternative is that the series is stationary around a fixed mean.

The results in part A of table 1 are generally supportive of the view that short- and long-term interest rates are cointegrated, with the

[20] Engle and Watson (1985) did some regressions similar to ours, using a similar data set on stock prices and dividends. They used the variable S_t rather than SL_t. Their results differ from ours in that they found no evidence of Granger causality from S_t to Δy_t, but they did not reject the present value model more strongly than we do.

[21] The dividend data differ slightly from those used in Shiller (1981b), Mankiw et al. (1985), West (1987), and others. It has recently come to our attention that the second (1939) edition of Cowles's book contains some corrections to the dividend series presented in the original 1938 edition, and these corrections have been incorporated here.

[22] The results are qualitatively unchanged by looking at other statistics from the Dickey–Fuller regression or by varying the order of the serial correlation correction between one and 10.

cointegrating vector equal to $(-1\ 1)$ as implied by the expectations theory. Over the short sample 1959–78, one cannot reject the hypothesis that short and long rates have a unit root at even the 10 per cent level; however, there is strong evidence that *changes* in interest rates are

TABLE 1. Unit root tests (Test Statistic $Zt\alpha$)

Variable	With trend	Without trend
A. In the term structure		
Sample 1959–78:		
y_t	−2.78	−1.72
Y_t	−2.76	−.46
Δy_t	−17.40 (1%)	−17.44 (1%)
ΔY_t	−15.30 (1%)	−15.32 (1%)
S_t	−3.15 (10%)	−3.08 (5%)
ξ_t	−15.22 (1%)	−15.25 (1%)
Sample 1959–83		
y_t	−3.83 (2.5%)	−2.32
Y_t	−2.51	−.50
Δy_t	−17.05 (1%)	−17.08 (1%)
ΔY_t	−15.27 (1%)	−15.29 (1%)
S_t	−4.77 (1%)	−4.67 (1%)
ξ_t	−15.18 (1%)	−15.19 (1%)
B. In the Stock Market		
y_t	−2.88	−1.28
Y_t	−2.19	−1.53
Δy_t	−8.40 (1%)	−8.44 (1%)
ΔY_t	−9.91 (1%)	−9.96 (1%)
$\theta = 31.092$:		
SL_t	−4.35 (1%)	−4.31 (1%)
ξ_t	−9.93 (1%)	−9.99 (1%)
$\theta = 12.195$:		
SL_t	−2.68	−2.15
ξ_t	−9.76 (1%)	−9.69 (1%)

Note: Test statistics for a variable X_t are based on the *t*-statistics on α in the regression $\Delta X_t = \mu + \beta t + \alpha X_{t-1}$ (with trend) or the regression $\Delta X_t = \mu + \alpha X_{t-1}$ (without trend). The *t*-statistic is corrected for serial correlation in the equation residual in the manner proposed by Phillips and Perron (1986) and Phillips (1987). Significance levels are: with trend: 10%, −3.12: 5%, −3.41; 2.5%, −3.66; 1%, −3.96; without trend: 10%, −2.57; 5%, −2.86; 2.5%, −3.12; 1%, −3.43.

stationary. The hypothesis that the long-short spread has a unit root is rejected at the 10 per cent level when a trend is estimated and at the 5 per cent level when the trend is excluded from the regression. Finally, the excess return ξ_t also appears stationary; this, together with the results for Δy_t and ΔY_t, is indirect evidence for stationarity of the spread because of the linear dependence discussed in Section 1.

Results are fairly similar over the full sample 1959–83. There is even stronger evidence that the spread is stationary, and the unit root hypothesis for short rates can be rejected unless a trend in interest rates is ruled out on a priori grounds.[23]

In part B of the table, we repeated these tests for the stock market data. Once again y_t and Y_t appear to be integrated of order one. In the stock market, the parameter θ is not determined by the present value model as it is in the term structure. Therefore, we must compute SL_t and ξ_t using estimates of θ obtained from the data. Strictly speaking, this invalidates the Phillips–Perron tests for SL_t and ξ_t, but we report the statistics as data description.

Table 2 gives details of alternative estimation procedures for θ. The cointegrating regression estimates θ at 31.092; the corresponding real discount rate (the reciprocal of θ) is 3.2 per cent, which is lower than

TABLE 2. Estimation of the cointegrating vector and test for cointegration in the stock market

	R^2	Estimate of θ	Implied discount rate (%)
1. $Y_t = -12.979 + 31.092y_t$	.842	31.092	3.2
2. $\Delta y_t = .101 + .165\Delta y_{t-1} + .010\Delta Y_t$			
$\quad - .157y_{t-1} + .004Y_t$	.373	37.021	2.7
3. Sample mean return = 8.2%	. . .	12.195	8.2

Tests of no cointegration: Engle and Granger (1987) ξ_2 statistic for eq. (1) residual, 3.58; significance levels: 10%, 3.03; 5%, 3.37; 1%, 4.07. Engle and Granger (1987) ξ_3 statistic for eq. (1) residual, 2.64; significance levels: 10%, 2.84; 5%, 3.17; 1%, 3.77.

[23] The results in table 1, pt. A, are more favourable to the hypothesis of cointegration between long and short rates than are the results reported by Phillips and Ouliaris (1986). They reject the null hypothesis of no cointegration at only the 15 per cent level (their table 6). However, their procedure does not impose the cointegrating vector a priori, and this may involve a loss of power.

the average dividend–price ratio and considerably lower than the sample mean return of 8.2 per cent.[24] The error-correction regression delivers a fairly similar estimate of θ, 37.021 with an implied real discount rate of 2.7 per cent. We proceed to construct SL_t using discount rates of 8.2 per cent and 3.2 per cent as a check on the robustness of our methods.

Engle and Granger's tests for no cointegration, based on the residual from the cointegrating regression, give mixed results: the ξ_2 statistic rejects at the 5 per cent level, while the ξ_3 statistic narrowly fails to reject at the 10 per cent level. The Phillips–Perron tests in part B of table 1 are also mixed. Both SL_t and ξ_t appear to be stationary when the 3.2 per cent discount rate is used, but at an 8.2 per cent discount rate the tests fail to reject the unit root null for SL_t even though they reject for Δy_t, ΔY_t, and ξ_t. There seems to be some evidence for cointegration between stock prices and dividends, but it is weaker than the evidence for cointegration in the term structure.[25]

The results in table 1 do not suggest that a 'rational bubble' is present in the term structure or the stock market since a bubble would cause both ΔY_t and S_t to be nonstationary. Accordingly, we interpret the test statistics below in terms of predictable excess returns.

In table 3, part A, we report summary statistics for a VAR test of the expectations theory of the term structure. The VAR includes Δy_t and S_t as variables, and the number of lags is chosen by the Akaike information criterion (AIC).[26] White's (1984) heteroscedasticity-consistent covariance matrix estimator is used in constructing standard errors and test statistics. The VARs are estimated for the short sample 1959–78 and the full sample 1959–83; they have eleven and six lags, respectively.

In both sample periods the lagged variables have a fair degree of explanatory power for the change in short rates. The R^2 for the Δy_t equation is 21.6 per cent in the short sample and 17.1 per cent in the

[24] The estimate of θ that corresponds to the sample mean return is 12.195. The higher estimate in the cointegrating regression is associated with a negative constant term; under the present value model, the constant should be proportional to the unconditional mean change in dividends, so it should be positive rather than negative. An estimated discount rate lower than the mean dividend–price ratio is consistent with the model only if dividends are expected to decline through time, the historical rise being due to sampling error.

[25] Phillips and Ouliaris (1986) did not reject the null hypothesis of no cointegration between stock prices and dividends at even the 25 per cent level (their table 6). Campbell and Shiller (1986) report unit root tests for log dividends, log prices, and the log dividend–price ratio. There is some evidence for trend stationarity of log dividends, no evidence against the unit root null for log prices, and strong evidence for stationarity of the dividend–price ratio.

[26] That is, we pick the number of lags to minimize $(-\ln \text{ likelihood} + \text{number of}$ parameters) in the VAR. Sawa (1978) has argued that the AIC tends to choose models of higher order than the true model but states that the bias is negligible when $p < T/10$, as it is here. The test statistics in table 3 are not highly sensitive to small changes in the lag length of the VAR system.

full sample. This argues against the view of Mankiw and Miron (1986) that short-rate changes are essentially unpredictable in the postwar period in the United States. Furthermore, there is strong evidence that spreads Granger-cause short-rate changes, as they should do if the expectations theory is true. The hypothesis of no Granger causality can be rejected at the 0.01 per cent level for the short sample and the 0.3 per cent level for the full sample.

A formal test of the expectations theory restrictions in equation (8) rejects very strongly. The null that excess returns on long bonds are unpredictable can be rejected at less than the 0.005 per cent level in the short sample and at the 0.03 per cent level in the full sample. The R^2 values for excess returns are 26.3 per cent and 16.7 per cent, respectively.[27] In the corresponding regression (4), which has the change in the long rate as its dependent variable, the coefficient on the spread has the wrong sign (-0.020 in the short sample and -0.039 in the full sample).[28]

Despite these negative results, the summary statistics in table 3, part A, suggest that there is an important element of truth to the expectations theory of the term structure. The spread does seem to move very closely with the theoretical spread, the unrestricted forecast of the present value of future short-rate changes. In both sample periods the variance of the spread is insignificantly different from the variance of the theoretical spread (i.e. our 'levels variance ratio' does not reject), and the two variables have similar innovation variances and an extremely high correlation. In the 1959–78 period the correlation between the actual and theoretical spreads is 0.978 with a standard error of 0.011, while in the 1959–83 period it is 0.956 with a standard error of 0.098. Figure 1 illustrates the comovement of S_t and S'_t in the short sample.[29]

What this suggests is that tests of predictability of returns are highly sensitive to deviations from the expectations theory—so sensitive, in fact, that they may obscure some of the merits of the theory. An example illustrates the point. Suppose long and short rates differ from the expectations theory in the following manner: $S_t = S'_t + w_t$, where w_t is serially uncorrelated noise. As Campbell and Shiller (1984) point out,

---

[27] Nonlinear Wald tests of eq. (7) reject at signficance levels of less than 0.005 per cent in the short sample and 8.4 per cent in the full sample.

[28] This is consistent with the results of Shiller et al.(1983).

[29] The high correlation of these variables in postwar U.S. data might also have been inferred from results in Modigliani and Shiller (1973) (see particularly their fig. 6). Despite the evidence reported in Modigliani and Shiller and in the present paper, one of us (Shiller 1979) presented evidence suggesting that long-term interest rates are too volatile to accord with the expectations theory. By contrast with Modigliani and Shiller and the present paper, Shiller (1979) assumed that *levels* of short rates are stationary, an assumption more clearly appropriate for prewar data sets.

TABLE 3.   Tests of present value model

A. In the term structure

Sample 1959–78:
   Akaike criterion selects 11-lag VAR
   Δy equation R^2 = .216; S Granger-causes Δy at 0.01% level
   S equation R^2 = .877; Δy Granger-causes S at 0.3% level
   Test of present value model: $\chi^2(22)$ = 83.02; P-value < 0.005%
   Summary statistics:

$E(\Delta y)$ = .016	$\sigma(S)$	= 1.060
$E(S)$ = 1.144	var(S)/var(S')	= .987 (.360)
$E(S')$ = .016	corr(S, S')	= .978 (0.11)
$\sigma(\Delta y)$ = .442	var(ξ)/var(ξ')	= 1.160 (1.146)

Sample 1959–83:
   Akaike criterion selects ix-lag VAR
   Δy equation R^2 = .171; S Granger-causes Δy at 0.3% level
   S equation R^2 = .772; Δy Granger-causes S at 1.3% level
   Test of present value model: $\chi^2(12)$ = 35.63; P-value = 0.03%
   Summary statistics:

$E(\Delta y)$ = .021	$\sigma(S)$	= 1.320
$E(S)$ = 1.138	var(S)/var(S')	= 3.394 (3.948)
$E(S')$ = .021	corr(S, S')	= .956 (.098)
$\sigma(\Delta y)$ = .793	var(ξ)/var(ξ')	= .502 (.506)

B. In the stock market

Sample 1871–1986:
θ = 12.195 (8.2% discount rate): Akaike criterion selects four-lag VAR
   Δy equation R^2 = .400; SL Granger-causes Δy at < 0.001% level
   SL equation R^2 = .837; Δy Granger-causes SL at 63.3% level
   Test of present value model with mean restriction: $\chi^2(9)$ = 15.74;
P-value = 7.2%
   Test of present value model without mean restriction: $\chi^2(8)$ = 15.72;
P-value = 4.7%
   Summary statistics:

$E(\Delta y)$ = .017	$\sigma(SL)$	= 15.51
$E(SL)$ = 16.07	var(SL)/var(SL') =	67.22 (86.04)
$E(SL')$ = 2.563	corr(SL, SL') =	−.459 (.801)
$\sigma(\Delta y)$ = .168	var(ξ)/var(ξ') =	11.27 (4.49)

θ = 31.092 (3.2% discount rate): Akaike criterion selects two-lag VAR
   Δy equation R^2 = .378; SL Granger-causes Δy at < 0.001% level
   SL equation R^2 = .516; Δy Granger-causes SL at 1.8% level
   Test of present value model with mean restriction: $\chi^2(5)$ = 14.90;
P-value = 1.1%
   Test of present value model without mean restriction: $\chi^2(4)$ = 5.75;
P-value = 21.8%

TABLE 3.   (*cont.*)

B. In the stock market (*cont.*)

Summary statistics:

$E(\Delta y)$ =	.017	$\sigma(SL)$	= 9.937
$E(SL)$ =	−12.52	var (SL)/var (SL')	= 4.786 (5.380)
$E(SL')$ =	16.66	corr (SL, SL')	= .911 (.207)
$\sigma(\Delta y)$ =	.167	var (ξ)/var (ξ')	= 1.414 (.441)

excess bond returns will be predicted by S_t and a regression of ΔY_{t+1} on S_t may find that the coefficient has the opposite sign from that predicted by (4), even if the variance of w_t is quite small. However, a regression of S_t^* on S_t will find that the coefficient has the same sign as predicted by (3), and downward bias caused by w_t will be small if the variance of w_t is small. Moreover, the variance ratios var(S_t)/var(S_t') and var(ξ_t)/var(ξ_t') may not be much greater than one. In this example the spread predicts short-rate movements almost correctly, even though it badly misforecasts long-rate movements. Deviations from the present value model are transitory rather than persistent, so the metric of equation (10) reveals the strengths of the expectations theory that are obscured by the metric of equation (11). [30]

In part B of table 3, we repeated the exercises above for stock prices and dividends. We worked with one sample period but two discount rates. The Akaike criterion selected a four-lag representation for the data when the sample mean discount rate 8.2 per cent was used and a two-lag representation when the cointegrating regression discount rate 3.2 per cent was used.

The VAR estimates suggest that dividend changes are rather highly preditable; the R^2 values for the equations that explain them are around 40 per cent. There is very strong evidence that price-dividend spreads Granger-cause dividend changes, which is what one would expect if there is any truth to the present value model for stock prices.

We conducted two formal tests of the model. The first restricted the mean of the price-dividend difference, while the second left the mean unconstrained and restricted only the dynamics of the variable. (In the case of the term structure, the mean spread is always unconstrained because we allowed a constant risk premium.)

The results of these tests include some statistical rejections at conventional significance levels, but they are not nearly as strong as the

---

[30] We do not claim that this example is literally correct for our data. The model $S = S' + w$ can be tested, for any MA(q) process for w, by regressing ξ on information known $q + 2$ periods earlier. We found that this test rejected the model for q up to 8 using the bond data for 1959–78.

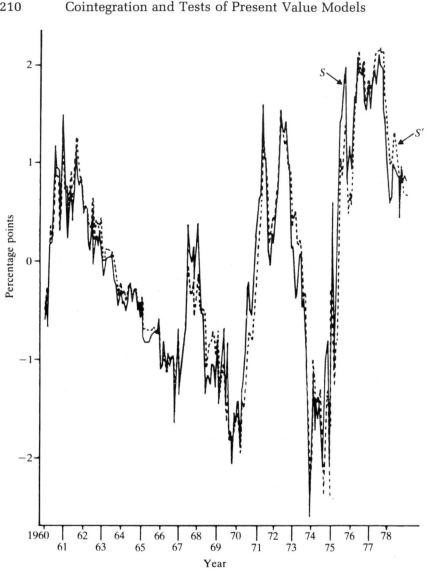

Fig. 1. Term structure: deviations from means of long-short spread S_t and theoretical spread S'_t.

rejections in the term structure. The pattern of results is sensitive to the choice of discount rate. When the sample mean return is used, the mean restriction of SL_t is satisfied almost exactly. Therefore, the test of only the dynamic restrictions in equation (8) rejects more strongly, at the 4.7 per cent level as compared with the 7.2 per cent level for the full set of restrictions. When the discount rate from the cointegrating regression is used, the complete set of restrictions is rejected as the 1.1 per cent level while the significance level for the dynamic restrictions is only 21.8 per cent.[31] For both discount rates, a regression of ΔY_{t+1} on SL_t gives a coefficient estimate with a negative sign rather than the positive sign implied by the present value model.[32]

These tests are 'portmanteau' tests of the present value model against an unspecified alternative. We also present variance ratios in order to test against the specific alternative that stock prices 'move too much' in levels or innovations. The point estimate of the levels variance ratio var(SL_t)/var(SL_t') is dramatically different from unity, at 67.22, when the sample mean discount rate is used. Not surprisingly, the variance ratio is smaller when future dividend changes are discounted at the lower rate estimated by the cointegrating regression, but it is still considerable at 4.79. However, the asymptotic standard errors on these ratios are huge, and one cannot reject the hypothesis that both of them equal unity.

The innovations variance ratios var(ξ_t)/var(ξ_t') are also estimated larger than unity, and here the standard errors are less extreme. In the sample mean discount rate case, one can reject at the 5 per cent level the hypothesis that the innovation variance ratio is unity; it is estimated to be 11.27, with a standard error of 4.49. With the lower discount rate, the ratio is estimated at 1.41, with a standard error of 0.44.

Plots of the price–dividend difference and the unrestricted VAR forecast of dividend changes give a visual image of these variance results. At an 8.2 per cent discount rate (fig. 2), SL_t and SL_t' are negatively correlated (but there is a very large standard error on the correlation) and the excess volatility of the spread is very dramatic. At a 3.2 per cent discount rate (fig. 3), SL_t and SL_t' have a correlation of 0.911 (with standard error 0.207) and the excess volatility is much less dramatic.[33]

To compare our results on volatility with results using earlier methods, we also computed sample values of S_t^* using the terminal condition $S_T^* = S_T$, where T is the last observation in our sample. We computed SL_t^* analogously. Equation (3) implies $\sigma(S_t^*) > \sigma(S_t)$ and $\sigma(SL_t^*) > \sigma(SL_t)$. For the bond data in the period 1959–78, $\sigma(S_t^*) = 1.217$, while $\sigma(S_t) = 1.060$, so the inequality is satisfied. For the stock data at an 8.2 per cent discount rate, $\sigma(SL_t^*) = 7.928$, while $\sigma(SL_t) = 15.506$, so the inequality is sharply violated. The inequality is

---

[31] Nonlinear Wald tests of the dynamic restrictions in the form (7), rather than (8), reject at less than the 0.005 per cent level for the 8.2 per cent discount rate and at the 7.3 per cent level for the 3.2 per cent discount rate.

[32] The coefficient is −0.064 for the 8.2 per cent discount rate and −0.079 for the 3.2 per cent discount rate.

[33] It should be emphasized that excess volatility of the spread SL_t is not quite the same as the excess volatility discussed in Shiller (1981b). That analysis suggested that stock prices should very nearly follow a trend. If that were in fact what was observed, the spread SL_t would be quite volatile because of dividend movements.

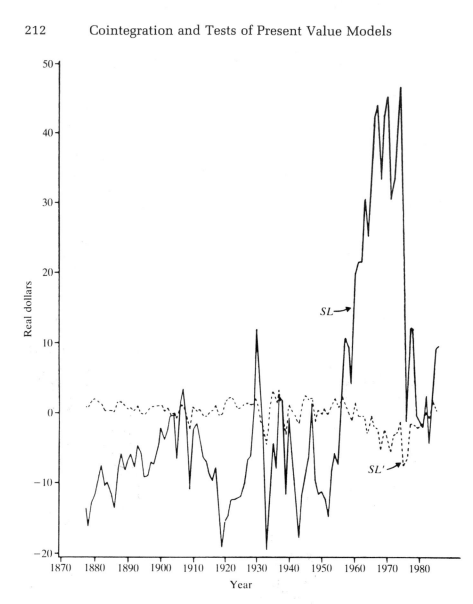

FIG. 2. Stock market: deviations from means of actual spread (SL_t = Price$_t$ − θ. Dividend$_{t-1}$) and theoretical spread SL'_t, θ = 12.195.

again satisfied by the stock data at a 3.2 per cent discount rate, where $\sigma(SL^*_t)$ = 12.888 and $\sigma(SL_t)$ = 9.937.

Following Scott (1985), we also regressed S^*_t on S_t and a constant. If the present value model is true, the coefficient on S_t should be one. The same holds for the corresponding regression with SL^*_t and SL_t. For bonds in 1959–78, we estimated the coefficient at 0.81; for stocks at an

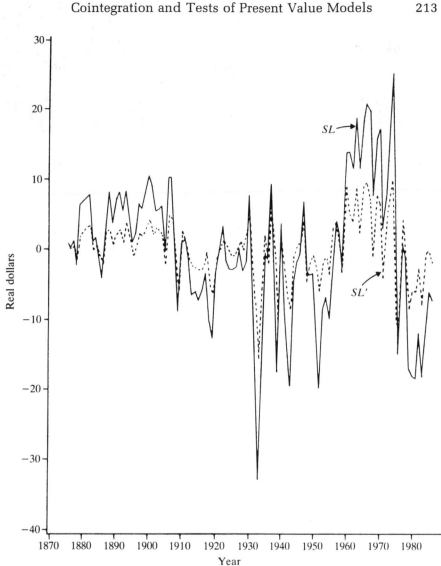

FIG. 3. Stock market: deviations from means of actual spread (SL_t = Price$_t$ − θ. Dividend$_{t-1}$) and theoretical spread SL'_t, $\theta = 31.092$.

8.2 per cent discount rate we estimated it at 0.16, while for stocks at a 3.2 per cent discount rate we estimated it at 0.02. Thus the results using S^*_t and SL^*_t generally support the conclusion that the present value model for bonds fits the data comparatively well, whereas the model for stocks has a poor fit even though it cannot be rejected statistically at high levels of confidence.

We close with a caveat about the plots and summary statistics generated by the VAR system. The VAR simulation method may be misleading if the wrong value of θ is chosen so that the spread variable is nonstationary. For example, if θ is chosen too large, the movements of S_t are dominated by the movements of $-\theta y_t$. The VAR results are then approximately those one would get if one regressed Δy_t and $-\theta y_t$ on lagged values óf these variables. It is well known that in finite samples estimates of autoregressive parameters for nonstationary variables are biased downward, and this problem will afflict the VAR if θ is too large.

In a simple case in which y_t follows an AR(1) process with a unit root and the VAR includes one lag only, one can show that the estimated VAR companion matrix will have first column zero and second column $((1 - \rho)/\theta\,\rho)'$, where ρ is a downward-biased estimate of the unit root. This companion matrix satisfies the restrictions of equation (9) almost exactly, whatever the behaviour of the variable Y_t. A symptom of this misspecification would be that mean returns would not obey the model, even though the dynamics of returns would appear to satisfy the restrictions.

It is possible that a problem of this sort affects our results for the stock market when we use a low 3.2 per cent discount rate corresponding to a high θ of 31.092. The cointegrating regression that generates this θ estimate—a regression of the level of Y on the level of y—is dominated by the enormous postwar hump in stock prices. Since this hump coincided with a much milder hump in real dividends, the regression estimates a coefficient for y that is much larger than the historical average price–dividend ratio. The negative intercept prevents the fitted value from overpredicting Y over the sample period as a whole. As a result, over the bulk of the sample period, the spread SL_t is distinctly negatively correlated with the lagged dividend.[34] The VAR estimates place considerable weight on this earlier part of the sample period because the dividend equation is specified in terms of dividend changes that are more variable before 1946. Thus the high correlation of SL_t and SL_t' may be to some extent spurious.

This view is supported by the results from regressing SL_t^* on SL_t. This is a levels regression that is dominated by the postwar hump in stock prices, and here we find the coefficient to be essentially zero rather than one as required by the model. Further support comes from the fact that we strongly reject the implications of the model for the mean of the data when we impose a 3.2 per cent discount rate.

---

[34] Over the period 1871–1946, the spread has a correlation of -0.7 with the lagged dividend when θ is set equal to 31.092.

4. Conclusion

In this paper we have shown how a present value model may be tested when the variables of the model, y_t and Y_t, follow linear stochastic processes that are stationary in first differences rather than in levels. If the present value model is true, a linear combination of the variables — which we call the spread — is stationary. Thus y_t and Y_t are cointegrated. The model implies that the spread is linear in the optimal forecast of the one-period change in Y_t and also in the optimal forecast of the present value of all future changes in y_t. We have shown how to conduct formal Wald tests of these implications.

We have also proposed an informal method for evaluating the 'fit' of a present value model. A VAR is used to construct an optimal unrestricted forecast of the present value of future y_t changes, and this is compared with the spread. If the model is true, the unrestricted forecast or 'theoretical spread' should equal the actual spread. We computed the variances and correlation of the two variables and plotted their historical movements.

We applied our methods to the controversial present value models for stocks and bonds. We found that both models can be rejected statistically at conventional significance levels, with much stronger evidence for bonds. However, in our data set, the spread between long- and short-term interest rates seems to move quite closely with the unrestricted forecast of the present value of future short-rate changes. This can be interpreted as evidence that deviations from the present value model for bonds are transitory. In contrast, our evaluation of the present value model for stocks indicates that the spread between stock prices and dividends moves too much and that deviations from the present value model are quite persistent, although the strength of the evidence for this depends sensitively on the discount rate assumed in the test.

References

BAILLIE, RICHARD T., ROBERT E. LIPPENS, and PATRICK C. MCMAHON, (1983), 'Testing rational expectations and efficiency in the foreign exchange market', *Econometrica*, **51**, 553–63.

BLANCHARD, OLIVIER J., and MARK W. WATSON (1982), 'Bubbles, rational expectations and financial markets', in *Crises in the Economic and Financial Stucture: Bubbles, Bursts and Shocks*, ed. Paul Wachtel (Lexington, Mass., Lexington).

CAMPBELL, JOHN Y. (1987), 'Does saving anticipate declining labor income? An alternative test of the permanent income hypothesis', *Econometrica*, **55**, 1249–73.

—— and SHILLER ROBERT J. (1984), 'A simple account of the behavior of long-term interest rates', *A.E.R. Papers and Proc.* **74** 44–8.

—— —— (1986), 'The dividend–price ratio and expectations of future dividends and discount factors', Working Paper no. 2100. Cambridge, Mass.: NBER.

COWLES, ALFRED (1939), *Common-Stock Indexes*, 2nd edn. (Bloomington, Ind., Principia).

DIBA, BEHZAD T., and HERSCHEL I. GROSSMAN (1984), 'Rational bubbles in the price of gold', Working Paper no. 1300, Cambridge, Mass.: NBER.

DICKEY, DAVID A., and WAYNE A. FULLER (1981), 'Likelihood ratio statistics for autoregressive time series with a unit root', *Econometrica*, **49**, 1057–72.

ENGLE, ROBERT F., and CLIVE W. J. GRANGER (1987), 'Cointegration and error-correction: representation, estimation and testing', *Econometrica*, **55**, 251–76.

—— and MARK W. WATSON (1985), 'Appliciations of Kalman filtering in econometrics', paper presented at the World Congress of the Econometric Society, Cambridge, Mass.

FAMA, EUGENE F. (1970), 'Efficient capital markets: a review of theory and empirical work', *J. Finance*, **25**, 383–417.

GREGORY, ALLAN W., and MICHAEL R. VEALL (1985), 'Formulating Wald tests of non-linear restrictions', *Econometrica*, **53**, 1465–8.

HAMILTON, JAMES D., and CHARLES H. WHITEMAN (1985), 'The observable implications of self-fulfilling expectations', *J. Monetary Econ.* **16**, 353–73.

HANSEN, LARS PETER, and THOMAS J. SARGENT (1981*a*), 'Exact linear rational expectations Models: Specification and Estimation', Staff Report no. 71. Minneapolis Fed. Reserve Bank.

—— —— (1981*b*), 'Linear rational expectations models for dynamically interrelated variables', in *Rational Expectations and Econometric Practice*, ed. Robert E. Lucas, Jr., and Thomas J. Sargent (Minneapolis Univ. Minnesota Press).

KLEIDON, ALLAN W. (1986), 'Variance bounds tests and stock price valuation models', *J.P.E.* **94** 953–1001.

LEROY, STEPHEN F., and RICHARD D. PORTER (1981), 'The present-value relation: tests based on implied variance bounds', *Econometrica*, **49**, 555–74.

MANKIW, N. GREGORY, and JEFFREY A. MIRON (1986), 'The changing behavior of the term structure of interest rates', *Q.J.E.* **101**, 211–28.

—— DAVID ROMER, and MATTHEW D. SHAPIRO (1985), 'An unbiased re-examination of stock market volatility', *J. Finance*, **40**, 677–87.

—— and MATTHEW D. SHAPIRO (1985), 'Trends, random walks, and tests of the permanent income hypothesis', *J. Monetary Econ.* **16**, 165–74.

MARSH, TERRY A., and ROBERT C. MERTON (1986), 'Dividend variability and variance bounds tests for the rationality of stock market prices', *A.E.R.* **76**, 483–98.

MELINO, ANGELO (1983), 'Essays on estimation and inference in linear rational expectations models', Ph.D. dissertation, Harvard Univ.

MODIGLIANI, FRANCO, and ROBERT J. SHILLER (1973), 'Inflation, rational expectations and the term structure of interest rates', *Economica*, **40**, 12–43.

PHILLIPS, P. C. B. (1987), 'Time series regression with unit roots', *Econometrica*, **55**, 277–302.

—— and S. N. DURLAUF (1986), 'Multiple time series regression with integrated processes', *Rev. Econ. Studies*, **53**, 473–95.

—— and S. OULIARIS (1986), 'Testing for cointegration', Discussion Paper no. 809. New Haven, Conn.: Yale Univ., Cowles Found.

—— and P. PERRON (1986), 'Testing for unit roots in time series regression', Discussion Paper. New Haven, Conn.: Yale Univ., Cowles Found.

QUAH, DANNY (1986), 'Stationary rational bubbles in asset prices', Manuscript. Cambridge: Massachusetts Inst. Tech.

SARGENT, THOMAS J. (1979), 'A note on maximum likelihood estimation of the rational expectations model of the term structure', *J. Monetary Econ.* **5**, 133–43.

SAWA, TAKAMITSU (1978), 'Information criteria for discriminating among alternative regression models', *Econometrica*, **46** 1273–91.

SCOTT, LOUIS O. (1985), 'The present value model of stock prices: regression tests and Monte Carlo results', *Rev. Econ. and Statis.* **67**, 599–605.

SHILLER, ROBERT J. (1979), 'The volatility of long-term interest rates and expectations models of the term structure', *J.P.E.* **87**, 1190–1219.

—— (1981*a*), 'Alternative tests of rational expectations models: the case of the term structure', *J. Econometrics*, **16**, 71–87.

—— (1981*b*), 'Do stock prices move too much to be justified by subsequent changes in dividends?', *A.E.R.* **71**, 421–36.

—— (1984), 'Stock prices and social dynamics', *Brookings Papers Econ. Activity*, no. 2 pp. 457–98.

—— (1987), 'Conventional valuation and the term structure of interest rates', in *Macroeconomics and Finance: Essays in Honor of Franco Modigliani*, ed. Rudiger Dornbusch, Stanley Fischer, and John Bossons. (Cambridge, Mass., MIT Press).

—— JOHN Y. CAMPBELL, and KERMIT L. SCHOENHOLTZ (1983), 'Forward rates and future policy: interpreting the term structure of interest rates', *Brookings Papers Econ. Activity*, no. 1 pp. 173–217.

STOCK, JAMES H. (1987), 'Asymptotic properties of least squares estimates of cointegrating vectors', *Econometrica*, **55**, 1035–56.

WEST, KENNETH D. (1987), 'A specification test for speculative bubbles', *Quarterly J. of Economics*, **102**, 553–80.

—— (1988), 'Dividend innovations and stock price volatility', *Econometrica*, **56**, 37–61.

WHITE, HALBERT (1984), *Asymptotic Theory for Econometricians* (Orlando, Fla., Academic Press).

11

Merging Short- and Long-Run Forecasts

An Application of Seasonal Cointegration to Monthly Electricity Sales Forecasting*

R. F. ENGLE, C. W. J. GRANGER, and
J. J. HALLMAN

Abstract

When forecasts of a series Y_t must be made for several horizons, it is a common practice to build different models to forecast different horizons. This paper shows how the information in the several models can be combined in an error-correction framework to yield a single set of forecasts which outperform those from the separate models. The notions of seasonal integration and cointegration are introduced. The methods are applied to forecasting monthly commercial electricity sales with some success. Also reported are results of some simulation experiments designed to evaluate their effectiveness.

1. Introduction

When forecasts of a series of Y_t must be made for several horizons, it is common practice to build different models for different horizons. For ease of exposition just two models will be considered, the short-run (or 'monthly') model and the long-run (or 'annual'). The models are generally used to produce forecasts over different horizons and to help with

* Research supported by Electric Power Research Institute and under NSF grants SES 84–20680 and SES 85–13858 to the first and second authors, respectively. The third author was supported under a National Science Foundation Graduate Fellowship while preparing this work.

Printed with permission of: *Journal of Econometrics*, 40, (1989), pp. 45–62.

different types of decisions. There will be only a single data-generating process (d.g.p.) for Y_t, of course, but the two models can be thought of as approximating different parts of this generating process. This paper will discuss the question of how the two models can be merged, or combined, so that a better overall approximation for the d.g.p. can be obtained. This new model could produce superior forecasts at some horizons and also overcomes the practical difficulty of having two different conflicting forecasts at some horizons.

The two models may well have quite different specifications with non-overlapping sets of explanatory variables. If Y_t is the monthly demand for electricity for some region or utility, the short-run model may concentrate on rapidly changing variables such as those that are strongly seasonal, particularly temperature and other weather variables. The long-run model will be largely based on slowly moving variables, such as population characteristics, appliance stock and efficiencies or a local GNP measure. The variables will be chosen because they are believed to be particularly appropriate and data is available. One model does not ignore the explanatory variables of the other model because they are thought to be of no importance, but because they are thought to be relatively unimportant. To use all of the variables in the short-run model may make it too complicated, and the long-run explanatory variables may not enter significantly when a minimization of a one-month forecast variance is used as a criterion. It will usually also be true that monthly values are not available for some of the slowly changing variables.

In this paper, it will be assumed that the builders of the short-run model are given the task of merging the two models but that they may not have available the past values of the explanatory variables used in the long-run model.

The paper begins by considering the concept of integration and seasonal integration and then the idea of cointegration which proves useful for coordinating the models. A practical example and the results of a simulation study are also presented.

2.   The Cointegration Model

If Y_t is a series such that dth differences $(1 - B)^d Y_t$ are stationary, it is called integrated and denoted I(d). A stationary series may be designated I(0). An I(1) series is much smoother or slower-changing than an I(0) series. If a vector of series Y_t, W_t, is I(1) but there exists a linear combination

$$z_t = Y_t - \alpha' W_t, \tag{1}$$

that is I(0), then the series are said to be cointegrated. A typical pair of I(1) series will not have this property. If cointegration occurs, then the data generation process of Y_t can be represented by an 'error-correction' model of the form

$$\Delta Y_t = \delta - \gamma z_{t-1} + \beta' V_t + \varepsilon_t, \qquad (2)$$

where V_t are I(0) explanatory variables which could therefore include lags of ΔW or stationary lag polynomials of ΔY. The idea of cointegration, some implications, test procedures and applications can be found in Granger (1986), Engle and Granger (1987) and in the special issue of the *Oxford Bulletin of Economics and Statistics* (August 1986), **88**; 3.

For the problem being considered here, it may be assumed that Y_t contains an I(1) component that is being forecast by the long-run model, so that

$$Y_t = C_0 + C_1' W_t + \eta_t, \qquad (3)$$

where W_t is a vector of I(1) components and it is anticipated that $C_1 = \alpha$. The short-run model is assumed to take the form

$$\Delta Y_t = b_0 + b_2' V_t + \varepsilon_t, \qquad (4)$$

where V_t are I(0) variables. As z_t in (2) is based on long-run variables, it is probably not used in the short-run model. Thus, the short-run model is assumed to differ from the error-correction d.g.p. (2) by the omission of the γz_{t-1} term.

In this formulation, there are three forecasting models. The complete 'true' model is given by (2), the long-run forecast will be based on (3) (possibly with η_t being given a simple time-series structure, such as an assumed AR(1) model), and the short-run forecasts are formed from (4).

If data are available frequently enough, say monthly, for all the variables in W_t and X_t, the complete model (2) can be constructed. One-step forecasts can be found by writing (2) as

$$Y_t = \delta - (1 - \gamma)Y_{t-1} + \gamma\alpha' W_{t-1} + \beta' V_t + \varepsilon_t, \qquad (5)$$

and replacing V_t by its forecast. Given forecasts of W_t and V_t, multi-step forecasts of Y_t are found by iterating (5) out to the required horizon. Let $f_{n,h}$ denote the h-step ahead of a forecast made at time n, and suppose we are forecasting just a particular month (say January) in each year in the future. Then the long-run forecasts of the I(0) variables V_t will be just constants (their mean for that month) and so

$$f_{n,h}^Y \approx \delta^* + (1 - \gamma)f_{n,h-1}^Y + \gamma\alpha' f_{n,h-1}^W,$$

or

$$f_{n,h+1}^Y - f_{n,h}^Y \approx \delta^* - \gamma(f_{n,h}^Y - \alpha' f_{n,h}^W).$$

If the left-hand side is small, or approximately a constant, then the right-hand side shows that

$$f_{n,h}^Y \approx \alpha' f_{n,h}^W + \text{constant}, \tag{6}$$

as given by the long-run model (3) if $C_1 = \alpha$. Thus, using the complete model one gets short-run forecasts similar to those given by (4) (possibly improved due to the presence of z_{t-1} in (2)), while the long-run forecasts are nearly the same as those from the long-run model (3).

In practice, the complete model is not available, so approximations have to be used. (2) is a convenient form because the long-run specification enters only through z_{t-1} and the short-term through V_t. The modeller is assumed to have the full information set except the W_t series. Note that to build (2) one only needs the components of z_{t-1}, which are Y_{t-1} and $\alpha' W_{t-1}$. The latter term is the forecast of Y_{t-1} made from the long-term model. (If W_t is not observed monthly, some interpolation procedure may be required.) If $\hat{f}_{n,h}^Y$ is the forecast of Y_{n+h} made at time n from the long-term model, then an estimate of z_t is

$$\hat{z}_t = Y_t - \hat{f}_{t-1,1}^Y.$$

An approximation to the full model is found by regressing ΔY_t on a constant, $\hat{z}_{t-1}$ and V_t giving

$$\Delta Y_t = \delta - \gamma \hat{z}_{t-1} + \bar{\beta}' V_t + e_t. \tag{2'}$$

This model is fairly easily achieved once the $\hat{f}_{t-1,1}^Y$ and V_t terms are obtained, and can be immediately used to form one-step forecasts. It also can be iterated out to form medium and long-term forecasts and the long-term forecasts will be essentially the same as those obtained from (1). Putting $t = n + h$ in (2') and replacing everything by its best forecast, one gets

$$f_{n,h}^Y = f_{n,h-1}^Y + \delta - \gamma(f_{n,h-1}^Y - \hat{f}_{n,h-1}^Y) + \beta' f_{n,h}^V,$$

assuming the e_t in (2') to be zero-mean white noise. Running these equations for $h = 1, 2, \ldots$ and using $f_{n,0}^Y = Y_n$ etc., one can generate by iteration the forecasts $f_{n,h}^Y$ from the model (2'). Naturally they will not be quite the same as those obtained from the 'true' model (2), but they do represent a reasonable synthesis of the short-run model data and the long-run model forecasts, having the correct long-horizon (large h) properties.

If forecasts are made for every month, the short-run forecast model will provide forecasts of the seasonal component. The long-run model will have nothing to say about this component. Naturally, if just a single month each year is considered, or an annual aggregate, then the seasonal component is of no consequence.

3.   Theory of Seasonal Cointegration

In this section the theory of integration and cointegration at different frequencies, particularly the zero and seasonal frequencies, is introduced. A series may be said to be integrated of order d at frequency θ if the series has a spectrum $f(\omega)$ which takes the form

$$f(\omega) = c(\omega - \theta)^{-2d},$$

for ω near θ, denoted $x_t \sim I_\theta(d)$. For example, a series is integrated just at the zero frequency if $(1 - B)^d x_t = C(B)\varepsilon_t + \mu$ and if the spectrum of $C(B)\varepsilon_t$ is bounded away from zero and infinity at all frequencies. If μ is non-zero, the series is $I_0(d)$ with drift. A series may be integrated at any of the seasonal frequencies $\omega_s = 2\pi j/s$, $j = 1, \ldots, s/2$, where data is recorded s times a year. For convenience in this paper it will be assumed that a series is always integrated of the same order at all seasonal frequencies. For example, if x_t is generated by

$$S(B)^d x_t = C(B)\varepsilon_t + \mu,$$

where

$$S(B) = \frac{1 - B^s}{1 - B} = (1 + B + B^2 + \ldots + B^{s-1}),$$

and the spectrum of $C(B)\varepsilon_t$ is bounded as before, then x_t is seasonally integrated of order d, $x_t \sim SI(d)$, with drift if $\mu \neq 0$.

If $x_t \sim {}_\theta(d)$, $d > \frac{1}{2}$ and the series has been generated for an indefinitely long time, it will have an infinite variance. In particular, if $d = 1$, the variance will be proportional to t, the time since initiation. It is clear from these definitions that a series may be integrated at more than one frequency. For example, if x_t is generated by

$$(1 - B^s)x_t = \varepsilon_t,$$

it is $I_0(1)$ and also $SI(1)$.

A vector of series x_t, each component of which is $I_\theta(d)$, may be said to be cointegrated at that frequency if there exists a vector α_θ such that

$$z_t^\theta = \alpha_\theta' x_t$$

is integrated of lower order at θ. The case of practical importance is when $d = 1$, so that $z_t^\theta \sim I_\theta(0)$.

It is convenient to add one further piece of notation. If a series x_t is $I_0(d_0)$ and $SI(d_s)$ it will be denoted $x_t \sim SI(d_0, d_s)$. Thus, if $d_0 = 1$, $d_s = 1$, x_t is integrated of order one at both zero and seasonal frequencies.

These definitions are potentially important for modelling electricity demand as this demand is very likely to be $SI(1, 1)$ due to important long-run and seasonal components. Further, if the model has been carefully specified, then the long-run model explanatory variables, $\gamma' W_t$ in (1), should be cointegrated with the seasonally adjusted components of Y_t, and the short-run model explanatory variables, $\beta' V_t$ in (3), should be seasonally cointegrated with differenced Y_t.

Virtually all of the current literature on cointegration fails to consider the effects of seasonal integration. In this literature, it is usual to estimate the cointegrating parameter α in the bivariate case by regressing x_{1t} on x_{2t}, which is called the cointegrating regression. If the resulting residual z_t is I(0), then a superefficient estimate of α results, with a distribution derived by Stock (1987). For series which are seasonally integrated, this result may be lost as shown in the theorem below.

Let $X' = [x_1, \ldots, x_T]$ be the data for the electricity sales, income and other variables so that $X = [Y, W]$. The cointegrating regression minimizes the sum of squared residual $z'z$, from $z = X\alpha$ subject to a normalization restriction such as a unit coefficient on the selected dependent variable.

THEOREM. *Let X_t be a vector of random variables partitioned so that $X'_t = (x_{1t}, x_{2t}, x_{3t})$, where x_{1t} is SI(1,1), x_{2t} is SI(1,0) and x_{3t} is SI(0,1).*

(a) If X_t is seasonally cointegrated at zero frequency but not seasonal frequencies, then the value of α which minimizes $\alpha' X' X \alpha$ (with $\alpha_3 = 0$) subject to $\alpha'\alpha = 1$ will not generally be consistent, however the α which minimizes $\alpha' \bar{X}' \bar{X} \alpha$ (with $\alpha_3 = 0$) will be consistent where $\bar{x}_t = (1 + B + \ldots + B^{s-1})x_t = S(B)x_t$ and $\bar{X}' = (\bar{x}_1, \ldots, \bar{x}_T)$.

(b) If instead X_t is seasonally cointegrated at seasonal frequencies but not at zero frequency, then the value of α which minimizes $\alpha' X' X \alpha$ (with $\alpha_2 = 0$) will not generally be consistent, however, the α which minimizes $\alpha' \tilde{X}' \tilde{X} \alpha$ (with $\alpha_2 = 0$) will be consistent where $\tilde{x}_t = (1 - B)x_t$ and $\tilde{X}' = (\tilde{x}_1, \ldots, \tilde{x}_T)$.

(c) If, instead, x_{1t} and x_{2t} are SI(1,1) with drift and SI(1,0) with drift, respectively, but there is an α with $\alpha_3 = 0$ for which $\alpha' X_t \sim I(0)$ without drift, then the value of α which minimizes $\alpha' X' X \alpha$ will be consistent.

PROOF. (a) To show that α estimated from the time averaged data will be consistent it is sufficient to show that these data are cointegrated in the usual or Engle–Granger sense. First we show the $\bar{x}_t$ is I(1).

$$(1 - B)\bar{x}_t = (1 - B)S(B)x_t = C(B)\varepsilon_t,$$

hence $\bar{x}_t$ will be I(1) for x_{1t} which is SI(1, 1). For x_{2t} which is SI(1, 0), $\bar{x}_t$ is also I(1) because $d = 1$ is the smallest integer satisfying the definition of integration and the zeros in the spectrum at seasonal frequencies are not relevant. To show that $\alpha' \bar{x}_t$ is I(0), one merely notes that, since $\alpha' x_t \sim SI(0, 1)$, by definition $S(B) \alpha' x_t = \alpha'(S(B) x_t) = \alpha' \bar{X}_T \sim I(0)$. Hence, $\alpha' \bar{x}_t$ is I(0) and $\bar{x}_t$ is CI(1, 1).

To show that the cointegrating regression on the untransformed variables x_t will not necessarily lead to a consistent estimate of α it is sufficient to produce a counterexample. This particular counterexample, however, is revealing of precisely the issue faced in monthly electricity demand modelling. Suppose the data are generated by the process

$$y_t = \alpha x_t + u_t,$$

$$(1 + B + \ldots + B^{s-1}) u_t = \varepsilon_t,$$

$$x_t = x_{t-1} + v_t,$$

where ε and v are serially independent with arbitrary contemporaneous covariance. Multiplying the first equation by $(1 - B^s)$ gives

$$(1 - B^s) y_t = S(B) v_t + (1 - B) \varepsilon_t,$$

where ε and v are serially independent with arbitrary contemporaneous covariance. Multiplying the first equation by $(1 - B^s)$ gives

$$(1 - B^s) y_t = S(B) v_t + (1 - B) \varepsilon_t,$$

establishing that y is SI(1, 1) and not I(1). However, x_t is I(1). The linear combination of $(1, -\alpha)$ times $(y, x)'$ yields a random variable u, which has a finite spectrum at zero frequency although it has spikes or poles at all the seasonals. This vector does not eliminate all seasonal poles so X_t is seasonally cointegrated at zero frequency but not at seasonal frequencies. The regression of y on x can be expressed as

$$\hat{\alpha} = \alpha + (x'x/T^2)^{-1} x'u/T^2.$$

It is well known since Fuller (1976) that $x'x/T^2$ converges in distribution to a random variable rather than a constant. Some tedious algebra shows that in this case $x'u/T^2$ has also a variance which is of O(1) since both x and u have infinite variances, and the ratio will not have a probability limit as required for consistency of the estimator. This counterexample establishes in this particularly simple case that the cointegrating equation on levels is not consistent in the presence of seasonal unit roots unless x is fully cointegrated.

(b) To establish the similar result for cointegration at seasonal frequencies, exactly the same steps are taken and will not be repeated here. The requirement that $T^{-2} \tilde{X}' \tilde{X} = O_p(1)$ in this case has been established by Chan and Wei (1988).

(c) To establish the consistency of the cointegrating regression when there are drifts, it must be established that the trends implied by the drifts dominate the seasonality thereby reinstating the consistency of the cointegrating regression. This is essentially shown in Sims, Stock and Watson (1986) and will not be reproduced here.

There are several implications of the theorem for the situation being considered in this paper. It has been assumed that electricity sales are available monthly and that long-run explanatory variables, W_t may not be available monthly, only annually. Since the W_t variables represent income, appliance saturations and so forth which are not seasonal, the use of monthly observations on W_t to estimate the cointegrating regression would not result in inconsistent estimates of the long-run parameters α unless there are dominating trends. Only if the sales data were filtered with the $S(B)$ filter, would such a least-squares regression give consistent estimates of α. The use of annual observations on sales and W_t is an example of such filtering and is therefore recommended as an approach to estimating the long-run model without the need to model the seasonality. This is a very simple and old conclusion but is newly justified by the analyses of seasonal cointegration.

4. An Empirical Example of the Error-Correction Synthesis

Monthly commercial electricity sales for Massachusetts Electric Company, a retail subsidiary of New England Electric Power Service Company was analysed from January 1975 through May 1985. The same data were analysed in Pastuszek and Watson (1985) who develop a short-run forecasting model. A stylized version of their model regresses the level of sales on two lagged values, cooling and heating degree days, eleven monthly dummies and a constant. The results are reported in table 1.

From the examination of table 1, the short-run model appears to be well specified. The effects of weather are sensible and the second-order lag in sales should eliminate most serial correlation. However, examination of table 2, which includes a series of diagnostic tests, suggests that there may be problems with the model. There seems to be some first-order serial correlation remaining and some evidence of heteroskedasticity. More serious is the evidence that the variables *ECTEST2* and *ERROR CORRECTION* were inappropriately omitted from the regression. These are the long-run forecast $\hat{f}^Y_{t-1,1}$ and the error correction terms $\hat{z}_{t+1}$, respectively, which will be described in more detail below. They indicate that the model seriously omits the long-run or trend component in its modelling. Within the sample, the accuracy of the forecast is highly commendable, however as the model is used to forecast five years into the future, the forecasts exhibit a substantial and

TABLE 1. Short-run model of monthly sales

Variable	Coefficient	Std. error	t-statistic
MCD	0.14	0.03	4.10
MHD	0.03	0.01	2.25
MCD[−1]	−0.07	0.03	−2.05
MHD[−1]	−0.01	0.01	−1.10
M[−1]	0.64	0.08	7.18
M[−2]	0.28	0.08	3.31
_FEB	−23.93	6.71	−3.56
_MAR	−33.67	8.78	−3.83
_APR	−37.18	11.02	−3.37
_MAY	−25.95	13.56	−1.91
_JUN	−11.38	16.16	−0.70
_JUL	−22.46	18.73	−1.19
_AUG	−9.84	20.14	−0.48
_SEP	−18.99	19.48	−0.97
_OCT	−23.84	16.50	−1.44
_NOV	−18.68	12.08	−1.54
_DEC	0.88	7.28	0.12
_CONST	25.22	20.87	1.20

Number of observations	124
Mean value of M	289.20
Standard deviation of M	28.77
Standard error of forecast	9.07
R-square (corrected for mean)	0.091
$F(18, 106)$	62.81
Adjusted R-square	0.89
Durbin–Watson statistic	2.29
AIC error statistic	9.70
Schwartz error statistic	11.90

TABLE 2. Diagnostic test statistics

ECTEST2	Chi-square(1)	30.65	$p = 1.000$
ERROR CORRECTION	Chi-square(1)	27.51	$p = 1.000$
AUTO[−1] serial correlation	Chi-square (1)	14.67	$p = 1.000$
NONLINEARITY in x test	Chi-square(6)	2.14	$p = 0.093$
HETEROSCEDASTICITY TIME	Chi-square(1)	0.03	$p = 0.144$
HETEROSCEDASTICITY with X	Chi-square(18)	31.51	$p = 0.975$
HETEROSCEDASTICITY YFIT	Chi-square(1)	5.27	$p = 0.978$
ARCH[−1] process test	Chi-square(1)	21.21	$p = 1.000$
ARCH[−12] process test	Chi-square(1)	0.00	$p - 1.027$
CHOW test	$F(18, 88)$	1.27	$p = 0.804$

uncharacteristic decline. Because the estimated process for sales is stationary, it eventually returns to its unconditional mean.

A possible improvement to this short-run model is to impose the unit root restriction and estimate the model in differences. In this case, the historical trend will be extrapolated, which again may not be desirable.

The long-run model is just a contemporaneous OLS regression that is estimated in two ways for this example. The first uses monthly data, while the second is based on annual data obtained from summing the monthly values. In most applications only the latter will be available. Because there are only ten years of data an extremely simple long-run model is estimated. The basic explanatory variable is the number of Massachusetts Electric commercial customers, labeled MC (or AMC in the annual model). In addition, local economic conditions may determine the level of intensity of use by these customers so the local unemployment, MU (or AMU in the annual model), is also used. Some experiments with relative prices suggest that price would not help the model. The results are presented in tables 3 and 4. Because these regressions are cointegrating regressions, the disturbances are assumed merely to be stationary, not white noise. Thus the t-statistics will not be reliable guides to the inclusion of variables in these regressions. One test for the cointegration hypothesis, which is only appropriate in the non-seasonal case, is based on the Durbin–Watson statistic for the cointegrating regression. The value of 0.95 from the monthly regression would easily confirm the conjecture that these three variables are cointegrated if there were no seasonality. The precise nature of such tests in the presence of seasonality is a topic for further research.

The forecasts from these two models were constructed for five years or until 1990. In the first case, the forecasts were monthly, while in the second the forecasts were annual but were interpolated to monthly values using spline interpolation. The series have no seasonality and are

TABLE 3.   Long-run model estimated from monthly data

Variable	Coefficient	Std. error	t-statistic
MU	-2.614946	1.494347	-1.74
MC	0.006263	0.000915	6.84
_CONST	-105.922279	66.974351	-1.58

Number of observations	112
Mean value of M	293.00
(Standard deviation)	(27.03)
Standard error of forecast	19.88
Adjusted R-square	0.45
Durbin–Watson statistic	0.95

TABLE 4. Long-run model from annual data

Variable	Coefficient	Std. error	t-statistic
AU	−40.963840	8.001853	−5.11
AC	0.071864	0.006373	11.27
_CONST	−991.846822	460.045640	−2.15
	Number of observations	10	
	Mean value of AM	3435.16	
	(Standard deviation)	(243.86)	
	Standard error of forecast	34.84	
	Adjusted R-square	0.097	
	Durbin–Watson statistic	2.73	

best interpreted as 'weather and seasonally adjusted sales' forecasts. Since these series are to be used in error-correction models, they are called *ECTEST1* and *ECTEST2*, respectively. In each case the out of sample forecasts were based upon simple Box–Jenkins models of *MC* and *MU*. Thus the historical trends in these series were projected to continue and, consequently, the prediction is that sales will continue to increase. In actual forecasting, however, electric utilities often have more information on the likely path of the independent variables. This leads to the construction of one or more forecast scenarios. In *EC-TEST3*, it is assumed that unemployment and customers remain constant over the next five years. This series is identical with *ECTEST2* except during the post-sample period. *ECTEST1* and *ECTEST2* scenarios are plotted with the historical data on *M* in fig. 1.

Error-correction models were then estimated using each of the long-run forecasts in the error-correction term. That is, a regressor $M[-1] - ECTEST1[-1]$ was introduced into the short-run model and is anticipated to have a negative coefficient. When *M* is above its long-run forecast, there is downward pressure on *M* next period. The short-run model is built on the first difference of sales and has as explanatory variables, lagged changes in sales and current and lagged weather variables. The lagged weather is anticipated to be important through billing cycle effects. The only trend variable is the long-run forecast which is constrained in the error-correction term to have the same coefficient as the lagged level of *M*. If there were no error-correction term, then the trend would be modelled solely by the intercept in the first difference model as illustrated by the short-run model above. The results are presented in tables 5 and 6 for the two long-run forecasts.

The estimates for both models are highly encouraging. In each case the error-correction term is highly significant and of the correct sign.

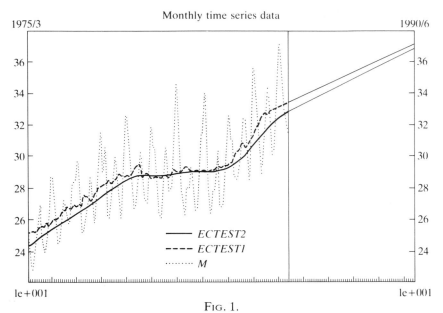

Fig. 1.

Table 5. Error-correction model using monthly long-run model

Variable	Coefficient	Std. error	t-statistic
MCD	0.128022	0.014416	8.88
MHD	0.055242	0.004204	13.14
MCD[−1]	0.035419	0.020368	1.73
MHD[−1]	0.000271	0.006114	0.04
M[−1] − *M*[−2]	0.226384	0.061441	3.68
M[−1] − *ECTEST1*[−1]	−1.130600	0.098280	−11.50
CONST	−41.220136	4.422205	−9.32

Number of observations	124
Mean value of __DM_	0.35
(Standard deviation)	(18.80)
Standard error of forecast	7.83
Adjusted R-square	0.82
Durbin–Watson statistic	2.15

The weather variables are significant although the lags are probably not necessary. The diagnostic tests for the monthly model found that the model is quite clean against a wide range of possible misspecifications. There is some evidence that seasonal dummy variables would improve the fit, but there is no test which rejects at the 99 per cent level, which

TABLE 6.   Error-correction model using annual long-run forecast

Variable	Coefficient	Std. error	t-statistic
MCD	0.141101	0.015230	9.26
MHD	0.055315	0.004530	12.21
$MCD[-1]$	0.014629	0.021370	0.68
$MHD[-1]$	−0.004948	0.006501	−0.76
$M[-1] - M[-2]$	0.190117	0.065617	2.89
$M[-1] - ECTEST2[-1]$	−1.010415	0.101993	−9.90
CONST	−33.543761	4.400422	−7.62

Number of observations	124
Mean value of $\_DM$	0.35
(Standard deviation)	(18.80)
Standard error of forecast	8.43
Adjusted R-square	0.79
Durbin–Watson statistic	1.91

is unusual when so many tests are carried out. There is somewhat more evidence against the *ECTEST2* version of the error-correction model.

These two models were then used to forecast Massachusetts commercial sales for the next five years. The forecasts for *ECTEST2* are presented in fig. 2. Superimposed in this figure are the original series *M*

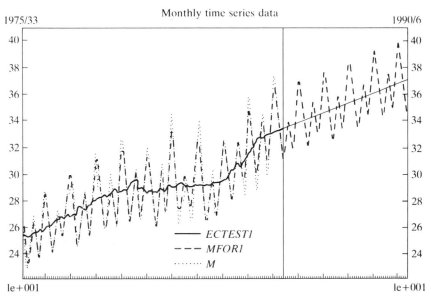

FIG. 2.

through 1985, the long-run forecast within sample and out of sample, and the merged forecast labeled *MFOR*. The forecasts using *ECTEST1* are similar but lower, and those from *ECTEST3* are that in the post-sample period. These forecasts are seen to accomplish the purpose of providing a short-run forecast which accurately predicts the seasonality and short-run movements in sales but which is consistent with the long-run forecast over the longer period.

5. A Simulation Study

To evaluate the effectiveness of the various techniques introduced above, a simulation study was conducted. Data were generated using a model which has properties similar to the electricity data and used to build long-run, short-run and merged models. From each of these data sets and models, multi-step forecasts were constructed and the results compared for accuracy on post-sample data. In each case, the independent variables were forecast assuming that the form of the equation was known but not its coefficients. Therefore, all forecasts are interpreted as unconditional forecasts. Surely forecasts conditional on the long-run variables would dramatically favour the long-run and merged models. Thirty-eight years of data were generated for each replication. The first 28 were used to fit the models, and then the final 10 years of 120 months were forecast conditional only on the first 28-year data set. Mean squared forecast errors of each forecast horizon were computed across 500 replications. Thus the forecast errors are not constructed by rolling the sample period forward but corresponds to a fixed time period.

The data for electricity sales, y_t, was generated from

$$y_t = m_1 + 0.6y_{t-1} + w_t + v_t + \varepsilon_{1t}, \tag{7}$$

where w_t is the long-run component generated by

$$w_t = m_2 + 0.5w_{t-12} + 0.5w_{t-24} + \varepsilon_{2t}, \tag{8}$$

and the seasonal or temperature-based component was generated by

$$v_t = v_{t-12} + \varepsilon_{3t} - \varepsilon_{3t-1}. \tag{9}$$

These parameter values imply that w_t is SI(1, 1) if $m_2 = 0$ and SI(1, 1) with drift otherwise, while v_t is SI(0, 1). This is easily seen by rewriting (8) and (9) as

$$(1 - B^{12})(1 + 0.5B^{12})w_t = m_2 + \varepsilon_{2t},$$

$$S(B)v_t = \varepsilon_{3t}.$$

From (7) it is immediately deduced that y is $SI(1, 1)$ if $m_2 = 0$ and $SI(1, 1)$ with drift otherwise, and that y and w are seasonally cointegrated at zero frequency but not at seasonal frequencies. The relationship at zero frequency says that

$$y_t = 2.5w_t + u_t,$$

where u_t still has seasonal unit roots as well as stationary components. It also appears that y and v are seasonally cointegrated at seasonal frequencies; however, a slightly more general definition of seasonal cointegration is required here to incorporate the dynamic relationship for these variables. As this is not needed for our analysis we leave this point.

To mimic actual data, the initial values of the seasonal were taken to be 90, 80, 60, 40, 20, 50, 70, 80, 60, 30, 60, 80, so that the series peak in January and August. All ε_t are assumed to be $N(0, 1)$ white noise. In the simulation first reported $m_1 = 1$ and $m_2 = 12$ so that annualized w_t is essentially a linear trend. In the second simulation, $m_2 = 1$ so that the trend is a minor component of the series.

The short-run model relates the change in y_t to the changes in the seasonal variables and to lagged changes in y_t. The equation estimated is

$$\Delta y_t = \delta_0 + \delta_1 \Delta y_{t-1} + \delta_2 \Delta v_t + e_{1t}. \tag{10}$$

This equation can be derived by differencing (7) and then treating $\Delta(w_t + \varepsilon_{1t})$ as e_{1t}. One might expect that this error would be serially correlated and therefore higher-order lags were introduced into (10), but there was not very much difference in the performance of the equation. The lagged dependent variable presumably captured much of this effect.

The long-run model was estimated using a cointegrating regression under one of three data assumptions. Letting τ index annual data,

$$y_\tau = \alpha_0 + \alpha w_\tau + e_{2\tau}. \tag{11}$$

The three assumptions are:

(i) All data are used so that the model is estimated as though the long-run explanatory variable w_t is available monthly and the subscript τ in (11) is implicitly replaced with t.

(ii) Every twelfth data point is used so that the long-run explanatory variable is treated as a stock and point sampled. The December observation is chosen.

(iii) Twelve-month averages are used for the data in (11) under the assumption that w_t is a flow variable. The Theorem in section 3 suggests that this version will be consistent, whereas version (i) will not when there is no drift. However, version (i) uses twelve times as many observations and may have a smaller variance, and when there is a drift in w_t, the Theorem implies that version (i) will be consistent as well. In practice usually only one of these series on w would be available, so there is no choice.

Three error-correction models were estimated corresponding to these three long-run models. These take the form

$$\Delta y_t = \beta_0 + \beta_1 v_t + \beta_2(\hat{y}_t - y_{t-1}) + e_{3t}, \tag{12}$$

where $\hat{y}_t$ is the monthly forecast of y_t made by a long-run model. The monthly version of the long-run model immediately produces monthly forecasts, however the other two versions do not. For these a simple linear interpolation was used. Although this introduced errors into $\hat{y}$, these appeared to be small as the series was inherently smooth being the long-run prediction.

If the monthly observations on w are available, then the investigator may estimate the true relation (7). As a basis for the comparison we consider estimates of

$$y_t = \theta_0 + \theta_1 y_{t-1} + \theta_2 w_t + \theta_3 s_t + e_t, \tag{13}$$

which should provide the best estimate of both the short- and long-run effects. In practice, we believe that such estimates are not available either because w_t is not measured monthly or because the short- and long-run forecasters cannot agree to use a single model.

The mean square forecast errors for horizons from 1 through 120 months of the various estimators were obtained. The annual model using every twelfth data point is generally inferior to the one using annual averages and so is the associated error-correction model. For this reason, and because the scheme is not even feasible in many cases, we will not mention these models again. Table 7 extracts from the results information on the forecasts of some Januaries from the other models; this controls for the seasonality which makes the interpretation of the long-run models particularly complex.

The results in table 7 are rather clear. Forecasting sales ten years in the future is inherently more uncertain than one year. Forecasting with

TABLE 7.   Summary January mean squared forecast errors

Year	Actual	Esti-mated	Long-run model		Error-correction model	
			Annual	Monthly	Annual	Monthly
1	4.1	4.1	2024	2053	14.9	4.3
2	6.9	7.2	2022	2055	19.7	8.0
3	9.3	9.7	2017	2054	21.7	10.6
5	13.8	15.7	2011	2064	27.4	16.9
10	21.6	28.0	2023	2092	40.3	29.8

the correctly specified model is only slightly less accurate than using the true parameters. The short-run model is not shown, but was found to perform substantially worse both at short and at long horizons. It was about nine times worse than estimating the true model for one-month forecasts and six times worse for a ten-year horizon. The long-run models, however, are even worse than the short-run model at all horizons. This is primarily because they make no attempt to model the seasonality so that the bulk of the mean squared forecast error is presumably the bias from seasonality. It was found that although the MSFE for the monthly long-run model is 2053 for the one-month forecast, it was only 93 for the three-month forecast.

The most interesting results therefore are the error-correction models. Both the monthly and annual error-correction models perform very well. The monthly is only slightly inferior to estimation of the full correctly specified model, while the annual is not quite as good but still much better than the short- or long-run models themselves. The annual model incurs the added error due to the interpolation of the long-run forecasts and the forecast of the w series using aggregate data and an AR(2) specification. One might expect that this estimation would be considerably less precise than the monthly estimate. Because there is a substantial drift in w_t, part (c) of the Theorem from section 3 suggests on all grounds that the monthly error correction model should be the best.

This simulation experiment bears out the expectations of the theory. It is possible to combine short- and long-run forecasts using an error-correction formulation which conveniently encapsulates the long-run forecast information in a single variable. If there is a choice between estimating the long-run model on monthly data or annual data, one should choose the annual version if seasonality is a large component of the monthly variance but use the monthly data if the trend is the dominant component of the monthly variance.

Simulation experiments have also been tried with other parameter values, no drift, more lags in (10) and somewhat different data generation processes for W_t. The results are similar to those reported here. When forecasts are made conditional on W_t, the models using the extra information far outperform (10) as expected. Further detailed results can be obtained from the authors.

6. Conclusions

If there exist two forecasting models, one aiming at the long run and the other at the short run, our suggestion is that the two sets of forecasts be merged by adding an 'error-correction' term into the short-run model. This term consists of the difference between the most recent actual value for the series and the long-run model's forecast of that value. The coefficient on this term will have to be estimated and then the resulting model run forward in time to provide forecasts of a horizon. The experience so far accumulated suggests that this technique will be successful.

References

CHAN, N. H., and C. Z. WEI (1988), 'Limiting distributions of least squares estimates of unstable autoregressive processes', *Annals of Statistics*, **16**, 367–401.

ENGLE, ROBERT F., C. W. J. GRANGER (1987), 'Cointegration and error correction: Representation, estimation, and testing', *Econometrica*, **55**, 251–76.

FULLER, W. (1976), *Introduction to Statistical Time Series* (New York, Wiley).

GRANGER, C. W. J. (1986), 'Development in the study of co-integrated economic variables', *Oxford Bulletin of Economics and Statistics*, **68**, 213–28.

PASTUSZEK, LYDIA and MARK WATSON (1985), 'Developments in short run forecasting: A comparison of monthly forecasting electricity sales', in Steve Braithwait (ed.), *Sixth load Forecasting Symposium: Forecasting in an era of marketing, conservation, and competition*, San Antonio (EPRI, Palo Alto, CA).

SIMS, CHRISTOPHER, JAMES STOCK, and MARK WATSON (1986), 'Inference in linear time series models with some unit roots', manuscript (Stanford University, Stanford, CA).

STOCK, JAMES (1987), 'Asymptotic properties of least squares estimators in error correction models', *Econometrica*, **55**, 1035–56.

12

Cointegrated Economic Time Series: An Overview with New Results*

ROBERT F. ENGLE and B. SAM YOO

Abstract

This paper surveys the theoretical developments surrounding cointegrated systems. It discusses the representation, estimation, and testing of such systems. By using the Smith–McMillan–Yoo decomposition of polynomial matrices, the paper directly extends this analysis to the case of multiple unit roots, complex or seasonal unit roots, and multiple cointegrating vectors. A new and careful analysis of the case of $I(2)$ cointegration is presented which coincides with Granger's multicointegration and with Hendry and von Ungern Sternberg's integral control mechanism.

The paper compares the Engle–Granger two-step estimation model with FIML and its approximations recently introduced by Johansen, Juselius and Phillips. A new three-step estimator is proposed which achieves the benefits of FIML with only an additional least squares regression starting from the two-step estimator.

An empirical example of production, sales and inventories from Granger and Lee is used to illustrate the three-step estimator in the case of $I(2)$ cointegration.

1.   Introduction

The motivation for the concept of cointegration is as intuitive as is the first lecture on least squares regression. In regression, we decompose

* This paper was prepared by invitation for the European Meeting of the Econometric Society in Copenhagen, 24–8 August 1987, and has been substantially revised and extended. Research was supported by NSF Grants to the first author. The authors are indebted to many people for helpful discussions, but particular mention should be made of Professors Granger, Johansen, MacKinnon, Phillips, Park, Stock, Watson, and an anonymous reviewer, all of whose insights have improved this draft of the paper although they cannot be held responsible for remaining deficiencies.

the movements of one random variable, the dependent, into movements which are associated with the independent variables, and a purely random-error term. That is, a linear combination of the dependent and independent variables is white noise. For cointegration we require only that the slowly moving or trending movements in the dependent variable equal linear combinations of similar movements in the independent variables. The remainder need not be purely random; it can be a general stationary process.

A second difference between the introductory least squares lecture and the cointegration analysis is that in the latter case there is no need to designate one of the variables as 'exogenous'. The decomposition of the movement of two series is symmetric so that if x and y are cointegrated, then y and x are cointegrated. The question is often phrased whether there is a linear combination of two non-stationary series which is stationary. If some form of exogeneity assumption is made, then this can be used to restrict the parameterization as is discussed to some extent below.

This interpretation of cointegration focuses on trends and unit roots as the 'interesting' features of a time series, but there are other similar features which could provoke the same arguments. For example, seasonality in different series could be the important features and one could relate the seasonal behaviour of one series to the seasonal behaviour of another and suppose that the remainder is stationary. This approach was taken by Hylleberg *et al.* (1990) and will be discussed below. One could also apply this approach to features such as heteroskedasticity. A series with a certain type of heteroskedasticity, or a fat-tailed distribution, or even certain types of contamination by outliers could be potentially decomposed into the movement of a similar series and a stationary residual without any of these key features. Apparently, it would only be in special cases that this decomposition could be accomplished and such situations would usually imply that the variables are fundamentally related.

This paper will briefly discuss integrated processes in Section 2. One may refer to Diebold and Nerlove (1989) for a detailed survey on unit root processes. It will then examine various representations or ways to write cointegrated systems in Section 3 for the most common unit root case. In Section 4 extensions will be considered building on the representations obtained in Section 3. Section 5 examines the $I(2)$ case in detail and its connection with integral control mechanisms. Section 6 introduces the estimation and testing problems for cointegrated systems which are examined in detail in later sections. Section 7 presents the Engle–Granger two-step method; Section 8 considers more than one cointegrating vector; Section 9 presents FIML estimation and Section 10 introduces a new three-step estimator. Section 11 contains an empirical example and Section 12 concludes.

2. The Integration of Economic Time Series

A random variable with no deterministic components will be defined to be integrated of order d if the dth difference of the random variable is wide sense stationary and therefore can be represented by a stationary invertible ARMA process. Notice that if the random variable is differenced too many times, the moving average will have a unit root in it and will not be invertible. If it is differenced too few times, the autoregressive part will contain a unit root so that the ARMA process is not stationary. Of course not all non-stationary time series can be made stationary by differencing, so that the assumption that a variable is $I(d)$ is possibly special. Nevertheless, Box and Jenkins (1970) and more recently Nelson and Plosser (1982) find evidence that many time series appear to fall into this category. In fact, most macroeconomic time series appear to be $I(1)$ with possible exceptions of unemployment which could be $I(0)$ and some price or nominal money supply aggregates which may be $I(2)$.

An $N \times 1$ vector of random variables, x_t, each of which is $I(0)$ and has no deterministic component, can always, by the Wold decomposition theorem, be written as an infinite order vector moving average. Letting $C(B)$ be an $N \times N$ matrix polynomial in the backshift operator B, and ε_t be an $N \times 1$ vector of contemporaneously and serially uncorrelated random variables, we may therefore write:

$$x_t = C(B)\varepsilon_t, \tag{1}$$

with $E(\varepsilon_t \varepsilon_t') = I$, $E(\varepsilon_t \varepsilon_{t-i}') = 0$ for $i \neq 0$, and $C(0)$ lower triangular. Such a vector of random variables has a multivariate spectral representation given by

$$F_{xx}(\omega) = C(e^{i\omega})C'(e^{-i\omega}) \tag{2}$$

where ω is the frequency and $i = \sqrt{-1}$. The diagonal elements of $F_{xx}(\omega)$ give the univariate spectrum of each component of the random vector. The assumption that each element of x is $I(0)$ means that these spectra are nowhere either zero or infinite. In particular, this must be true at $\omega = 0$ since it is the zero frequency or long-run component of a series which is reduced by differencing. The zero frequency spectrum is given by

$$F_{xx}(0) = C(1)C'(1) \tag{3}$$

which will have a zero diagonal element if a row of $C(1)$ is identically zero and will have an infinite diagonal element if any element of $C(1)$ is infinite.

Similarly, if each element of x_t is $I(1)$ so that $x_t \sim I(1)$, then

$$\Delta x_t = C(B)\varepsilon_t \tag{4}$$

with the same conditions. This equation can be solved for the level of x_t as $x_t = \Delta^{-1} C(B)\varepsilon_t$ or more precisely:

$$x_t = x_0 + (1 + B + B^2 + \ldots + B^{t-1})C(B)\varepsilon_t \qquad (5)$$

which is again a moving average process with a component x_0 which is treated as deterministic conditional on the presample information. The sum of moving average coefficients is now $tC(1)$ which will grow infinitely large for large t unless $C(1) = 0$. The 'spectrum' of x_t for large t will therefore go to infinity at zero frequency. The second difference of x_t in this case will be given by

$$\Delta^2 x_t = (1 - B)C(B)\varepsilon_t$$

so that the moving average representation will have a sum of moving average coefficients which is zero and therefore a spectrum which is zero at zero frequency. This illustrates the point that underdifferencing leaves a zero frequency pole in the spectrum while overdifferencing produces a zero in the spectrum.

This feature of integrated random variables has recently attracted much attention. The long-term forecasts of economic variables are easily expressed in the moving average representation. From (5),

$$x_{t+h} = x_0 + \sum_{i=1}^{t+h} \left(\sum_{j=0}^{t+h-i} C_j \right) \varepsilon_i$$

$$= x_0 + \sum_{i=1}^{t} \left(\sum_{j=0}^{t+h-i} C_j \right) \varepsilon_i + \sum_{i=1+t}^{t+h} \left(\sum_{j=0}^{t+h-i} C_j \right) \varepsilon_i$$

so that the forecast of x_{t+h} given information at time t is simply the first two terms or

$$x_{t+h/t} = x_0 + \sum_{i=1}^{t} \left(\sum_{j=0}^{t+h-i} C_j \right) \varepsilon_i. \qquad (6)$$

The effect of the shock in period t on the forecast in period $t + h$ is therefore simply

$$\partial x_{t+h} / \partial \varepsilon_t = \sum_{j=0}^{h} C_j \quad \xrightarrow{h \to \infty} \quad C(1). \qquad (7)$$

Thus the persistence of a shock to a random variable depends upon the sum of the moving average coefficients of the differences of the random variable. Notice that if x is truly $I(0)$, then a shock today will have no effect on the forecast many steps in the future. If it is truly $I(1)$ then the persistence can be measured by (the square root of) the spectrum at zero frequency. The effect of a shock can be greater or less on the distant future than it was in time t since $C(1)$ can be greater or less than one. If the series is actually $I(2)$, then the effect of the shock grows monotonically with the forecast horizon. Thus the implications of the integratedness of macroeconomic time series can be very important. If a shock to GNP is persistent, as argued by Mankiw and Shapiro (1986), then a cost benefit analysis would suggest substantial measures to prevent downward shocks and create upward shocks. If consumption responds to permanent income, then the response of consumption to a shock in income depends importantly on the integratedness of income. The excess sensitivity of consumption to income shocks as reported, for example, by Flavin (1981) then becomes undersensitivity if income is highly persistent. See, for example, Deaton (1986), Campbell (1987), Campbell and Deaton (1987), and Hall (1989). Finally, Fama and French (1986), and Cochrane and Sbordone (1988) have presented evidence that asset prices are not Martingales and possibly that shocks are eventually reversed implying that high returns in one period will eventually lead to lower returns as prices return to their stationary distribution. Regardless of the eventual consensus on these issues, the integratedness of economic time series is of substantial interest and multivariate extensions of the concepts will similarly have important implications as will be developed in this paper.

3.   Representations for Cointegrated Systems

Granger (1981) first introduced the concept of cointegration which was further developed in Granger and Weiss (1983). Engle and Granger (1987) presented a representation theorem originally contained in Granger (1983) and new estimation and testing procedures. A special issue of the *Oxford Bulletin* in 1986 presented several important overviews, empirical applications and Monte Carlo studies of the estimation and testing strategies in Engle and Granger. This collection of studies has now been joined by a wide range of applications and theoretical developments. In this section, several simple theoretical representations of cointegrated systems will be presented including several new formulations which greatly simplify the analysis and extensions.

A system of purely non-deterministic random variables is said to be cointegrated if each of the elements is individually $I(1)$ while r linearly independent linear combinations are $I(0)$. Later in this paper we consider cointegration of variables which are not $I(1)$ but this is the most empirically important case.

Let again x_t be an $N \times 1$ purely non-deterministic random vector with all elements $I(1)$. Then from (4)

$$\Delta x_t = C(B)\varepsilon_t.$$

Rewriting $C(B) = C(1) + (1 - B)C^*(B)$, which can always be done without loss of generality, (4) becomes

$$\Delta x_t = C(1)\varepsilon_t + \Delta C^*(B)\varepsilon_t \tag{8}$$

so that a linear combination $z_t = \alpha'x_t$ will have representation

$$\Delta z_t = \alpha'C(1)\varepsilon_t + \Delta\alpha'C^*(B)\varepsilon_t \tag{9}$$

and therefore if $\alpha'C(1) \neq 0$, z_t will also be $I(1)$. If $\alpha'C(1) = 0$, then

$$z_t = \alpha'C^*(B)\varepsilon_t \tag{10}$$

which will generally be $I(0)$. Under the weak additional assumption that $C(B)$ is a rational polynomial matrix meaning that each element is a ratio of two finite polynomials, then $\alpha'C^*(1)$ can be shown to be finite. In this case it remains possible that $\alpha'C^*(1) = 0$ in which case z_t has a non-invertible moving average representation and could therefore be $I(-1)$. At the moment, we assume $\alpha'C^*(1) \neq 0$ for simplicity and consider more general cases in Section 5.

The condition for cointegration is therefore that $C(1)$ has reduced rank. Any vector lying in the null space of $C(1)$ is a cointegrating vector and the cointegrating rank is the rank of this null space. This implies from (3) that the spectral density matrix at zero frequency is singular. Phillips and Ouliaris (1988) have suggested a test for cointegration based on this observation.

An implication of cointegration for forecasting is immediately apparent from equation (7). The persistence of any shock on a linear combination of random variables is simply given by that vector times $C(1)$. Such a cointegrating linear combination $\alpha'x_t$ is stationary and will show no persistence. Although individual series can only be forecast with increasingly wide confidence intervals, the cointegrating linear combination has a finite confidence interval. For more details, see Engle and Yoo (1987). This observation is consistent with the interpretation of the cointegrating error term as being a measure of disequilibrium.

Stock and Watson (1988) have proposed an intuitively satisfying representation for such systems called by them the 'common trends representation'. From (8) they solve for the level of x_t just as done in (5).

$$x_t = x_0 + (1 + B + B^2 + \ldots B^{t-1})(C(1) + (1 - B)C^*(B))\varepsilon_t \tag{11}$$

$$= x_0 + C(1)(1 + B + \ldots B^{t-1})\varepsilon_t + C^*(B)\varepsilon_t.$$

Because $C(1)$ has rank $N - r$, it can be written as the product of two rectangular matrices, an $N \times (N - r)$ matrix A and an $(N - r) \times N$ matrix J, giving $C(1) = AJ$. Defining

$$\tau_t = \tau_{t-1} + J\varepsilon_t$$

$$= (1 + B + \ldots + B^{t-1})J\varepsilon_t$$

as an r-dimensional random walk with initial condition $\tau_0 = 0$, (11) becomes

$$x_t = x_0 + A\tau_t + C*(B)\varepsilon_t. \qquad (12)$$

This is the common trends representation which receives its name from the interpretation of τ as the trends in a set of time series. Because there are fewer random walks than variables in the system, the trends are 'common'. Because $C(1) = AJ$, $\alpha'A = 0$ so that the cointegrating linear combinations will not have any random walk component. From an economic point of view the assumption that trends are common is often appealing as there may be latent variables which are responsible for the growth of many separate random variables. In King *et al.* (1987), for example, the common trend is identified as an accumulation of past technology shocks.

For estimation and inference, a much more useful representation is the Autoregressive Representation. This involves inverting the matrix polynomial $C(B)$. Because the matrix is singular at one value of its argument, the inverse exists at all other points, but care must be taken to isolate the reduced rank component. Recently Yoo (1986) has adapted the Smith–McMillan form for polynomial matrices to this problem. The version he applies, will be called the Smith–McMillan–Yoo form to make clear the properties of the expressions.

LEMMA: For any rational matrix $C(B)$ which is finite for all B on or within the unit circle,

$$M(B) = V(B)C(B)U(B) \qquad (13)$$

where

(1) All the roots of $\det U(B) = 0$ and $\det V(B) = 0$ lie outside the unit circle;
(2) $M(B)$ is diagonal with all roots of $\det M(B) = 0$ on or within the unit circle.

For a proof of this lemma see Yoo (1986). The key step in the proof is to recognize that by simple row operations involving polynomial linear combinations, any finite order polynomial matrix can be triangularized. This is the Hermite form of a polynomial matrix and the product of all the elementary row operators will have a determinant which is independent of the argument B. Such a matrix is called 'unimodular', and necessarily has a finite order polynomial inverse. By post multiplying by a second unimodular matrix the diagonal or 'Smith' form is obtained. The Smith–McMillan form recognizes that a rational matrix can be converted to a finite order polynomial matrix by multiplying by the least common divisor of all the elements. Yoo then factors the diagonal matrix of rational polynomials into a component with zeros on or within the unit circle and a component with zeros outside the unit disk. The latter has an inverse and is combined with the unimodular matrices to achieve the form in the lemma.

From (13) it follows that for any rational vector moving average process with no poles

$$C(B) = U^{-1}(B)M(B)V^{-1}(B)$$

since $U(B)$ and $V(B)$ have inverses, so that

$$\Delta x_t = U^{-1}(B)M(B)V^{-1}(B)\varepsilon_t. \tag{14}$$

The rank of $C(1)$ must be the same as the rank of $M(1)$ which is here assumed to be $N - r$. By the assumptions of the Smith–McMillan–Yoo form, $M(B)$ can be expressed as

$$M(B) = \begin{bmatrix} I_{N-r} & 0 \\ 0 & \Delta I_r \end{bmatrix} \tag{15}$$

where I_s is the $s \times s$ identity matrix. Cases with higher powers of Δ will not be called $I(1)$ systems and will be considered in Section 5.

The autoregressive form is easily achieved in three steps. First premultiply both sides of (14) by $U(B)$ to obtain

$$\Delta U(B)x_t = M(B)V^{-1}(B)\varepsilon_t \tag{16}$$

The last r rows of this equation have a Δ on both sides, therefore the equation can also be written as

$$\bar{M}(B)U(B)x_t = V^{-1}(B)\varepsilon_t \tag{17}$$

where

$$\bar{M}(B) = \begin{bmatrix} \Delta I_{N-r} & 0 \\ 0 & I_r \end{bmatrix} \tag{18}$$

Finally multiplying by $V(B)$ gives the autoregressive form:

$$A(B)x_t = V(B)\bar{M}(B)U(B)x_t = \varepsilon_t \tag{19}$$

Notice that $A(B)$ will have full rank for all values of B within the unit circle, but will have only rank r for $B = 1$. Clearly if $U(B)$ and $V(B)$ are finite polynomial matrices, this will be a finite autoregression; otherwise, it will be an infinite order autoregression which is more conveniently treated as a vector ARMA. This process could initially be defined as an autoregression and then transformed into the moving average representation since each step is easily reversed. This derivation is far simpler than that used by Engle and Granger (1987) and reveals the essential nature of the inversion of the singular polynomial matrices.

From the autoregressive form, the error correction representation is easily derived. Partitioning V and U conformably with M as

$$V(B) = [V_1(B), \gamma(B)], \qquad U'(B) = [U_1(B), \alpha(B)]$$

$$A(1) = V(1)\bar{M}(1)U(1) = \gamma(1)\alpha'(1) \equiv \gamma\alpha'$$

where $\gamma \equiv \gamma(1)$ and $\alpha \equiv \alpha(1)$. Because both U and V have full rank for all values of B within or on the unit circle, $U(1)$ and $V(1)$ are of full rank and therefore both γ and α must have full column rank which is here equal to r. Following the same strategy as used for the moving average, the polynomial matrix $A^*(B)$ can be defined by

$$A(B) = A(1)B + A^*(B)\Delta \tag{20}$$

so that

$$A^*(B)\Delta x_t = -\gamma\alpha'x_{t-1} + \varepsilon_t. \tag{21}$$

This representation includes only variables which are $I(0)$. The dependent variable is a vector autoregression in the changes in x_t which are therefore $I(0)$, and the right-hand side includes just the linear combination of the levels of x which is stationary, $\alpha'x_t = z_t$. The name error correction model derives from the interpretation of this type of model as an optimal control rule where z_t is viewed as an error which is partially corrected in the next period by setting x_{t+1} according to (21). The name was first suggested by Davidson et al. (1978) following Sargan (1964) and is further developed in Hendry and von Ungern-Sternberg (1981). Because all the variables are stationary, estimation and inference on the parameters in A^* and γ can proceed under the usual assumptions if α is known.

If there is no cointegration, then all the elements of $A(1)$ are zero and so the error correction term does not enter the model. Hence, if it is assumed that the data follow a vector autoregression in the differences, it is in effect assumed that there is no cointegration. Thus the model in differences will be misspecified if there is cointegration. The unrestricted estimation of the vector autoregression in levels is an alternative strategy, using (19) without restrictions. In this case, estimation of the system is straightforward, but inference on the estimates will be difficult as discussed in later sections.

An alternative derivation of the error correction form will be useful below. From the form of $\bar{M}(B)$ it is clear that

$$\bar{M}(B) = \Delta I_N + B \begin{bmatrix} 0 & 0 \\ 0 & I_r \end{bmatrix}$$

so (19) becomes

$$V(B)U(B)\Delta x_t = -\gamma(B)\alpha'(B)x_{t-1} + \varepsilon_t \tag{22}$$

which suggests a polynomial cointegrating vector, PCIV as first proposed by Yoo (1986), and polynomial distributed lags on the error correction term. From this construction it is assured that $V(B)U(B)$ will be a stable autoregressive matrix; it is not guaranteed that this will be true of $A^*(B)$. Because

$$\gamma(B)\alpha(B) = \gamma\alpha' + \Delta[\gamma(B)\alpha'(B)]^*,$$

direct substitution establishes that

$$A^*(B) = V(B)U(B) + B[\gamma(B)\alpha'(B)]^*$$

From the Smith–McMillan–Yoo form a latent variable interpretation of cointegration is directly available. Equation (17) represents the system when it is only partly converted to autoregressive form. Letting

$$\begin{bmatrix} y_t \\ z_t \end{bmatrix} \equiv U(B)x_t$$

equation (17) can be rewritten as

$$\begin{bmatrix} \Delta y_t \\ z_t \end{bmatrix} = V^{-1}(B)\varepsilon_t \tag{23}$$

where Δy is $(N-r) \times 1$ and z is $r \times 1$. Thus the system can be described in terms of latent variables y and z where y is $I(1)$ and z is $I(0)$. There are as many z's as cointegrating vectors and as many y's as common trends. Inverting $U(B)$ the observable x vector is a general distributed lag of linear combinations of y and z. Thus each element of x again has components which are $I(1)$ and $I(0)$.

From the partition of $U(B)$, $z_t = \alpha'(B)x_t$ so that a polynomial cointegrating vector produces a stationary random variable. As argued above, the fixed cointegrating vector $\alpha(1)$ also generates a stationary random variable. However, as discussed by Yoo and as will be discovered below, only polynomial cointegrating vectors can generally reduce multiple time series to stationarity in more complex situations.

4.   Extensions of the Theory of Cointegration

Since the original structure of cointegrated systems was proposed, there have been many theoretical extensions to more general settings. The original work focused upon first-order systems while Granger (1986), Yoo (1986), and Johansen (1985) have discussed extensions to higher orders. Hylleberg *et al.* (1989) and Engle, Granger, and Hallman (1990) discuss seasonal unit roots and cointegration. Yoo (1986), Sims, Stock, and Watson (1987), and Granger (1986) introduce time trends into such systems and Yoo also considers explosive processes. Finally, Granger (1987) and Escribano (1987) explore some possibilities for non-linear cointegration. Granger considers cases where the attractor set is a non-linear function of the observable variables, and Escribano considers linear attractor sets but non-linear rates of adjustment towards the cointegration relation.

In a rather different vein, Engle (1982) considered time series models for second moments rather than first moments as described throughout this paper. These Autoregressive Conditional Heteroskedastic or ARCH processes were extended by Engle and Bollerslev (1986) to include integrated variance processes. More recently, Bollerslev and Engle (1990) have pointed out that in a multivariate setting there may be some linear combinations of random variables which have integrated variance while others do not. This provides a natural definition of cointegration in variance.

In this paper, several of the linear model extensions can immediately be developed using the techniques described in the previous section. The generic model will allow for two potentially different unit roots in the time series and therefore potentially two sets of partially cointegrating vectors.

Let $\delta_1(B)$ and $\delta_2(B)$ be lag polynomials with $\delta_1(B) = 0$ for $B = \theta_1$ with $\delta_2(B) = 0$ for $B = \theta_2$ where both θ_1 and θ_2 may be complex and lie on or inside the unit circle. In some examples these could be multiple roots. A vector of time series x_t is assumed to have some non-stationary elements at these roots such that filtering by the product $\delta_1(B)\delta_2(B)$ is sufficient to achieve a finite moving average representation:

$$\delta_1(B)\delta_2(B)x_t = C(B)\varepsilon_t.$$

Notice that it is not assumed here that all elements of x have the same order. This generic model covers several important models. If $\delta_1(B) = \delta_2(B) = \Delta$ the model will describe cointegration in $I(2)$ models. If $\delta_1(B) = \Delta$ but $\delta_2(B) = (1 + B)$ the model describes seasonal behaviour where the seasonal repeats every two observations. This is the only seasonal periodicity for semi-annual data but it is only one of the possible seasonal roots for more frequently sampled data. For quarterly data, $\delta_2(B) = (1 + B^2)$ generates a cycle every four periods, and $\delta_2(B) = (1 + B + B^2 + B^3)$ combines the annual and biannual seasonal patterns to give a complete description for seasonal unit root quarterly models. If $\delta_2(B) = 1 - aB$ for $a > 1$, explosive processes are incorporated.

The Smith–McMillan–Yoo form for $C(B)$ implies

$$\delta_1(B)\delta_2(B)x_t = U^{-1}(B)M(B)V^{-1}(B)\varepsilon_t, \tag{24}$$

$$M(B) = \begin{bmatrix} I_{N-r_1-r_2-r_3} & & & 0 \\ & \delta_1(B)I_{r_1} & & \\ & & \delta_2(B)I_{r_2} & \\ 0 & & & \delta_1(B)\delta_2(B)I_{r_3} \end{bmatrix} \tag{25}$$

so that the rank of $C(\theta_1)$ is $N - r_1 - r_3$ and the rank of $C(\theta_2) = N - r_2 - r_3$. Multiplying both sides of (24) by $U(B)$ gives the expression

$$\bar{M}(B)U(B)x_t = V^{-1}(B)\varepsilon_t$$

$$\bar{M}(B) = \begin{bmatrix} \delta_1(B)\delta_2(B)I_{N-r_1-r_2-r_3} & & & 0 \\ & \delta_2(B)I_{r_1} & & \\ & & \delta_1(B)I_{r_2} & \\ 0 & & & I_{r_3} \end{bmatrix}. \tag{26}$$

Partitioning $U(B)$ conformably

$$U'(B) = [U_1(B), \alpha_1(B), \alpha_2(B), \alpha_3(B)]$$

gives

$$\begin{bmatrix} U_1'(B)\delta_1(B)\delta_2(B)x_t \\ \alpha_1'(B)\delta_2(B)x_t \\ \alpha_2'(B)\delta_1(B)x_t \\ \alpha_3'(B)x_t \end{bmatrix} = V^{-1}(B)\varepsilon_t. \tag{27}$$

Therefore each row of (27) describes a stationary vector of random variables. For example, $\alpha_1(B)$ eliminates the root at θ_1 and when multiplied by $\delta_2(B)$ there remain no non-stationary components. $\alpha_3(B)$ apparently eliminates both roots itself. Because $U(B)$ has full rank, each of these matrix polynomials are restricted to be of full column rank at all values of B including the roots θ_1 and θ_2 so that trivial solutions such as $\alpha(\theta_1) = 0$ are excluded.

In each case, the cointegrating vector appears to be a cointegrating polynomial. However, it may often be possible to find a cointegrating vector simply by substituting the value of the relevant root. For example,

$$\alpha_1(B) = \alpha_1(\theta_1) + \delta_1(B)\alpha_1{}^*(B) \tag{28}$$

defines $\alpha_1{}^*(B)$. Substituting in the second line of (27) gives

$$\alpha_1(B)\delta_2(B)x_t = \alpha_1(\theta_1)\delta_2(B)x_t + \alpha_1{}^*(B)\delta_1(B)\delta_2(B)x_t.$$

Since the first and third terms are $I(0)$ by construction, the second must also be. Therefore $\alpha_1(\theta_1)$ is a cointegrating vector with constant coefficients which has the property that $\alpha_1(\theta_1)'x_t$ has no root at θ_1. When multiplied by $\delta_2(B)$ the time series is stationary.

This argument cannot be applied for $\alpha_3(B)$ since this polynomial must be expanded around two roots. An alternative expansion can be applied when the roots are distinct:

$$\alpha_3(B) = \alpha_3(\theta_1)\delta_2(B)/\delta_2(\theta_1) + \alpha_3(\theta_2)\delta_1(B)/\delta_1(\theta_2)$$

$$+ \alpha_3*(B)\delta_1(B)\delta_2(B). \tag{28'}$$

Notice that when $B = \theta_1$ and when $B = \theta_2$ the equation is satisfied and for other values of B, α_3* can produce the equality. Because $\alpha_3(B)x_t$ is $I(0)$ and $\alpha_3*(B)\delta_1(B)\delta_2(B)x_t$ is $I(0)$, the sum of the two intermediate terms must be $I(0)$. There is, however, no constant cointegrating vector which produces the $I(0)$ random variable. The same conclusion holds when the two roots are the same. Whenever more than one root is being eliminated by a polynomial cointegrating vector, there is no guarantee that a constant cointegrating vector can be found. We now formulate this statement as a theorem.

DEFINITION: Let $\delta(B)$ be a scalar polynomial of degree J with roots θ_i, all of which lie on or within the unit circle, and let x_t be an $N \times 1$ purely non-deterministic vector time series with:

$$\delta(B)x_t \sim I(0), \qquad \text{for all elements.}$$

If there exists an $N \times 1$ vector polynomial $\alpha(B)$ such that $\alpha(\theta_i) \neq 0$ for all i, and $\alpha'(B)x_t \sim I(0)$, then $\alpha(B)$ is a *polynomial cointegrating vector for* θ_i, $i = 1, \ldots, J$. Similarly, if there exists an $N \times 1$ vector $\alpha \neq 0$ with the property that $\alpha'x_t \sim I(0)$ then α is a *cointegrating vector for* θ_i, $i = 1, \ldots, J$.

THEOREM: When $J = 1$ in the definition above, there exists a cointegrating vector whenever there exists a polynomial cointegrating vector. When $J > 1$, the existence of a PCIV does not imply the existence of a cointegrating vector.

PROOF: For $J = 1$, the proof comes by construction with $\alpha = \alpha(\theta_1)$ as in (28). For $J > 1$, the proof comes from the construction of a system with a PCIV but no cointegrating vector. Consider the simple common trend or latent variable form:

$$x_{1t} = w_{t-1} + \varepsilon_{1t}$$

$$x_{2t} = w_t + \varepsilon_{2t}$$

$$\delta(B)w_t = \varepsilon_{3t}$$

and ε_{it} are all $I(0)$ and independent. Clearly $\alpha(B) = (1, -B)'$ is a polynomial cointegrating vector. However, $\alpha = (\varphi, 1)'$ will only be a cointegrating vector if $(1 + \varphi B)w_t$ is $I(0)$. This can only be achieved if $\delta(B)$ has a single root but it explicitly is assumed to have more than one. The counter example clearly generalizes to $N > 2$.

Coming back to system (27), we now obtain the error correction form. Premultiplying (26) by $V(B)$ and separating $\bar{M}(B)$ into two parts gives

$$V(B)U(B)\delta_1(B)\delta_2(B)x_t = V(B)[\delta_1(B)\delta_2(B)I_N - \bar{M}(B)]U(B)x_t + \varepsilon_t.$$

Now partitioning $V(B)$ as before into

$$V(B) = [V_1(B), \gamma_1(B), \gamma_2(B), \gamma_3(B)]$$

the error correction model can be expressed as

$$V(B)U(B)\delta_1(B)\delta_2(B)x_t = -\gamma_1(B)\alpha'_1(B)\delta_2(B)(1 - \delta_1(B))x_t \quad (29)$$
$$-\gamma_2(B)\alpha'_2(B)\delta_1(B)(1 - \delta_2(B))x_t$$
$$-\gamma_3(B)\alpha'_3(B)(1 - \delta_1(B)\delta_2(B))x_t\varepsilon_t$$

which contains three error correction terms. Each of these terms is stationary and because $\delta(0) = 1$ for both factors each error correction term depends only upon lagged x's

Now consider the applications of this expression. If $\delta_1(B) = \delta_2(B) = \Delta$ and $r_2 = 0$, then this is a system of $I(2)$ random variables. The first set of r_1 cointegrating polynomials given by $\alpha_1(B)$ [and the cointegrating vectors $\alpha(1)$], reduces the integration of these linear combinations to $I(1)$. The r_3 PCIV $\alpha_3(B)$ reduce the degree to $I(0)$. However, $\alpha_3(1)x_t$ will not be $I(0)$ in general.

If $\delta_1(B) = \Delta$ and $\delta_2(B) = (1 + B + B^2 + \ldots + B^{s-1})$ where S is the seasonal periodicity, then $\delta_1(B)\delta_2(B) = (1 - B^s)$ but it is quite possible to have different cointegrating polynomials for each of these terms. Furthermore, the first can be treated simply as a cointegrating vector, but the second and third must be considered as cointegrating polynomials as they all consist of more than one root. In the error correction form, there is potentially a low-frequency term in the 'seasonally adjusted' data, $\delta_2(B)x_t$, which is the conventional error correction term, an error correction in the 'detrended' data, $\delta_1(B)x_t$, which may need a polynomial cointegrating vector, and an error correction term in the raw data which eliminates both the seasonal and the low frequency non-singularities. This formulation has been applied in Engle, Granger, and Hallman (1990) to electricity data.

In Hylleberg et al. (1989) this line of argument is extended to allow each of the seasonal roots to have its own error correction term. Thus in quarterly data the roots of $(1 - B^4)$ are ± 1, $\pm i$. The paper tests for each of these roots in a univariate process and develops the relevant error correction process.

This section has given a unified approach to a variety of extensions which have been developed to the cointegration of linear systems.

5. Cointegration for I(2) Systems

A direct application of the results in the preceding section can be found in the analysis of systems of variables which are $I(2)$. Although most economic variables are presumably $I(1)$ or $I(0)$, the cumulative sums of such variables would be $I(2)$ or $I(1)$ respectively. Thus a vector of $I(2)$ random variables can be constructed without loss of generality, regardless of the integratedness of the original data. In fact a vector of $I(d)$ random variables can similarly be constructed for any integer d, hence we need a definition of a dth order system. If we now write such a system as

$$\Delta^d x_t = C(B)\varepsilon_t = U^{-1}(B)M(B)V^{-1}(B)\varepsilon_t \qquad (30)$$

where $M(B)$ depends only on Δ, we have the following definition:

DEFINITION: The system (30) is an $I(d)$ system if the maximum power of Δ in $M(B)$ is d while the minimum power is zero.

Notice that if the minimum power of Δ were not zero, then Δ could be factored out of the right-hand side and cancelled with Δ^d to get a system of order $d - 1$. For a dth order system, there must be some polynomial combinations of $\Delta^d x_t$ which are $I(0)$. If the maximum were $d + 1$ rather than d, then by redefinition of the variables an $I(d + 1)$ system is obtained. This can be written as

$$\Delta^{d+1}(\Sigma x_t) = C(B)\varepsilon_t$$

without changing $C(B)$ since $\Delta\Sigma x_t = x_t$ with appropriate initial values. The variable Σx_t is the cumulation of x_t and is now viewed as the original data series.

To examine the properties of $I(2)$ systems, consider the Smith–McMillan–Yoo form in (25) for a bivariate system. In this case $N = 2$, $r_1 = r_2 = 0$, $r_3 = 1$ and $\delta_1(B) = \Delta$, and $\delta_2(B) = \Delta$ so that:

$$M(B) = \begin{bmatrix} 1 & 0 \\ 0 & \Delta^2 \end{bmatrix} \qquad (31)$$

Then the autoregressive form is simply

$$[V_1(B) \quad \gamma(B)]\begin{bmatrix} \Delta^2 & 0 \\ 0 & 1 \end{bmatrix}\begin{bmatrix} U_1'(B) \\ \alpha'(B) \end{bmatrix} x_t = \varepsilon_t \qquad (32)$$

and the error correction representation is

$$V(B)U(B)\Delta^2 x_t = -\gamma(B)(1 - \Delta^2)\alpha'(B)x_t + \varepsilon_t.$$

Rewriting this in a more convenient form, we express $\alpha(B)$ as

$$\alpha(B) = \alpha(1) + \Delta\alpha^*(B) = \alpha(1) + \Delta\alpha^*(1) + \Delta^2\alpha^{**}(B)$$

and define $A(B) = V(B)U(B) + \gamma(B)(2 - B)\Delta^2\alpha^{**}(B)B$, and $\gamma_1(B) = \gamma(B)(2 - B)$. Using these, (32) can be rewritten as

$$A(B)\Delta^2 x_t = -\gamma_1(B)[\alpha'(1) + \alpha^*(1)'\Delta]x_{t-1} + \varepsilon_t. \tag{33}$$

The error correction equation in (33) now includes both levels and changes of the two variables. Just as before, each term in (33) is $I(0)$ and thus estimation and inference is straightforward once $\alpha(1)$ and $\alpha*(1)$ are known. Note that in this system there are two levels of cointegration. Because $\alpha(1)x_t + \alpha*(1)\Delta x_t$ is $I(0)$, and the second term is at most $I(1)$, the first must be at most $I(1)$. Thus, $\alpha(1)$ reduces x_t from $I(2)$ to $I(1)$ and is therefore a cointegrating vector in the Engle–Granger sense with $d = 2$, $b = 1$. In other words, $\alpha(1)$ is a cointegrating vector for Δx_t. The cointegrating polynomial forms a linear combination of four variables, two levels and two changes. However, because the two changes are themselves cointegrated, it is only necessary to consider linear combinations of the two levels and one of the changes to find a fully general cointegrating vector.

Suppose the original data were labelled y_t and were $I(1)$. Then let x_t in equation (30) be defined as $\Delta x_t \equiv y_t$, or $x_t = \Delta^{-1}y_t = \Sigma y_t$. Then the error correction representation in (33) becomes

$$A(B)\Delta y_t = -\gamma_1(B)[\alpha(1)'\Delta^{-1} + \alpha*(1)']y_{t-1} + \varepsilon_t. \tag{34}$$

As mentioned before $\alpha(1)'y_t$ is $I(0)$ so $\alpha(1)'\Delta^{-1}y_t$ is $I(1)$ which in turn is cointegrated with $\alpha^*(1)'y_t$. Because of the cumulation of y_t in the error correction term, Hendry and von Ungern-Sternberg (1981) call this an integral control mechanism. If this is a behavioural model, the agent setting y_t responds not only to the previous value of y_t but to the cumulation of past values, which can often be interpreted as the stock counterpart of the flow variables y_t.

An interesting example of this form is contained in Granger and Lee (1988). They consider the relation between production and sales for firms and industry groups. In general they find that production and sales are $I(1)$ variables and are cointegrated. However, there is more structure in the data. The cumulation of production minus sales is inventories and they find that inventories are cointegrated with production. Because production and sales are cointegrated, the change in inventories is stationary and hence inventories are $I(1)$ and potentially cointegrated with production or sales. The final polynomial cointegrating vector relates cumulated production, cumulated sales, and sales to form a stationary random variable. This is an example of the integral control mechanism described above.

6. Estimation and Testing

The rapid progress of theoretical work in cointegration has been matched by new developments in estimation and testing. Perhaps the most surprising result is the simplicity of the two-step methods proposed by Engle and Granger (1987). These have proved to be useful tools in applications and have now been extended to increase the range of circumstances in which they are applicable. A series of alternative testing strategies are now being proposed for more complex cases. Recently a full maximum likelihood approach has been suggested by Johansen (1988) which is extended in Johansen and Juselius (1988) to include testing procedures for linear restrictions on the cointegrating vectors based upon the likelihood ratio principle. They show that the distribution of the test statistics is asymptotically χ^2. Phillips (1988) also provides a more general discussion on the inference problem for cointegrated systems. He shows among others two important results. First, given the knowledge of the cointegrating rank, the classical asymptotic inference applies to the FIML estimators of error correction models. Secondly, this is in general possible only if all the unit root and cointegrating restrictions are imposed. Hence, for example, the standard inference procedure is not in general applicable if a cointegrated system is modelled by the unrestricted vector autoregression. This confirms the earlier result by Sims, Stock, and Watson (1986): in an unrestricted VAR, only the parameters that can be rewritten as coefficients on zero-mean, $I(0)$ variables are asymptotically normal.

To get an intuitive idea of these developments, consider the following simple bivariate system:

$$y_t = \alpha x_t + u_t \tag{35}$$

$$\Delta x_t = \gamma \Delta y_{t-1} + \delta(y_{t-1} - \alpha x_{t-1}) + v_t \tag{36}$$

where u_t and v_t are zero-mean, mutually uncorrelated, jointly Gaussian iid random variables with variances σ_u^2 and σ_v^2 respectively. We also assume that y_t and x_t are both zero-mean $I(1)$ and thus cointegrated with the cointegrating vector $(1 - \alpha)$. Turning (35) into an error correction form and thereby obtaining a multivariate error correction form will be straightforward. However, since the following discussion does not depend on the representation chosen, but only on whether the unit root restrictions as well as the cointegrating restrictions are imposed, as discussed by Phillips (1988), we choose to proceed with (35). As it is, conditional upon the information set consisting of the two variables up to $t - 1$, (35) represents the conditional mean of y_t on x_t, and (36) depicts the marginal of x_t. We now discuss the cases in which various restrictions are correctly imposed on the equations. One of the cases requires a system estimation and thus the uncorrelatedness assumption on the errors does not sacrifice anything. In fact, it allows us to see the problem step by step from single to simultaneous equations. For the sake of brevity, we shall be less formal in discussing the asymptotic results and use previously established lemmas freely without necessarily referencing them. Most of the lemmas can be found from the works by Phillips and his students, notably Park and Phillips (1988, 1989). Our notations on stochastic calculus are also consistent with theirs.

CASE 1: Neither the unit root nor the cointegration restrictions are imposed.

The system in this case becomes an unrestricted *VAR* and the distributions of the estimates are in general nonstandard as shown by Sims, Stock, and Watson (1986), among others.

CASE 2: $\gamma = \delta = 0$.

Under this set of restrictions, x_t is strictly, and strongly, exogenous. Cointegrating regressions with strongly exogenous regressors as (35) are extensively studied in Park and Phillips (1988). Similar regressions without $\delta = 0$ imposed, i.e. cointegrating regression with strongly exogenous $I(0)$ as well as $I(1)$ regressors, are also studied by Park and Phillips (1989). Obviously, the FIML estimator of α in this case is obtained simply by OLS on (35), and (37) $T(\hat{\alpha} - \alpha) = (T^{-2}\sum x_t^2)^{-1} T^{-1}\sum x_t u_t$ converges in distribution to

$$\left[\int B_v^2\right]^{-1} \int B_v \, dB_u \tag{38}$$

where B_u and B_v are Brownian motions, with variances respectively σ_u^2 and σ_v^2, obtained essentially as the limiting processes of the two random walk processes whose innovations are respectively given by u_t and v_t. Since the two random walks are independent, so are the two Brownian motions. Consequently, the conditional distribution of (38) on B_v is normal, i.e.

$$\left[\int B_v^2\right]^{-1} \int B_v \, dB_u \sim N\left[0, \ \sigma_u^2\left(\int B_v^2\right)^{-1}\right]. \tag{39}$$

Note that the distribution of (37) conditional on the whole sample of x

is normal for all T, although this is a direct consequence of the Gaussian assumption on u_t, and thus the normality conclusion (39) is not really surprising. It should be noted, however, that the Gaussian assumption is made to facilitate the discussions; the asymptotic results (38) and (39) hold without the assumption. Normalizing the sum of squares of x_t by T^2 is because x_t is $I(1)$ and so its sum of squares explodes much faster than the conventional rate T.

It is straightforward to show that the t-statistic of $\hat{\alpha}$ is asymptotically a standard normal. Because the ML estimator of the variance of the error term is consistent, which is also straightforward given the consistency of $\hat{\alpha}$, the facts used in obtaining (38) are essentially all that are needed to show the asymptotic normality of the t-statistic.

CASE 3: $\delta = 0$.

Under this restriction, x_t is weakly (but not strongly) exogenous for α. Hence OLS on equation (35) will provide the FIML estimator of α. In order to see the asymptotic normality of this estimator, we first rewrite the system in common trends form ignoring unimportant initial values.

$$
y_t = \frac{\alpha}{(1 - \alpha\gamma)} S_{vt} + u_t^* - \alpha v_t^*
$$

$$
x_t = \frac{1}{(1 - \alpha\gamma)} S_{vt} + \gamma u_{t-1}^* - v_t^*
$$

(40)

where S denotes the summation operator so that

$$
S_{vt} = \sum_{j=1}^{t} v_j
$$

and starred variables are $I(0)$ whose innovations are given by the corresponding i.i.d. variables without stars:

$$
u_t^* = (1 - \alpha\gamma B)^{-1} u_t
$$

$$
v_t^* = \alpha\gamma(1 - \alpha\gamma)^{-1}(1 - \alpha\gamma B)^{-1} v_t.
$$

As far as asymptotics are concerned, the exact content of these starred variables is not important because they are dominated in the limit by the common trend component S_{vt}. The only useful fact is that the starred variables in x_t are uncorrelated with current u_t, which is one of the reasons behind the asymptotic equivalence of the second equation in (41). Using $\equiv$ to denote asymptotic equivalence in probability, it then follows that

$$
T^{-2}\Sigma x_t^2 \equiv T^{-2}\Sigma S_{vt}^2/(1 - \alpha\gamma)^2 \xrightarrow{\ d\ } \int B_v^2/(1 - \alpha\gamma)^2 \quad (41)
$$

$$
T^{-1}\Sigma x_t u_t \equiv T^{-1}\Sigma S_{vt} u_t/(1 - \alpha\gamma) \xrightarrow{\ d\ } \int B_v\, dB_u/(1 - \alpha\gamma)
$$

and so

$$T(\hat{\alpha} - \alpha) \xrightarrow{\text{d}} (1 - \alpha\gamma) \left[\int B_v^2 \right]^{-1} \int B_v \, dB_u. \qquad (42)$$

Hence, we again have the normality conclusion: conditional on B_v, the limiting distribution of the FIML estimator of α is normal. The t statistic of $\hat{\alpha}$ can easily be seen to be asymptotically a standard normal as in the previous case.

CASE 4: $\gamma = 0$.

Under this restriction, x_t is predetermined as in case 3 but no longer weakly exogenous due to the cointegrating restriction appearing in the second equation. Hence the FIML requires the joint estimation of the system. Instead of going through analytic maximization of the likelihood function, we simplify the problem by assuming δ and the variance ratio $g = \sigma_v^2/\sigma_u^2$ are known. The resulting FIML estimator of α is then of course a function of these parameters and in practice the asymptotically equivalent estimate is obtained by evaluating the function with any consistent estimators of δ and g, which for example can be obtained by the Engle–Granger two-step procedure. The simplifying assumption on δ and g therefore entails no loss of generality asymptotically.

The FIML estimator of α is then given by

$$\hat{\alpha} = [g\Sigma x_t^2 + \delta^2\Sigma x_{t-1}^2]^{-1}[g\Sigma x_t y_t - \delta\Sigma x_{t-1}(\Delta x_t - \delta y_{t-1})] \qquad (43)$$

which can be easily obtained by stacking the two equations into one with heteroskedasticity corrected and then simply performing OLS on the resulting equation. This stacking is, of course, possible because the two equations share the same coefficient. Simple substitution then shows

$$\hat{\alpha} - \alpha = [g\Sigma x_t^2 + \delta^2\Sigma x_{t-1}^2]^{-1}[g\Sigma x_t u_t - \delta\Sigma x_{t-1}v_t]. \qquad (44)$$

In order to examine the limiting behaviour of this random variable, first write x_t in the common trend form:

$$x_t = \delta S_{ut-1} + S_{vt} \qquad (45)$$

which shows that the corresponding Brownian motions satisfy

$$B_x = \delta B_u + B_v \qquad (46)$$

with the correspondence indicated by subscripts. It then follows that

$$T^{-2}[g\Sigma x_t^2 + \delta^2\Sigma x_{t-1}^2] \xrightarrow{\text{d}} (g + \delta^2) \int B_x^2$$

$$T^{-1}[g\Sigma x_t u_t - \delta\Sigma x_{t-1}v_t] \xrightarrow{\text{d}} \int B_x(g \, dB_u - \delta \, dB_v). \qquad (47)$$

Hence

$$T(\hat{\alpha} - \alpha) \xrightarrow{\ d\ } \left[(g + \delta^2) \int B_x^2 \right]^{-1} \int B_x(g\,\mathrm{d}B_u - \delta\,\mathrm{d}B_v). \qquad (48)$$

Notice that the Brownian motions B_x and $gB_u - \delta B_v$ are uncorrelated and thus, being Gaussian processes, are independent of each other. Consequently, conditional on B_x, the limiting distribution is again normal.

It is interesting to note that if the cointegrating restriction in the second equation (36) is ignored and OLS is performed on (35), then the resulting OLS estimator $\tilde{\alpha}$ follows

$$T(\tilde{\alpha} - \alpha) \xrightarrow{\ d\ } \left[\int B_x^2 \right]^{-1} \int B_x\,\mathrm{d}B_u \qquad (49)$$

which is nonstandard since B_x and B_u are correlated. This result shows that predetermined regressors do not imply that the OLS estimates will have a standard distribution.

In summary, we note that in all cases except the first one, the t statistics of the FIML estimators are asymptotically standard normal which is immediate from the distributional results on the coefficient estimators.

7.   A Three-Step Estimator for Cointegrated Systems

Although the two-step estimates of all the parameters of the $I(0)$ variables are asymptotically efficient, the estimates of the cointegrating relations are not. The above discussion which builds on Johansen and Juselius (1988) and Phillips (1988) indicates that the distribution theory for maximum likelihood estimates of the coefficients of the cointegrating vector is quite simple while that for the two-step estimates is not. In this section, we propose a simple third step which gives estimates of the cointegrating vectors and their standard errors which are asymptotically equivalent to FIML. The solution is simply to compute one step of scoring; this is especially easy in this case as many of the regressors are easily shown to be asymptotically irrelevant. In fact, in the easiest case only a regression of the residuals from the error correction model on the $I(1)$ variables is required.

We consider the general Gaussian error correction model of (21) which is

$$A^*(B)\Delta x_t = -\gamma\alpha' x_{t-1} + \varepsilon_t$$

with $\varepsilon_t \sim N(0, \Omega)$ so that the log likelihood is proportional to

$$L = \sum_t L_t(\theta_1, \theta_2; \Delta x_t) = -(T/2)\log\det\Omega - (1/2)\sum_t \varepsilon_t'\Omega^{-1}\varepsilon_t \qquad (50)$$

where θ_1 are the parameters in A^*, γ, and Ω, and θ_2 are the parameters α. One step of iteration from estimates $\tilde{\theta}$ can be described as

$$\hat{\theta} = \tilde{\theta} + Q^{-1}(\theta)\partial L/\partial\theta, \qquad (51)$$

where Q is an estimate of the information matrix of which the most convenient form is given by:

$$Q = \sum_t E_{t-1}[\partial L_t/\partial\theta \; \partial L_t/\partial\theta'] \qquad (52)$$

where the information set implied by the expectation includes all past x's plus the current x's which can be treated as predetermined. It can be easily shown that the diagonal elements of Q corresponding to θ_1 are $O_p(T)$ while those for θ_2 are $O_p(T^2)$. Similarly, the scores for θ_1 are $O_p(T^{1/2})$ while those for θ_2 are $O_p(T)$. Hence terms of lower order than indicated can be omitted to simplify the computation without changing the limiting distribution. In particular, the information matrix can be treated as block diagonal between the two sets of parameters since the terms in the off-diagonal blocks are at most $O_p(T)$ but are normalized by $T^{3/2}$ and thus converge to zero after normalization.

Since the information matrix is block diagonal, estimates of θ_1 which are asymptotically equivalent to FIML can be obtained simply by updating estimates of θ_1 taking consistent estimates of θ_2 as given. This is the explanation for the full efficiency of the estimates obtained at the second step in the two-step method which use consistent estimates of the cointegrating vector, θ_2, to compute efficient estimates of θ_1. This argument applies equally for the coefficients in the cointegrating relations: asymptotically efficient estimates of θ_2 can be computed by taking as given any consistent estimate of θ_1 such as those available from the second step. Only the equations for θ_2 are needed to calculate the estimates, hence the estimates sought in the third step are given by:

$$\hat{\theta}_2 = \tilde{\theta}_2 + Q_{22}^{-1}\partial L/\partial\theta_2, \qquad Q_{22} = \sum_t E_{t-1}[\partial L_t/\partial\theta_2\partial L_t/\partial\theta_2'] \quad (53)$$

which can be computed in general by a least squares regression. As a by-product of this computation, Q_{22}^{-1} is computed which has the property

$$Q_{22}^{1/2}(\hat{\theta}_2 - \theta_2) \xrightarrow{\;d\;} N(O, I) \qquad (54)$$

under the assumptions made by Johansen, Juselius, and Phillips.

To apply this formula in the simplest case we suppose there is only one cointegrating vector and that the recursive form of the model only has the error correction term in the first equation. That is, if we parameterize the model so that $A^*(O)$ is upper triangular with Ω diagonal, which can always be done, then the error correction term vanishes in the other equations. If we normalize α so that the first variable, x_1 has a coefficient 1 while the rest, x_2, have coefficients a, then we notice that x_2 are weakly exogenous in the sense of Engle, Hendry, and Richard (1983) for the parameters of the first equation, including α. The first equation in this notation becomes:

$$\Delta x_{1t} = -\gamma(x_{1t-1} - a'x_{2t-1}) + \beta_{02}\Delta x_{2t} + \beta_{11}\Delta x_{1t-1} + \beta_{12}\Delta x_{2t-1}$$
$$+ \ldots + e_{1t}$$

where we have supressed the subscript on γ as it should not lead to confusion since the γ's in all other equations are assumed to be zero. The two-step method of estimating this equation first estimates a by a least squares estimate of x_1 on x_2 to get $\tilde{a}$. The second step estimates the error correction form taking $a = \tilde{a}$ and obtains residuals $\tilde{e}_{1t}$, and an estimate of γ denoted $\tilde{\gamma}$. By construction e_{1t} is uncorrelated with Δx_{2t} and by Gaussianity, independent. Now,

$$\partial L_t/\partial \theta_2 = \partial L_t/\partial a = \sigma_1^{-2}e_{1t}x_{2t-1}\gamma$$

so that the third step gives:

$$\hat{a} = \tilde{a} + \left[\tilde{\gamma}\sum x_{2t-1}x'_{2t-1}\right]^{-1}\sum x_{2t-1}\tilde{e}_{1t}$$

$$Q_{22}^{-1} = \sigma_1^2\left[\tilde{\gamma}^2\sum x_{2t-1}x'_{2t-1}\right]^{-1}. \tag{55}$$

The three-step estimates are obtained simply by regressing the residuals from the error correction model on the lagged variables from the cointegrating relation, each multiplied by the estimate $\tilde{\gamma}$ available from the second step. The coefficients of this regression are the corrections to the two-step estimates, and the standard errors from this regression are appropriate for asymptotic Gaussian inference. The multiplication by the estimated $\tilde{\gamma}$ can be done after the regression as it is simply a constant in this case. Since x_2 is weakly exogenous, FIML is achieved from estimation of only the first equation and the algorithm developed is simply an approximation to FIML for this case. It could, of course, be iterated, however the gains to be expected may be small. Since the third step involves a regression of an $I(0)$ variable $\tilde{e}_{1t}$ on a set of $I(1)$ variables, x_{2t}, the regression coefficient should be quite small. Hence, further iteration of steps 2 and 3 would most likely produce little change.

In the more common case, x_2 is not weakly exogenous. Again assuming a triangular structure for $A^*(0)$ and diagonal for Ω, the log likelihood can be written as

$$L = -(1/2)\sum_{it}\sum e_{it}^2/\sigma_i^2 - (1/2)\sum_i T\log\sigma_i^2. \tag{56}$$

The derivative of L_t with respect to a becomes

$$\partial L_t/\partial a = \sum_i e_{it}\gamma_i x_{2t-1}/\sigma_i^2. \tag{57}$$

The third step can therefore be most easily applied by stacking the weighted residuals from the equations, $\tilde{e}_i$ with $\tilde{e}_i = (\tilde{e}_{1i}, \ldots, \tilde{e}_{Ti})'$, and $\tilde{\sigma}_i^2 = \tilde{e}_i'\tilde{e}_i/T$, into a large vector $\tilde{E} = (\tilde{e}_1'/\tilde{\sigma}_1, \tilde{e}_2'/\tilde{\sigma}_2, \ldots, \tilde{e}_N'/\tilde{\sigma}_N)'$, which is $NTx1$, and stacking the weighted $\tilde{\gamma}_i x_2$ into $X = (\tilde{\gamma}_1 x_2'/\tilde{\sigma}_1, \ldots, \tilde{\gamma}_N x_2'/\tilde{\sigma}_N)'$ with $x_2' = (x_{20}, \ldots, x_{2T-1})$ which is an $NTx(N-1)$ vector assuming that the cointegrating vector includes all N variables. In this notation, $\partial L/\partial a = X'E$ and $Q_{22} = X'X$. Evaluating these terms at $\tilde{\theta}_1$, the three-step estimate of α is given by

$$\hat{a} = \tilde{a} + [X'X]^{-1}X'\tilde{E} \tag{58}$$

$$[X'X]^{1/2}(\hat{a} - a) \xrightarrow{d} N(0, I)$$

and $\tilde{E}'\tilde{E}/NT \equiv 1$.

A similar procedure is available when there are more than one cointegrating vector. In this case there is a regression like (58) which updates the estimates of all the cointegrating vectors. In the error correction form of (21), α is now an Nxr matrix where there are r cointegrating vectors. Normalizing so that the first element of x appears in each cointegrating vector with a coefficient of one, the error correction form of the ith equation can be written as:

$$\{A^*(B)\Delta x_t\}_i = \{-\gamma\alpha'x_{t-1} + \varepsilon_t\}_i \tag{59}$$

$$= -\gamma_{i1}(x_{1t-1} - a_1'x_{2t-1}) - \gamma_{i2}(x_{1t-1} - a_2'x_{2t-1}) -$$

$$\ldots - \gamma_{ir}(x_{1t-1} - a_r'x_{2t-1}) + \varepsilon_{it}$$

where the subscripts on a and γ refer to the r cointegrating relations and the notation $\{\ \}_i$ refers to the ith row of a matrix. Each of the α's must have coefficient (typically zero) restrictions so that they are linearly independent. That is, the first cointegrating vector could establish a long-run relation between x_1 and the first element of x_2 while the second establishes a long-run relation between x_1 and the second element of x_2. This implies that the first two elements of x_2 are themselves cointegrated but that relationship would not appear as part of the error correction mechanism.

Using the notation above (58) with $X^1, \ldots, X^r$ referring to the stacked weighted matrices of regressors included in the first through rth cointegrating vectors, the scores for each can be written as:

$$\partial L/\partial a_1 = X^1{}'E, \ldots, \partial L/\partial a_r = X^r{}'E$$

and hence the derivative of L with respect to the full set of coefficients $\theta_2 = \text{vec}(a)$, and the estimate of the information matrix Q_{22} are given by

$$\partial L/\partial \text{vec}(a) = \mathcal{X}'E, \qquad \text{and } Q_{22} = \mathcal{X}'\mathcal{X} \tag{60}$$

where $\mathcal{X} = (X^1, \ldots, X^r)$. Thus the updating equations for the three-step method are simply expressed as

$$\text{vec}(\hat{a}) = \text{vec}(\tilde{a}) + (\mathcal{X}'\mathcal{X})^{-1}\mathcal{X}'E \tag{61}$$

$$[\mathcal{X}'\mathcal{X}]^{-1}(\text{vec}(\hat{a}) - \text{vec}(a)) \xrightarrow{d} N(0, I). \tag{62}$$

8. Empirical Example

We now examine an empirical example of inventories developed by Granger and Lee (1989) which is an example of $I(2)$ cointegration, and apply the three-step estimation method.

The final model estimated by Granger and Lee is based on production, p, and sales, s, of monthly aggregate manufacturing and trade:

$$\Delta p_t = \begin{matrix} 1.83 \\ (5.06) \end{matrix} - \begin{matrix} .75 \\ (3.94) \end{matrix} z_{t-1} - \begin{matrix} .05 \\ (3.15) \end{matrix} u_{t-1} + \begin{matrix} .19 \\ (1.20) \end{matrix} \Delta p_{t-1} - \begin{matrix} .37 \\ (2.15) \end{matrix} \Delta s_{t-1}$$

$$(63)$$

$$\bar{R}^2 = 0.06 \qquad DW = 1.98$$

$$\Delta s_t = \begin{matrix} 1.00 \\ (2.82) \end{matrix} - \begin{matrix} .04 \\ (.20) \end{matrix} z_{t-1} - \begin{matrix} .01 \\ (.72) \end{matrix} u_{t-1} - \begin{matrix} .42 \\ (2.51) \end{matrix} \Delta s_{t-1} + \begin{matrix} .24 \\ (1.53) \end{matrix} \Delta p_{t-1}$$

$$\bar{R}^2 = 0.03 \qquad DW = 2.01$$

where absolute t-values are in parentheses. The two cointegrating terms are defined as follows:

$$z_t = p_t - s_t$$
$$u_t = I_t - 13.01 - 1.53 s_t.$$

The data series for inventory, I_t, and sales are taken from the Citibank data base and are the aggregate figures of three industries: manufacturing, merchant wholesalers, and retail trade. The data are in 1982 constant dollars and seasonally adjusted. They range from January 1967 to April 1987 providing a sample of size 244. The data for p_t are generated as sales plus the change in inventory, i.e. $p_t = s_t + \Delta I_t$. Consequently, the error correction term z_t, which is identical to ΔI_t, is directly available from the data. The other term u_t is estimated by OLS as a cointegrating regression. Of course, prior to the estimation, p_t and s_t are tested to be $I(1)$ by the augmented Dickey–Fuller test. The same univariate test is applied to z_t which rejects the $I(1)$ hypothesis in favour of $I(0)$. Cointegration of I_t and s_t are tested by the Engle–Granger test and again non-cointegration is rejected in favour of cointegration. Granger and Lee then estimate the full error correction model to get (63). The term u_t contains I_t which is an integration of another error correction term $\dot{z}_t$. Hence the model contains an integral correction term and as a whole u_t and z_t constitute a polynomial cointegrating vector discussed by Yoo (1986). It is an example of $I(2)$ cointegration as described above. The model is in reduced form and thus describes the conditional mean of the two dependent variables based on the information up to $t-1$. It is a restricted vector autoregression.

Our interest here is in estimating a triangular relation between production and sales. This is often called a structural model. Intuition tells us that the current changes in sales will affect the current changes in production, but the reverse is not likely unless the market is continuously in excess demand. Hence we put the current change in sales into the first equation maintaining the second to be the marginal mean of sales given the past information set. In estimating this structural error correction model, we have omitted all insignificant variables from the equations and the outcome is

$$\Delta p_t = \underset{(7.43)}{.91} + \underset{(38.68)}{.95} \Delta s_t - \underset{(12.80)}{.74} z_{t-1} - \underset{(7.50)}{.04} u_{t-1} + \tilde{e}_{1t} \quad (65)$$

$$\bar{R}^2 = .87 \qquad DW = 2.0$$

$$\Delta s_t = \underset{(3.55)}{.95} - \underset{(2.89)}{.18} \Delta s_{t-1} + \tilde{e}_{2t}$$

$$\bar{R}^2 = 03 \qquad DW = 1.97$$

where e_{1t} and e_{2t} are residuals and other variables are defined the same as above. The highly significant contemporaneous term in the first equation reveals the strong correlation between the production and sales residuals in the reduced form.

Sales are weakly exogenous in this model for the parameters in the first equation, because the error correction term u_{t-1} does not enter the second equation, and thus the FIML estimator of the cointegrating vector together with its standard errors can be easily calculated as described in the preceding section. Regressing the residuals from the first equation on the constant and $\tilde{\gamma}s_{t-1} = 0.04s_{t-1}$, yields:

$$\tilde{e}_{1t} = - \quad .31 \quad + \quad .02 \quad (\tilde{\gamma}s_{t-1}) \qquad \tilde{\gamma} = .04 \qquad (66)$$
$$(.649) \qquad (.046)$$

where the numbers in parentheses are standard errors. Hence the three-step estimate of a is obtained as

$$\hat{a} = 1.53 + .02 = 1.55 \qquad (67)$$

with the standard error .046 and so the t-value is 33.7. When the updating in (66) was done on all the coefficients of (65) simultaneously by regressing $\tilde{e}_1$ on the three stationary regressors as well as $\tilde{\gamma}s_{t-1}$, virtually identical results were obtained indicating that the sample size here is sufficiently large that the $I(0)$ and $I(1)$ variables are effectively orthogonal.

9.   Conclusions and Directions for Further Research

The theoretical and empirical analysis of cointegrated systems is a rapidly developing and highly exciting field. Many of the techniques which have been developed are already in use and a variety of interesting economic hypotheses have been rephrased and tested in the context of cointegration. Further results can be expected from application to more general systems which had previously been analysed by vector autoregressions or structural econometric models.

The use of the Smith–McMillan–Yoo polynomial representation provides a neat and simple way to extend the analysis of cointegration from the $I(1)$ case to higher order real unit roots and to other roots on the unit circle. It reveals directly the possibility of polynomial cointegrating vectors which is confirmed empirically and economically by the inventory example of Granger and Lee. This paper presents a complete and new analysis of the $I(2)$ case.

Estimation and testing of cointegrated systems in the standard $I(1)$ case now includes not only the simple two-step methods of Engle and Granger, but also FIML methods of Johansen and Juselius and Phillips. The FIML methods have the advantages of increased asymptotic efficiency and a Gaussian limiting distribution theory for the t-ratios. They have the disadvantage of computational complexity. This paper has proposed an intermediate alternative: a three-step estimator which achieves the same limiting distribution as FIML in an additional least squares regression from the two-step estimate. This estimator looks like a promising addition to the arsenal of tools for analysing cointegrating systems.

References

BANERJEE, A., J. J. DOLADO, D. F. HENDRY, and G. W. SMITH (1986). 'Exploring equilibrium relationships in econometrics through static models: Some Monte Carlo evidence', *Oxford Bulletin of Economics and Statistics*, **48:3**, 253–77.

BOLLERSLEV, T., and R. ENGLE (1990), 'Common Persistance in Conditional Variances', manuscript.

BOX, G. E. P., and G. M. JENKINS (1970), *Time Series Analysis, Forecasting and Control* (San Franciso, Holden-Day).

CAMPBELL, JOHN (1987), 'Does saving anticipate declining labor income: An alternative test of the permanent income hypothesis?', *Econometrica*, **55**, 1249–73.

—— and A. DEATON (1987), 'Is consumption too smooth?', Working Paper 2134, NBER.

COCHRANE, JOHN, and A. M. SBORDONE (1988), 'Multivariate estimates of the permanent components of GNP and stock prices', *Journal of Economic Dynamics and Control*, **12**, 255–96.

DAVIDSON, J. E., D. F. HENDRY, F. SRBA, and S. YEO (1978), 'Econometric modelling of aggregrate time series relationships between consumer's expenditure and income in the U.K.', *Economic Journal*, **91**, 704–15.

DEATON, A. (1987), 'Life-cycle models of consumption: Is the evidence consistent with the theory', in T. F. Bewley (ed.), *Advances in Econometrics, Fifth World Congress*, ii. 121–48.

DIEBOLD, F., and M. NERLOVE (1989), 'Unit roots in economic time series: A selective survey', in T. B. Fomby and G. F. Rhodes (eds.), *Advances in Econometrics; Cointegration, Spurious Regression and Unit Roots* (Greenwich, Ct. JAI Press).

DICKEY, D. A., and W. A. FULLER (1979), 'Distribution of the estimators for autoregressive time series with a unit root', *Journal of the American Statistical Association*, **84**, 427–31.

ENGLE, R. F. (1982), 'Autoregressive conditional heteroscedasticity with estimates of the variance of U.K. inflation', *Econometrica*, **50**, 978–1008.

—— and T. BOLLERSLEV (1986), 'Modelling the persistence of conditional variances', *Econometric Reviews*, **5(1)**, 1–50.

—— and C. W. J. GRANGER (1987), 'Co-integration and error correction: representation, estimation and testing', *Econometrica*, **55**, 251–76.

—— —— and J. HALLMAN (1990), 'Merging short and long-run forecasts: an application of seasonal co-integration to monthly electricity sales forecasting', *Journal of Econometrics*, **40**, 45–62.

—— D. F. HENDRY, and J. F. RICHARD (1983), 'Exogeneity', *Econometrica*, **51**, 277–304.

—— and B. SAM YOO (1987), 'Forecasting and testing in co-integrated systems', *Journal of Econometrics*, **35**, 143–59.

ESCRIBANO, ALVARO (1987), 'Error-correction systems: Nonlinear adjustments to linear long-run relationships', CORE Discussion Paper 8730.

FAMA, E. F., and K. R. FRENCH (1986), 'Common factors in the serial correlation of stock returns', CRSP Working Paper 200.

FLAVIN, F. A. (1981), 'The adjustment of consumption to changing expectations about future income', *Journal of Political Economy*, **89**, 1020–37.

FULLER, W. A. (1976), *Introduction of Statistical Time Series*, (New York, Wiley).

GRANGER, C. W. J. (1981), 'Some properties of time series data and their use in econometric model specification', *Journal of Econometrics*, **16**, 121–30.

—— (1983), 'Co-integrated variables and error-correcting models', unpublished UCSD Discussion Paper 83–13.

—— (1986), 'Developments in the study of cointegrated economic variables', *Oxford Bulletin of Economics and Statistics*, **48:3**, 213–28.

—— (1987), 'Introduction to stochastic processes having equilibria as simple attractors: The Markov Case', manuscript, UCSD.

—— and T. W. LEE (1988), 'Multicointegration', in T. B. Fomby and G. F. Rhodes (eds.), *Advances in Econometrics; Cointegration, Spurious Regression and Unit Roots* (Greenwich, Ct., JAI Press).

—— —— (1989), 'Investigation of production, sales and inventory relationships using multicointegration and nonsymmetric error correction models', forthcoming, *Journal of Applied Econometrics*.

—— and P. NEWBOLD (1974), 'Spurious regressions in econometrics', *Journal of Econometrics*, **2**, 111–20.

—— and A. A. WEISS (1983), 'Time series analysis of error-correcting models', in *Studies in Econometrics, Time Series, and Multivariate Statistics* (New York, Academic Press), 255–78.

HALL, ROBERT (1987), 'Consumption', in R. J. Barro (ed.), *Modern Business Cycle Theory* (Harvard University Press), 153–77.

HENDRY, D. F. and T. VON UNGERN-STERNBERG (1981), 'Liquidity and inflation effects on consumer's expenditure', in *Essays in the Theory and Measurement of Consumer's Behaviour*, ed. A. S. Deaton, (Cambridge, Cambridge University Press).

HYLLEBERG, S., R. F. ENGLE, C. W. J. GRANGER, and B. S. YOO (1990), 'Seasonal integration and co-integration', forthcoming, *Journal of Econometrics*, 44, 215–38.

JOHANSEN, SØREN (1985), 'The mathematical structure of error correction models', preprint, KUIMS.

—— (1988), 'Statistical analysis of cointegration vectors', *Journal of Economic Dynamics and Control*, **12**, 231–34.

—— and KATARINA JUSELIUS (1988), 'Hypothesis testing for cointegration vectors—with an application to the demand for money in Denmark and Finland', Preprint, IMS, University of Copenhagen.

KING, R., C. I. PLOSSER, J. H. STOCK, and M. W. WATSON (1987), 'Stochastic trends and economic fluctuations', mimeo, Stanford University.

KAILATH, T. (1980), *Linear Systems* (Prentice Hall).

MACKINNON, JAMES (1990), 'Critical values for cointegration tests', in Engle and Granger (eds.), this volume.

NELSON, C. R., and C. I. PLOSSER (1982), 'Trends and random walks in macroeconomic time series', *Journal of Monetary Economics*, 129–162.

PARK, J. Y., and P. C. B. PHILLIPS (1988), 'Statistical inference in regressions with integrated processes: Part I', *Econometric Theory*, **4**, 468–97.

—— (1989), 'Statistical inference in regression with integrated processes: Part 2', *Econometric Theory*, **5**, 95–131.

PHILLIPS, P. C. B. (1986), 'Understanding spurious regressions in econometrics', *Journal of Econometrics*, **33**, 311–40.

—— (1987), 'Time series regression with a unit root', *Econometrica*, **55**, 277–301.

—— (1988), 'Optimal inference in cointegrated systems', Cowles Foundation, Discussion Paper 866.

—— and S. N. DURLAUF (1986), 'Multiple time series with integrated variables', *Review of Economic Studies*, **53**, 473–96.

—— and S. OULIARIS (1986), 'Testing for cointegration', Cowles Foundation, discussion paper 809.

—— —— (1987), 'Asymptotic properties of residual based tests for cointegration', Cowles Foundation, discussion paper 847.

—— and P. PERRON (1988), 'Testing for a unit root in time series regression', *Biometrika*, **75**, 335–46.

SAID, S. E., and D. A. DICKEY (1984), 'Testing for unit roots in autoregressive moving average models of unknown order', *Biometrika*, **71**, 599–607.

SARGAN, J. D. (1964), 'Wages and prices in the United Kingdom: A study in econometric methodology', in *Econometric Analysis for National Economic Planning*, ed. by P. E. Hart, G. Mills, and J. N. Whittaker (London, Butterworths).

SIMS, C. A., J. H. STOCK, and M. W. WATSON (1986), 'Inference in linear time series models with unit roots', manuscript, University of Minnesota, forthcoming, *Econometrica*.

STOCK, J. H. (1987), 'Asymptotic properties of least squares estimators of cointegrating vectors', *Econometrica*, **55**, 1035–56.

—— and M. W. WATSON (1988), 'Testing for common trends', *Journal of the American Statistical Association*, **83**, 1097–107.

YOO, B. SAM (1986), 'Multi-cointegrated time series and generalized error-correction models', Economics Department, University of California, San Diego, working paper.

—— (1987), 'Co-integrated time series: Structure, forecasting and testing, unpublished Ph.D. dissertation, UCSD.

13

Critical Values for Cointegration Tests*

JAMES G. MACKINNON

Abstract

This paper provides tables of critical values for some popular tests of cointegration and unit roots. Although these tables are necessarily based on computer simulations, they are much more accurate than those previously available. The results of the simulation experiments are summarized by means of response surface regressions in which critical values depend on the sample size. From these regressions asymptotic critical values can be read off directly, and critical values for any finite sample size can easily be computed with a hand calculator.

1. Introduction

Engle and Granger (1987) suggested several techniques for testing the null hypothesis that two or more series, each of which is $I(1)$, are not cointegrated. This paper is concerned with the most popular of these techniques, which I shall refer to as Engle–Granger (or EG) tests even though they were not the only tests proposed by those authors. EG tests are closely related to some of the tests suggested by Fuller (1976) and Dickey and Fuller (1979) to test the unit root hypothesis; I shall refer to these as Dickey–Fuller or DF tests. EG and DF tests are very easy to calculate, but they suffer from one serious disadvantage: the test statistics do not follow any standard tabulated distribution, either in finite samples or asymptotically.

Engle and Granger (1987), Engle and Yoo (1987), Yoo (1987), and Phillips and Ouliaris (1990) all provide tables for one or more versions

* This research was supported, in part, by the Social Sciences and Humanities Research Council of Canada. It was undertaken while the author was visiting the University of California, San Diego. I am grateful to all of the econometricians there for providing such a hospitable research environment, and to the editors of this volume for comments on an earlier version.

of the EG test. But these tables are based on at most 10,000 replications, which means that they are quite inaccurate. Moreover, they
contain critical values for only a few finite sample sizes; asymptotic
critical values, which are in many cases the most interesting ones, are
not provided.

This paper provides tables of critical values for two versions of the
EG test and three versions of the DF test. Although they are based on
simulation, they should be accurate enough for all practical purposes.
The results of the simulation experiments are summarized by means of
response surface regressions, in which critical values are related to
sample size. The coefficients of the response surface regressions are
tabulated in such a way that asymptotic critical values can be read off
directly, and critical values for any finite sample size can easily be
computed with a hand calculator.

2.   Engle–Granger and Dickey–Fuller tests

EG tests are conceptually and computationally quite simple. Let the
vector $\mathbf{y}_t \equiv [y_{t1} \ldots y_{tN}]^T$ denote the tth observation on N time series,
each of which is known to be $I(1)$. If these time series are cointegrated,
there exists a vector $\boldsymbol{\alpha}$ such that the stochastic process with typical
observation $z_t \equiv [1 \ \ \mathbf{y}_t]^T \boldsymbol{\alpha}$ is $I(0)$. If they are not cointegrated, there
will exist no vector $\boldsymbol{\alpha}$ with this property, and any linear combination of
y_1 through y_N and a constant will still be $I(1)$.

To implement the original form of the EG test one first runs the
cointegrating regression

$$y_{t1} = \alpha_1 + \sum_{j=2}^{N} \alpha_j y_{tj} + \mu_t, \tag{1}$$

for a sample of size $T + 1$, thus obtaining a vector of coefficients
$\hat{\boldsymbol{\alpha}} = [1 -\hat{\alpha}_1 \ldots -\hat{\alpha}_N]$. One then calculates

$$\hat{z}_t = [1 \ \ \mathbf{y}_t]^T \hat{\boldsymbol{\alpha}} = y_{t1} - \hat{\alpha}_1 - \hat{\alpha}_2 y_{t2} - \ldots - \hat{\alpha}_N y_{tN}$$

and tests to see if $\hat{z}_t$ is $I(1)$ using a procedure essentially the same
(except for the distribution of the test statistic) as the DF test. The null
hypothesis of non-cointegration corresponds to the null hypothesis that
$\hat{z}_t$ is $I(1)$. If one rejects the null, one concludes that y_1 through y_N are
cointegrated.

To test whether $\hat{z}_t$ is $I(1)$ one may either run the regression

$$\hat{z}_t = \rho \hat{z}_{t-1} + \varepsilon_t \tag{2}$$

and calculate the ordinary t statistic for $\rho = 1$, or run the regression

$$\Delta \hat{z}_t = \gamma \hat{z}_{t-1} + \varepsilon_t, \tag{3}$$

where $\Delta\hat{z}_t \equiv \hat{z}_t - \hat{z}_{t-1}$, and calculate the ordinary t statistic for $\gamma = 0$. In either case one drops the first observation, reducing the sample size to T. These two procedures evidently yield identical test statistics. Because there is a constant term in (1), there is no need to include one in (2) or (3). The regressand $\hat{z}_t$ will necessarily have mean zero. The regressor $\hat{z}_{t-1}$ will not have mean quite equal to zero, because of the omission of $\hat{z}_1$, but it will always have mean very close to zero except when T is small and $\hat{z}_1$ is unusually large in absolute value. Hence adding a constant to (2) or (3) would have a negligible effect on the test statistic.

The way the EG test is computed is somewhat arbitrary, since any one of the y's could be given the index 1 and made the regressand of the cointegrating regression (1). As a result, the value (but not the distribution) of the test statistic will differ depending on which series is used as the regressand. One may therefore wish to repeat the procedure with different y's serving as regressand, thus computing up to N different test statistics, especially if the first one is near the chosen critical value.

If $N = 1$ this procedure is equivalent to one variant of the ordinary DF test (see below), in which one runs the regression:

$$\Delta z_t = \alpha_1 + \gamma z_{t-1} + \varepsilon_t$$

and tests for $\gamma = 0$. As several authors have shown (see West 1988 and Hyllèberg and Mizon 1989), the latter has the Dickey–Fuller distribution only when there is no drift term in the data-generating process for z_t, so that $\alpha_1 = 0$. When $\alpha_1 \neq 0$, the test statistic is asymptotically distributed as $N(0, 1)$, and in finite samples its distribution may or may not be well approximated by the Dickey–Fuller distribution. The original version of the EG test likewise has a distribution that depends on the value of α_1; since all tables assume that $\alpha_1 = 0$, they may be quite misleading when that is not the case.

There is a simple way to avoid the dependence on α_1 of the distribution of the test statistic. It is to replace regression (1) by the regression

$$y_{t1} = \alpha_0 t + \alpha_1 + \sum_{j=2}^{N} \alpha_j y_{tj} + u_t, \tag{4}$$

that is, to add a linear time trend to the cointegrating regression. The resulting test statistic will now be invariant to the value of α_1, although it will have a different distribution than the one based on regression (1).[1] Adding a trend to the cointegrating regression often makes sense

---

[1] It will not be invariant to the value of α_0, however; to achieve that, one would have to add t^2 to the regression.

for a number of other reasons, as Engle and Yoo (1991) discuss. There are thus two variants of the Engle–Granger test. The 'no-trend' variant uses (1) as the cointegrating regression, and the 'with-trend' variant uses (4).

In some cases, α (or at least α_2 through α_N) may be known. We can then just calculate $z_t = y_{t1} - \alpha_2 y_{t2} - \ldots - \alpha_N y_{tN}$ and use an ordinary DF test. In this case it is easiest to dispense with the cointegrating regressions (1) or (4) entirely and simply run one of the following regressions:

$$\Delta z_t = \gamma z_{t-1} + \varepsilon_t \tag{5}$$

$$\Delta z_t = \alpha_1 + \gamma z_{t-1} + \varepsilon_t \tag{6}$$

$$\Delta z_t = \alpha_0 t + \alpha_1 + \gamma z_{t-1} + \varepsilon_t \tag{7}$$

The t statistics for $\gamma = 0$ in these three regressions yield the test statistics that Fuller (1976) refer to as $\hat{\tau}$, $\hat{\tau}_\mu$, and $\hat{\tau}_\tau$ respectively; he provides some estimated critical values on page 373. We will refer to these three test statistics as the 'no-constant', 'no-trend', and 'with-trend' statistics. Note that the tabulated distribution of the no-constant statistic depends on the assumption that $z_0 = 0$, while those of the other two are invariant to z_0. The tabulated distribution of the no-trend statistic depends on the assumption that $\alpha_1 = 0$ (see West 1988 and Hylleberg and Mizon 1989), while that of the with-trend statistic depends on the assumption that $\alpha_0 = 0$.

Up to this point it has been assumed that the ε_t's are serially independent and homoskedastic. These rather strong assumptions can be relaxed without affecting the asymptotic distributions of the test statistics. The test statistics do not even have to be modified to allow for heteroskedasticity, since, as Phillips (1987) has shown, heteroskedasticity does not affect the asymptotic distribution of a wide class of unit root test statistics. They do have to be modified to allow for serial correlation, however. The easiest way to do this is to to use Augmented Dickey–Fuller (ADF) or Augmented Engle–Granger (AEG) tests. In practice, this means that one must add as many lags of $\Delta \hat{z}_t$ to regressions (2) or (3), or of Δz_t to regressions (5), (6), or (7), as are necessary to ensure that those regressions have residuals that appear to be white noise.

A different approach to obtaining unit root tests that are asymptotically valid in the presence of serial correlation and/or heteroskedasticity of unknown form was suggested by Phillips (1987) and extended to the cointegration case by Phillips and Ouliaris (1990). The asymptotic distributions of what Phillips and Ouliaris call the $\hat{Z}_t$ statistic are identical to those of the corresponding DF, ADF, EG, and AEG tests. Phillips and Ouliaris tabulate critical values for two forms of this statistic (corresponding to the no-trend and with-trend versions of the DF and

EG statistics) for several values of N. Unfortunately, these critical values are based on only 10,000 replications, so that they suffer from considerable experimental error. Moreover, they are for 500 rather than an infinite number of observations, so that they are biased away from zero as estimates of asymptotic critical values. As can be seen from Table 1 below, this bias is by no means negligible in some cases.

3. The Simulation Experiments

Instead of simply providing tables of estimated critical values for a few specific sample sizes, as previous papers have done, this paper estimates response surface regressions. These relate the 1 per cent, 5 per cent, and 10 per cent lower-tail critical values for the test statistics discussed above, for various values of N, to the sample size T.[2] Recall that T refers to the number of observations in the unit root test regression, and that this is one less than the total number of observations available and used in the cointegrating regression. Response surfaces were estimated for thirteen different tests: the no-constant, no-trend, and with-trend versions of the DF test, which are equivalent to the corresponding EG tests for $N = 1$, and the no-trend and with-trend versions of the EG test for $N = 2, 3, 4, 5$, and 6. Thus a total of thirty-nine response surface regressions were estimated.

The DF tests were computed using the one-step procedures of regressions (5), (6), and (7), while the EG tests were computed using two-step procedures consisting of regressions (1) or (4) followed by (3). These are the easiest ways to calculate these tests. Note that there is a slight difference between the degrees-of-freedom corrections used to calculate the regression standard errors, and hence t statistics, for the DF tests ($N = 1$) and for the EG tests ($N \geqslant 2$). If the no-trend and with-trend DF tests were computed in the same way as the corresponding EG tests, they would be larger by factors of $((T - 1)/(T - 2))^{1/2}$ and $((T - 1)/(T - 3))^{1/2}$ respectively.

Conceptually, each simulation experiment consisted of 25,000 replications for a single value of T and a single value of N.[3] The 1 per cent, 5 per cent, and 10 per cent empirical quantiles for these data were then calculated, and each of these became a single observation in the response surface regression. The number 25,000 was chosen to make the

---

[2] The upper tail is not of any interest in this case, and the vast majority of hypothesis tests are at the 1 per cent, 5 per cent, or 10 per cent levels.

[3] In fact, results for $N = 2$, 3, 4, and 5 were computed together to save computer time. Results for $N = 1$ were computed separately because the calculations were slightly different. Results from $N = 6$ were computed separately because it was not decided to extend the analysis to this case until after most of the other calculations had been completed.

Explanation

N: Number of $I(1)$ series for which null of non-cointegration is being tested.

Size: Size of one-tail test.

Obs.:   Number of observations used in response surface regression. Possible values are 600, 560, 520, and 480. If Obs. = 600, the regression used forty observations from each of $T = 18$, 20, 22, 25, 28, 30, 32, 40, 50, 75, 100, 150, 200, 250, and 500. If Obs. = 560, observations for $T = 18$ were not used. If Obs. = 520, observations for $T = 18$ and $T = 20$ were not used. If Obs. = 480, the regression used forty observations from each of $T = 20$, 22, 25, 28, 30, 32, 36, 40, 50, 100, 250, and 275.

β_∞:   Estimated asymptotic critical values (with estimated standard errors in parentheses).

β_1:   Coefficient on T^{-1} in response surface regression.

β_2 Coefficient on T^{-2} in response surface regression. Set to zero if t statistic was less than one in absolute value.

For any T the estimated critical value is

$$\beta_\infty + \beta_1/T + \beta_2/T^2.$$

For example, for $T = 100$ the 5 per cent critical value for the with-trend EG test with $N = 5$ is

$$-4.7154 - 17.432/100 - 16.50/100^2 = -4.8914$$

---

bias in estimating quantiles negligible, while keeping the memory requirements of the program manageable.

For all values of N except $N = 6$, forty experiments were run for each of the following sample sizes: 18, 20, 22, 25, 28, 30, 32, 40, 50, 75, 100, 150, 200, 250, and 500. For $N = 6$ the sample sizes were: 20, 22, 25, 28, 30, 32, 36, 40, 50, 100, 250, and 275. Most of the sample sizes were relatively small because the cost of the experiments was slightly less than proportional to the sample size, and because small sample sizes provided more information about the shape of the response surfaces.[4] However, a few large values of T were also included so that the response surface estimates of asymptotic critical values would be sufficiently accurate. The total number of replications was 12 million in 480 experiments for

[4] The experiments would have required roughly 900 hours on a 20 Mh. 386 personal computer. All programs were written in FORTRAN 77. About 70 per cent of the computations were done on the PC, using programs compiled with the Lahey F77L-EM/32 compiler. Some experiments, representing roughly 30 per cent of the total computational burden, were performed on other computers: an IBM 3081G, which was about 7.5 times faster than the PC, and an HP 9000 Model 840, which was about 15 per cent faster.

[5] The experiments for $N = 6$ were done later than the others, and were designed in the light of experience with them. It was decided that the extra accuracy available by doing more experiments for large values of T was not worth the extra cost.

$N = 6$ and 15 million in 600 experiments for the other values of N.[5]

Using a correct functional form for the response surface regressions is crucial to obtaining useful estimates. After considerable experimentation, the following form was found to work very well.

$$C_k(p) = \beta_\infty + \beta_1 T_k^{-1} + \beta_2 T_k^{-2} + e_k. \tag{8}$$

Here $C_k(p)$ denotes the p per cent quantile estimate for the kth experiment, T_k denotes the sample size for that experiment, and the β's are parameters to be estimated. The parameter β_∞ is an estimate of the asymptotic critical value for a test of size p, since as T tends to infinity T^{-1} and T^{-2} both tend to zero. The other two parameters determine the shape of the response surface for finite values of T.

The ability of (8) to fit the data from the simulation experiments was remarkably good. To test its adequacy it was compared to the most general specification possible, in which $C_k(p)$ was regressed on fifteen dummy variables (twelve when $N = 6$), corresponding to the different values of T. It was rejected by the usual F test in only a very few cases where it seemed to have trouble fitting the estimated critical values for the very smallest value(s) of T. The adequacy of (8) was therefore further tested by adding dummy variables corresponding to the smallest values of T, and this test proved slightly more powerful than the first one. When either test provided evidence of model inadequacy, the offending observations ($T = 18$ and in one case $T = 20$ as well) were dropped from the response surface regressions.

Several alternative functional forms were also tried. Adding additional powers of $1/T$ never seemed to be necessary. In fact, in several cases fewer powers were necessary, since the restriction that $\beta_2 = 0$ appeared to be consistent with the data. In most cases one could replace T^{-2} by $T^{-3/2}$ without having any noticeable effect on either the fit of the regression or the estimate of β_∞; the decision to retain T^{-2} rather than $T^{-3/2}$ in (8) was based on very slim evidence in favour of the former. On the other hand, replacing T by $(T - N)$ or $(T - N - 1)$, the number of degrees of freedom for the cointegrating regression in the no-trend and with-trend cases, often (but not always) resulted in a dramatic deterioration in the fit of the response surface.

The residuals e_k in regression (8) were heteroskedastic, being larger for the smaller sample sizes. This was particularly noticeable when (8) was run for larger values of N. The response surface regressions were therefore estimated by feasible GLS. As a first step, $C_k(p)$ was regressed on fifteen (or twelve) dummy variables, yielding residuals $\acute{e}_k$. The following regression was then run:

$$\acute{e}_k^2 = \delta_\infty + \delta_1(T_k - d)^{-1} + \delta_2(T_k - d)^{-2} + \text{errors}, \tag{9}$$

where d is the number of degrees of freedom used up in the cointegrating regression and the δ's are coefficients.[6] The inverses of the square roots of the fitted values from (9) were then used as weights for feasible GLS estimation of (8). The feasible GLS estimates were generally much better than the OLS ones in terms of loglikelihood values, but differed very little from them numerically.

The final results of this paper are the feasible GLS estimates of regression (8) for thirty-nine sets of experimental data. These estimates are presented in Table 1. The estimates of β_∞ provide asymptotic critical values directly, while values for any finite T can easily be calculated using the estimates of all three parameters. The restriction that $\beta_2 = 0$ has been imposed when the t-statistic on $\hat\beta_2$ was less than one in absolute value.

Estimated standard errors are reported for $\hat\beta_\infty$ but not for $\hat\beta_1$ or $\hat\beta_2$, since the latter are of no interest. What is of interest is the standard error of

$$\hat{C}(p, T) = \hat\beta_\infty + \hat\beta_1 T^{-1} + \hat\beta_2 T^{-2},$$

the estimated critical value for a test at the p per cent level when the sample size is T. This varies with T and tends to be smallest for sample sizes in the range of 80 to 150. Except for very small values of T (less than about twenty-five), the standard error of $\hat{C}(p, T)$ was always less than the standard error of the corresponding $\hat\beta_\infty$, so that if the standard errors of the $\hat\beta_\infty$'s were accurate they could be regarded as upper bounds for the standard errors of $\hat{C}(p, T)$ for most values of T.

However, the standard errors for $\hat\beta_\infty$ reported in Table 1 are undoubtedly too small. The problem is that they are conditional on the specification of the response surface regressions. Although the specification (8) performed very well in all cases, other specifications also performed well in many cases, sometimes outperforming (8) insignificantly. Estimates of β_∞ sometimes changed by as much as twice the reported standard error as a result of minor changes in the specification of the response surface that did not significantly affect its fit. Thus it is probably reasonable to think of the actual standard errors on the $\hat\beta_\infty$'s as being about twice as large as the reported ones. Even so, it seems likely that few if any of the estimated 1 per cent critical values in Table 1 differ from the true value by as much as .01, and extremely unlikely that any of the estimated 5 per cent and 10 per cent critical values differ from their true values by that much.

---

[6] Considerable experimentation preceded the choice of the functional form for regression (9). It was found that omitting d had little effect on the fit of the regression, although on balance it seemed preferable to retain it. In this respect regression (9) is quite different from regression (8), where using $T_k - d$ rather than T_k sometimes worsened the fit substantially.

TABLE 1.   Response surface estimates of critical values

N	Variant	Size (%)	Obs.	β_∞	(SE)	β_1	β_2
1	No constant	1	600	−2.5658	(.0023)	−1.960	−10.04
		5	600	−1.9393	(.0008)	−0.398	0.0
		10	560	−1.6156	(.0007)	−0.181	0.0
1	No trend	1	600	−3.4335	(.0024)	−5.999	−29.25
		5	600	−2.8621	(.0011)	−2.738	−8.36
		10	600	−2.5671	(.0009)	−1.438	−4.48
1	With trend	1	600	−3.9638	(.0019)	−8.353	−47.44
		5	600	−3.4126	(.0012)	−4.039	−17.83
		10	600	−3.1279	(.0009)	−2.418	−7.58
2	No trend	1	600	−3.9001	(.0022)	−10.534	−30.03
		5	600	−3.3377	(.0012)	−5.967	−8.98
		10	600	−3.0462	(.0009)	−4.069	−5.73
2	With trend	1	600	−4.3266	(.0022)	−15.531	−34.03
		5	560	−3.7809	(.0013)	−9.421	−15.06
		10	600	−3.4959	(.0009)	−7.203	−4.01
3	No trend	1	560	−4.2981	(.0023)	−13.790	−46.37
		5	560	−3.7429	(.0012)	−8.352	−13.41
		10	600	−3.4518	(.0010)	−6.241	−2.79
3	With trend	1	600	−4.6676	(.0022)	−18.492	−49.35
		5	600	−4.1193	(.0011)	−12.024	−13.13
		10	600	−3.8344	(.0009)	−9.188	−4.85
4	No trend	1	560	−4.6493	(.0023)	−17.188	−59.20
		5	560	−4.1000	(.0012)	−10.745	−21.57
		10	600	−3.8110	(.0009)	−8.317	−5.19
4	With trend	1	600	−4.9695	(.0021)	−22.504	−50.22
		5	560	−4.4294	(.0012)	−14.501	−19.54
		10	560	−4.1474	(.0010)	−11.165	−9.88
5	No trend	1	520	−4.9587	(.0026)	−22.140	−37.29
		5	560	−4.4185	(.0013)	−13.641	−21.16
		10	600	−4.1327	(.0009)	−10.638	−5.48
5	With trend	1	600	−5.2497	(.0024)	−26.606	−49.56
		5	600	−4.7154	(.0013)	−17.432	−16.50
		10	600	−4.4345	(.0010)	−13.654	−5.77
6	No trend	1	480	−5.2400	(.0029)	−26.278	−41.65
		5	480	−4.7048	(.0018)	−17.120	−11.17
		10	480	−4.4242	(.0010)	−13.347	0.0
6	With trend	1	480	−5.5127	(.0033)	−30.735	−52.50
		5	480	−4.9767	(.0017)	−20.883	−9.05
		10	480	−4.6999	(.0011)	−16.445	0.0

4. Conclusion

It is hoped that the results in Table 1 will prove useful to investigators testing for unit roots and cointegration. Although the methods used to obtain these results are quite computationally intensive, they are entirely feasible with current personal computer technology. The use of response surface regressions to summarize results is valuable for two reasons. First, this approach allows one to estimate asymptotic critical values without actually using infinitely large samples. Secondly, it makes it possible to tabulate results for all sample sizes based on experimental results for only a few. Similar methods could be employed in many other cases where test statistics do not follow standard tabulated distributions.

References

DICKEY, D. A., and W. A. FULLER (1979), 'Distribution of the estimators for autoregressive time series with a unit root', *Journal of the American Statistical Association*, **84**, 427–31.

ENGLE, R. F., and C. W. J. GRANGER (1987), 'Co-integration and error correction: Representation, estimation and testing', *Econometrica*, **55**, 251–76.

—— and B. S. YOO (1987), 'Forecasting and testing in co-integrated systems', *Journal of Econometrics*, **35**, 143–59.

—— —— (1991), 'Cointegrated economic time series: A survey with new results', this volume.

FULLER, W. A. (1976), *Introduction to Statistical Time Series* (New York, Wiley).

HYLLEBERG, S., and G. E. MIZON (1989), 'A note of the distribution of the least squares estimator of a random walk with drift', *Economics Letters*, **29**, 225–30.

PHILLIPS, P. C. B. (1987), 'Time series regression with a unit root', *Econometrica*, **55**, 277–301.

—— and S. OULIARIS (1990), 'Asymptotic properties of residual based tests for cointegration', *Econometrica*, **58**, 165–93.

YOO, B. S. (1987), 'Co-integrated time series: Structure, forecasting and testing', unpublished Ph.D. dissertation, University of California, San Diego.

WEST, K. D. (1988), 'Asymptotic normality, when regressors have a unit root', *Econometrica*, **56**, 1397–417.

14

Some Recent Generalizations of Cointegration and the Analysis of Long-Run Relationships

CLIVE W. J. GRANGER

1. Introduction

In the form usually discussed and tested in the economics literature the basic building blocks of cointegration are a pair of $I(1)$ series x_t, y_t such that there is a unique combination $z_t = x_t - Ay_t$ that is stationary (or $I(0)$). It follows that there must be a common factor representation

$$x_t = Aw_t + \tilde{x}_t$$

$$y_t = w_t + \tilde{y}_t \tag{1.1}$$

where $\tilde{x}$, $\tilde{y}$ are zero mean $I(0)$ components, and the common factor w_t is $I(1)$. Since an $I(1)$ series plus an $I(0)$ series is $I(1)$ it follows that x_t, y_t are both $I(1)$, their '$I(1)$ness' being derived from the same common source, w_t. It is clear that as

$$z_t = A\tilde{x}_t - \tilde{y}_t$$

is a linear combination of $I(0)$ components it will be $I(0)$ with mean zero (or just possibly $I(d)$, $d < 0$). If x_t, y_t are generated by (1.1) then they will be cointegrated and vice versa, if they are cointegrated they must have a common factor representation such as (1.1). An error-correction model is given by

$$\Delta x_t = \rho_1 z_{t-1} + \text{lags in } \Delta x_t, \Delta y_t + \varepsilon x_t$$

$$\Delta y_t = \rho_2 z_{t-1} + \text{lags in } \Delta x_t, \Delta y_t + \varepsilon y_t \tag{1.2}$$

with the additional property that at least one of ρ_1 or ρ_2 must be non-zero, where $z_t = x_t - Ay_t$ and also $0 > \rho_1 - A\rho_2 > -2$. If x_t, y_t are generated by such an error-correction model they must be cointegrated and vice versa, if they are cointegrated they must have an error-correction model representation.

A useful interpretation of these concepts is that the economy prefers to remain near the line $x = Ay$, which may then be thought of as an attractor, and this may be equated with certain forms of economic equilibrium. To have the interpretation it is essential that z_t be $I(0)$ and have mean zero, which implies that the univariate series z_t has zero as its attractor. If z_t has zero mean and is generated by an AR(p) model

$$(1 - \lambda_1 B)(1 - \lambda_2 B) \ldots (1 - \lambda_p B)x_t = \text{white noise,}$$

a possible measure of the strength of attraction is

$$\lambda = \max_{1 \leq k \leq p} \lambda_k,$$

as for h large the optimum forecast of x_{t+h} made at time t is approximately $\lambda^h x_t$. In fact, one might expect that if the attraction is due to market forces or government controls, then the strength of attraction would increase as the size of z increases, suggesting a non-linear model generating z_t. If $x = Ay$ is an attractor, or an equilibrium, then the error-correction model is the disequilibrium mechanism.

There are obviously many ways to generalize this set of statements about cointegration. In this survey various of these generalizations will be discussed briefly, with concentration on the concepts involved rather than rigorous statements and proofs. An obvious direction of generalization is to replace the pair of series, x_t, y_t by a vector x_t having n components. Each component could be $I(1)$ but there could be r vectors, $\alpha_1, \ldots, \alpha_r$ each of which is such that $z_{jt} = \alpha_j' x_t$ is $I(0)$. This generalization is discussed in Engle and Granger 1987, Johansen 1988, and elsewhere, and so is not covered further in this survey.

Another natural generalization is to remove the requirement that x_t, y_t are exactly $I(1)$. Suppose that it is possible to define a dominant property of a series, denoted $x_t \sim D$ and if a series does not have D, then denote $x_t \sim ND$. The dominance property ensures that if x_t, y_t both have D, then generally so will any linear combination of these series and, also if $x_t \sim D$, $y_t \sim ND$ then $q_t = ax_t + By_t \sim D$, if $\alpha \neq 0$. Further, if x_t, y_t are both ND, then so is any linear combination. Suppose now that x_t, y_t both have D but there exists a linear combination $z_t = x_t - Ay_t \sim ND$. A common factor representation such as (1.1) may follow from these properties, with $\tilde{x}, \tilde{y}$ both ND, x, y both D and $w \sim D$. Further, if there exists some linear (or nonlinear) filter $d(B)$ such that if $x_t \sim D$, then $d(B)x_t \sim ND$ a form of error-correction model (1.2), with Δ replaced by $d(B)$, will be possible, provided the white noise residuals are ND. Examples of D are processes having roots very near but not quite at one, such as a AR(1) processes with parameter just slightly over one, series having unit or near unit roots of frequencies other then zero, deterministic trends in mean such as t^α or exp t, broken trends in mean, a group of outliers, processes that are $I(d)$, $d > 0$, steps in mean, structural changes and so forth. Not all of these cases have quite the same implication as standard cointegration. For instance, if a pair of series consists of a linear trend plus a stationary component then there will *always* exist a linear combination which has no trend, which is not true if the linear trend is replaced with an $I(1)$, unit root common factor.

In the remainder of this survey, the dominant property will be taken to be $I(1)$ although in many cases some other D can be used and similar results obtained. In linear structures it is clear that an $I(0)$ series x_t cannot be cointegrated with an $I(1)$ series y_t. However, forming the accumulated x_t, by

$$Sx_t = \sum_{j=0}^{t} x_j$$

will give $Sx_t \sim I(1)$ and then Sx_t and y_t could be cointegrated. For the more general dominance property, $Sx_t = \Delta^{-1} x_t$, with $\Delta = 1 - B$, would be replaced by $[d(B)]^{-1}$. An extension of this idea is where x_t, y_t are both $I(1)$ and are cointegrated with $z_t = x_t - Ay_t$ being $I(0)$. Then the accumulation Sz_t will be $I(1)$ and if Sz_t, x_t (or y_t) are cointegrated then x_t and y_t are said to be multi-cointegrated, with $q_t = x_t - cSz_t \sim I(0)$. The theory of this case is discussed by Granger and Lee (1988), where it is shown that the error-correction model now explains Δx_t, Δy_t in terms of lagged z_t, q_t and Δx_t, Δy_t. An obvious application is when x_t, y_t are respectively the production and sales of some industry, $z_t = x_t - y_t$ is the change of inventory and Sz_t is the level of inventory which may be cointegrated with sales. This application is considered in Granger and Lee 1989 for a group of US industries, at various levels of aggregation, and some evidence found in favour of multi-cointegration. However, the strongest evidence in favour is with error-correction models containing a simple form of nonlinearity. Defining $z_t^+ = z_t$ if $z_t \geq 0$, z_t^- if $z_t \leq 0$ and similarly for q_t^+, q_t^-, these error-correction models have Δx_t, explained by lagged z^+, z^-, q^+, q^- and lagged Δx_t, Δy_t, and possibly also for Δy_t. With x_t production, all four error-correction terms sometimes came in significantly and with different coefficients.

Multi-cointegration is a particular case of what has been called polynominal cointegration (Yoo 1988) in which a pair of filtered series $\alpha_1(B)x_t, \alpha_2(B)y_t$ are cointegrated. Another particular example is if x_t is $I(2)$, so that $(1 - B)x_t$ is $I(1)$ and y_t is $I(1)$.

One entry into nonlinear generalizations of the basic form of cointegration is the nonlinear error-correction form

$$\Delta x_t = g(z_{t-1}) + \text{lags } \Delta x_t, \Delta y_t + \text{residual.}$$

It is generally true that if z_t is $I(0)$ then so will be $g(z_t)$, provided that z_t is stationary in all moments. The function $g(\ )$ can be either chosen to have a particular parametric form, such as a cubic in z, or may be estimated non-parametrically. Both strategies are considered by Escribano (1987a, b) who provides applications to US money demand using a cubic function of z_t.

The nonlinear error-correction model is just one of several ways in which nonlinearity can enter the simple cointegration form, as will be seen. It can be interpreted as saying that the 'strength of attraction' of the cointegration line varies with the size of z_t.

2.   Common Factors, Aggregation and Seasonality

2(i)   Common factors

In the simple bivariate cointegration case, the necessary existence of the common I(1) factors leads to the obvious question of how should this common factor be estimated? The constraints implied by the equations (1.1) are insufficient to identify the common factor. One way to proceed is to use the error-correction (EC) directly to provide an estimate, which is made unique by adding some extra constraint. Consider for example the EC model

$$\Delta x_t = \rho_1 z_{t-1} + a_1 \Delta x_{t-1} + b_1 \Delta y_{t-1} + \varepsilon_{1t}$$
$$\Delta y_t = \rho_2 z_{t-1} + a_2 \Delta x_{t-1} + b_2 \Delta y_{t-1} + \varepsilon_{2t}. \tag{2.1}$$

Consider the pair of transformed series

$$z_t = x_t - A y_t$$
$$w_t = \rho_2 x_t - \rho_1 y_t \tag{2.2}$$

where $z_t \sim I(0)$, and generally $w_t \sim I(1)$. Applying the weights in the transformed to (2.1) gives

$$\Delta z_t = (\rho_1 - A\rho_2)z_{t-1} + (a_1 - Aa_2)\Delta x_{t-1} + (b_1 - Ab_2)\Delta y_{t-1} + \text{res.} \tag{2.3}$$

and

$$\Delta w_t = (a_1\rho_2 - a_2\rho_1)\Delta x_{t-1} + (b_1\rho_2 - b_2\rho_1)\Delta y_{t-1} + \text{res.} \tag{2.4}$$

x_t, y_t can be solved from (2.2) in terms of z_t, w_t, giving

$$x_t = (1 + A\lambda\rho_2)z_t - A\lambda w_t$$
$$y_t = \lambda\rho_2 z_t - \lambda w_t$$

while

$$\lambda = (\rho_1 - A\rho_2)^{-1}.$$

Substituting these into (2.3), (2.4) gives a pair of equations of the form

$$\Delta z_t = (\rho_1 - A\rho_2)z_{t-1} + \phi_1\Delta z_{t-1} + \phi_2\Delta w_{t-1} + \mathrm{res}_{1t}, \qquad (2.5)$$

and

$$\Delta w_t = \theta_1\Delta z_{t-1} + \theta_2\Delta w_{t-1} + \mathrm{res}_{2t}. \qquad (2.6)$$

For z_t to be $I(0)$ it is necessary that in (2.5)

$$0 < (\rho_1 - A\rho_2) < -2$$

A useful decomposition is

$$w_t = w_{1t} + w_{2t}$$

where

$$\Delta w_{1t} = \theta_2\Delta w_{1t} + \mathrm{res}_{2t} \qquad (2.7)$$

and

$$w_{2t} = \theta_1 z_{t-1} + \theta w_{2,t-1} \qquad (2.8)$$

provided only that $\mathrm{res}_{2t} \neq 0$, all t, it follows from (2.7) that w_{1t} is $I(1)$ and it is a candidate for the common factor. It has the distinct property that w_{1t} is not (Granger) caused by z_t. The EC system (2.1) can then be decomposed into a mechanism that drives the system along the line $x = Ay$, which may be considered as an attractor—this is the common factor w_{1t}—and a second mechanism that keeps the point (x_t, y_t) near the attractor, described by z_t. In this example, the common factor representation takes the form

$$x_t = - A\lambda w_{1t} + (1 + A\lambda\rho_2)z_t - A\lambda\theta z_{t-1}$$
$$y_t = - \lambda w_{1t} + \lambda\rho_2 z_t - \lambda\theta z_{t-1}$$

with w_{1t} the common $I(1)$ factor. All the coefficients can be found directly from the EC model, after a little algebra. Stock and Watson (1988) have a similar decomposition which uses a different identification procedure. Their common factor and the w_{1t} derived here differ by a $I(0)$ factor. It should be noted from (2.2) that if ρ_1, say, is zero, then x_t becomes the common factor.

2(ii)   Aggregation

Many observed economic series have been achieved after some form of aggregation, either cross-sectional or temporal. It is easily shown that the $I(1)$-ness of a series, and also cointegration, is preserved under temporal aggregation. Thus, if a series is generated over one time interval (a week, say) but is recorded over a longer interval (such as a month) the cointegration is not disrupted, although the terms in the error-correction model will be changed. With cross-sectional aggregation the situation is more complicated. If macro variables are simple sums of micro variables (such as consumption for a country is the sum of consumptions at each state or district), then cointegration at the macro level (say between income and consumption) does not necessarily imply cointegration between similar variables at the state level. Similarly, if income and consumption are cointegrated for each state they need not be at the macro level, as the cointegrating vector $(1, -A)$ can differ across states. Gonzalo (1989) gives a description of these various possibilities and provides conditions that ensure aggregation from micro to macro cointegration and also vice versa.

2(iii)   Seasonal cointegration

Defining $S(B) = (1 - B^a)/(1 - B)$, where a is the number of observation time periods in a year, so that $a = 4$ if data is recorded quarterly and $a = 12$ if monthly, the series S_t generated by

$$S(B)S_t = \text{white noise}$$

may be thought as being strongly seasonal. It will have a spectrum with infinite peaks at the seasonal frequencies, a variance that increases linearly with time, and shocks will have a permanent impact. A series having a unit root at frequency θ may be denoted $x_t \sim I_\theta(1)$. If $a = 12$ and x_t is strongly seasonal, θ will take the values $2\pi/12$, $2\pi/6$, etc. Consider a pair of series x_t, y_t having a pair of common factors

$$x_t = A_1 w_t + A_2 S_t + \tilde{x}_t$$

$$y_t = w_t + S_t + \tilde{y}_t$$

where $\tilde{x}$, $\tilde{y}$ are $I(0)$ and with zero mean, w_t is $I_o(1)$, and S_t is strongly seasonal, denoted $S_t \sim I_s(1)$. It is clear that $z_{1t} = x_t - A_1 y_t$ is $I_s(1)$ but not $I_o(1)$, and that $z_{2t} = x_t - A_2 y_t$ is $I_o(1)$ but not $I_s(1)$. Thus full cointegration can occur, with a linear combination of x_t, y_t which is $I(0)$ only if $A_1 = A_2$. It has been found that if $A_1 \neq A_2$ and an attempt is made to test for cointegration at zero frequency the test will be likely to perform badly when the series also contain strong seasonal components. The questions that naturally arise are (a) how does one test for seasonal unit roots, (b) how does one test for cointegration at zero frequency when seasonal components are present, (c) how to test for cointegration at seasonal frequencies, (d) if cointegration is found both at zero and at seasonal frequencies, what form does the error-correction model take, and (e) are there any examples of seasonal cointegration being found with actual economic data?

The first of these questions is discussed in Hylleberg *et al.* 1990. Starting with a single series x_t, three other series are defined (if the series is recorded quarterly), each of which eliminates all of the potential unit roots except one, i.e.

$$y_{1t} = (1 + B + B^2 + B^3)x_t$$

unit root left at zero frequency

$$y_{2t} = -(1 - B)(1 + B^2)x_t$$

unit root left at π frequency

$$y_{3t} + (1 - B)(1 + B)x_t$$

unit root left at $\pi/2$ frequency.

Then the regression is run:

$$(1 - B^4)x_t = \pi_1 y_{1,t-1} + \pi_2 y_{2,t-1} + \pi_3 y_{3,t-2} + \pi_4 y_{3,t-1}$$
$$+ \text{ lags } (1 - B^4)x_t + e_t$$

using p lags, say.

This is an extension of the augmented Dickey–Fuller test. The series has a unit root at zero if $\pi_1 \neq 0$, at frequency π if $\pi_2 \neq 0$ and at frequency $2\pi/4$ if π_3 or $\pi_4 \neq 0$. Using the t-statistics for parameters as test-statistics, critical values are provided in Hylleberg *et al.* 1989 based both on theory and simulations. It is shown that the standard augmented Dickey–Fuller tables can be used for π_1 and π_2. It is also found that if x_t does contain seasonal roots and if this is ignored when performing a standard (augmented) Dickey–Fuller test for a unit root at zero frequency, the test will be inconsistent and lack power. At the very least, one should filter out the seasonal component before performing the test for a zero frequency unit root.

The maximum likelihood estimates of an error-correction model can provide tests for cointegration and, in a vector situation, also tests for how many cointegrating vectors are present. These tests are discussed in Johansen 1988, and simulation studies find them to be both more powerful and more robust than some alternative tests. The procedures have been generalized to seasonal unit roots and seasonal cointegration by Lee (1989). Applications of these techniques have found some evidence of both seasonal unit roots and of seasonal cointegration using data from Britain, Japan, and Canada.

If a pair of series $\mathbf{x}_t$ are cointegrated both at the zero and the seasonal frequencies, as above, with z_{1t} being $I_s(1)$ but $I_o(0)$ and z_{2t} being $I_s(0)$ but $I_o(1)$, the error-correction model takes the form

$$\mathbf{D}(B)\Delta_4\mathbf{x}_t = \lambda_1 S(B)z_{1,t-1} + \lambda_2\Delta z_{2,t-1} + \text{white noise}$$

where $S(B) = (1 - B^4)/(1 - B)$. It is seen that if there is seasonal cointegration, but it is ignored in the modelling process, then a misspecified error-correction model will result, leading to inferior forecasting and long-run interpretation. It follows that countries who do not make seasonally unadjusted data generally available are reducing the potential quality of the econometric models for the economy of that country.

3. Some Nonlinear Generalizations

If x_t, y_t have some dominant property, the obvious nonlinear generalization of cointegration is to ask if there are nonlinear functions $g(x_t, y_t)$ which do not have this property. One possible and useful way to define a dominant property for nonlinear processes is by considering long- and short-memory properties. If I_t is an information set available at time t, consisting of $x_{t-j}, j \geq 0$ and possibly also $\mathbf{q}_{t-j}, j \geq 0$ where $\mathbf{q}$ is some vector of other observed variables consider the conditional distribution of x_{n+h}, given $I_t, f(x_{n+h} \mid I_t)$. If, for h large, this conditional distribution is not a function of I_t, the x_t may be called short-memory in distribution. Similarly, x_t is short-memory in mean if $f_{t,h} = E[x_{t+h} \mid I_t] \to m$ as $h \uparrow \infty$, where m is a constant. Thus, the optimum, least-squares forecast of x_{t+h}, given the proper information set I_t, for h large tends to the constant m and is thus independent of I_t. An example is the AR(1) process given by

$$x_t = \alpha x_{t-1} + \varepsilon_t$$

where $E[\varepsilon_t\varepsilon_{t-j}] = 0$, all $j \neq 0, \varepsilon_t$ is independent of $x_{t-j}, j \geq 0$ and $|\alpha| < 1$, so that the optimum forecast is

$$f_{t,h} = \alpha^h x_t$$

which clearly tends to zero as h increases. If a process is short-memory in distribution it follows that all functions $g(x_t)$ such that $E[g(x_t)]$ exists are short-memory in mean. Short-memory in distribution is equivalent to uniform mixing, as discussed in the probability literature. If $f(x_{t+h} \mid I_t)$ does depend on I_t for all h, the process can be called long-memory in distribution and similarly, if $f_{t,h}(I_t)$ is a function of I_t for all h, the processes is long-memory in mean. If a process x_t is long-memory in distribution it follows that some functions are long-memory in mean, but the linear function need not be. An example of a process that is long-memory in variance but not in mean is

$$x_t = \varepsilon_t S_{t-1}$$

where

$$S_t^2 = S_{t-1}^2 + \varepsilon_t^2, \ S_o^2 = 0.$$

and ε_t is i.i.d. with mean zero.

These definitions are not quite the same as found in some parts of the time series literature, where x_t is said to be long-memory if its spectrum goes to infinity as frequency tends to zero.

Nonlinear cointegration can be taken to occur if $g_1(x_t)$, $g_2(y_t)$ are both long-memory in mean but $z_t = g_1(x_t) - Ag_2(y_t)$ is short-memory in mean. The attractor set is then $g_1(x) = Ag_2(y)$ and as z_t is short-memory this line can also be interpreted as an equilibrium. Clearly, other definitions are possible using the same basic ideas. Hallman (1989) discusses the use of the ACE algorithm (see Brieman and Friedman 1985) to estimate the functions $g_1(x_t)$, $g_2(y_t)$ to maximize the correlation between these transformed variables. He provides some simulations to indicate the success of this procedure and also some examples using actual economic data. It is shown, for example, that the 3-month Treasury Bill interest rate and real money base are not linearly cointegrated but do appear to have a nonlinear attractor. The most likely use of these techniques is where x_t, y_t are both long-memory in mean and to consider functions of the form $x_t - g(y_t)$ to be short-memory in mean.

An alternative form of nonlinear model is activated by using time-varying parameters. As an example, the error-correction model may have equations:

$$\Delta x_t = \rho_1(t)z_{t-1} + \text{lags } \Delta x_t, \Delta y_t + \text{residual}$$

where now $z_t = x_t - A_t y_t$. The easiest cases to analyse are when either A_t or $\rho_1(t)$ are constant, in the first case the equilibrium or attractor is changing over time, perhaps as technology, laws or policy evolve, and in the second case there is a constant attractor but the extent of 'error-correction' is varying over time. It is possible to estimate the time-varying system in either of these two simple cases by using the Kalman filter algorithm but if both ρ and A are time-varying the question of how to estimate them is less clear. If ρ_1 is a constant, and A may vary there are several simple cases that are easily covered, such as when A varies because of some other observable variable q_t so that $A_t = \beta_1 q_t$ or if it varies because of some known exogenous shock or policy change, or if A_t is a constant plus an $I(0)$ process. A more difficult case is if A_t is a constant plus an unobserved $I(1)$ process, as then the Kalman filter may pick A_t in $z_t = x_t - A_t y_t$ to be nearly x_t/y_t (assuming y_t is non-zero). This is clearly a unacceptable solution and the estimates of A_t have to be constrained away from it. Although the question of how to test for time-varying cointegration, that is with A varying over time, has not been truly resolved, it does show promise. A suggestive example is with the two types of US money, $m1$ and $m2$ which are not linearly cointegrated but may appear to be time-varying cointegrated, probably due to the changes in composition of $m2$ in the early 1980s.

The majority of studies conducted so far have concentrated on the linear attractor with $z_t = x_t - Ay_t$ being $I(0)$ in mean. However, if z_t is $I(1)$ in variance, it is difficult to interpret the line $x = Ay$ as an attractor, as z_t will wander widely around, and through, this line. Using the IARCH specification (see Engle and Bollerslev 1986) there has been found evidence of long-memory in variance of financial data. It is possible for a pair of series to be $I(1)$ in variance but for a linear combination to be $I(0)$ in variance, a case that might be called cointegrated in variance. An example would be

$$x_t = w_t'\beta x + r_{xt}$$

$$y_t = w_t'\beta y + r_{yt}$$

where w_t are explanatory variables for the mean,

$$r_{xt} = \varepsilon_{xt} q_{1t}, r_{yt} = \varepsilon_{yt} q_{2t}$$

with q_{1t}^2, q_{2t}^2 cointegrated, as then

$$r_{xt}^2 - Ar_{yt}^2 = \sigma_x^2 q_{1t}^2 - A\sigma_y^2 q_{2t}^2 + \text{residual}$$

and A can be chosen to make this first term $I(0)$. If residuals are found to be $I(1)$ in variance this possibility is clearly an interesting case to investigate.

4.   Conclusion

This survey has mentioned briefly some of the more obvious ways in which the simple form of cointegration can be generalized. Clearly, many other directions for generalization are possible and it seems that this area will remain a rich area for research topics in the near future.

References

BRIEMAN, L., and J. H. FRIEDMAN (1985), 'Estimating optimal transformations for multiple regression and correlation', *J. Amer. Stat. Assoc.* **80**, 580–97.

ENGLE, R. F., and T. BOLLERSLEV (1986), 'Modelling the persistence of conditional variances', *Econometric Reviews*, **5**, 1–50.

—— and C. W. J. GRANGER (1987), 'Cointegration and error-correction: Representation, estimation and testing', *Econometrica*, **55**, 251–76. (Chapter 5 of this volume.)

ESCRIBANO, A. (1987a), 'Cointegration, time co-trends and error-correction systems: An alternative approach', Core discussion paper 8715, Universite Catholique de Louvain.

—— (1987b), 'Error-correction systems: Nonlinear adjustments to linear long-run relationships', Core discussion paper 8730, Universite Catholique de Louvain.

GONZALO, J. (1989), 'Cointegration and aggregation', working paper, UCSD, Economics Department.

GRANGER, C. W. J., and T.-W. LEE (1988), 'Multi-cointegration', to appear in G. F. Rhodes, Jr., T. B. Fomby, Jai Press (eds.), *Advances in Econometrics*. (Chapter 9 of this volume.)

—— —— (1989), 'Investigation of production, sales and inventory relationships using multi-cointegration and non-symmetric error-correction models', *J. of Applied Econometrics* **4**, 5145–59.

HALLMAN, J. (1989), 'Topics in linear and nonlinear time series', Ph.D thesis, UCSD, Economics Department.

HYLLEBERG, S., R. F. ENGLE, C. W. J. GRANGER, and B. S. YOO (1990), 'Seasonal integration and cointegration', *J. of Econometrics*, **44**, 215–38.

JOHANSEN, S. (1988), 'Statistical analysis of cointegration vectors', *J. of Econ. Dynamics and Control*, **12**, 231–54. (Chapter 7 of this volume.)

LEE, HAHN S. (1989), 'Maximum likelihood inferences on cointegration and seasonal cointegration', working paper, UCSD, Economics Department.

STOCK, J. H. and M. W. WATSON (1988), 'Testing for common trends', *J. Amer. Stat. Assoc.* **83**, 1097–107. (Chapter 8 of this volume.)

YOO, B. S. (1988), 'Cointegrated time series: Structure, forecasting and testing', Ph.D. thesis, UCSD, Economics Department.

Index of Subjects

Index compiled by Frank Pert

Index of Names